MENC Handbook of
Research Methodologies

MENC HANDBOOK OF RESEARCH METHODOLOGIES

Edited by

Richard Colwell

OXFORD

UNIVERSITY PRESS

2006

OXFORD
UNIVERSITY PRESS

Oxford University Press, Inc., publishes works that further
Oxford University's objective of excellence
in research, scholarship, and education.

Oxford   New York
Auckland   Cape Town   Dar es Salaam   Hong Kong   Karachi
Kuala Lumpur   Madrid   Melbourne   Mexico City   Nairobi
New Delhi   Shanghai   Taipei   Toronto

With offices in
Argentina   Austria   Brazil   Chile   Czech Republic   France   Greece
Guatemala   Hungary   Italy   Japan   Poland   Portugal   Singapore
South Korea   Switzerland   Thailand   Turkey   Ukraine   Vietnam

Published by Oxford University Press, Inc.
198 Madison Avenue, New York, New York 10016

www.oup.com

Oxford is a registered trademark of Oxford University Press

Library of Congress Cataloging-in-Publication Data
MENC handbook of research methodologies / edited by Richard Colwell.
      p. cm.
    Includes bibliographical references and index.
    ISBN-13 978-0-19-518945-2; 978-0-19-530455-8 (pbk.)
    ISBN 0-19-518945-0; 0-19-530455-1 (pbk.)
      1. Music—Instruction and study.   I. Colwell, Richard.   II. Music Educators
    National Conference (U.S.)

MT1.R512 2006
780'.71—dc22   2005048095

9 8 7 6 5 4 3 2 1

Printed in the United States of America
on acid-free paper

Preface

Important projects require considerable cooperation and this book is no exception. Ms Kim Robinson and Eve Bachrach of Oxford University Press teamed with Mike Blakeslee and John Mahlmann of the National Association for Music Education—MENC to make this project possible. It was their idea and their inspiration that allowed me to be a part of this important undertaking.

The Handbook of Research on Music Teaching and Learning published in 1992 was possible because of the foresight of Maribeth Payne of Schirmer Books and John Mahlmann of the Music Educators National Conference. *The New Handbook of Research on Music Teaching and Learning* published in 2002 required even more cooperation from Payne and Robinson of Oxford and the music education conference. Both handbooks were immediate successes. Ms Robinson contacted Mike Blakeslee to explore ways that the material in the handbooks could be made more accessible to students, faculty, and libraries. Their solution was to identify material that was essential for all scholars in the profession and to make this material available in small, economical, publications.

It has been my pleasure to work with them and not only to have the responsibility of identifying the critical chapters but to work with the authors in updating the material to reflect events affecting the profession since the original publication. It should be of great interest to the profession to see which areas of research in music teaching and learning have changed significantly and which continue to be based upon fundamental philosophies and procedures. In seeking the best minds in the profession, it will come as no surprise that our authors are based in Great Britain and Canada as well as the United States. In two of the nine chapters we found it advisable to have co-authors from outside the profession thus allowing us to avoid the in-profession bias that often accompanies some research procedures.

The chapters are unique and can be read in any order. Bennett Reimer, however, sets the stage by identifying the research issues that require the attention of all scholar/researchers in the profession. Following his introductory material, our authors portray the essential knowledge one must have to understand historical, philosophical, assessment, qualitative and quantitative research. I am confident that this book will set a standard for publishing in many disciplines and it is noteworthy that Oxford and the National Association for Music Education have taken this leadership step.

Contents

Contributors

EDWARD P. ASMUS is professor of music at the University of Miami. His research has centered on affective response to music, music motivation, nonmusical outcomes of music instruction, quantitative methodology, and evaluation of music programs. He earned his B.M.E. at Ohio State University and his advanced degrees from the University of Kansas.

LEE R. BARTEL is associate professor of music education at the University of Toronto and is director of the Canadian Music Education Research Center. His primary research interests include research methods, response to music, and aspects of social psychology. Bartel is an associate of the Centre for Health Promotion, on the research staff at the Bloorview MacMillan Rehabilitation Centre, and a research associate of the John Adaskin Project. He is a former editor of the *Canadian Journal of Research in Music Education* and currently edits *Canadian Music Educator*.

LIORA BRESLER is a professor at the College of Education at the University of Illinois at Urbana Champaign, where she also held positions at the Center for Instructional Research and Curriculum Evaluation and at the Bureau of Educational Research. She holds degrees in piano performance, philosophy, and musicology from Tel-Aviv University and a degree in education from Stanford. Her research interests include arts and aesthetic education and qualitative research methodology. She is co-editor of *Arts and Learning Journal* and the electronic *International Journal for Education and Arts*, and guest edits for International Issues in *Arts Education Policy Review, Educational Theory, Research Studies in Music Education*, and *Visual Arts Research*.

RICHARD COLWELL, professor emeritus of the University of Illinois and the New England Conservatory of Music, has long been involved with assessment and evaluation. In 1970, he published *An Evaluation of Music Teaching and Learning*. Beginning in the late 1960s and continuing into the 1980s he published 22 music achievement tests. He served as a consultant to the states of New York, Illinois, Indiana, and Minnesota in the development of their state music tests and is presently working in the same capacity with the Boston Public Schools. He was the editor of the first *Handbook of Music Teaching and Learning* and co-editor of the new handbook. His *Teaching Instrumental Music* is in its third edition and he recently published, with Lizabeth Wing, *An Orientation to Music Education: Structural Knowledge for Teaching Music.*

GORDON COX is senior lecturer in education, University of Reading, UK. His publications include *Folk Music in a Newfoundland Outport* (1980), *A History of Music Education in England 1872–1928* (1993), *Living Music in Schools 1923–1999: Studies in the History of Music Education in England* (2002), and *Sir Arthur Somervell on Music Education: His Writings, Speeches and Letters* (2003). He is co-editor of the *British Journal of Music Education*, and is on the editorial board of the *Journal of Historical Research in Music Education.*

DAVID J. FLINDERS is an associate professor of education at Indiana University, Bloomington. His professional interests focus on qualitative research and curriculum theory. His own qualitative research was first published as a monograph *Voices from the Classroom* (1989). He has also co-authored *Responsive Teaching* (1990) with C.A. Bowers, and co-edited *Theory and Concepts in Qualitative Research* (1993) with Geoffrey Mills and the *Curriculum Studies Reader* (1997) with Stephen Thornton.

JACK J. HELLER is professor of music at the University of South Florida, Tampa, and music director of the Tampa Bay Symphony and Spanish Lyric Theater of Tampa. He received his undergraduate training at the Juilliard School, his M.Mus. from the University of Michigan, and his Ph.D. from the University of Iowa. He has held postdoctoral fellowships at Ohio State and Yale Universities. He taught in the public schools of Ohio and Iowa and was concertmaster of the Toledo Orchestra for several years. He has served on the editorial committees of the *Council for Research in Music Education Bulletin*, the *Journal of Research in Music Education*, *Research Perspectives in Music Education*, and *Psychomusicology.*

ESTELLE JORGENSEN is professor of music education at Indiana University in Bloomington. She obtained her terminal degree from the University of Calgary. She founded the *Philosophy of Music Education Review* and continues as its editor. She is the author of *Search of Music Education* (1997) and *Transforming Music Education* (2002).

EDWARD J. P. O'CONNOR is professor emeritus at the University of Connecticut, where he taught courses in music education, research, and world music. He served as evaluator for more than a dozen schools and special music programs. His primary area of research has been in multicultural music education. He co-authored "Czech Republic and Slovakia" in the *Garland Encyclopedia of World Music: Europe* and held an International Research and Exchanges Board fellowship to Czechoslovakia. He received his doctorate from Teachers College, Columbia University.

RUDOLF E. RADOCY received his B.S. from Ohio State University, his M.M. from the University of Michigan, and his Ed.D. from Pennsylvania State University. After teaching instrumental and vocal music in Michigan public schools, he joined the faculty in music education and music therapy at the University of

Kansas. He is professor emeritus at Kansas. He co-authored *Psychological Foundations of Music Behavior and Measurement* and *Evaluation of Musical Experiences* with David Boyle. He was named outstanding alumnus by Ohio State and Penn State and has received the MENC Senior Researcher Award.

BENNETT REIMER is the John W. Beattie Professor of Music Emeritus at Northwestern University, Evanston, Illinois, where he was chair of the Music Education Department, director of the Ph.D. program in music education, and founder and director of the Center for the Study of Education and the Musical Experience. He is the author or editor of fifteen books and over 125 articles, chapters, and reviews. His writing, teaching, and lecturing have ranged over a diversity of topics including philosophy of music education, curriculum theory, research theory, multicultural issues, musical intelligences, interdisciplinary arts principles, teacher education, international music education issues, and applications of cognitive psychology to music learning. He has been director of or participant in many national and international projects, including the MENC Goals and Objectives Project and the MENC Task Force that wrote the National Standards for Music Education, and served as a Research Exchange Scholar to China and as one of six authors of position papers for the MENC Vision 20/20 project. He has lectured and presented keynote addresses all over the world. Reimer received the rare Legends of Teaching Award from the Northwestern University School of Music and an honorary doctorate from DePaul University, Chicago, both in 1997, the year of his retirement. A special double issue of *The Journal of Aesthetic Education*, "Musings: Essays in Honor of Bennett Reimer," was published in Winter 1999. At the 2002 MENC convention Reimer was inducted into the Music Educators Hall of Fame.

CAROL P. RICHARDSON is professor of music in music education at the School of Music, University of Michigan. She won a National Academy of Education/ Spencer postdoctoral fellowship for her 1995 study of children's music-listening processes. Her most recent book is *Music Every Day: Transforming the Elementary Classroom*, with co-author Betty Atterbury. She is a 2004–2005 Fellow with the American Council on Education (ACE) mentored by Chancellor Nancy Cantor at Syracuse University and President Mary Sue Coleman at the University of Michigan.

ROBERT E. STAKE is a professor of education and director of the Center for Instructional Research and Curriculum Evaluation (CIRCE) at the University of Illinois. He is a specialist in the evaluation of educational programs, an author, and a researcher. In 1988 he received the Lazarfeld Award from the American Education Research Association. He is the author of *Quieting Reform, Evaluating the Arts in Education, The Art of Case Study Research*, and *Standards-Based and Responsive Evaluation*.

MENC Handbook of
Research Methodologies

Toward a Philosophical Foundation for Music Education Research

1

BENNETT REIMER

This chapter explores several important issues that need to be addressed if a philosophical foundation for music education research is to be built. Implicit in this task are three presumptions: (1) that music education research is not at present and has not in the past been guided by foundational philosophical principles, (2) that it would be beneficial for the research enterprise if such principles were articulated and applied, and (3) that careful consideration of several key issues will be necessary if music education research is to be grounded in a coherent philosophical-epistemological perspective.

What is *not* offered here is a philosophy of music education research. Although I will not attempt to disguise whatever preferences and proclivities I hold, I will also not aim toward a particular resolution of the philosophical issues to be raised. It is my hope that sufficient debate about these (and other such) issues will lead interested and capable individuals to formulate philosophical principles that would guide our research efforts.

Because I will be discussing something that does not yet exist, the consequences of its absence, and the ways our work is likely to improve if we were to have it, I will naturally tend to focus on shortcomings within music education research. After all, if no shortcomings existed, there would be little reason to posit that we are in need of something we do not yet have. It is not particularly pleasant to set out to draw attention to weaknesses as a way of establishing that we have much room for improvement and to indicate some of the ways we need to improve. This is especially the case in a book of this sort, which to a large degree exists, correctly and aptly, to celebrate the achievements in one dimension of music education research. That such achievements have been considerable in music education research in general is admirable, given that this field has a very short research history because it lies outside those disciplines in which research is the central or at least a major defining activity. That its research endeavor has grown so rapidly, has mastered so many of the complexities of the activity, has developed so many highly competent specialists, has established training programs for preparing new recruits, and has developed a large, wide-ranging literature is ample testimony that high levels of success have been achieved. Yet it can also be argued that the continuing viability of music education research will depend on significant foundational improvements. This chapter suggests what these might be and how they may be achieved.

The Lack of a Philosophical Grounding for Music Education Research

From among the many ways the term *philosophy* can be construed, I focus here on its meaning as "a system of principles for guidance in practical affairs" (*Random House Dictionary*). The term *system* implies that the principles be ordered according to a set of beliefs that achieves a convincing level of consistency and validity.

Philosophical principles, to be valid and useful, cannot simply be a random collection of assumptions. A unifying core of precepts, sufficiently congruent to provide coherence, sufficiently broad to cover the scope of the enterprise, and sufficiently in consonance with what is accepted as well founded according to the criteria established by the community in question, is necessary for a convincing and useful set of philosophical guidelines to exist.

The term *principles* refers to a particular level of mental operation. Principles provide general rules, laws, or guidelines from which specific actions or beliefs might logically spring. As generalities that capture the determining characteristics or essential qualities of a phenomenon or activity, principles provide the nexus for consistent doing and being. Without a set of principles for guidance, practical affairs can be only accidental, lacking the unity of purpose that is required for effectiveness.

Music education research is an enterprise employing disciplined inquiries[1] in an attempt to understand and improve the teaching and learning of music. It has been undertaken, I suggest, without a sufficient level of grounding in a coherent system of guiding principles. With the advent of the initial *Handbook of Research on Music Teaching and Learning* and *The New Handbook of Research on Music Teaching and Learning*, a few substantial, far-reaching explorations of foundational issues relating to music education research have been produced.[2] Few other discussions exist in the general music education literature about the basic questions that must be grappled with for a set of sound and useful principles to emerge. We find in various articles and in the well-established music education research textbooks a heavy weighting toward a particular (positivist) conception of science as the basis for the endeavor. Issues are seldom raised as to what is valid music education research;

how music education research should be organized and conducted; who should do music education research; what science means; how science has radically questioned its own nature during the twentieth century; the uncertain relationship of the physical and biological sciences with the so-called social sciences; the uncertain relationship of the physical, biological, and social sciences with the domain of art; the vexing dilemmas of the relation of basic research to applied research; and a host of questions about the compatibility of education as a social-political endeavor to the particular model of scientific research that music education has tended to adopt uncritically as its modus operandi.[3] This is not to say that the quantitative, positivist definition of science and research that has dominated the history of music education research until only recently is, ipso facto, mistaken or misguided. It *is* to say that we have been mistaken and misguided not to have examined, carefully, critically, and continually since its inception, how and why and when such a definition might be or might not be appropriate for our research purposes. I am not questioning here the substantive issue of the adequacy of positivistic science as a basis for music education research. (Under the section "Several Key Issues . . . ," I later return to this issue in some detail.) I am raising the question of our historical need, and our failure, to think about music education research at a metacognitive level. That is the level from which principles could emerge that might have helped our research become more efficacious. It is important to think at that level. We have not yet, I suggest, sufficiently engaged in professional discussions about the basic issue of what scientific truth might mean and not mean. We have not yet adapted our research practices to be in accordance with a more thoughtful grounding for them. Therefore, we remain uncomfortably mired in the traditions established in the earlier years of our research endeavor.

By contrast, we have traditionally thought a great deal about the various modes or methodologies by which music education research might be carried on. Few articles or textbooks on research neglected to discuss the differences among types of research, such as philosophical, historical, descriptive, experimental, and variations thereof. Perhaps the most inclusive treatment was provided by Robert Sidnell, who, after reviewing several classifications, proposed a three-dimensional matrix including methods of inquiry (historical, descriptive, experimental, philosophic), central variables (the teacher, the learner, the interaction of teacher and learner, content, and environment), and disciplines (education, musicology, psychology, sociology, anthropology, history).[4] Our substantial interest in types of research (there is far less discussion of central variables or disciplines) reflects the characteristic focus by music educators on issues of methodology. In every aspect of music education, from the most practical to the most theoretical, we have historically been fascinated by (if not fixated on) methodological concerns. This may stem, in part, from our need to demonstrate our capacity to be scholarly, but it is also likely to be a result of our concentration, from the early colonies to the present, on the teaching of performance, with all the attendant needs for regularity, careful sequencing, technical finesse, and constant monitoring and assessing. Such requirements and the remarkable success the profession has achieved in meeting them raise methodological issues to high levels of consciousness and inevitably transfer to endeavors not directly related to performance, such as research.

Therefore, discussions of the various research types or modes have focused largely on the methods and techniques by which they should properly be carried out. Given the long-standing dominance of quantitative research, the great number and intricacy of technical details related to it, whether descriptive or experimental or correlational, and the special languages, computations, and symbolic representations they require, major attention has been and is now given in the music education research literature and in research courses to their methodological particulars. Such (necessary) attention to detail fits well not only with the positivist and quantitative bent mentioned previously but also with the seemingly natural predilections of many music educators.

Little similar attention has been paid to philosophical issues related to the various research methodologies. It is generally agreed that all of them are necessary, but questions of why, and in what ways, have seldom received more than cursory treatment. A step toward principles was taken by Charles Leonhard and Richard J. Colwell in their 1976 review of research and projections for the future, by their suggestion that in order to achieve better clarity about significant research topics, philosophers and scientists will have to collaborate.[5] But we have not built on this suggestion by trying to define what the characteristics of significant research topics might be, whether the research types we have traditionally identified are relevant to or sufficient for dealing with such topics, how each type of research might be expected to contribute toward useful knowledge, how and for what purposes each type (including those more recently identified) might collaborate or interact with the others, whether particular types may be incompatible with one or more of the others in the context of some topics, and whether combining two or more types might yield insights larger than the sum of the parts included. Lacking examination of these issues, we cannot simply assume that so long as we have various types of research being undertaken, we are doing our work responsibly. We need to attend to the principles lurking beneath the surface of our previous, largely technological discussions of the ways research can be conducted, by focusing on issues such as (1) what each type allows us to know, (2) what good such knowings are, and (3) how our knowings might be enhanced by combinations and juxtapositions currently not attempted because of our limited understanding of which dimensions and dynamics of music education each type can be expected to clarify.

Few generalizations would seem more self-evident than that different types or modes of research yield different pictures of reality. In addition to being clearer about how that occurs so we can exercise more intelligent control over it, we also need to be clearer about what realities we are interested in exploring through research. Little sustained discussion exists in the music education research literature of the issue of what it is we need to

know in order to improve music education. The Leonhard and Colwell article mentioned previously attempts to suggest a set of "major research questions," and other attempts have been made over the years to delineate topics
that might drive the research enterprise.[6] The most frequent way such topics
are suggested, however, is through the "Recommendations for Further Research" sections of doctoral dissertations and other studies, but these are
generally limited to extensions of the particular topic of the dissertation or
study. No mechanism exists to gather, coordinate, and prioritize the many
recommendations made. Further, such recommendations are ex post facto—
they suggest follow-ups to topics that were chosen without the guidance of
an overarching plan leading to that specific research effort. No such plan
exists because no widely adopted philosophical principles for music education research exist to provide a foundation for such planning.

One more issue should be mentioned regarding the lack of philosophical
guidelines for music education research. To what degree do we expect music
education research to relate to, influence, or in any way be connected with
practices of teaching and learning music? We often give strong indications
that we expect research to have practical consequences, as in our attempts
to translate research results into language nonresearchers can understand
and to make these user-friendly reports available in a variety of ways. This
is under the assumption that research frequently is or should be applicable
to practice. That assumption has often been questioned. The general literature on educational research reflects an intense examination of whether and
how research relates to schooling and why it often does not, an examination
carried on with particular energy in our sister field of art education. We have
not paid similar attention to the theoretical issues of why research in music
education seems to have such little relevance for the great majority of music
teachers. This has been noted outside our own field, as in the comment by
Beverly Jones and June McFee in the *Handbook of Research on Teaching*
(3rd edition): "The controversy regarding separation of research from practice which is pervasive in art education is conspicuously absent in the literature of music education."[7]

I return to this issue in my discussion of the question of who should do
research. The point here is that a carefully devised set of principles for music
education research would offer guidance as to whether and when we should
expect practical payoffs from research and how such payoffs might be
achieved. We do not at present have such guidance available to us, accounting in large part for our disorganization as to how we approach the conduct
and application of research. Such disorganization, ironically, is quite atypical
of music education as a whole. Why, then, can it be argued, as I believe it
validly can be, that music education research, which should be characterized
by thoughtful, effective structures within which its diverse activities can be
generated and carried on coherently, is largely devoid of such structures, all
existing structures being ex post facto? The answer lies, to a large degree,
in the lack of a solid foundation on which a research structure can be built.

The Need for a Philosophical Foundation for
Music Education Research

The discussion in the preceding section focused on several important factors demonstrating that we have carried out our research endeavors in the absence of guiding principles. We have not attempted to define sufficiently what we mean by science, what we can and cannot expect from science, and how we can utilize science to help us with the problems we think are important. Therefore, we cannot exercise optimum control over how we engage in science in our research endeavors. Instead, we tend to "do science" in ways only vaguely related to a definition of science that is itself quite vague.

There is a historical basis for this situation. A good deal of music education research in the past and continuing to the present has been influenced by the assumptions of behavioristic psychology, which is the paradigm case in the human sciences of positivism as it has existed in the physical and biological sciences. There is a tendency to regard such research as being the very model of science, and those who have done it most and best as being our most "scientific" researchers. We have not discussed whether this particular model is (1) viable within the larger fields of philosophy of science, psychology, and educational research; (2) pertinent for the needs of music education; and (3) supportive of values we hold for both music and education. If we had discussed the issue with some thoroughness and rigor, we would have discovered that (1) behavioristic assumptions were being severely questioned in both philosophy and psychology at the very time we began adopting them as the basis for much of our own research, (2) they do offer important insights and guidelines for certain aspects of music education, and (3) they do support certain values we tend to hold but are inimical to others.

What difference would it have made if we had achieved a reasonable level of clarity about such matters through our ongoing discussions of them? Perhaps we would have been able to use behaviorism more insightfully and powerfully, taking advantage of what it can do very well from the perspective of what it cannot do very well. Perhaps we would have been better aware that other models from psychology were and are viable for our research and could have pursued them with the energy they deserved, achieving a balance in psychological orientations more relevant to the diverse nature of music education than we otherwise were able to achieve. We would have been able, perhaps, to recognize the importance of behavioristic research in light of its particular strengths while also being cognizant of its inherent weaknesses. In short, our philosophical-theoretical groundings could have made our research endeavors more sensible.

We are now in a new era in psychology with almost wholesale abandonment of the interest in and the credibility of behaviorism and the rise of cognitive psychology along with the broader domain of cognitive science, and we are beginning to see this change reflected to some degree in music education research. It is disconcerting to think that we might now embrace cognitive psychology as unthinkingly as we did behavioral psychology. Although new developments in psychology clearly seem to be immensely fruitful for the music education enterprise as a whole and for research in particular, we would benefit from history if we recognized that, rather than buying in uncritically to a particular psychological orientation, we would be better served to reflect on what we want and are able to get from it that might help us accomplish what we define as being important to accomplish. We would then not become servants of a particular psychological view, as was our tendency with behaviorism, but controllers of our scholarly destinies, using psychology as another powerful means for attaining benefits we seek.

On the issue of research modes, a set of principles guiding our actions might have led us to realize that, although each must be carried on in methodologically sound ways, the more important issues have to do with the nature of each type of inquiry and with their limitations and interrelations. Such issues are raised by the complexities of the three essential factors with which the field of music education must deal—music, people, and education. For each factor, there is a three-part set of fundamental realities as to its nature.

In regard to music, it exists, in certain respects, as a phenomenon with a nature transcending time and place. No matter when in human history and no matter where in human communities, music has qualities setting it apart from all other human endeavors. Yet in certain other respects, it is a product of particular times and particular places. The universal nature of music is exemplified in specific cultural contexts, which are always complex because there are many manifestations of music and many cross-cultural influences in particular cultures. Finally, in still other respects, music exists in singular manifestations—this specific process or piece at this specific moment for this specific occasion. Music, after all, is phenomenon underneath generality.

Human beings exhibit the very same tripartite nature. In certain respects, all human beings are alike—they manifest universal qualities that set them apart from all other creatures and things. But simultaneously, people always exist as members of particular societies at particular times, and that membership pervades all they are and can be. At this level, the complexities are enormous because differences in gender, age, and role (among other factors) affect the playing out of social membership. Also, people are usually members of several cultural groupings, at several levels of engagement, simultaneously, especially in the modern world where cultural isolation is rare. But further, each human being is, in certain respects, sui generis, with characteristics distinctive to each particular individual. People are, underneath any commonalities, unique identities.

Because music education is one part of a larger endeavor, the domain of education itself must be accounted for in the mix of factors with which our research must deal. Here also we find the same tripartite division. In certain senses, education is an undertaking with transhistorical, transcultural characteristics. In other senses, it is embedded in history and in particular cultures, with the infinite number of political, social, psychological, and economic issues that fact entails. But further, every act of learning is incomparable, requiring an engagement by a unique person at a particular moment in that person's life with sets of conditions experienced only as that person can experience them. Education, after all, occurs in a single person's inner being.

Given these realities, research modes should be seen as mechanisms to throw light on one or several dimensions of music, people, and education and on the interaction of these dimensions. Certain kinds of research are particularly helpful at certain levels but are limited in providing insights at other levels. Experiments, for example, are particularly useful in probing for insights at the transpersonal level but are less useful in yielding understanding of what occurs in unique situations for particular individuals. Case studies reverse the situation. History can be organized to illuminate broad, general trends, but in doing so it can miss the nuances of specific occurrences in their manifold complexities. Every possible way to carry on research has its strengths and limitations.

Because music education deals with the interrelations of music, people, and education, each of them existing at three general levels of reality, research attempting to understand and enhance those interrelations must be both diverse and coordinated. No single approach to research can possibly cope with all levels, and no scattershot array of studies can possibly yield understandings of the organic nature of the interactions music education must influence. Until we have rationalized how and why we can employ various research modes relevantly and cohesively, we will continue to be more unscientific—that is, more unsystematic, uncoordinated, imprecise, and unfocused—in our search for disciplined knowledge than we should strive to be. To construct philosophical principles for music education research is, precisely, to provide guidance as to how we can achieve better science.

These considerations lead directly to the understanding of science as the rationalized search for solutions to human problems rather than as a prescriptive technology one is obligated to follow. Our technological orientation has tended to lead us to think that "doing science" is a matter of following prescribed routines as exactly and "objectively" as possible. I return to this notion of science later. Here, the issue needing to be raised has to do with what it is that drives the research enterprise in the first place. What purposes (other than completing a dissertation, getting published, achieving tenure) do we expect research to serve? I would suggest that if research in music education is to be scientific in a meaningful sense, it should serve the purposes of more effective, useful, and relevant teaching and learning of music. But what would that consist of? Clearly, that is a philosophical question at base: It is a question of values. Effective for what? Useful for what? Relevant for what? What *do* we want music education to achieve, so that research might help us achieve it and thereby fulfill the function of being science?

I do not intend here to answer this question, of course, having used up several hundred gallons of ink (if not blood) elsewhere in trying to answer it. I do intend to suggest that science is and must be a value-driven enterprise, and the values it is driven to help achieve are, by necessity, human values because science is a human construct and an activity pervaded with human valuing. Objective it is not; disciplined it must be. What disciplines it, I would argue, is its pursuit of meaningful values and the rigor of that pursuit. Therefore, a philosophical foundation for music education research will have to relate in several ways to a philosophy of music education, which can provide it with its significant research topics. Unless our research modes and techniques are aimed in meaningful directions—that is, employed for valid and important purposes—we will too often give the impression of being "scientoid" rather than scientific, as resembling science rather than being science.

It is not enough to argue that researchers must or at least should pursue topics of interest—even of pressing interest—to themselves. Certainly, we should hope and expect that researchers will be devoted to the topics on which they will be expending the significant investments of time and energy that sizable research studies require. The issue is not the interest and devotion of particular researchers; it is the structure within which research interests and commitments are encouraged to arise and be sustained.

At present, no profession-wide structure exists to generate, coordinate, and disseminate music education research. In the absence of a planned, rationalized structure of goals to give direction to choices for individual and group efforts, research topics tend to be generated randomly. The source of topics is too often one's present interest, one's intuition as to what might be of interest to others, the availability of a technology or research process compatible with one's skills, a search for something that can be claimed as one's territory, or a hunt in the literature for loose threads that can be picked up. There are any number of ways that one might light on a reasonably persuasive and reasonably accomplishable topic.

Occasionally, particular research settings determine the choice of topic: places where an influential historian, experimentalist, tests and measurements expert, philosopher, or the like influences (or persuades) others to do similar work, or where an individual or group of researchers interested in a particular area such as therapy, behavioral techniques, or performance problems similarly influences others to join in the endeavor. Such settings go a long way to fill the vacuum that exists when no direction at all is discernible to guide the choice of research topics. Although it would seem that maximum freedom to choose a topic exists where no prior research direction exists, such "freedom" is actually a function of vacuity—an absence of interests and commitments to which a researcher might gravitate. When any topic can be chosen, choice can be only by chance or impulse, and the freedom to choose becomes an empty exercise. The existence of a goal structure within which the freedom to choose is governed by meaningful parameters, with meaningful consequences, allows freedom to be balanced with responsibility, thereby giving freedom significance. As in the creation of art, where choices must be made within a structure of artistic constraints that give the choices a necessary function, research choices must be made within a structure of professionally defined constraints. These give particular choices of research a purposive function within a larger, meaningful structure.

Freedom without structure is anarchic, and music education research has suffered from an excess of disorder because its structure has been insufficient to give meaning to freedom of choice. Although the constraints in choices previously mentioned have helped provide cohesion in particular instances, they are not the products of a rationalized plan to which they are consciously contributing, but rather the result of chance events that led particular people with particular interests to exert influence on those with whom they came into contact. Our profession deserves better. We deserve to build, by our conscious, directed efforts, a planned research program focusing on the significant problems and issues of music education for which research can provide assistance, and in which all those engaged in research or preparing to engage in research can find a useful contribution to make in light of their individual intellectual strengths and personal-professional interests. Of course, a structured research program can be so restrictive and prescriptive as to forestall freedom. That is the opposite end of the continuum from there being so little structure as to render freedom insignificant. Between the untenable extremes lies the possibility for balances in which an overarching plan allows our research to become directed toward the important goals we define for it, and in which individual researchers can freely find a contribution to make toward the achievement of progress also being sought by others.

The development of such plans requires the guidance of articulated principles for generating significant research topics and viable research contexts within which the topics can be pursued. Such contexts would provide optimum working conditions of people, facilities, and resources in pursuit of defined professional goals over sufficient periods of time for progress to be expected to occur. That is how effective science works. Science does not proceed by a random accretion of uncoordinated, unfocused studies chosen by individuals working in isolation from communities of like-minded, similarly goal-driven colleagues. If that is how science had proceeded, we would, in the larger sphere of science, be faced now with what faces us in music education research—bits and pieces of insights insufficiently coordinated to add up to a larger picture.

We have done much excellent research of a variety of sorts in a variety of fields, as this and other volumes in this series attest. Imagine, for a moment, if all this research had been guided by well-defined goals focusing on topics mutually defined as central to the improvement of music education. Imagine, further, that this research had been carried out in contexts providing optimum coordination, so that individual (or group) studies were accomplished in ways that enhanced all possible interstudy congruences. Imagine that the studies had been carefully linked to build on fruitful leads, to fill in needed gaps of knowledge, to replicate and expand successful attempts, to provide longitudinal data (so lacking in our research,) to probe theoretical-philosophical weaknesses, and to put resulting findings into practice in a variety of relevant education settings with careful monitoring and follow-ups. Surely we would have been able, under such conditions, to have approximated more closely the astonishing gains made in the traditional (and new) sciences during the past three or four decades—gains that could not possibly have been made without extraordinary degrees of coordination. Although some would argue (correctly, I believe) that our subject matter is more complex than theirs, it is nevertheless reasonable to assume that we would have made far more progress than we have made, and would have done so in contexts also promoting genuine communities of cooperating scholars. The human benefit of doing so is not to be lightly dismissed, in that such communities are far more likely to attract people to become professional researchers than the "scientist as isolationist" image we have tended to portray.

There are a variety of ways to build ongoing research contexts, the research center as existing in the sciences by the hundreds if not thousands being the clearest example. This chapter is not the place to describe and discuss the details of research centers or of other ways to provide the coordination from which music education research would benefit dramatically. The point is that the development of philosophical guidelines for music education research would entail, as a necessary adjunct, building operational research structures and policies to carry out the guidelines intelligently and cohesively. I will return to this matter in the concluding section of this chapter.

Several Key Issues Underlying a Philosophical Foundation for Music Education Research

Foundational issues for which philosophical principles are needed arise from a particular agenda. For example, a philosophy of music education is likely to grapple with issues such as the nature of music, its various social functions, what musical creation consists of, what musical experience consists of, how music "means," and how education can be organized to achieve the values the philosophy claims for it. The defining issues for music education research are likely to include the nature of scientific knowing, the modes of scientific knowing, how such knowings relate to the knowings music education is concerned with, the structures within which science can take place effectively in a field such as music education, and how findings can be implemented. The previous two sections touched on some of the kinds of issues for which philosophy might be expected to provide guidance for music education research.

Here I want to offer a few illustrative examples of foundational issues to which philosophical thinking about research is likely to have to attend, so that the nature and scope and level of the work might become more apparent. To attempt to cover most or all such issues would be tantamount to writing a complete philosophy, so, obviously, only a small sample can be handled in this section. First, I discuss in some detail the dilemma being caused by the recent major shifts in the philosophy of science and the repercussions those shifts have had in the field of educational research. We, too, in music education research, will have to adapt to the new intellectual realities being thrust on us, and it is a function of philosophical guidelines to help us do so effectively.

Second, I discuss briefly a conceptualization of the various ways one particular research mode (in this case, history) might be construed to operate, to illustrate that research, no matter of what sort, requires a basis in philosophical commitments—in value choices—in order to be carried on at all. Research, we need to understand explicitly, cannot be value-free, so we must be clear about the value choices being made in any particular research methodology or endeavor and in the subsequent educational recommendations it might yield.

Finally, I raise the issue of who should be engaged in doing research and in what settings it can be carried on most fruitfully. This issue leads directly to the domain of research policy, much neglected if not ignored in music education but about which philosophy might be expected to offer some clarity.

How "Scientific" Is Science?

From the beginnings of modern science some four centuries ago until the revolution in conceptions of science that occurred around the middle of the twentieth century, science was largely conceived to be the domain in which assured, inerrant knowledge (1) was assumed to be possible and (2) could be achieved through the use of appropriate methodologies. Scientific knowledge was considered to be, by its very nature, founded upon the existence of a reality beyond human subjectivity, variability, and uncertainty. That solid, unchallengeable reality could be discovered reliably by either the careful application of the human senses (bolstered by instrumentation), as empiricists like John Locke and George Berkeley believed, or by the application of reason, as rationalists like René Descartes believed. Scientific knowledge depended on the objective application of the senses or of reason. Subjectivity was taboo because it intruded between the human observer and the "real" being observed. That "real"—that objectively existent actuality—could be represented accurately, once discovered, by language (construed to include symbol systems such as mathematics).

The general term for this belief system is *positivism*. Although some thinkers before the middle of the twentieth century were skeptical about this view (John Dewey notably among them), most adopted it, or some form of it, as the basis for their work. And although the view was developed as applicable to the "hard" sciences, whose subject matter was the natural world, it was an easy and seemingly logical step to assume that it applied equally to human affairs. The methodologies of natural science and the quest for existent actualities could be transferred from the traditional sciences to the human domain—the social sciences. Research in social science could be as objective and reality-seeking as in the sciences exploring the natural world; methodologies for ensuring objectivity and control of variables, as well as the use of statistical power, could be used to duplicate in social science what was occurring in natural science.

It was an even easier step to assume that education, as part of social behavior, could be understood to be a domain in which objectively existent reality could be uncovered through the applications of scientific methodology. Educational research, often teamed with the psychology most amenable to the positivist scientific model—behaviorism—adopted and implemented this model as its foundation. Music education research did likewise. Such research in education generally and in the subdomain of music education was predicated on the principle on which positivism was founded—that objective truth could be discovered by scientific methodologies. In education, such truth would consist of verifiable propositions applying to all learners and teachers and disciplines in all education contexts. As Gary A. Cziko explained,

> The adoption by the behavioral sciences toward the end of the nineteenth century of the research perspective and methodology used in the physical sciences is usually considered to mark the birth of "scientific" sociological, psychological, and educational research. The emphasis on quantification, objectivity, experimentation, and inferential statistical techniques still found in mainstream behavioral science clearly show the influence of the research methods of the physical sciences on those of the behavioral sciences.[8]

Inevitably, then, the major focus for research was the first level—the universal level—of the tripartite reality in which music, people, and education exist, with some attention to the group-culture level but less attention to the individual level except as another way to reveal universals. What science is after, in the positivist view, are those underlying truths applicable in all circumstances. Such truths must be statistically verifiable: An incomparable, individual experience cannot, by its nature, be generalized to the level of a universal principle. Statistical methodologies must be constructed to subsume the particular within the general because scientific principles are always general principles. And the possibility of observer or experimenter bias—the particular personality, belief system, expectation system, and emotional investment of the person(s) doing the research—needs to be controlled for. The more one controls for all the possible ways universality might be compromised, the better—the more "scientific"—the research.

The foundational beliefs of positivism, Cziko pointed out, were so severely called into question, beginning with the middle of the twentieth century, as to constitute what many people have called a revolution, or "paradigm shift," in the philosophy of science, leading to the period of postpositivism, including postmodernism and its various offshoots, in which we are now living.[9] Every concept, from the notion of objectivity to the idea of reliable observation, and to the assumptions of verifiability, discoverable reality, control, and universal principles and constants—all were probed for inherent weaknesses. All were found to be vulnerable, not only in the human sciences, where they were obviously and painfully so, but also in the natural sciences, most notably in physics, where they had once seemed invincible. By the late 1970s, it was possible for the distinguished education researcher Donald Campbell to sum up the paradigm shift of accumulating skepticism toward long-held assumptions about science as follows:

> Nonlaboratory social science is precariously scientific at best. But even for the strongest sciences, the theories believed to be true are radically underjustified and have, at most, the status of "better than" rather than the status of "proven." All commonsense and scientific knowledge is presumptive. In any setting in which we seem to gain new knowledge, we do so at the expense of many presumptions. . . . Single presumptions or small subsets can in turn be probed, but the total set of presumptions is not of demonstrable validity, is radically underjustified. Such are the pessimistic conclusions of the most modern developments in the philosophy of science.[10]

If it is so, as is now commonly accepted in the field of philosophy of science, that science is necessarily perspectival rather than disinterested, the perspectives and values of investigators determining what will be discovered, how it will be discovered, why it should be discovered, and what the discovery will then mean; that science is necessarily systemic rather than linear, the system in which it exists being validly described as more biological and psychological than mechanical; that science is essentially theory based, culture based, and language based, with language being a social construct itself inherently and deeply metaphorical rather than abstractly logical; that evidence can be generated only by using procedures that are themselves the products of historically embedded human value structures; that evidence gained is never sufficient to eliminate alternative theories that might explain the data equally well, so that all theories are inherently and by nature underdetermined; and that everything seemingly "objective" is itself a product of a historical value system and belief system itself subjectively determined, then several conclusions seem inevitable. The notion of truth as something reducible to single entities (the notion of "rival paradigms" in which each is a rival for the single possible truth) will have to be expanded to include the notion of truth as being multiple and organic ("complementary paradigms" providing different perspectives and foci on different dimensions of a complex, multitudinous system of interactive components). The myth of science as objective, and therefore value-free, needs to be recognized as being itself a value position, and this position judged against emerging others that stress not only that "value-free science" is an inherent impossibility but also that the idea itself is ethically dangerous, misleading, dehumanizing, and neutralizing, preventing us from acting in responsible ways to improve the human condition according to values we can embrace openly. Such emergent values, Cziko argued, are based on a view of reality as being not "objectively given" but instead as inherently dynamic, conflictual, relative, acausal, idiosyncratic, socially constructed, and historically based. Language itself is value laden, the "appropriately scientific" language we have inherited being a historically devised political mechanism to promote the subject-object dualism then valued. When values are no longer focused on promoting this dualism, language can be recognized to be a psychological-aesthetic-social phenomenon and be employed openly and freely to act that way in disciplined inquiries. The conception of science as a search for objective truth can be reconceived as a search for more useful, more satisfying human meanings. Such are the assertions now current in the philosophy of science.

As one can imagine, the response to all this by the community of education researchers was massive, complex, and contentious. As regular readers of the publications of the American Educational Research Association during those years (most notably the *Educational Researcher*) know, it was also ongoing and persistent. Few issues of the journals in education research did not contain articles dealing in some way and at some level with one or another of the research implications of the shifting paradigm in science from positivism to some version of postpositivism and postmodernism. The arguments ranged across a continuum from radical critiques of most past and present educational research assumptions and practices, and proposals to abandon them, to attempts to adapt and retain older ideas by bending them to fit the new ones. Entirely off the continuum, in that they did not engage in the debate at all, were those who were unaware that any changes had taken place, or who are unwilling or unable to acknowledge that change had occurred, and who simply went on doing what they had always done. This, I believe, characterized music education research, then and to this day, to an uncomfortable degree.

For those unaware of the philosophical changes that took place in science or who chose (and continue to choose) to ignore them, the notion of education research as being devoted to the prediction and control of behavior remains convincing. But some who continue to hold deterministic views argue nonetheless that it is likely to be impossible to make predictions of human behavior that are both accurate and nontrivial. As Cziko suggested, it is possible to retain a belief in behavior as being "lawful" and theoretically predictable but also as too complex to expect that reliable predictions could ever be made.[11] This was pointed out early in the debates about the nature and prospects of educational research by Lee J. Cronbach and Richard Snow, who argued that individual differences interact with educational treatments over time in such massively complicated, accumulative ways as to defy research discoveries. They concluded that "comprehensive and definitive experiments in the social sciences are not possible and that the most we can ever realistically hope to achieve in educational research is not prediction and control but rather only temporary understanding."[12]

But this may not have gone far enough, for Cronbach and Snow implied that it is only a matter of complexity that prevents prediction and therefore control. Others argued that what influences human behavior is not the environment or other objective, external stimuli that are, theoretically, researchable but, instead, the *meanings* ascribed to life events by each individual. Such meanings are inherently resistant to any research techniques based on positivist notions because they are a function of the totality of all of a person's previous experiences, and therefore access to them is impossible to gain. Further, even within a positivist framework, the magnitude of individual differences is so stupendous (Carl Sagan estimated that the human brain has some 10^{13} synapses permitting something like 2 raised to the power 10^{13} different possible states, a number far greater than the total number of elementary particles—electrons and protons—in the entire universe) that no two humans, even identical twins raised together, "can ever be really very much alike."[13] Add to this all the complicating factors of education, and one begins to appreciate the limited nature of the idea that educational research can predict and control behavior and that it should operate according to the premise that it should be devoted entirely or primarily to doing so.

But other factors add still more implications, as Cziko explained. Under the Newtonian view on which positivistic science was founded and from which positivistic education research sprang, it was assumed that all relevant variables could be measured objectively and that all events were determined by (and therefore predictable by knowledge of) preceding events. The world and its people, therefore, are causally determined, and those causes can be identified and measured reliably. Although the physical sciences have discarded this view, it remains, anomalously, a dominant perspective in contemporary, mainstream "scientific" educational research.

One major discovery in the physical sciences that led to an altered view of prediction was chaos theory, in which, although each individual step in any process may be conceived to be determined causally, it is theoretically impossible to predict the outcome of any *sequence* of steps in the process, even with the most precise possible knowledge of the relevant initial conditions.[14] Initially tiny differences in conditions lead to large, unpredictable differences in results because of the nonlinear effects of chaos, so that, for example, E. N. Lorenz, an important chaos theorist, was led to the conclusion that accurate, long-range forecasting of the weather was impossible, no matter how much and how precise the data and how powerful the computer power to process it. Chaos theory would seem to be particularly germane to educational research because the processes occurring in education seem fruitfully conceived as following nonlinear histories in which accumulative events lead to unpredictable outcomes. This seems to be at least as descriptive of what tends to occur in educational reality (and in human reality) as deterministic explanations have been.

In addition to theories expanding on and altering deterministic views, several important nondeterministic positions have been articulated as bearing directly on what educational research can be in essence. The first is that human learning is an evolutionary process in which, as in biological evolution, chance, randomness, and "creative" (acausal) leaps play essential roles. If human cognitive learning is to any degree creative and free rather than determined and mechanical, results cannot be predicted or controlled, nor should they be. Research, under this view, is an activity intended not to deduce predictable outcomes of particular inputs but to describe as fully as possible the varieties of conditions under which an optimal variety of learning outcomes might occur.

Another factor leading to a different sense of research than the positivistic one has to do with consciousness, self-determination, and openness of choice rather than restriction of choice. Consciousness, it has been suggested, plays an interactive role in human reality, being influenced by the reality in which it exists but also influencing what that reality can be. Despite many restrictions, the possibility of choosing freely from many alternatives is real in human life and learning because consciousness, allowing awareness of alternative possibilities, leads to unpredictable choices in that (1) choices can be freely made and (2) alternative future possibilities cannot be predicted. Prediction (and control) of complex, creative human behaviors would have to take account of the regulatory role of consciousness but cannot do so because consciousness cannot be made known to researchers and is likely to be only dimly and partially known to individuals in that it is more like a lived process than an existent entity. Therefore, the attempt to predict behavior, especially in that most complex of all settings—education—would seem to be futile, except, perhaps, in cases so restricted to nonconscious or preconscious mental functions (classical operant conditioning, perhaps) as to relinquish any meaningful definition of the term *education,* especially when education is conceived as a cognitive enterprise.

Finally, the advent of quantum mechanics has clarified that the physical universe operates by processes far different from the Newtonian deterministic ones, in that randomness and unpredictability seem built into phenomena at the subatomic level. Observation (measurement) of particles changes the particles, entities can exist in two apparently contradictory conditions at the same time, and interconnections exist among all phenomena in ways of which we are only beginning to be aware. The implications of all this for human functioning, as in education, are complex and uncertain. (Cziko discusses a variety of factors.) But it would seem reasonable to entertain the notion that human beings may reflect in their nature some, at least, of the aspects of the indeterminacy of all matter.

If unpredictability in any or all of its guises is a foundational aspect of human learning and education, the definition of educational research as "scientific" in a positivist sense would seem highly questionable, if not largely irrelevant. But many educational theorists continue to argue that at certain levels and for certain purposes and under certain conditions it is still useful (or essential) to continue to employ the kinds of research based on positivist, deterministic assumptions because to *some* degree they can help us regularize what would otherwise seem chaotic, and to *some* degree, at *some* levels, they can be reasonably predictive, especially statistically, and it is helpful if not necessary to be able to predict, if only at the level of probabilities, among groups sufficiently large to allow some probabilities to appear.[15] But even advocates of probabilistic research are likely to agree that the essential (or at least operative) unpredictability of human behavior explains why traditional educational research has not advanced, exerted the influence, or achieved the hopes for it, as might have been expected from the large amount of work done. D. C. Phillips has been a major advocate of the idea that objectivity can still serve as a regulative principle, in that research can be opened to criticism its evidence subjected to scrutiny, and its conclusions potentially refuted by better explanations. The key to objectivity, for Phillips, is not a positivist worldview but that research should be carried out in a "critical spirit."[16] Yet even Phillips is led to agree that "social scientists have not been able to discover generalizations that are reliable enough, and about which there is enough professional consensus, to form the basis for social policy. . . . While the situation may suddenly turn around . . . there seems to be no good reason for this to happen."[17]

One major response to the issues raised by the decline in the credibility of positivism was the rise of qualitative research as an alternative or addition (depending on how one stood on the question of the viability of positivism) to quantitative research. Qualitative research focuses on descriptions of an openly interpretive sort, even to the point of using language overtly for its aesthetic qualities.[18] It concentrates on individuals, as in case studies, because of the conviction, as put most directly by H. E. Gruber, that "averaging across subjects blurs our view of exactly that which we want to study"[19] and that attempts must be made to plumb the depths of what people actually experience when they learn. Qualitative research, it is believed, opens up possibilities for understanding individuals rather than seeking transpersonal essences or pervasive laws. For these and for a host of other reasons,[20] qualitative approaches to educational research made significant inroads within the dominant culture of positivistic orientations, although this movement caused a sociological struggle of major dimensions, the term *warfare* often being used to describe the tenor of the debate that took place.[21] It is not just the simple matter that qualitative research provides another useful methodology, as sometimes assumed by music education researchers. It is that qualitative approaches construe human reality as being very different from the reality assumed by traditional science, raising the issue as to whether reality must continue to be conceived as unidimensional or whether it is possible for it to be multidimensional.

Where might all this ferment in educational research, brought about by the disruptions occurring in the twentieth century in our understandings of science, lead the profession? In a clever article, the eminent researcher Nate L. Gage looked back at the period of the 1980s from the imagined vantage point of the year 2009, projecting three possible scenarios for the twenty years after 1989.[22]

First, he paints the picture of what actually occurred by 1989, a year in which the "Paradigm Wars" came to a climax. During the 1980s, he says, research in education such as had been carried on in the 1960s and 1970s took a severe beating, characterized as "at best, inconclusive, at worst, barren" and as "inadequate to tell us anything secure and important about how teachers should proceed in the classroom." The attempt to lay a scientific basis for teaching had failed, the critics claimed, and the application of science to education had proven futile. Even if positivistic social science had succeeded, it would have been applicable only in "authoritarian, manipulative, bureaucratic systems."

Three classes of critiques were leveled in the late 1980s at the previous two or three decades of educational research. The antinaturalist critique claimed that human affairs cannot be studied with natural science techniques (and hence the term *social science* is an oxymoron) because human learning is essentially intentional, purposeful, and humanly meaningful. There are no causal, direct connections between teacher behavior and student learning. Human behavior is inherently not stable and uniform over time, space, and context. Teacher planning is itself subject to nonlinear events and responses, as are student learnings. Educational research, therefore, should not deal with fictions such as prediction and control but should attempt to provide insights similar to those yielded by moral philosophers, novelists, artists, and literary critics.

The interpretivist critique focused on the immediately meaningful nature of acts of learning, in which the learner's interpretation, including volition, variability, created meanings, and constructed social realities, are all essential factors in what can be learned and how it can be learned. Positivistic research, focusing on prediction and control, should be supplanted by interpretive research, which examines the conditions of meaning created by interactions of teachers, students, subject matters, and contexts of learning.

The critical theorist's critique was aimed at the technological, rationalist, efficiency-driven, objectivist, and measurement-focused nature of mainstream educational research, which neglected what is most important in education—its social, political, and economic agenda. Traditional education serves traditional value systems and power systems, whereas properly motivated education can redress social inequities and help reconstruct society. Teaching and research of a positivist nature is essentially trivial, aiming at the finer technical details of schooling and neglecting the social imperatives for which education exists.

All this, says Gage, had actually occurred by 1989, and that was the actual state of affairs at that time. Now, what did he imagine happening in the two decades following?

Scenario 1   The critics triumphed, and the kind of objectivist-quantitative "scientific" research that had been so dominant for most of the twentieth century ground to a halt. Courses in tests and measurements, statistical techniques, and research design disappeared. No one any longer used structured observations, achievement or aptitude tests, or statistical treatment of data. Journals no longer published articles in any way reporting tests of statistical significance, correlation coefficients, effect sizes, meta-analyses or the like. Research became a matter of observing carefully and reflecting deeply, and teachers became active researchers rather than recipients of research done by others.

The results were all positive. Teachers became aware of small differences in teaching that made big differences in student learning. Student differences, both individual and cultural, finally began to be taken fully into account, so that individuals were able to optimize their learnings in settings where teachers provided optimal conditions for each child. Pupils also were sensitized to deep social issues underlying what they learned, so that far greater equality began to be achieved among previously disenfranchised groups. Education became more individually effective and more socially constructive.

Scenario 2   In this version of the future, says Gage, the focus on individual learning and on social improvement did take place as in scenario 1, producing the hoped-for results. But what did *not* take place was the demise of quantitative, positivistic research, because a "great awakening" occurred in the recognition that alternative modes of research were compatible and that the "incompatibilists," who had argued that quantitative and qualitative approaches could not coexist, were simply wrong. Philosophical analysis provided a basis for pragmatic solutions in which it was recognized that paradigm differences do not require paradigm conflicts. Different approaches to research were concerned with different but important aspects of education and learning, and interdisciplinary, cooperative research began to be the norm. Subject-specific issues, ethnographic issues, and meaning-generation issues were all recognized to be amenable to deeper understanding through a variety of research approaches, and the reality levels of universals, cultural characteristics, and individualities were seen to be dimensions requiring a variety of research perspectives that could be mutually reinforcing.

The social sciences, it came to be recognized, need not blindly adopt assumptions about uniformity in nature as a given. But although many aspects of human reality are changeable and incomparable, some are relatively permanent and uniform, and some research should be devoted to explaining the uniformities in human life, culture, and education without adopting a strict positivist bias.

Process-product research, so strongly criticized, continued to be carried on, focusing not only on mechanical, predictable laws, such as had previously been the quest, but also on interpretive and cognitive teacher processes and on student products conceived as outcomes that could be reasonably investigated through essays, real-life performances, group processes, student products, and so forth, in addition to standardized testing. A great mixture

of research methodologies began to occur, and a broader spectrum of educational issues and topics were investigated, reflecting psychological, anthropological, and various subject matter perspectives. Rivalries among perspectives gave way to respectful cooperation, as the hegemony of the established
psychological-quantitative-positivist position opened up to include those approaches to research based on different epistemologies and discipline bases.

> Thus from the jungle wars of the 1980s, educational researchers, including
> those concerned with teaching, emerged onto a sunlit plain—a happy and
> productive arena in which the strengths of all three paradigms (objective-
> quantitative, interpretive-qualitative, critical-theoretical) were abundantly re-
> alized, with a corresponding decrease in the harmful effects of their respective
> inadequacies. Educational researchers today look back with amused tolerance
> at the invidious recriminations that the paradigm-loyalists had hurled at other
> paradigms in the 1980s.[23]

Scenario 3   Finally, Gage recognized, the possibility exists that the next
twenty years will bring no significant change. The paradigm wars continued
to be waged, and the traditional positivist view continued to hold sway with
increasingly bitter attacks by those proposing "alternative paradigms." Each
camp reflected differences in temperament as much as intellectual positions—
the tough-minded against the tender-minded, scientific against humanistic,
nomothetic against ideographic, statistical against clinical, positivist against
hermeneutic—so that purely rational considerations tended to become embedded in community identification issues, and the conflicts spun on and on
to the detriment of both education and educational research. "How long the
war will last, and whether it will lead to the demise of social and educational
research, including research on teaching, are questions that cannot be answered in the year 2009."[24]

Which scenario would prove accurate? The answer, Gage suggested, depended on how the educational research community would act. From the
vantage point of 2005, (only a few years short of Gage's projection to 2009),
we can observe that qualitative research did in fact succeed in becoming far
more than the "alternative" it was regarded to be at its outset. Many would
argue, on the basis of its quickly accepted veracity and utility and its fast-
growing presence in the education literature, that it did, in fact, approach
scenario 1, and in due time, research achieved, to an admirable degree, scenario 2. At first, although qualitative approaches did not replace or eliminate
the older quantitative mind-set, it made that belief system and research endeavor seem enervated, even, to a degree, irrelevant. At many conventions
of the American Educational Research Association in the 1990s, and to some
degree to the present, the sense was palpable that sessions were (are) dominated by the new, more vigorous, more "with it" approaches to research
spawned by qualitative ways of thinking, the positivists having to be content
to hunker down in neglected enclaves where they continue to preach, to a
dwindling audience, the old gospel.

With the growing strength of what once was considered alternative, the debilitating effects began to fade of regarding the continuing quantitative research efforts as "quasi" on the basis that they were necessarily not as fully controlled as the hard sciences can be. Experiments in educational research, it began to be realized, are not quasi (approximate, imitative, false, not genuine, not authentic) but instead can be regarded as being as valid—as scientific—in its setting as strict control is in its very different setting. So even the ongoing quantitative work, although losing some of its cachet, was still regarded as not inherently inferior to what could be accomplished in the physical sciences but as entirely genuine for the issues with which it must deal. If that is the case, the door is opened also to regarding a host of other modes of evidence gathering, in addition to those already established, as being authentic instances of research. The debate as to what, then, qualifies to be regarded as "research" (a poem? a painting? a musical composition or performance? a prayer or meditation? a session with an analytical psychotherapist?) has become serious, contentious, and portentous for the future of this field.[25] We need, perhaps, another Nate Gage to predict our possible futures.[26]

One dimension in the future, if present events persist, is likely to be the politicization of educational research. Although government at the federal level has often exerted influence on education and therefore on educational research, despite state and local level responsibilities, the advent of the No Child Left Behind initiative, under the administration of President George W. Bush, elevated federal authority dramatically. Under its unremitting focus on the universal aspects of education, in which the contents of learning, the required levels of achievement, the rates of attaining that achievement, the method of ascertaining achievement, and the rewards and penalties of conforming or not conforming to each of those stipulations, the notion of equality of educational opportunity ("No Child . . .") was translated into identicality of process and product. Cultural differences went out the window. Individuality as well. Ignored was the reality that each and every child is distinctive in regard to endowments in the many ways people can be intelligent, in the many ways of learning, in the many ways learning can be demonstrated, in the infinite gradations in learning rates among the various subject matters within the individual's mental, physical, and emotional capacities, and in propensities to learn, both in general and in each particular subject area. Add to this the inevitable variations in opportunities to learn, including the variable levels of support for learning from parents, peers, teachers, schools, and communities, and the enormously variegated nature of learning became reduced to a simplistic formula.

The dangers for research follow directly. Given the required uniformity of all variables in the content and processes of education, evidence of compliance must be equally as uniform if the system is to have its peculiar veracity. One method of securing evidence qualifies superbly—testing. "Evidence-based education" requires evidence-based research to back it up.

When evidence is construed to be valid only at the universal level, the experiment and other supportive quantitative research methodologies become paramount once again, as does the mechanism of testing to ascertain whether stipulated objectives are being met. Despite the protests of the qualitative research community that evidence cannot be reduced to test results, and in fact that the belief that it can be perverts and undermines even the universal level of human reality, let alone the cultural and individual dimensions, the force of politics had become so powerful that little could be done to halt or slow the swinging of the pendulum back to where it was when positivism held sway. Although the newly revived positivism may be tempered to some degree by all the work accomplished since its loss of hegemony, few could argue that the pendulum swing has been insignificant in regard to the fortunes of education and educational research.

All of these historical and occurring events are immediately applicable to the present and future not only of educational research in general but also of music education research. As to the future, I suggest that what music education research becomes in the next couple of decades depends on how the music education research community digests what has occurred and is occurring in the larger field of research and responds in considered, complementary ways. We have lived through periods of ideological warfare about which, to judge by what has been debated in the field of music education, we have paid scant attention.[27] I hope we can engage ourselves in the major research issues of our day because we cannot claim full membership in the community of scholars if we remain as outside the center of activity as we now are. But I hope we can do so in ways that avoid fruitless battles, as occurred during the paradigm wars. We need to grapple with the larger issues of research in ways that lead us toward intelligent, informed control over our destiny rather than aimless drifting on whatever winds we get caught in from the debates going on all around us. Philosophical reflection about music education research should help us understand the complex issues and alternatives now being addressed in research in the social sciences generally and education in particular and, based on our own history, nature, and needs, provide some useful guidelines for how we might develop to a more mature level in light of alternative possible futures. I would personally hope that we could develop as Gage's scenario 2 suggests, in a reconciliation of the quantitative and qualitative positions, along with others more recently brought to attention that demonstrate their efficacy. Synergistic beliefs and actions in research, encompassing various modalities as being interrelated and mutually supportive, have proliferated[28] and deserve, I believe, our sympathetic endorsement because of my conviction that the three levels of our reality call for us to employ as many research modes and as many interactions among them as can assist us in understanding and optimizing the enormous complexities with which we must deal. Philosophical guidance is needed to clarify whether and why this is the case and how we could organize our research accordingly.

Related Issues in Doing Research Responsibly

As mentioned in the first two sections of this chapter, a good deal of interest is shown in the field of music education research about the various research modes, but most of this interest is methodological and technical rather than substantive. Few discussions exist about the epistemology of research modes—what they can help us know and how their presumptions influence what they allow us to know.[29] We have tended to assume that if one follows correct procedures for doing whatever type of research one is doing, the results are then assured to be valid. Unfortunately, this does not begin to address the complexities of the issue. Underneath the level of methodology is the dilemma that research choices always both reveal and conceal—reveal by focusing on a particular aspect of reality (and giving the impression that this particular aspect therefore constitutes the reality) and conceal by neglecting a great many alternative realities not being focused upon (thereby invalidating them).

All research modes are subject to this fundamental dilemma, so our consciousness needs to be raised as to how this occurs and how we can be better aware of it both in doing research and in using and assessing research. To exemplify this, I will raise the issue, necessarily briefly, in regard to the doing of history.

Our explanations of history as a mode of music education research are, typically, methodological. Certain procedures must be followed to do history correctly. We must choose a researchable, manageable, and, it is to be hoped, original topic. We must gather data of a variety of sorts by building a bibliography, we must ask a multitude of precise questions, and we must refine the topic and read for general context. We should use source materials carefully, including primary and secondary, easily available and less available, newly discovered and oral. We should be careful to authenticate and verify our materials both externally and internally. We should report objectively, leaving our personal biases out. We should write up the results clearly and in a well-organized fashion. And so forth. Do all this, it is implied, and good history will have been accomplished.

Certainly all of this is valid, but when historical research is construed to consist of only these matters, as tends to be the case in the music education research literature, it distorts and misrepresents the issues that the doing of history entails. By necessity, history must infer and explain. Historical facts become "evidence" only within a framework of explanations; they are incapable, in and of themselves, of being meaningful. What are the issues raised by the necessity of explaining historical facts? *That* is what we need to grapple with in our discussions of history as a mode of research.

David B. Tyack addresses this and other basic issues of historical research.[30] He intends to demonstrate the influence exerted by the explanatory model a researcher chooses to present a particular history. He uses, as the basis for his demonstration, the rise of compulsory schooling in the United States over the century from the 1850s to the 1950s. By presenting several alternative explanatory models for this phenomenon, he hopes to give evidence of (and to avoid) the reductionism that results when only one particular thesis (or none at all) is the basis for a history. First, he offers a sketch of the salient events and issues relating to the compulsory school attendance movement. Although many would consider such an overview to be, in and of itself, "history," it only scratches the surface of what historical research requires. Tyack then offers five different explanatory accounts of these events and issues. Each deals with the same situation, but, because each stems from a different disciplinary or ideological framework, each defines the problems differently, chooses different units of analysis, and offers different pictures of what occurred.

Those taking the view that the advent of compulsory education is to be understood as a political phenomenon emphasize the role of the government and the use of education as a means to incorporate people into a nation-state and to legitimize the status of those who will be citizens and those who will be leaders. The ethnocultural orientation, however, sees the phenomenon of compulsory schooling quite differently, focusing on the influence of ethnic and religious groups and their attitudes and beliefs as playing the major roles in what could have occurred and in what therefore did occur. The organizational perspective offers a still different interpretation, probing the bureaucratic, institutional implications and downplaying the influence of religion and ethnicity. Human capital theorists, alternatively, paint a picture of the family as the decision unit in calculating what the costs and benefits of compulsory education might be, and they draw implications for how the nation as a whole was led to its decisions on the basis of a human investment paradigm. Finally, a Marxian analysis is offered, in which class struggle is the source of the dialectic mechanisms that produce societal change, and capitalist assumptions and values drive the events and decisions.[31]

What does one make of these diverse ways of construing the history of the same phenomenon? Each is valid, each is explanatory, and each directs attention to certain kinds of evidence that could be used to confirm or disprove its assertions of causation. Each is, in every sense, a "history." Can one then simply add them all up to get the sum total, constituting the "real" history?

Tyack thinks not. Each of the models deals with social reality on a different level, and each is based on a different conception of what it is that underlies social change. Simple eclecticism would cause a blurring of the separate visions and a confusion of the purpose of each. So we are confronted by a principle of history—that it is not a single entity, and most assuredly not an "objective presentation" of facts, but a construction determined by values and choices, in which the assumptions and interests and preconceptions of those doing the constructing inevitably influence that which is constructed as a result.

One of my purposes in this essay has been to extend the boundaries of discussion about the history of American education. I have become convinced that much of the recent work in the field . . . has used causal models too implicitly. It has also tended to constrict the range of value judgments. . . . Entertaining explicit alternative models and probing their value assumptions may help historians to gain a more complex and accurate perception of the past and a greater awareness of the ambiguous relationship between outcome and intent—both of the actors in history and of the historians who attempt to recreate their lives.[32]

Adding to the issues Tyack raises about what constitutes history and how it might be carried out fruitfully is the emerging conception of education, and of educational research, as consisting of the telling of narrative stories. This view encompasses much of what is now occurring in qualitative research. It throws new light on the kinds of stories told, not told, and obscured by quantitative, "objective" research.

This perspective holds that humans are, essentially, storytelling organisms who lead storied lives as individuals and as social groups. To understand human reality requires the study of the ways humans experience their world, and human experience can be grasped most truthfully by exploring the stories that tell about the truths being lived. In a complex, detailed, and wide-ranging explanation of this way of conceiving history and the present, and its implications for understanding what educational research can be and how it might be carried out more effectively, F. Michael Connelly and D. Jean Clandinin build the case that the "real" is what humans construe to be so, and that what is most real is the life story we live.[33] Researchers are also humans living their stories—not disembodied spirits endowed with extra-human powers of objectivity. Education and research on education, including research on the history of education, require

> a mutually constructed story created out of the lives of both researcher and participant. We therefore think in terms of a two-part inquiry agenda. We need to listen closely to teachers and other learners and to the stories of their lives in and out of classrooms. We also need to tell our own stories as we live our own collaborative researcher/teacher lives. Our own work then becomes one of learning to tell and live a new mutually constructed account of inquiry in teaching and learning. What emerges from this mutual relationship are new stories of teachers and learners as curriculum makers, stories that hold new possibilities for both researchers and teachers and for those who read their stories.[34]

So many changes have been and are occurring in fundamental ideas about educational research, including how we tell the story of the history of education, that to carry on our work in music education in disregard of or ignorance about what is going on in the larger field of educational research would seem to be professionally irresponsible. Where are the ongoing, probing discussions about how the history of music education might be accomplished in ways reflecting recent scholarship about history as an endeavor?[35] Where are the counterpart discussions of every other mode of doing research, each of which is being as thoroughly reexamined as is history? Where, in short, is a philosophical grounding for research that can make our work as researchers more meaningful? Clearly we do not have one, nor do we have the lively exchange of ideas about research out of which philosophical principles might be encouraged to emerge. I am not suggesting that we must stop doing research until we have attended to our philosophical needs, or that the research we have done and are doing is invalid because of the lack of guiding principles. But surely we are operating in less than an optimal professional situation, and it would seem important for us to begin to pay the attention it deserves to how we might improve the situation. That is, we would benefit from efforts to forge a convincing philosophical foundation for music education research that could serve as the basis for needed changes in our research policies.

Policy Issues for Music Education Research

I have pointed out elsewhere that philosophy and policy are, or should be, intimately related, in that a philosophy provides the foundation for valid policy while policy deals with issues raised by but beyond the purview of a philosophy.[36] Because efforts to philosophize about music education research were seldom made until very recently and only sporadically in the present, there has been little basis for coherent policy making, so the research policies and practices that have emerged are generally retrospective and reactive rather than anticipatory and proactive. We have attempted to respond to perceived needs but have done little to create anticipative policies that carry out a philosophically grounded agenda. What policy issues might emerge, then, as needing to be taken into account if a set of foundational principles underlying music education research was developed?

Just as it is likely that such philosophical thinking will raise issues relating to the nature of the scientific enterprise itself, it is also likely to raise issues about the appropriate locus for the enterprise of music education research. We have assumed, along with the field of educational research generally, that research is an activity most reasonably and appropriately carried out in university settings by university professors. An entire culture of research has arisen in both education and music education and that culture is almost completely centered in higher education, as is evident in this book and the others in this series. Well, what is wrong with that?

A good many people in educational research are now arguing that there is a great deal wrong with it. As pointed out by Marilyn Cochran-Smith and Susan L. Lytle, two paradigms for doing educational research have dominated over the last two decades (p. 2).[37] The first, process-product research, has assumed that effective teaching can be understood by correlating particular processes such as teacher behaviors with particular products, usually defined as student achievement. This cause-effect model "emphasizes the actions of teachers rather than their professional judgments and attempts to capture the activity of teaching by identifying sets of discrete behaviors re-producible from one teacher and one classroom to the next." Under this view of the teacher as a technician, the teacher's role "is to implement the research findings of others concerning instruction, curriculum, and assess-ment. With this view, the primary knowledge source for the improvement of practice is research on classroom phenomena that can be observed. This research has a perspective that is 'outside-in'; in other words, it has been conducted almost exclusively by university-based researchers who are out-side the day-to-day practices of schooling."[38]

A second paradigm, the qualitative, deals with studies of "classroom ecol-ogy," providing detailed, descriptive accounts of classrooms and other school settings that shed light on their meanings. Here, too, while there are a small number of reports coauthored by university-based researchers and school teachers, practically all are the products of university researchers, who frame and mediate teachers' perspectives through their own perspectives as re-searchers.

> We propose that current research on teaching within both process-product and interpretive paradigms, constrains, and at times even makes invisible, teachers' roles in the generation of knowledge about teaching and learning in classrooms. The contents of the *Handbook of Research on Teaching* (Witt-rock, 1986), widely viewed as the most comprehensive synthesis of research in the field, is indicative of this exclusion . . . the 1037-page handbook con-tains 35 research reviews. Although a few of these include studies carried out by university researchers in cooperation with teachers, and several focus ex-plicitly on teachers' thinking, knowledge, and the cultures of teaching . . . none are written by school-based teachers nor . . . are published accounts of teachers' work cited. Rather, in most of the studies included, teachers are the objects of researchers' investigations and then ultimately are expected to be the consumers and implementors of their findings. Missing from the hand-book are the voices of the teachers themselves, the questions that teachers ask, and the interpretive frames that teachers use to understand and improve their own classroom practices.[39]

Out of analyses such as these an important movement has been generated to reconsider whether the traditional place for educational research to be conducted—the university, with schools serving as data sources—is, in fact, the best place for achieving meaningful school change as a result of research. The term *teacher research* has arisen as indicating a need to change research from an activity presently dominated by nonschool professionals and non-school locations to one in which teachers trained to also be active researchers become partners in the endeavor. We may move in the direction of a chang-ing balance in the research culture, in which teachers themselves assume more responsibility for disciplined inquiry about the work they do, using university personnel as a source for particular needs the teacher researchers identify. If the painful gap between research as it is presently conducted and school use of that research is to be bridged, it would seem that a shift in the control and conduct of research would help significantly.[40] And that raises another issue directly related—how would such teacher researchers be trained?

At present, music educators in training at the undergraduate level seldom if ever are introduced to, let alone trained in, research. At the master's level, students who will be taking (or returning to) school jobs are generally given one course in research. My sense is that most "Introduction to Research in Music Education" courses are intended to prepare more receptive, knowledgeable consumers of research that has been carried on by university faculty members or by doctoral students. (I would assume there are exceptions to this, in which the model of the teacher as potential researcher is followed.)

The issues here plead for policy guidance. What would, in fact, be the optimal way to structure an introductory research course, and how might a series of courses and other offerings be developed to prepare teachers to become effective school-based researchers? To what extent should the study of philosophical issues related to research be foundational for the study of research techniques and designs, given the value choices such techniques and designs necessarily entail? How do we address the issue of doctoral level research preparation, given the complexity inherent in a situation in which many doctoral students are likely to take jobs having little to do with research?[41] What kinds of studies would be most effective for the few choosing to specialize in research—a common program for all such students, some common elements with subsequent specialization in a particular mode, or specialization from the start? As with the other questions I have attempted to raise in this chapter, I do not here intend to offer answers—only to suggest that we should, as a profession, be seeking answers to such pressing concerns through our professional activities—journals, symposia, and so forth. Our neglect of matters of philosophy inevitably has caused a concomitant neglect of matters of policy, so that our research infrastructure is insufficiently solid to support our activities securely.

This situation applies as well to our research coordination and dissemination practices. Our present research journals, including *The Journal of Research in Music Education,* the *Council for Research in Music Education,* and a steadily growing variety of other research publications, serve to bring particular studies to attention. This is a valuable function, but it tends also to exacerbate the problem of diffuseness, in that the studies reported represent a bewildering variety of topics and approaches demonstrating plainly the existing disordered state of our research endeavor. Even in the related, focused journals, such as *Psychology of Music,* the desired level of coordination among studies is absent because little such coordination exists. The various Special Research Interest Group newsletters help to reach and define communities of shared interests, which is certainly healthy, but they also must present the research in their topic areas as it exists in its disorganization.

What we seldom if ever find in any of the journals are discussions of the research enterprise qua enterprise. That, I am proposing, is precisely what we require, not only in our journals, but among all the members of the music education research community. We require it because we need guidelines for our actions, and such guidelines are not likely to emerge in the absence of a rich and ongoing professional dialogue as to what they might be. Our journals should, I think, actively seek articles on basic issues of the music education research enterprise, with occasional single-focus issues to which several people are invited to contribute. A music education research planning council, ongoing with rotating membership, might be charged with the formulation of policies to be suggested to the research community for their discussion and exploration. We need to encourage young scholars to become researchers, not only as practitioners but also as theoreticians about the issues of research, and we need to demonstrate in our publications that theorizing about research is as necessary as doing particular research studies. Out of such ferment of ideas we are likely to generate unifying views— philosophical principles—that can bring sufficient order to our endeavors to help research become more valid as science and more influential in the larger sphere of music education than it has been to the present, through policies that implement the philosophical guidelines suggested.[42] Movement in this direction would mean that "at long last, arts education researchers would be able to orient their work to shared, explicit research priorities. This reorientation could dramatically reduce the piecemeal nature of arts education research and increase its value to arts teachers, policy makers, and administrators."[43]

The issues raised in this chapter, I have suggested, are fundamental to the music education research enterprise, and progress in resolving them is fundamental to the improvement of that enterprise. If we actually do address such issues, every aspect of music education research will be affected, some or many of them significantly. I believe the stresses of change—even major change—are worth facing, because I believe that research should play a far more significant role in music education than it ever has played or is ever likely to play under its present a philosophical condition. It is time, I suggest, for music education research itself to be subjected to serious and ongoing disciplined inquiry about its nature, value, and modes of functioning.

NOTES

1. The term disciplined inquiry as the essential characteristic of research was suggested by Shulman (1988, 3–17).

2. See Stubley (1992, 3–20) and Elliott (2002, 85–102), in addition to this chapter. For a critique of the theoretical foundations of music education and its research, see Westbury (2002, 144–161).

3. For representative examples over the years of the unquestioned acceptance of a mechanistic, positivist scientific model as a valid basis for music education research, see Beattie (1934, 89–92), Wilson (1935, 163–166), Schneider and

Cady (1965, 36–43), Petzold (1963, 18–23), Kaplan (1966, 206), Colwell, (1967, 73–84), Greer (1975, 3–11), Phelps (1980), and Rainbow and Froehlich (1987).

4. Sidnell (1972, 17–27).

5. Leonhard and Colwell (1976, 1–29).

6. An early example of a thoughtful attempt to do so was Choate (1965, 67–86). A publication of MENC also addresses this issue (Lindeman et al., 1998).

7. Jones and McFee (1986, 912).

8. Cziko (1989, 18).

9. An extensive literature exists on the scientific revolution leading to post-positivism. A few basic sources are Feyerabend (1978), Giere (1987), Hanson (1958), Hempel (1966), Hull (1989), Kuhn (1962), Macdonald and Pettit (1981), Newton-Smith (1981), Phillips (1987), Popper (1968), Scheffler (1967), Toulmin (1961), and Weimer (1979).

10. Campbell (1978, 185).

11. Cziko (1989, 17–19).

12. Quoted in ibid., 17.

13. Quoted in ibid., 18.

14. An explanation of chaos theory accessible to laypeople is Glieck (1987).

15. Ideas of this sort are presented in Lehrer, Serlin, and Amundson (1990).

16. Phillips (1990, 35).

17. Quoted in Cziko (1989, 23).

18. As suggested by Eisner (1979).

19. Quoted in Cziko (1989, 23).

20. A good overview is given in Eisner and Peshkin (1990).

21. A fascinating glimpse of the struggle in educational research to include nonpositivistic, nonquantitative methodologies is given in the editorial by Urban (1990), in which he explains how difficult it was to get the educational research community to allow publication of nontraditional studies. Also, for a penetrating treatment of the conflictual sociology of quantitative versus qualitative research in education, see Reinharz (1990). A cogent history of the rise of qualitative research and its influences on music education research is Flinders and Richardson (2002).

22. Gage (1989).

23. Ibid., 9.

24. Ibid.

25. See, for example, Eisner and Barone (1997) and Irwin and Cosson (2004).

26. One such attempt is Eisner (1993).

27. It is difficult to find, in our research literature, discussions of issues such as are raised in my explanation here of recent events in the philosophy of science and in educational research. Notable exceptions are Heller and Campbell (1976), my response to that chapter (Reimer 1977), Campbell and Heller (1980), and Reimer (1985). See also, of course, the references in note 2.

28. For an excellent overview of the movement toward a synergistic posture in educational research, see Johnson and Onwuegbusie (2004).

29. An important exception is the critique of historical research in music education by Cox (2002).

30. Tyack (1988).

31. This very brief overview does little justice to the richness and complexity of the explanations Tyack (1988) offers of how each point of view determines the history it describes. Interested readers will want to study his entire chapter.

32. Tyack (1988, 58).

33. Connelly and Clandinin (1990).

34. Ibid., 12.

35. A hint of awareness of these issues is given by Heller (1990, 73), in which he recognizes that, according to several histories of American music education, men play nearly all the major roles, twentieth-century achievements are neglected, racial and ethnic minorities are hardly mentioned, and music education for the handicapped is entirely absent. In Heller and Wilson (1992), the discussion is entirely of procedural matters.

36. Bennett Reimer (1989, 7–10). In Reimer (2003), chapter 2 discusses several alternative value claims for music education and suggests a philosophical-cum-policy position that incorporates all of them.

37. Cochran-Smith and Lytle (1990).

38. Ibid., 2, 3.

39. Ibid., 3.

40. For readings on the issue of the teacher as researcher, see the references in Cochran-Smith and Lytle (1990) and the bibliographies in Oja and Smulyan (1989), Goswami and Stillman (1987), Schon (1987), Kincheloe (1990), and Winter (1989). Also see Zeichner and Noffke (2001).

41. See, for a discussion of doctoral level study as requiring a philosophical foundation now lacking, including the issue of how effective research training remains a central unaddressed dimension, Reimer (2004).

42. Other related issues pertinent to the research-practice gap are discussed by Eisner (1984).

43. Pankratz (1989).

REFERENCES

Beattie, J. W. (1934). The function of research. *Yearbook of the music educators national conference* (pp. 89–92).

Campbell, T. C. (1978). Qualitative knowing and action research. In M. Brenner, P. Marsh, & M. Brenner (Eds.), *The social contexts of method* (p. 185). New York: St. Martin's Press.

Campbell, W., & Heller, J. (1980). An orientation for considering model of musical behavior. In D. Hodges (Ed.), *Handbook of music psychology.* Lawrence KS: National Association for Music Therapy.

Choate, R. A. (1965). Research in music education. *Journal of Research in Music Education, 13(2)*, 67–86.

Cochran-Smith, M., & Lytle, S. L. (1990). Research on teaching and teacher research: The issues that divide. *Educational Researcher, 19(2)*, 2–11.

Colwell, R. J. (1967). Music education and experimental research. *Journal of Research in Music Education, 15(1)*, 73–84.

Connelly, F. M., & Clandinin, D. J. (1990). Stories of experience and narrative inquiry. *Educational Researcher, 19(5)*, 2–14.

Cox, G. (2002). Transforming research in music education history. In R. Colwell

& C. P. Richardson (Eds.), *The new handbook of research on music teaching and learning* (pp. 695–706). New York. Oxford University Press.

Cziko, G. A. (1989) Unpredictability and indeterminism in human behavior: Arguments and implications for educational research. *Educational Researcher, 18(3),* 18.

Eisner, E. W. (1979). *The educational imagination.* New York: Macmillan.

Eisner, E. W. (1984). Can educational research inform educational practice? *Phi Delta Kappan, 65(7),* 447–452.

Eisner, E. W. (1993). Forms of understanding and the future of educational research. *Educational Researcher, 22(7),* 5–11.

Eisner, E. W., & Barone, T. (1997). Arts-based educational research. In R. Jaeger (Ed.). *Complimentary methods of educational research.* New York: Macmillan.

Eisner, E. W., & Peshkin, A. (Eds.). (1990). *Qualitative inquiry in education.* New York: Teachers College Press.

Elliott, D. J. (2002). Philosophical perspectives on research. In R. Colwell & C. P. Richardson (Eds.), *The new handbook of research on music teaching and learning* (pp. 85–102). New York: Oxford University Press.

Feyerabend, P. (1978). *Against method.* London: Verso.

Flinders, D. J., & Richardson, C. P. (2002). Contemporary issues in qualitative research and music education. In R. Colwell & C. P. Richardson (Eds.), *The new handbook* of research on music teaching and learning (pp. 1159–1175). New York: Oxford University Press.

Gage, N. L. (1989). The paradigm wars and their aftermath: A "historical" sketch of research on teaching since 1989. *Educational Researcher, 18(7),* 4–10.

Giere, R. (1984). *Explaining science: A cognitive approach.* Chicago: University of Chicago Press.

Glieck, J. (1987). *Chaos: Making a new science.* New York: Viking.

Greer, R. D. (1975). Music instruction as behavior modification. In C. K. Madsen, R. D. Greer, & C. H. Madsen (Eds.), *Research in music behavior* (pp. 3–11). New York: Teachers College Press.

Hanson, N. R. (1958). *Patterns of discovery.* Cambridge: Cambridge University Press.

Heller, J., & Campbell, W. (1976). Models of language and intellect in music research. In A. Motycka (Ed.), *Music education for tomorrow's society* (pp. 40–49). Jamestown: GAMT Music Press.

Heller, G. N. (1990). Music education history and American musical scholarship: Problems and promises. *The Bulletin of Historical Research in Music Education, 11(2),* 73.

Heller, G. N., & Wilson, B. D. (1992). Historical research. In R. Colwell (Ed.). *Handbook of research on music teaching and learning* (pp. 102–114). New York: Schirmer.

Hempel, C. (1966). *Philosophy of natural science.* Englewood Cliffs, Prentice Hall.

Hull, D. (1989). *Science as process.* Chicago: University of Chicago Press.

Irwin, R., & de Cosson, A. (Eds.) (2004). a/r/tography: *Rendering self through arts-based living inquiry.* Vancouver: Pacific Educational Press.

Johnson, R. B., & Onwuegbusie, A. J. (2004). Mixed method research: A research paradigm whose time come. *Educational Researcher, 33(7),* 14–26.

Jones, B. J., & McFee, J. K. (1986). Research on teaching arts and aesthetics. In M. C. Wittrock (Ed.), *Handbook of research on teaching*, 3rd ed. (p. 912). New York: Macmillan.

Kaplan, M. (1966). *Foundations and frontiers of music education*. New York: Holt, Rinehart, and Winston.

Kincheloe, J. (1990). *Teachers as researchers: Qualitative inquiry as a path to empowerment*. New York: Falmer.

Kuhn, T. S. (1962). *The structure of scientific revolutions*. Chicago: University of Chicago Press.

Lehrer, R., Serlin, R. C., & Amundson, R. (1990) Knowledge or certainty? A reply to Cziko. *Educational Researcher, 19(6)*, 16–19.

Leonhard, C., & Colwell, R. J. (1976). Research in music education. *Bulletin of the Council for Research in Music Education, 49,* 1–29.

Lindeman, C., Flowers, P., Jellison, J., Kaplan, P. R., & Price, H. E. (1998). *A research agenda for music education: Thinking ahead*. Reston, VA: Music Educators National Conference.

MacDonald, G., & Pettit, P. (1981). *Semantics and social science*. London: Routledge and Kegan Paul.

Newton-Smith, W. H. (1981). *The rationality of science*. London: Routledge and Kegan Paul.

Oja, S. N., & Smulyan, L. (1989). *Collaborative action research: A developmental approach*. London: Falmer.

Pankratz, D. B. (1989). Policies, agendas, and arts education research. *Design for Arts in Education, 90(5),* 2–13.

Petzold, R. G. (1963). Directions for research in music education. *Bulletin of the Council for Research in Music Education, 1,* 18–23.

Phelps, Roger P. (1980). *A guide to research in music education*, 2nd ed. Metuchen, NJ: Scarecrow Press.

Phillips, D. C. (1987). *Philosophy, science, and social inquiry*. Oxford: Pergamon.

Philips, D. C. (1990). Subjectivity and objectivity: An objective inquiry. In E. W. Eisner, & A. Peshkin (Eds.), *Qualitative inquiry in education* (p. 35). New York: Teachers College Press.

Popper, K. (1968). *Conjectures and refutations*. New York: Harper.

Rainbow, E. L., & Froelich H. C. (1987). *Research in music education*. New York: Schirmer.

Reimer, B. (1977). Language or non-language models of aesthetic stimuli. *Journal of Aesthetic Education, 11(3)*.

Reimer, B. (1985). Toward a more scientific approach to music education research. *Bulletin for the Council for Research in Music Education, 83,* 1–21.

Reimer, B. (1989). *A philosophy of music education*, 2nd ed. Englewood Cliffs, NJ: Prentice Hall.

Reimer, B. (2003). *A philosophy of music education: Advancing the vision*. 3rd ed. Upper Saddle River, NJ: Prentice Hall.

Reimer, B. (2004, October). Building the foundations for doctoral programs in music education. Paper presented to the Consortium for International Cooperation, Evanston, IL.

Reinharz, S. (1990). So-called training in the so-called alternative paradigm. In E. Guba (Ed.), *The paradigm dialog*. Beverly Hills, CA: Sage.

Scheffler, I. (1967). *Science and subjectivity*. New York: Bobbs-Merrill.

Schneider, E. H., & Cady, H. L. (1965). Competency of research. In *Evaluation and synthesis of research studies relating to music education*. Columbus: Ohio State University Research Foundation.

Schon, D. A. (1987). *Educating the reflective practitioner*. San Francisco: Jossey-Bass.

Shulman, L. S. (1988). Disciplines of inquiry in education: An overview. In R. M. Jaeger (Ed.), *Complementary methods for research in education*. Washington: American Education Research Association.

Sidnell, R. (1972). The dimensions of research in music education, *Bulletin of the Council for Research in Music Education, 49*, 17–27.

Goswami, D., & Stillman, P. P. (Eds.) (1987). *Reclaiming the classroom: Teacher research as an agency for change*. Upper Montclair, NJ: Boynton.

Stubley, E. V. (1992). Philosophical foundations. In R. Colwell (Ed.), *Handbook of research on music teaching and learning* (pp. 3–20). New York: Schimer.

Toulmin, S. (1961). *Foresight and understanding*. New York: Harper and Row.

Tyack, D. B. (1988). Ways of seeing: An essay on the history of compulsory schooling. In R. M. Jaeger (Ed.), *Complementary methods for research in education*. Washington, DC: American Education Research Association.

Urban, W. J. (1990). The social and institutional analysis section: Context and content. *American Educational Research Journal, 27(1)*, 1–8.

Weimer, W. B. (1979). *Notes on the methodology of scientific research*. Hillsdale, NJ: Lawrence Erlbaum.

Westbury, I. (2002). Theory, research, and the improvement of music education. In R. Colwell & C. P. Richardson (Eds.), *The new handbook of research on music teaching and learning* (pp. 144–161). New York: Oxford University Press.

Wilson, E. (1935). The teacher's use of research. In *Yearbook of the music educators national conference* (pp. 163–166).

Winter, R. (1989). *Learning from experience: Principles and practice in action research*. New York: Falmer.

Zeichner, K. M., & Noffke, S. E. (2001). Practitioner research. In V. Richardson (Ed.). *Handbook of research on teaching*, 4th ed. Washington, D.C.: American Educational Research Association.

Maintaining Quality in Research and Reporting

2

JACK J. HELLER
EDWARD J. P. O'CONNOR

Scholarly Inquiry and a Research Perspective

What Is Research?

In order to evaluate competence in research, the evaluator must first have a clear conception of what constitutes research as opposed to other scholarly activities. There are many scholarly pursuits that may in a broad sense fall under the category "research." The word research (from the French *rechercher*, which means to travel through or survey) implies a going back to search for something. With respect to research in music education, however, that concept is too broad. We are concerned primarily with the systematic search for solutions to problems based on empirical observation. This is not meant to disparage scholarly endeavors that fall outside our more restricted definition. Of course, research searches for something. But that something should be very specific and it should be stated at the outset of any research report. The researcher must have a very clear idea of what the question is that will be investigated. The techniques and methodology used to search for an answer to a question should be appropriate to the question posed. Good research is that which provides as unbiased an answer as possible to a question supported by empirical evidence. "Empirical" here is meant to be viewed as "observations."

The view of the nature of observations has changed over time. Based on the seminal monograph of Campbell and Stanley (1963), research in education during the 1970s and 1980s was dominated by the methodological

38

ideal represented by the premise expressed in that publication: that the "true" experiment was the model for educational researchers. That view was adopted by researchers in music education.

In recent times, however, research methodology became divided between quantitative and qualitative methodologies (see Fraenkel & Wallen, 2000; Grady, 1998). But the seeming dichotomy in current educational research literature between the value of qualitative and quantitative research is misguided. Once the researcher has identified a problem, appropriate means for addressing that problem should be decided. For most research questions, there are multiple techniques that can provide answers to the researcher's hypotheses. The issue should be which approach is appropriate for the question(s) asked.

The term "research" often is used to categorize precursors of the "scientific method." For example, data collection (going to a library to determine what others have written about a topic), taxonomy generation (generating well-thought-out lists), and "experimenting" (in the sense of seeking new experiences: "If I mix these sounds with that rhythm what will happen?") are all considered "research" in the popular use of the word. While these may be necessary activities, their importance is due to the part they play as tools in the total research process, not as research projects in themselves.

In order to seek answers to questions about music teaching or learning, researchers may use a method that has been labeled "historical" (e.g., which answers questions of past practice by examining original documents or artifacts); "descriptive" (e.g., determines the status or state of the art of a phenomenon such as examining process through surveys, case studies, trend studies); or "experimental" (e.g., applying or manipulating various conditions in controlled situations). All of these methods may use techniques that are qualitative or quantitative in nature to provide acceptable answers, depending on the nature of the question. The issue should be whether the answer to an educational question is defensible and persuasive to the informed reader.

Relationship of Theory to Practice and Research

Theory   The questions researchers seek to answer should not be unique to a given situation. Rather, research should be theory driven. In order to contribute anything useful to our knowledge about human behavior (musical or otherwise) research must have an underlying theory to test. However, theory does not develop in isolation. A theory should be based on a philosophical position supported by empirical evidence.

There are some that insist on adding "philosophical" to the methodologies of research. Philosophy is important; it can be scholarly; but it is not research. It is philosophy. Philosophical discourse is essential to a better understanding of music and music teaching and learning, but we do not consider philosophy research. (See Jorgensen, 1992.) Philosophy is a highly regarded scholarly activity.

Philosophical discourse (or, more precisely, model building) should lead to testable hypotheses that allow researchers to collect observations that support or refute a theory (or model). Theories about music teaching or learning can lead us to design research studies that may clarify practice in the music education enterprise. Price (1997) correctly points out that "all pursuits of knowledge inform all others. To ignore any is to be ignorant. Philosophical and historical inquiry uninformed by empirical evidence is very deep in a cave; conversely, empirical evidence without solid philosophical and historical foundation is a pursuit operating without illumination" (p. 4). Amen.

Practice   Practice in music education is driven by many factors: economics, political issues, religion, taxonomies of educational importance, philosophy of what it means to be "educated," and so on. Music educators encounter many pitfalls in their quest for clear and unambiguous answers to questions about the teaching/learning process in music. It is unlikely that the research enterprise, *as it is currently practiced,* will be able to inform the music education profession about the very complex process of becoming musically educated. This is because music education research often is fragmented, rarely led by theory, and too frequently supported by biased evidence.

Even though there are national standards, there is no united agreement among practicing music educators in the elementary, secondary, or tertiary schools in the United States about what it means to be musically educated. Curriculum specialists and philosophers have provided some help. They have generated the taxonomic framework and rationale for music education practice. The profession has had notable scholars who have provided guidance by using these important approaches. Herculean efforts have generated the national standards, goals and objectives, and assessment strategies for music education. But there seems to be little persuasive evidence *from research* that music teachers can use to help them become more successful teachers. While the profession has provided a number of journals (e.g., *The Journal of Research in Music Education, Council Bulletin, Psychology of Music, Update,* etc.) that do report some good research, teachers and professors do not always seem to read and take advantage of what is reported. Part of the reason for this gulf is the lack of substantial support in time and fiscal resources for research in music education.

Research   Examples of research fall into at least three general types: historical (mostly qualitative in technique), descriptive (qualitative or quantitative), and experimental (mostly quantitative). These categories are descriptions in a broad sense of the particular methodologies used to address a research question. They are not meant to exclude other divisions of the research process, or to exclude combinations of these three methodologies.

The nature of human learning in music is extremely complex. Many more carefully designed studies must be carried out in order to begin to understand how musical learning takes place. Psychologists, after more than a century of carefully constructed studies and huge amounts of funding, are only now beginning to understand the nature of human learning under very limited conditions. Even though good music teachers do generally understand the teaching/learning process, knowledge from research of the underlying processes might help improve current practice to a broader community.

Much of the reported research in music education continues to be the reworking of doctoral dissertations. Many of these studies represent a novice's efforts that usually contribute little to understanding the complex issues of music teaching and learning. Such studies do not add credibility to the music education research enterprise. This issue led to the birth of the *Bulletin of the Council for Research in Music Education* in 1963 under the able leadership of Richard Colwell (1969). One of the original purposes of this periodical was to offer critiques of doctoral dissertations in the hope that such critiques would improve future research, and ultimately, teaching practice. While the *Bulletin* certainly made the profession more acutely aware of the many problems that researchers faced and it did have a very positive effect on some subsequent research, the general problem of shoddy research still existed a quarter of a century after the *Bulletin* first was published (Colwell, 1988). Shoddy research still exists today. Doctoral advisers at too many universities are still not well equipped to direct research. University music schools and departments mostly give obeisance to research but do not give release time for faculty to develop their research skills and a research agenda. Teaching loads in music are typically extremely heavy and research funding is small compared to other social sciences, including education.

By contrast, psychologists, who are well-schooled in research techniques, have for many years carried out studies in music. Unfortunately, most of these studies seem to ask questions that are beside the point for music educators. Results of laboratory-type experiments in which computers generate stimuli often are generalized inappropriately to a musical situation. The Ann Arbor Symposium (Taylor, 1981) clearly demonstrated the lack of understanding by prominent psychologists of the issues concerning the music learning and teaching processes. This group of psychologists made it clear that they had no answers to the questions music educators raised. Their feeble attempts to address these questions showed their inability to provide answers, even tentative ones, for the music education profession.

More recently, psychology seems to have embraced music as a robust means to study human behavior. Organized conferences for and by psychologists have proliferated with music as the main topic. Most of the research reported at these meetings have excellent internal validity but questionable external validity. Generalizability to music education issues seems to be limited.

To expect that research in music education or psychology, as currently practiced, can tell music teachers how to improve their instruction is a figment of our collective imaginations. Until the field of music education can justify time release for music faculty to engage in meaningful research (including pre-K to college level teachers) and to provide reasonable funding for such research, not much hope for improvement can be expected. Even if the impairments of time and money were somehow magically removed, the generally low level of graduate research instruction in music still remains a serious problem.

Research is not considered here to be a panacea for the many problems and issues the music education profession faces. It is simply one more human activity that strives to answer perplexing, interesting problems inherent to music education. But good persuasive theorizing accompanied by good persuasive research may help to provide answers. Evidence to convince school boards and state departments of education to require music study as part of the basic school curriculum and to fund such programs properly must continue to be generated if high-quality music education programs are to become the norm rather than the exception.

The music education profession needs to raise the level of understanding about what good research means. And the necessary time must be allocated by administrators to encourage good systematic long-range research programs. University faculty development seminars should be offered for music education faculty so that they can update and upgrade their research skills. If several years (maybe even decades) can be devoted to well-designed research studies in music teaching and learning, then there is hope for research to play a significant role in meeting some of the many lofty goals music educators have.

Distinguishing Research From Other Forms of Scholarly Inquiry

The following taxonomy is an attempt to establish an ordinal scale for written and oral scholarly pursuits.[1] Its purpose is to focus attention on a restricted definition of the term "research," applied here to one endpoint of a continuum. There are many scholarly pursuits, presented in various forms (performance, debate, etc.) that do not properly fall under this definition of research. These forms can be organized into a taxonomy. The reader should keep in mind the distinction between work that is based on empirical observation and that which is not, even though it may masquerade under the term "research."

Eisner (1997) takes the view that *all* forms that are used to "inform" should be called research. In defense of his definition of qualitative research he writes that,

> there is an intimate relationship between our conception of what the products of research are to look like and the way we go about doing research. What we think it means to do research has to do with our conception of meaning, our conception of cognition, and our beliefs about the forms of consciousness

that we are willing to say advance human understanding—an aim, I take it, that defines the primary mission of research. What succeeds in deepening meaning, expanding awareness, and enlarging understanding is, in the end, a community decision. Conversation and publication are, in part, aimed at testing ideas in that community. (pp. 5–6)

What Eisner is talking about includes *all* human communication. The arts accomplish Eisner's notion of informing us about the world. Only in that broad sense are the arts then considered research. Eisner would probably call each of the categories that follow (i.e., Performance, Documentary, Position Paper, or Debates) research, as each can inform us about the world in some way. Yet, each of these categories misses some essential character of research. The essential character of research is that it must attempt to present unbiased evidence, with equal opportunity for an opposing point of view to be considered.

We do not accept Eisner's proposition. The many ways that may inform us about the education process are ubiquitous. They may tell us what the writer (or actor, or musician, or painter, etc.) believes, and they may be very powerful. But as the following taxonomy tries to show, these varied forms of human discourse or communication systems are not, by our definition, research. The taxonomy's purpose is to focus attention on a restricted definition of the term "research." If research, in this restricted sense, is carried out with care and systematic rigor, it hopefully will add a measure of knowledge about the music teaching/learning process.

The Taxonomy

Performance (Dance, Plays, Poems, Music)   The first activity in the taxonomy is performance. A performance is complete or sufficient by itself. That is, there is (usually) no direct reference to other similar productions, although knowledge of the genre, style, and of the milieu from which it springs is usually necessary for the reader's, listener's, or viewer's understanding of the work. Judgment of the merits of the work is an external function (literary criticism), not part of the "performance."

One can argue successfully that good performing artists (musicians, dancers, and actors) follow the general guidelines set out in the "scientific method." For example, the performer often identifies a problem, defines the problem more specifically, sets up a question (what will happen if I do this or that?) or an hypothesis (I think this will happen if I do that), collects data (tries out a particular passage to see if the hypothesis is correct), and draws conclusions about the evidence that was collected. That process does follow the steps generally given for the "scientific method." But this entire activity usually *is not explicit* and not available to others than the performer. The judgment of the performance by listeners is much like literary criticism, not research.

Documentary (News Reports, Book Lists, Catalogues)   A documentary is an enumeration of data or a reporting of "events" (a list of musical scores collected, documentary coverage of a convention, an enumeration of a school's assets). Often a taxonomy is generated to help organize a list into categories (étude taxonomies, curriculum taxonomies). In all documentaries, the choice of the data to be included implies an editorial function. Accuracy and completeness may suffer even with unbiased authors. Judgment of the work is external and is usually accomplished by comparison with an alternative presentation. Isomorphism (having similar or identical structure or appearance) is usually the standard of comparison.

The person responsible for producing the documentary chooses the data to be reported. This is the editorial function. The reporter's enlightenment may be very important to the success of the finished product and the end result may be very elucidating. In fact, it may lead to someone carrying out a research project to try to verify an aspect of the documentary. The documentary may be very well crafted and be very useful, but it is not research in our restricted sense.

As Colwell (1988) rightly points out, "Too often journals present 'this is the way it is' articles; conventions and workshops offer sessions on 'how to do it,' and our professional lives become crowded with in-service education that is primarily observation of 'successful' techniques rather than enlightening dialogue about the theoretical rationale, the value, and the effect of practices" (p. 5). Such reports and activities are not research. They are either documentaries or position papers.

Position Paper (Political Speeches, Sales Promotions)   The position paper presents its case in the strongest possible terms using arguments that do not admit to any essential deficiencies. Examples are monographs or essays supporting a particular point of view or dogma (pro arguments), polemics rejecting a particular point of view or dogma (con arguments), political speeches, commercials, and so on. Unending varieties of persuasion are employed (hard sell, soft sell, reverse psychology, etc.). Judgment is external and can be directed toward the merits of the argument or toward the (internal) virtuosity of the author, depending on the critic's agreement with or opposition to the point of view expressed.

Some position papers may be regarded as fine examples of scholarly endeavor. But, again, they are not research. Strong, even elegant, arguments for or against an issue do not meet the essential requirements for research. The researcher must take a neutral position and must make a strong attempt to minimize bias. *This chapter should be considered a position paper.*

Competitive Debate (High School or College Debating Team Competition)   In a competitive debate the pro and con arguments are presented by two groups under rules of procedure designed to provide a "fair" competition. A third group, the judges, observes. The outcome is based on the relative virtuosity of the participants, each of whom presents a *position paper.* The merit of the position is not a consideration, as the sides of the argument are assigned to the participants on a chance basis. Judgment is accomplished within the context of the debate.

Formal Debate (Town Meeting, Courtroom Trial)   In a formal debate (often on a referendum at a town meeting, or a civil or criminal trial) opposing views concerning a specified issue are presented by two individuals or groups. A third group (judge, jury, or voters) determines the outcome of the debate. The judgment is based, ideally, on the merits of the position presented. However, the relative virtuosity of the advocates often carries more weight. The "right to counsel" in legal proceedings is an example of the attempt to diminish the difference in virtuosity between the prosecution and the defense. Judgment is accomplished within the context of the debate.

Research (Historical, Descriptive, Experimental, and So On)   According to *Webster's Dictionary*, research is the "careful, systematic, patient study and investigation in some field of knowledge, undertaken to discover or establish facts or principles" (Agnes, 1999). This definition is somewhat naive. We prefer not to use "discover" in any definition of research. Research does not "discover or establish facts." "Facts" often change when new evidence is presented. Barzun and Graff (1992) assert, "The choice of facts and of relations is dictated by human interest as well as by nature. . . . [T]he facts, moreover, are seen through ideas (for example, the idea of a molecule) that are not immediately visible and ready to be noted down. They are searched for *with a purpose in mind*" [italics added] (p. 182). "Careful, systematic, patient study and investigation" (Agnes, 1999), nevertheless, must take place in research. Good research can verify principles and can address theory.

The researcher must develop arguments supported by careful observations that are clearly elucidated. These arguments should provide support for or against a particular theory that is being tested. The researcher acts as the prosecution, the defense, and as a preliminary judge. There is judgment (usually implicit, but sometimes explicit) of the methodology in terms of its appropriateness, sensitivity, and balance. With bias minimized or controlled, a natural balance is maintained, as both sides of the argument have the same advocate. The researcher in the statement of conclusions gives an initial critique of the merits of the issue under investigation. In addition, the researcher ties the research to the results and arguments of others through a careful presentation of references and bibliography, including opposing or contradictory points of view.

Interpretation of the Research Report

The *Bulletin of the Council for Research in Music Education* has since its inception in 1963 successfully provided critiques of doctoral dissertations (Colwell, 1969). Many of these critiques have demonstrated the lack of understanding in certain doctoral dissertations of what research means and what may appropriately be concluded from research reports.

Some of the criteria that should be used to determine the "goodness" of a particular research report are as follows.

1. Is there a theory or model that the research is designed to explore?
2. Is there a specific question or questions that the research will attempt to answer?
3. Does the research cite related research that seems appropriate to the study?
4. Are the techniques for data collection specified? These may be quantitative or qualitative in nature. Do these techniques seem appropriate to the questions asked?
5. If statistics are used, are the underlying assumptions for the statistical tests met?
6. Do the conclusions logically follow from the evidence collected?

Schneider and Cady (1967) provided an analysis of research in music education from 1930 to 1962. Their results showed that 273 research reports out of 1,818 analyzed (about 15%) could be considered "relevant and competent research" by their stated criteria for relevance and competence. Of course, the validity of these data is based on the authors' critical analyses. But whatever analytic techniques were used, their perception of competence in music education research was not very high.

While there have been other excellent content analyses of research in music education (e.g., Abeles, 1980; Hair, 2000; Standley, 1996; Yarbrough, 1984, 1996), these have not focused on the *competence* of the research cited. Grieshaber (1987) does provide a critical review but only in general terms does she note "many problems" with the cited research. Radocy and Boyle (1997) cite an extraordinary number and wide range of research topics in music education. While much of the research cited in their excellent book has been reported in prominent journals, the studies either tend to have poor external validity (to music) or the conclusions are not supported by reasonable evidence. Radocy and Boyle state that "much of it [music education experimental research] . . . lacks the rigorous control of the variables that would enable it to meet standards for research design in the behavioral sciences as delineated by Campbell and Stanley (1963), so interpretations must be made with caution" (p. 147).

In fact, many researchers cite related research without always selecting research reports that are exemplary in design and data collecting procedures. So, instead of building on the work of good previous research, often poorly designed studies are used as models. This practice seems to be fairly widespread in music education.

Often the conclusions reported in published research articles are not appropriate to the evidence provided. Some research reports generalize far beyond what the data analysis allows. In order to have confidence in any research, the reader must judge whether the research states a clear objective, follows an appropriate methodology, and draws reasonable conclusions.

The evaluator's first task is to attempt to reconstruct the research process from the report to determine if anything was missed or not carried out properly. (See the second section of this chapter.) Barzun and Graff (1992) have pointed out that one should recognize the difference between the research activity (developing hypotheses, collecting data, etc.) and the research report. They are two distinct activities. What viewers see in journals or hear in presentations is a summary of the research activity. All research reports are considered to be representations of the researcher's perspective. Barzun and Graff warn that, as unbiased as the researcher tries to be, the reader always should be on guard for unwarranted statements.

The overriding decisions about the "goodness" of a research report should adhere to the following guidelines. Whatever the research methodology or technique used, the researcher should have:

1. Clearly stated the purpose of the study (i.e., defined the problem).
2. Shown that she or he knows something about the area to be studied. This is generally accomplished by providing a section of related research. The related research should be assessed for its competence.
3. Clearly stated an hypothesis (or hypotheses) that points toward a solution to the problem and consequences that indicate what data should be collected.
4. Told the reader what techniques were used to gather evidence. This may range from studying artifacts or documents from an earlier century, to interviewing an artist, to giving a specific group a task oriented auditory stimulus tape, and so on.
5. Not generalized to situations other than what the evidence shows. Too often the author generalizes far beyond the data. For example, if musical scores of a particular composer demonstrate use of a specific harmonic technique, it may not be reasonable to generalize this information to other scores of that composer. The scores that were not examined may be quite different in the use of the harmonic technique. For an in-depth case study of an individual, it is not always proper to generalize to other individuals, even if the others seem to be similar to the case studied. There can, however, be one or more "principles" that the study has produced that can be generalizable.

    In an experimental study, if inferential statistics are not employed, the researcher should not generalize. In that situation, only the data from the sample(s) studied are all that should be discussed. Often, even when inferential statistics are employed, and the statistical tests turn out not to be significant, the author will point out that the data were almost significant. That is like being almost pregnant. If the statistical analysis from an inferential test is not significant, then there is no difference predicted in the population. The author may still discuss the data that were collected and their possible implications, but generalization beyond the sample data is not warranted or acceptable.
6. Decided whether or not a statistically significant difference between levels of a variable represents a meaningful or practical difference. Tunks (1978) suggested that a fairly straightforward procedure known as "Omega Squared" be used in order to estimate the strength of association between

or among variables. He points out that traditional statistical tests that have been used in a "substantial portion of published music education research . . . yield . . . limited information" (p. 28). Tunks (p. 33) gives the following suggestions for researchers and research readers:

- When reading research results, do not stop with statistical significance. If strength of association is reported, consider it; if not, calculate it.
- When reporting research, include a strength of association estimate, or at least calculate and consider it carefully before formulating conclusions that may be unfounded.
- If strength of association is not reported, include sufficient data for the reader to make the appropriate calculations.

Excellent discussions of other ways to address the issue of the magnitude of a statistically significant test in a research study can be found in Cohen (1994), Kirk (1996), Rosenthal (1991), Rostov and Rosenthal (1984), and Thompson (1996).

Cohen (1994) points out the "near-universal misrepresentation" of significant testing and suggests the use of graphs to describe effect size (p. 997). Without going into the details of the meaning of testing a null hypothesis here, suffice it to say that Cohen recommends that "we routinely report effect sizes in the form of confidence limits" (p. 1002). Cohen says the best way to reduce misinterpretation of a statistically significant result is to reduce the variance attributable to unreliable and invalid measurement. We agree that all observations (measurements) in a research study should be reliable and valid.

Kirk (1996) actually argues against null hypothesis testing. He asserts that there is only one way to know whether an effect size is due to chance sampling variability and that is to do a replication of the study (p. 756). He agrees with Cohen when he suggests utilizing confidence intervals for sample data.

Meta-analysis is described in great detail by Rosenthal (1991). This approach to estimating the magnitude of a relationship between two or more variables deals with quantification procedures for comparing and combining the results of a *series* of studies. That is, the researcher should not consider the results of *one* study to draw conclusions about the magnitude of an effect.

Rostov and Rosenthal (1984) discuss various ways to determine whether a statistical difference is a meaningful difference. The most straightforward is to define an effect size as "small," "medium," or "large" based on the correlation squared (r^2) among variables. They designate a correlation of .10 as small, .30 as medium, and .50 as large (p. 106).

Thompson (1996) argues that "many people who use statistical [significance] tests might not place such a premium on the tests if these individuals understood what the tests really do, and what the tests do not do" (p. 26). Among the approaches suggested to determine effect size are adjusted R^2, eta^2, and omega^2 (see Tunks, 1978, discussed earlier). Thompson encourages authors "to (a) correctly interpret statistical tests, (b) always interpret effect sizes, and (c) always explore result replicability" (p. 29).

The six guidelines presented above are intended to point out some of the most egregious weaknesses to look for in research reports. No doubt there are others. Careful researchers (in the critique of their own research and the research of others) should always be on guard for unwarranted bias and generalization. There are numerous volumes that describe in great detail various methodologies and techniques that can help to minimize bias in research and to allow the researcher to generalize results. The reader is encouraged to seek out this expertise in order to improve his or her own research skills.

Evaluating the Research Process and Reports

Critiquing the Research Process

As a field of research develops, we expect it to become more mature and sophisticated with an increasingly higher quality of production. But, we cannot take that for granted. Ultimately, quality in research depends on the rigor with which each researcher practices the craft. Unfortunately, rigor is not a finite quality. We cannot set a goal by which we expect researchers to demonstrate at least an 80% level of rigor. What we can do is periodically to remind our colleagues—both the practitioners and the readers of research—of the criteria by which research of quality may be achieved. Each individual must apply these criteria conscientiously and with discipline; in other words, with all the rigor that can be mustered.

The process of evaluating research parallels that of doing research. The model for research says, "State assumptions"; the model for evaluation says, "Were assumptions stated?" The key in either case is the application of criteria to determine whether the statement is adequate. Our goal here is to make these criteria explicit, particularly from the perspective of the evaluator. To do so, we will look at each step in the research process.

Researchers follow models in the same way composers follow forms. All works called symphonies will have certain structural features in common. Beyond that, each work will have unique characteristics that derive from the composer's creative, problem-solving process. The person analyzing a composition will attempt to identify the features of the work and understand the process the composer executed. Along the way, the analyst may make certain judgments, for example, "The work lacks rhythmic variety." Similarly, the person evaluating research starts with the report and, because the format of the report differs from the actual research process, attempts to reconstruct the steps the researcher took and to make some decisions about the adequacy of those steps.

We should note at this point that, if the evaluator is an advisor or member of an advisory committee, the evaluation will be an ongoing process as a student's research progresses. The same criteria will apply at each step.

Certain steps in the process must follow in a given order. It is impossible to define a research problem adequately if the subject has not been sufficiently delimited or is vaguely stated. Hypotheses cannot be identified if the problem is poorly conceived. Techniques for data gathering and analysis cannot be detailed if hypotheses do not point to the data that must be treated.

Other steps in the process occur whenever it is necessary to refine the study further. For example, assumptions may underlie the general topic, the specific subject, the research problem, or hypotheses. Similarly, terms must be defined whenever they arise. Concepts must be recognized and made explicit any time that it is necessary to be sure the reader understands what is being discussed. Limitations must be applied whenever it is essential to narrow the scope of the project further. It is the job of the evaluator to track these steps even if they are not made explicit in the report.

A couple of general observations may be useful. The art of research is the art of asking questions. The more questions that are asked, and the more incisive they are, the more likely the researcher is to uncover the pertinent variables of a study. The evaluator can judge whether sufficiently incisive questions have been asked. The science of research is the application of analysis and synthesis. Analysis does not occur only when the researcher has gathered data; it occurs at every step of the way. The general topic is analyzed to determine its major components and extract a specific subject; the subject is analyzed to identify something that is problematic; the problem is analyzed to discover relationships that may lead to hypotheses.

When the data have been analyzed, the process of synthesis begins. The data are categorized to show results; the results are examined to draw conclusions; the conclusions are placed in the context of the original topic. The research model should have a nice hourglass figure—broad at the level of the topic, narrow at the waist where individual points of data are identified, and again broad where the conclusions contribute some new insight to the field. The details of this process of questioning, analysis, and synthesis provide the framework for evaluating the research.

In his chapter, "Toward a Rational Critical Process," Gonzo (1992) presents several models for critiquing research, depending on the type of research or review. These models have a number of steps in common, differing primarily in the techniques for treating data. We will consider here the criteria for judging each of the common steps.

Topic or Theory Gonzo's models begin with the terms "Introductory model" or "Introductory rationale." Other terms for this beginning phase found in the literature include "topic," "theory," or "general hypothesis" (sometimes "working hypothesis"). The point is that an individual study should be related to the field and should help advance our knowledge in regard to some general concern; in other words, it will be one tile in a mosaic of a broad idea (see the section on theory and practice earlier in this chapter).

Sometimes we encounter a very specific problem. A person comes around a bend on a wooded trail and is face-to-face with a mother bear and cubs. The problem is evident immediately. It may be difficult in that situation to place the problem into the general context of animal behavior and hypothesize whether to run, freeze, or jump and scream like a maniac. Likewise, in teaching, we may encounter a bear of a problem—a particular approach is just not working with an individual student. To avoid trial and error (or screaming like a maniac), it is useful to put the problem into the context of some form of learning theory. This allows the researcher to bring a substantial body of literature to bear on the problem.

The evaluator's first question, therefore, may be whether there is a clearly stated topic, theory, or rationale for the study. How does one recognize a theory? Ironically, "learning theory" is not a single theory; it is a collection of theories. There are theories about individual learning styles, about the relation of maturation to music learning, and about how people learn to identify intervals.

Let us turn to a specific example of a well-stated theory. In *Africa and the Blues,* Kubik (1999) said:

> We proceed from the notion that there is no such thing as "roots" of the blues, but that the American blues were a logical development that resulted from specific processes of cultural interaction among eighteenth- to nineteenth-century African descendants in the United States, under certain economic and social conditions. (p. 4)

Substitute the word "theory" for "notion." Note that the theory, or topic, is not stated as a title, for example, "The Origin of the Blues." It begins by denying a common perception, that there is some primordial root of the blues, like the taproot of a tree. Rather, the blues resulted from cultural interaction, and there was an identifiable process involved. The process can be examined. Also, blues did not emerge in isolation, the product of some individual's creativity in the studio, but under particular economic and social conditions. How does this theory relate to general concerns in the field? Kubik said,

> In respect to its earlier history, most authors agree that the blues is a tradition that developed in the Deep South at the end of the nineteenth century under specific circumstances, molding together traits whose remote origins can be traced to distinctive African regions with other traits from Euro-American traditions, such as the use of ending rhymes in most of the lyrics, reference to I–IV–V degrees, strophic form, and certain Western musical instruments. The search for the blues' "African roots" has been a persistent concern in African-American studies. (pp. 3–4)

Following the previous statement of theory, Kubik posed questions: "Which African eighteenth- to nineteenth-century traditions preceded the blues, channeling experiences and energies into the formative processes of this music? And in which parts of Africa were these traditions established?" (p. 4). These questions form a general hypothesis establishing a direction for the research: to look for the origin of the blues in particular related African traditions and in specific African regions. To illustrate how the ending relates back to the theory, one of Kubik's conclusions was that ". . . most of the blues tradition in the rural areas of Mississippi has prevailed as a recognizable extension in the New World of a west central Sudanic style cluster" (p. 203).

Analysis of the Topic   The research report may go directly from the general theory to the specific subject of the study. However, in the process of identifying the subject, the researcher analyzes the topic quite thoroughly. The major components and subcomponents of the topic are determined, relationships between these components are examined, and a specific research subject is selected. The reason for identifying all of the components and subcomponents is to be sure that nothing that has bearing on the subject has been overlooked. If a researcher is primarily concerned with the learning activities in a classroom or rehearsal but has overlooked the impact of an administrative decision to shift to a block schedule, a major variable will have been missed.

In their large-scale study of the economics of the performing arts, Baumol and Bowen (1966, p. xv) began with three major components: the current state of affairs, the trends and their analysis, and sources of financial support. Each was further delineated. Under the current state of affairs they considered the organizations (in theater, opera, music, and dance); the cultural boom; the audience; the performer, composer, playwright, and choreographer; and the financial state of the organizations. In a work of this scope, each of these components became a chapter of the book. After a similar analysis of the other major components, they made the following statement: "The central purpose of this study is to explain the financial problems of the performing groups and to explore the implications of these problems for the future of the arts in the United States" (p. 4). This was professional research done over a few years with a large staff and substantial funding. A student project, starting with the same topic, might further subdivide the components to arrive at relationships between more specific aspects. The following subject might result: What effect would an expansion of advertising by the Hartford (CT) Symphony have on ticket sales for concerts, and would it be cost-effective?

Need   It may seem self-evident that there should be a recognized need for a study, but in practice it is not that simple. The researcher must review the literature thoroughly to be certain that the need has not already been met. One student proposed to his advisor to do a dissertation on a specific aspect of orchestration, only to be gruffly rebuffed. Later he discovered that the advisor's dissertation had been on the same subject. (This is not meant to suggest that a replication of a study may not be appropriate. If a student suggests a change in certain aspects of the original work, and that these changes may contribute to a better understanding of the underlying theory, the replication may be warranted.)

The evaluator of research, particularly an advisory committee member, will want to know whether the need for a study extends beyond a local situation. Will the results be generalizable, replicable, or disseminatable elsewhere? Is the subject of consequence or is it trivial? Will it contribute in some way to filling a gap in the literature or theory of the field? Even though there may be a legitimate need, can it be met at this time or are there intervening steps that must be taken first? Is there sufficient theory to back up the study; for example, if it involves some aspect of musical cognition, are there sufficient operational definitions of the cognition process to underlie the study?

There are at least two cautions that reviewers should bear in mind. First, was the need driven by expedience? Many researchers face the three-headed monster known as RPT (reappointment, promotion, and tenure). Was there a legitimate need for a particular study or was something rushed into print or onto a conference program in order for it to appear on a resume? Second, does the reviewer's own bias intervene? In response to a dissertation proposal in a graduate seminar, one class member blurted out, "Why in the world would anyone want to do that?" To him, the subject was a piece of meaningless minutia; to the proposer, it was an important missing link in his area of specialization. It is the responsibility of the researcher to state the need clearly and show its importance in the field; it is the responsibility of the reviewer to keep an open mind as to interests that may be different from his or her own.

Lomax presented a clear-cut example of a statement of need in *Folk Song Style and Culture* (1968) regarding his collection and analysis of folksongs and related cultural materials. "The work was filled with a sense of urgency. To a folklorist, the uprooting and destruction of traditional cultures and consequent gray-out or disappearance of the human variety presents [a] serious . . . threat. . . . The folk, the primitive, the non-industrial societies account for most of the cultural values of the planet" (p. 4).

Needs may be identified through the researcher's own teaching and musical experience, through conflicts and gaps in the literature, and through the suggestions for further research found at the end of most research reports. Researchers should be cautious, however, to weigh carefully the merit of suggstions for further research.

Purpose   The purpose of the study refers back to the "introductory rationale" but is somewhat more narrowly defined. It should point to the specific subject of the research after the topic has been analyzed and the need has been made explicit. It is important to distinguish between the need and the purpose. That is, it is not helpful to say, "There is a need to solve the problem. The purpose is to solve the problem." The purpose should be to apply and test new methodologies, make comparisons, derive principles, establish connections or correlations, and the like. To return to the Lomax example above, he stated:

> Our study began with the perception that there are powerful stylistic models shaping the majority of song performances in large regions of the world. The goal of our research was, first, to devise a descriptive technique [later called *cantometrics*] that would locate these grand song-style patterns in the recorded data itself and, second, to find what cultural regularities underlie and are relevant to these far-ranging and powerfully formative styles. (1968, p. 13)

The reviewer will want to make sure that the purpose (goal, intent, and such synonyms) is appropriate to the scope of the study. A purpose that is too grandiose and does not point to a specific subject is not likely to be met. The reviewer also will want to know what the study is intended to accomplish because the conclusions should show that the purpose has been fulfilled. In general, there should be just one purpose to a study, otherwise it is likely to go in divergent directions and never be resolved.

Survey of the Literature   While there may be a section or chapter in a dissertation or book titled Survey of Literature that reviews what the researcher has learned, in fact the process of reviewing literature is continuous throughout the study. Initially, the review helps the researcher select a topic and determine what is already known about it, including the theory on which it is based. It helps delimit the subject and identify variables having bearing on the subject. The literature will verify the existence of a problem.

To take a fairly simple example, one student wanted to determine whether beginning instrumental students will make better progress in groupings of like instruments (such as all single reeds) or unlike instruments. He found articles, four of which favored like instruments, four unlike, and four said the issue was inconclusive. Therefore, the problem remained. The literature should provide tools and techniques for data-gathering or, at least, guidelines and models for their design. The researcher also will find appropriate quantitative tools. Finally, the literature will keep the researcher up-to-date in the field. The reviewer may ask several questions about the way in which the literature was treated. Does the researcher show a sufficiently broad knowledge of the field? Did the individual examine the literature critically by determining whether authors were writing from the point of view of a particular philosophy? Were biases in the literature accounted for? Did the researcher determine whether recent literature extends, contradicts, or confirms past conclusions? Did the researcher determine whether certain data-gathering or analytical techniques have been supplanted or rendered obsolete by recent developments? Does the researcher present both (or all) sides of an issue and treat issues without bias; or does the researcher stack the deck with literature supporting a particular point of view? In the report, has the writer padded the bibliography with items that are beyond the scope of the study? Has appropriate form been used for citations and references?

The Subject   The convention of using the heading "Statement of the Problem" sometimes masks the need to distinguish between the research topic, the subject, and the problem. The topic is the broad field of interest, the subject is the specific phenomenon to be examined, and the problem is that which needs solution. Without the intervening step of defining the subject, the problem is likely to stay on too general a level to be resolved.

From a general topic, the researcher selects a specific subject to study. How specific should it be? The scope depends, in part, on the researcher's situation. A university faculty member may be engaged in a fairly large-scale, long-term project; a doctoral candidate will select a more limited subject that can come to completion probably within 1 to 3 years; a master's student will be wise to confine a thesis to a project that can be completed within the last year of study.

Regardless of scope, the rule of thumb is that a subject is adequately defined when all relevant questions about that subject have been asked within the scope of the study. For example, Landau (1960) wanted to know whether composers' compositional practices conform to the theories that they profess to follow. He selected Paul Hindemith, who had written about his theories in *The Craft of Musical Composition*. Because he could not answer all relevant questions about all of Hindemith's works, Landau selected chamber music extending over the composer's career and chose comparable sections to analyze, such as the first theme of sonata-allegro movements. So, the scope was limited to one composer, one genre, and one segment of form. The subject, then, was the relation between theory and practice in selected chamber works of Paul Hindemith. Landau could reasonably expect to answer all relevant questions about that subject. Notice, however, that there is nothing problematic about that statement. Before reaching the level of the problem, he had to define theory in terms of specific compositional rules and practice according to particular examples in the music. The problem was to determine the extent to which the examples conformed to the rules.

The person evaluating research needs to determine whether the subject is too broad for all relevant questions to be answered or, conversely, whether it is too narrow, failing to account for certain relevant questions. Questions that may be related to the subject but not relevant to the problem are set aside as limitations.

Analysis of the Subject   In order to arrive at a concrete problem that leads toward observable data, the subject must be analyzed. Proposals by some novice researchers smack of the following example:

Subject: A car

Problem: The car won't run.

Hypothesis: If the car is fixed, it will run.

Only after the hood is raised and the components of the mechanical system are identified—battery, wires, spark plugs, distributor, and so on—is it possible to begin to identify the problem.

The analysis of the subject may begin by asking the questions who, when, where, why, what, and how. If a subject statement contains an abstract term such as "teaching," the researcher can apply these questions: Who is the teacher (training, experience, duties)? When does teaching take place (schedule, use of time)? Where does it take place (use of space, relationships in space)? Why (philosophy, goals, objectives)? What is included (curriculum)? How is it administered (methods)? Relationships between these items may be examined to determine one or more research problems. In one school system, for example, administrative pressure for a performance-based program conflicted with the teachers' goal for a problem-solving approach.

At this point, other steps in the process may be applied to the analysis of the subject. Which elements are relevant and which may be set aside as limitations? Is it necessary to further clarify the meaning and characteristics of relevant items? Are there assumptions that need to be made explicit or questioned underlying the facts, explanations, and relations?

Literature can be of considerable help in analyzing the subject. For example, Buttram (1969) wanted to know what factors were involved in a person's ability to identify intervals correctly. Four factors were identified in the literature. This led to a problem in which the factors were compared to see which had the greatest influence on accuracy of interval identification.

The challenge for the person evaluating the research is not only to follow the researcher's analysis but also to determine whether any important steps are missing or misapplied.

Limitations   The application of limitations in a study serves important functions: It establishes the scope of the study, distinguishes the essential from the unessential, helps define steps in the process and determine pertinent variables, and informs both the reader and the researcher as to what is purposely being omitted. The report may contain a section in which limitations are listed. Or, they may be stated at any point in the text where it is necessary to inform the reader that something has been omitted. In either case, the researcher wants to anticipate the reader's concern, "But you didn't cover such-and-such point," by already having accounted for such points in the report as much as possible.

The evaluator will want to ask several questions about the limitations. Does the researcher have a rationale for the limitations? In Landau's study (1960), he did not discuss Hindemith's acoustical theories because they had no bearing on the rules for composition. In the study of groupings of instruments for lessons, the student eliminated the full ensemble because ensemble rehearsals tend to have different objectives than lessons. Has the researcher appropriately omitted items that would not lead toward observable data? Have certain limitations been set for expediency? Sometimes researchers want to limit the setting for a study to locations that are convenient, such as their own schools, when that might bias the sample by excluding certain ethnic groups, socioeconomic levels, and the like. It is possible to limit a study too narrowly. Has a sample been limited to a point that would affect the ability to generalize from the study? Has the researcher consulted literature that would help determine the appropriate size of a sample? Have any limitations been set that would cause relevant variables to be omitted? For example, if the participants in a study were limited to one grade level, it probably would eliminate maturation as a variable. Has the learning portion of a study omitted anything pertinent to the test? It is important for the evaluator to account for the fact that not all limitations are intentional or stated by the writer.

Definition of Terms and Concepts   The purpose of defining terms and concepts is to ensure that the researcher and reader have a common understanding, both in respect to the connotation of words and the perception of phenomena. The researcher also has to be conscientious about definitions in order to advance through the project. Vague terms and ill-considered ideas are stumbling blocks. If there are a number of technical terms, they may be grouped together in the report under the heading Definition of Terms. Otherwise, terms are defined in the text as they are encountered, often illustrated by an example beginning "such as. . . ."

The researcher should consider the audience in order to judge whether it is necessary to refine a term. For an audience of musicians, it is unnecessary to define an orchestra as an ensemble of strings, brass, woodwinds, and percussion. But, if the subject is the development of orchestration for the early concerto grosso, then a precise accounting of instruments at given points in time would be essential.

Concepts are somewhat more elusive, more difficult to recognize and define than terms. Essentially, they tell how people, including the researcher, think about things. Merriam (1964), in *The Anthropology of Music,* identifies a number of concepts about the practice of music and its role in society (pp. 63–84). These may be summarized as questions. How does any culture distinguish between music and nonmusic? What constitutes musical talent? What is the purpose or function of music in the society? What is the nature and importance of song texts? What is the optimum size for the performing group? What are the sources of music? Is music an emotion-producer? Who owns music? To what extent is there a preference for vocal or instrumental music? The answers to these questions tell how people of a given culture conceptualize their music.

Differing concepts about how people perceive music are embodied in the terms psychoacoustics and psychomusicology. One says that people respond to acoustical signals. The other says that two people may respond to the same acoustical signals differently (in a performance jury, one judge responded "Weak tone," another judge said "Refined tone.")

The evaluator needs to determine whether the researcher has consistently informed the reader about the meaning of terms and concepts, identifying any point at which the reader might say, "What do you mean by that?" The reviewer also should determine whether the research has been in any way hindered because the researcher has taken certain terms and concepts for granted and failed to recognize the impact that might have on a study. A careless researcher might base a study on older concepts that have since been rendered obsolete.

Assumptions   Assumptions serve a number of purposes in a study. First, they state conclusions and understandings from previous research. It is not necessary for the researcher to repeat previous research; rather, she or he may assume the validity of conclusions that others have reached as a point from which to develop something new or extend the previous research. Of course, the previous conclusions must be verifiable. Buttram cited previous research based on the assumption that "[A] highly developed awareness and understanding of musical intervals is considered basic to good musicianship. Interval discrimination has been used as an indicator of musical aptitude in tests . . . indicat[ing] that a close relationship exists between skill in sight-singing and interval identification" (1969, p. 309). However, since few attempts had been made to verify these views experimentally, he felt that there was a need for further research.

Second, assumptions may summarize the current status of thought in a particular field. In the book cited earlier, Merriam gave four assumptions about the then relatively new field of ethnomusicology (1964, pp. 37–39). First, "that ethnomusicology aims to approximate the methods of science"; second, "that ethnomusicology is both a field and a laboratory discipline"; third, "that ethnomusicology has been concerned primarily with non-Western cultures and most specifically with nonliterate societies"; and fourth, "while field techniques must of necessity differ from society to society, field method remains essentially the same in overall structure no matter what society is being investigated."

Third, assumptions state a point of view. In proposing a computerized system of score analysis, Forte (1966) said that the musical event is represented by the symbols on the page. Someone might say, "Wait a minute. You're ignoring the performance as part of the musical event." But, Forte was implying that musicians start developing an interpretation of the music (the musical event) by studying a score. A computer could count the number of secondary dominants in a score faster and as accurately as a person could. As long as a reader recognizes Forte's assumption that the score represents the musical event, it is possible to follow the logic of his train of thought through the study.

Some assumptions are not just those of the researcher but express commonly held views in the field. Buttram began his article with the following statement (substitute "assumed to be" for "considered"): "The musical interval may be considered the basic unit of musical construction. With its two tones presented sequentially, the interval is the basic melodic unit; with the tones presented simultaneously, the unit is harmonic" (1969, p. 309).

Fourth, assumptions help advance the analysis of the study by contributing to the definition of the problem. Often, assumptions are derived from concepts. If we conceive of something in a particular way, then certain things will follow. Buttram found that there were four factors that influenced interval identification. Each factor has an associated concept and assumption that might be summarized in this way:

1. Concept: Each interval has a distinctive character (quale) by which it is recognized.
   Assumption: The interval should be recognized instantly (it does not require time to figure it out).
2. Concept: The distance between pitches in an interval may be judged by the listener.
   Assumption: It takes time (a few seconds) to judge the distance between pitches.
3. Concept: Intervals do not normally appear in isolation but within a tonal context.
   Assumption: Hearing the interval within a tonal context will help the listener to identify the interval.
4. Concept: Certain intervals are more distinctive to the listener.
   Assumption: There will be a hierarchy of intervals in terms of accuracy of identification.

These concepts and assumptions led to a problem statement in which each factor was compared to a control set of intervals to determine accuracy of identification with college students as subjects.

As with other steps in the research process, assumptions should not be used for the sake of expediency. One student said, "For the purpose of this study, I will assume that all teachers are good teachers." Hardly.

The evaluator needs to determine whether stated assumptions are verifiable in fact or are open to question. If the assumptions cannot be supported, the results of the study are open to challenge. Has the researcher presented assumptions as fact or truth? Are there assumptions implied in the report that the researcher has not recognized and stated? Although it was never stated explicitly, in one study it was clear that minority students were assumed to have lower self-esteem than majority students. (In fact, minority students scored higher than majority students on both the pretest and posttest of the Coopersmith Self-Esteem Inventory.) Have assumptions connected to the conclusions and interpretation of results been stated?

Problem   A research problem represents a recognized difficulty, omission, question, conflict, or inaccuracy discovered through the analysis of a subject.

It may result from the need to extend, update, reinterpret, or validate earlier studies, or it may result from explorations in a new direction.

We encounter the term "problem" in three connotations, and this is a source of confusion to students. A student may say, "Scheduling classes, rehearsals, and lessons is a problem." No, it is a task, not a problem. The solution is already known. It may not be an easy task, it may be complicated to work out, but it is something teachers have been doing annually for decades. By contrast, if a teacher wanted to compare the effect of two or more scheduling patterns on the progress of beginning students, that might bear fruit as a problem. In other words, it is important to distinguish tasks from research problems.

Second is the connotation of a general "problem," in which the term is used synonymously with topic or subject (Statement of the Problem). Recognizing that teaching students to be creative is a problem in no way points toward a solution. At that level, it is not so much a problem as a general concern. By contrast, if we think of creativity as a process of weighing alternatives and seek to examine problem-solving skills, we are on the road to pinning down a concrete research problem.

A third connotation is the one we are concerned with at this stage of the research process. What is it, in concrete, explicit terms, that the analysis of the subject suggests needs to be solved? The following criteria may be applied to judge whether the problem has been adequately defined. Is it a specific problem? Does the statement contain abstract terms that require further definition? What variables have bearing on the problem? What variables may be accounted for by assumptions? Are any of the variables not relevant to the solution to the problem and, therefore, may be set aside as limitations? Does the problem lend itself to empirical observation? What relationships may be observed that would point toward the solution to the problem as stated in one or more hypotheses?

The more analysis the researcher can do to determine conditions related to the problem, the easier it will be to define hypotheses. Compare these examples:

> Problem: Will beginning students progress faster in groups of like instruments or unlike instruments?

> Problem: Will beginning students in groups of 6–8 show greater progress in classes of like or unlike instruments when taught by a single teacher using the Belwin Band Method for one semester as measured by the Watkins-Farnum Performance Scale?

If the problem has been well defined, the step to the hypothesis may be a short one.

Hypothesis   There are many definitions of the hypothesis in the literature, but let us keep it simple. As the step that follows the problem, it is a suggested solution to the problem, not yet tested to determine whether that solution is accurate.

Problem: The car's engine turns over, but it won't fire.

Hypothesis: Perhaps there is a loose wire. (We have not yet looked at the wires.)

In a sense, the hypothesis is a specialized assumption. We assume a solution to the problem and then test to see if that assumption can be accepted.

In the example of the instrumental groupings, we might hypothesize that students would make faster progress in groups of like instruments because we assume that the techniques of the instruments are similar and the teacher can address the group rather than individuals. But we cannot be certain until we test. We must let the data speak for themselves.

A single hypothesis may not be sufficient, not allowing the researcher to account for multiple conditions and variables, nor for interaction between variables. Buttram (1969) used four hypotheses to test the four factors:

1. There is no difference in accuracy of identification of intervals between a control version and one designed to reveal the influence of interval quale.
2. [The same statement ending with pitch distance.]
3. [The same statement ending with tonal context.]
4. There is no difference between the relative distinctiveness of intervals as identified in a control version and in versions designed to reveal the influence of quale, pitch distance, tonal context, and melody. (p. 312)

The evaluator should apply the following questions to the statement of an hypothesis: Does it contain a specific solution to the problem? Is that solution observable? Testable? Is there a basis for the solution in known fact? What variables are related to the solution? What alternative solutions might there be? Are there ambiguous or imprecise terms in the hypothesis? Does it point to the facts that must be collected? Does the hypothesis have multiple aspects, each of which should be accounted for in separate hypotheses? Are there interactions between variables that should be accounted for in separate hypotheses?

Once an hypothesis has been tested, it is either confirmed or rejected. If an hypothesis is rejected, it does not invalidate the study; it simply means that a different solution was the correct one. (It was not a wire; it was the distributor.) It is best to think of the hypothesis as a tool, not a truth.

Consequences of the Hypothesis   This step tends to be overlooked in research designs. The consequences tell what one would expect to observe if the hypothesis is confirmed. As such, it establishes the criteria for analysis of the data It is especially important to be aware that consequences are not conclusions (a source of confusion for students), because the data have not yet been collected and tested. The consequences tell what the researcher is going to look at to determine whether the hypothesis is confirmed. Virtually every statement of consequences should start with the phrase "We would expect to observe." To determine whether students in groups of like instruments made greater progress than those in the other groups, we would expect to observe greater accuracy in playing pitches, rhythms, dynamics, phrasing; better tone quality, and so on. These are the parameters of the test. Once the test has been scored, we can accept or reject the hypothesis.

Consequences must point to data that are observable and testable. The consequences must be logically implied by the hypotheses and must be stated precisely and unambiguously. The consequences should account for all relevant variables. They form the connection between the hypotheses and the test design—a smooth segue.

Guidelines for the Dissertation

The remainder of this chapter is addressed particularly to doctoral students and doctoral advisors. The discussion may seem at first glance to be almost self-evident, but, too often, a potentially important contribution to our knowledge about the teaching/learning process in music is missed, or a doctoral degree is not earned because some of the cautions suggested here are not followed.

Some graduate students look forward to the dissertation with the same anticipation they would to the gallows. However, it need not be that way. First, we suggest a practical perspective. A dissertation is not a magnum opus; it is the last practice in research of a person's student days. If eventually it leads to the publication of a book, fine, but that should not be the goal. The goal is to fulfill successfully a degree requirement. The primary audience is the doctoral committee. Once the dissertation is approved, the audience may expand to anyone who wishes to order it. A paper may be extracted from it for presentation at a meeting of a professional society or for publication in a journal, but those are eventualities and not a consideration for the dissertation itself.

It may help, also, to bear in mind that the dissertation is not of the magnitude of *War and Peace*. It is, in its series of chapters, a collection of short papers, not unlike those that students have written for various courses.

Length is not an important criterion for judging the quality of a dissertation. Papers that involve a good deal of description of data (case studies, musical analysis) will usually be longer than those in which quantitative data are presented in concise, graphic form.

Selection of the subject is a critical step in the research process. Close communication between the student and advisor is crucial. Some advisors feel that the student should work on something closely related to the advisor's own area of research so that the student may benefit from the advisor's expertise. The advisor may literally say, "I haven't gotten to this yet; do this." This has the additional advantage of immediately putting the student's work into the context of a theory-based field with a body of literature and perhaps some laboratory or field techniques already defined.

By contrast, the student may wish to pursue a field of interest that is outside the advisor's primary field. The advisor should have a sufficient knowledge of research procedures to be able to guide the student through the process in either case.

Ultimately, it is wise for the student to pick a subject in which she or he already has some professional expertise so that all of that prior knowledge may be brought to bear on the problem without having to master a new field. Would a particular subject require knowledge of a foreign language, and does the student have the time to learn the language sufficiently to deal with the literature? Is the subject likely to take the student into a related field that would require extensive study (for example, the subject of concept development in music could lead into a vast literature in psychology on concept development)? A further practical consideration is whether the student has the financial resources required to carry out the research, or whether there is a reasonable chance of obtaining a grant.

Other practical considerations in choosing a subject include the student's own personal circumstances. For example, does one really want to launch a longitudinal study if promotion, tenure, or salary increase are dependent on finishing the degree? The purist may say that these considerations are irrelevant to the research. But they are relevant to the quality of the research if such circumstances make the student feel pressured and therefore anxious and careless or inclined to take shortcuts.

There are some pitfalls for which both the student and advisor must be vigilant. One is the subject that is too broad. One student wrote a history of the string quartet. The paper was 1,500 pages long and took 5 years to complete. The doctoral studies office sent it back with the notation, "Since you did not use proper footnote form and will have to redo this, we suggest you do some drastic pruning." The advisor should never have approved such a broad subject.

At the opposite extreme is the trivial subject, either one that does not relate to general topics or theories in the field or is a confirmation of something already known by common experience of musicians and music educators. A couple of studies on the "discovery method" come to mind where children were left on their own to "discover" composition. As most teachers would predict, the studies simply confirmed that the children did not have the necessary skills to progress and, therefore, were soon frustrated.

A third pitfall is what we might call the "Messianic Concept." A person sets out to solve all of the problems of music education in one dissertation. That may sound facetious, but anyone who has sat through sessions of dissertation proposals will know exactly what we are talking about because this happens all too frequently. This concept results in a subject that is impossibly broad and is usually biased in tone.

A fourth pitfall is expedience. A person is the conductor of an ensemble and, therefore, chooses to do a study using his or her own ensemble. That may or may not prove to be feasible, and must be considered with great care. The possibilities of bias, inadequate sampling, and so on are strong.

In carrying out the research, following a well-established methodology is essential. Such methodologies are described elsewhere in this chapter, in these handbooks, and in the literature of various fields of study. For example, if a study involves a survey, there are textbooks on survey techniques.

Keeping up with the literature is critical to the dissertation. Not only does the literature tell about the history of the subject, but about current developments while the dissertation is in progress. One student's proposal was approved and he was well along in the design of a survey when, in the latest issue of *Dissertation Abstracts,* he discovered that someone else had completed a virtually identical study. Because replication did not seem appropriate in this case, he had to start over with a different subject. Journal articles tend to be more current than books, although for some journals there may be a backlog of as much as 2 years before an article appears in print. Presently, websites may have the most up-to-date information.

It is especially important for the student to look at the research literature critically. As mentioned previously, not all literature is of high quality. Have writers' assumptions and conclusions been verified, and were they theory-based? Was the methodology appropriate to the problem? Have certain errors been passed on from one writer to another? For example, one historian misidentified an early instrument. Several other writers who failed to verify his conclusion passed on his error.

As the dissertation progresses, ultimately it is the student's responsibility to see that all requirements are met. The first step is to check with the graduate school or doctoral studies office to obtain any printed regulations. These are likely to include the composition of the advisory committee, requirements for the oral examination, guidelines for form and style in the dissertation, and a series of deadlines that must be met. The student should start with the last deadline (when the final, approved copy must be submitted prior to commencement) and work backward to establish a calendar. It is wise to allow time for unanticipated delays. Also, an advisor or committee should not be expected to read and respond thoughtfully to a draft over night.

After the student and advisor agree on the subject of the study, it is time to establish the advisory committee. Procedures may differ from one institution to another. The committee usually has three to five members, one or two from the student's major field and others from related fields. The quality of the dissertation may depend in part on the constitution of the committee. For example, if the major advisor does not feel comfortable with guiding the student through a particular form of analysis, someone else may serve as the dissertation advisor. If the study involves analysis of complex contemporary music, it may be wise to have someone from the music theory faculty as the principal advisor. Persons from outside the department may be required, or at least desirable, on the committee. If complex quantitative analysis is involved, perhaps there should be someone from the statistics department on the committee.

The next step usually is the approval of the dissertation proposal. This may take the form of an outline presented orally to the committee or a graduate seminar, or it may be a formal, written proposal presented to the doctoral committee or to a committee of the graduate school that reviews proposals university-wide. While the student will not yet have done the actual gathering and testing of data, the study should, at this stage, be completely defined. The review of literature will essentially be complete, the problem and hypotheses defined, data-gathering techniques identified, and procedures for data analysis justified. Instead of conclusions, the proposal will suggest anticipated outcomes. The more rigorously the proposal is defined, the better its chances of approval. That may sound obvious, but we all have seen proposals submitted with the attitude, "Let's run it up the flagpole and see if anyone salutes," usually resulting in its being shot down.

In the process of preparing the proposal, the student needs to anticipate the need for other types of approval. Any study using human subjects may require written approval from parents, a public school administrator, or a special university office designated for such purposes. Before a questionnaire is distributed, it may require approval by some officer of the university if the student is viewed as a representative of the university.

When the data have been analyzed and it is time to write the dissertation, the student should inquire as to whether the graduate school has a prescribed format for the report (some do) and a prescribed manual of style. If none is prescribed, there are several guides to writing theses and dissertations as well as several manuals of style (some serve as both). The latest editions should be consulted because conventions change, especially as technology changes including citations from websites. It might be well to consult journals in the student's field to determine which manuals are customarily used. In any case, the rule of thumb is to pick one manual and use it consistently.

In general, writing a dissertation is no different from writing papers. But a few observations are in order, based on some common errors we have seen. First, the student should be sure that his or her own thoughts are prominent in the report. Some reports seem to be strings of quotations untouched by the human mind. The writer should introduce the material, provide transitions, paraphrase some material, and give assessments and explanations of the material. The reader should be led through the study with a logical train of thought.

Second, the writer should try to anticipate readers' questions. As much as possible, no questions should be left unanswered for the reader. This depends entirely on the writer's ingenuity. But, the goal is for the reader to say, "I may not agree with everything, but I understand exactly what you mean." Having others read the draft will help bring out any questions that need clarification. If the writer is uncertain whether something is clear, it is best not to engage in wishful thinking—"Maybe I can get by with that." It never works; revisions are in order.

Third, once all of the data are in hand, the writer should try to find a block of time to write straight through. It is extremely difficult to write in piecemeal fashion. One loses continuity of thought. It is a good idea to take a Christmas vacation, spread the papers out on the ping-pong table, let someone else cook the meals and run errands while the writing receives exclusive attention. It will soon be finished.

The student and advisor should agree on how the manuscript is to be presented. Some advisors like to see each chapter as it is finished; others like to see the complete dissertation so they can follow the continuity.

In the end, the quality of the dissertation depends on the conscientiousness of the student and the diligence of the advisor. If they have done their work thoroughly, the review by the committee and the scrutiny in the oral examination should go quite smoothly.

The Oral Examination (Defense of the Dissertation)

It is important for the student to understand the purpose of the oral examination because that will be a guide to preparation. The purpose is for the student to demonstrate that the subject of the dissertation has been so well mastered that the student can talk about it as well as having written about it. The committee knows that the student can write because they have already read the report. Some of us can write about a particular subject, and days later it seems as though someone else had written it; it does not seem familiar at all. We have put together a sequence of statements and lost track of the overall themes. The student needs to have the continuity of the subject in mind, be able to describe the process of the research, and relate the material to other aspects of the field through an oral presentation.

To plan for the oral examination, the student should check with the graduate school to determine the necessary steps to complete this requirement in a timely way. For example, it may be necessary to submit a copy of the dissertation to the graduate school at a date well in advance of the examination so that anyone interested in attending can read the manuscript beforehand. The graduate school may want to be certain that its requirements for the dissertation (from form and style to the bond of the paper) are met before the examination.

Usually, it is the student's responsibility to see that all procedures and requirements are met. It is up to the student to contact committee members, see that they have copies of the dissertation, and schedule the examination. Most institutions require that an announcement of the examination be published in a campus newspaper, or some other vehicle, at least 2 weeks before the scheduled time, so that interested persons may plan to attend. Oral examinations normally are open to the public. Other doctoral candidates are particularly interested in attending so that they may have a preview of what they will face.

The format of the oral examination will vary from one institution to another, but we can describe some general practices. First, the candidate may be asked to discuss how he or she arrived at the subject and then to talk through the research process. This not only shows the candidate's mastery of the material, but also provides a summary for guests who have not seen the report. The candidate is permitted to use notes, but the notes should be used sparingly. The individual should not read extensively from the notes because then it is no longer an oral examination.

It is acceptable to use handouts or projection, particularly when data may be presented in graphic form, such as the results of statistical treatments. Video may be used for the presentation of certain classroom activities or conducting situations. Audiotapes may be necessary for studies that test aural discrimination. When any audio-visual equipment is used, the student should check the equipment before the examination to be sure that it is working properly and have all taped examples cued up.

During the student's initial presentation, committee members may interrupt for clarification of certain points. However, the advisor should be sure that the discussion does not become sidetracked to the point that the student does not have an opportunity to finish the presentation.

Following the presentation, the committee members may ask questions. Some questions may be designed to test whether the student really understands the procedures that were used or was just blindly following prescribed procedures. A typical question might be, "What is meant by statistical significance?" Other questions may expose that which the candidate has taken for granted. One student's subject was orchestrational styles of two composers. The first question was, "What do you mean by style?" The student was stumped because he had taken for granted that everyone understood what that term meant. He had actually defined style in his analytical criteria, but was momentarily stunned by the question. Other questions may be designed to test the limits of a student's knowledge, deliberately going beyond what the student might reasonably be expected to know. It is all right for the student to say "I don't know" when faced with such a question, and the student should not consider that response to be a sign of failure.

A significant point is the fact that the student is expected to have knowledge beyond the subject of the dissertation. This is often overlooked in the preparation for an oral examination. For example, if the study deals with the works of a particular composer, questions may be asked as to how this composer's work relates to those who came before or after him, or to historical style trends. If the study has to do with individual learning styles, questions may arise as to how this relates to classroom management. While it is impossible for the student to anticipate all questions, it would be useful to consider the broader context of the subject and the definition of terms used in the study. It is a good idea to practice by giving a presentation to friends before facing the committee.

The results of an oral examination usually fall into one of three categories: no revisions, minor revisions, major revisions. The advisor is responsible for assuring that the appropriate forms are filled out and submitted to the graduate school with the results of the examination. If both the student and the advisor have been diligent and insured that committee members have reviewed the manuscript well in advance of the oral so that they could raise concerns and make suggestions, there should be no need for major revisions.

The Role of the Major Advisor

The term "advisor" seems self-explanatory, but, in fact, is not. Misunderstandings about the role and responsibilities of the advisor may lead to serious difficulties. The following guidelines should be considered.

First, it is well to check the university by-laws to determine whether the role and responsibilities of the advisor are defined. The by-laws may say that advising, including dissertation advising, is part of a faculty member's duties, but that final responsibility for meeting degree requirements rests with the student. Policy may vary from one institution to another. Because poor advising has been known to lead to litigation, the advisor should give serious thought to the nature of the duties. At the beginning of the dissertation process, the advisor and student should come to agreement as to the responsibilities of each in respect to such things as meeting deadlines, selecting the subject of the research, determining appropriate research procedures, editing the manuscript, and preparing for the defense of the dissertation.

Because a goal of the dissertation is to prepare the student to be an independent researcher on completion of the degree, the student should take as much initiative as possible at every step along the way. But because the student is a novice at research, the advisor should give close oversight. Extremes should be avoided. One advisor, trying to be accommodating, was overhead to say, "Oh, anything you want to do is fine with me." That gave the student no guidance at all. By contrast, an advisor may become too manipulative without thinking of the consequences. One student was preparing a performance edition of a folio of early music when he discovered that one of the tunes was the basis for a parody mass. The advisor insisted that he find every parody mass derived from that folio even though it was a tangent to the research problem. It proved to be an overwhelming task, but the advisor refused to relent. The student never finished, causing him to lose his job because he did not complete the degree in a specified time. Also, an advisor should not write the dissertation for the student. That seems almost too apparent to mention, but cases have been observed where a student struggles with the writing and the advisor, out of frustration and impatience, winds up writing most of the manuscript under the guise of editing. This leaves the student dependent rather than independent.

At the outset, the advisor should review with the student any guidelines and deadlines specified by the graduate school and establish a calendar by which the student will complete various steps in a timely manner. They also should review the student's personal situation to determine any limitations on time and resources. Will the student be working on the dissertation full-time, part-time, or piecemeal? Will the student be in residence at the institution or back on the job? Does the student have financial limitations? Is completion of the degree related to job retention?

The advisor should guide the student in the selection of a subject and help the student judge the appropriateness of the subject, both in terms of its relevance to the field and the student's capability to carry the study to completion.

The advisor is in a position to help the student select other committee members. Because of previous coursework, the student may feel comfortable or uncomfortable with certain faculty members. Or, the student may have had no contact with some who might contribute good advice to the study, especially persons from outside the department. Both student and advisor should be alert to when potential committee members will be on sabbatical. As much as possible, members should be chosen because their areas of expertise complement the subject and the methods of analysis. The student should determine with each committee member when that person wishes to be involved. All too often, the time for the oral examination arrives and a member of the advisory committee is asked to participate, having had almost no prior contact with the student and no opportunity to advise on the study.

If kept involved, the committee can perform a sometimes necessary function. An advisor and student may develop a close relationship, especially if the student is also the advisor's assistant. At times, this relationship can make it difficult for the advisor to remain objective or to say "No" when necessary. The committee provides a check on that happening. There have been times when members have had to say to the advisor, "Do you really want that study to represent you and this institution?" to which the advisor has usually responded, "No," and further work was in order.

The advisor should be sufficiently familiar with the research procedures and literature on the subject of the study to guide the student through the process with precision. Precision results primarily from the rigor with which the dissertation proposal is defined. If it is thoroughly and carefully defined, the rest of the project should be busy work, filling in the blanks, so to speak. Both the advisor and committee should feel that the study will be defensible at the time of the preliminary approval.

The advisor's role is critical in assuring that appropriate techniques are identified or designed for gathering and analyzing data. Many of these are described elsewhere in this Handbook and in other research literature, but it is the advisor's experience that should help point the student in the right direction. The advisor should be especially alert for the need to administer pilot versions of instruments with subsequent revisions. The advisor should take responsibility for informing the student of the need for approval of the use of human subjects, administration of questionnaires, and the like. This is especially true when the student is no longer in residence at the university and may not be in regular communication with the advisor. It is dismaying to discover that a student has sent out a poorly designed questionnaire under the name of the university without prior approval.

Some studies require more supervision than others. If a study involves primarily the analysis of music, and criteria for analysis have been agreed on, the student may work independently to complete the analysis and describe the results. But, if the study involves public school classroom activities where unanticipated turns of events may occur, it may be necessary for the student, advisor, and cooperating teachers to be in close communication throughout to account for any necessary adjustments.

When it comes time for the writing of the dissertation, the advisor and student should agree on how the material should be submitted: chapter by chapter or in larger segments. In either case, the advisor should take the responsibility to review the material promptly and thoroughly. One student who had turned in a draft was asked by a friend when she expected to finish. She replied, "Hopefully, within my lifetime." The advisor held the material for several months without responding. When reviewing the material, the advisor should watch for any evidence of plagiarism, intentional or unintentional.

Bearing in mind that the dissertation is still practice in research—still a learning experience—the advisor should not only critique the manuscript for content but also for form and style. It is not satisfactory for the advisor to say, "That's not good enough. Do it again." That provides no guidance. Perhaps it is helpful to remember that both the name of the advisor and the institution will appear in the dissertation and be eternally represented by that report.

The dissertation should be as polished as possible before the oral examination. The advisor should assure that all committee members have had ample time to review it and are satisfied with the results before the oral. (The same advice was given to the student. That avoids the possibility of each thinking the other had taken care of it.)

During the examination, the advisor serves as the moderator, gives instructions to the student, sees that the discussion stays on track, and may choose to invite questions from guests if there is time. It is especially important that the advisor not let the discussion deteriorate into a debate between faculty members, an all-too-frequent occurrence. At the conclusion of the oral, with the candidate and guests out of the room, the advisor chairs a meeting of the committee to determine the results of the oral and obtain the members' signatures on the appropriate form before informing the candidate of the results. Silly as it may seem to have to mention this—but it does happen—this meeting should not wander into unrelated discussions while the candidate suffers in the hallway.

The advisor's duties usually end with a signature on the approval page of the dissertation.

NOTE

1. We wish to acknowledge our former colleague, Professor Warren C. Campbell, in the development of this ordinal scale. Shared discussions over many years contributed to these ideas.

REFERENCES

Abeles, H. F. (1980). Responses to music. In D. A. Hodges (Ed.), *Handbook of music psychology* (pp. 105–140). Lawrence, KS: National Association for Music Therapy.

Agnes, M., Ed. in chief. (1999). *Webster's new world college dictionary* (4th ed.). Cleveland: Macmillan USA.

Barzun, J., & Graff, H. F. (1992). *The modern researcher* (5th ed.). New York: Harcourt Brace Jovanovich College Publishers.

Baumol, W. J., & Bowen, W. G. (1966). *Performing arts—The economic dilemma.* Cambridge, MA: MIT Press.

Buttram, J. B. (1969). The influence of selected factors on interval identification. *Journal of Research in Music Education, 17*(3), 309–315.

Campbell, D., & Stanley, J. (1963). *Experimental and quasi-experimental designs for research.* Chicago: Rand McNally.

Cohen, J. (1994). The earth is round ($p < .05$). *American Psychologist, 49*(12), 997–1003.

Colwell, R. J. (1969). *A critique of research studies in music education, final report.* U.S. Office of Education Research Project 6-10-245, Arts and Humanities Branch, University of Illinois at Urbana-Champaign.

Colwell, R. J. (1988). Editor's remarks. *Bulletin of the Council for Research in Music Education, 97*(Summer), 1–15.

Eisner, E. W. (1997). The promise and perils of alternative forms of data representation. *Educational Researcher, 26*(6), 4–10.

Forte, A. (1966). A program for the analytic reading of scores. *Journal of Music Theory, 10,* 330–64.

Fraenkle, J. R., & Wallen, N. E. (2000). *How to design and evaluate research in education* (4th ed.). New York: McGraw-Hill.

Gonzo, C. (1992). Toward a rational critical process. In R. Colwell (Ed.), *Handbook of research on music teaching and learning* (pp. 218–226). New York: Schirmer.

Grady, M. P. (1998). *Qualitative and action research: A practitioner handbook.* Bloomington, IN: Phi Delta Kappa Educational Foundation.

Grieshaber, K. (1987). Children's rhythmic tapping: A critical review of research. *Bulletin of the Council for Research in Music Education, 90,* 73–82.

Hair, H. (2000). Children's descriptions of music: Overview of research. *Proceedings of the 18th International Research Seminar, International Society for Music Education Research Commission: University of Utah, Salt Lake City,* 128–141.

Jorgensen, E. R. (1992). On philosophical method. In R. Colwell (Ed.), *Handbook of research on music teaching and learning* (pp. 91–106). New York: Schirmer.

Kirk, R. E. (1996). Practical significance: a concept whose time has come. *Educational and Psychological Measurement, 56*(5), 746–759.

Kubik, G. (1999). *Africa and the blues.* Jackson: University Press of Mississippi.

Landau, V. (1960). Paul Hindemith: A case study in theory and practice. *The Music Review, 21,* 38–54.

Lomax, A. (1968). *Folk song style and culture.* Washington, DC: American Association for the Advancement of Science.

Merriam, A. (1964). *The anthropology of music.* Evanston, IL: Northwestern University Press.

Price, H. E. (1997). Forum. *Journal of Research in Music Education, 45*(1), 3–4.

Radocy, R., & Boyle, J. D. (1997). *Psychological foundations of musical behavior* (3rd ed.). Springfield, IL: Charles Thomas.

Rosenthal, R. (1991). *Meta-analytic procedures for social research* (rev. ed.). Newbury Park, CA: Sage Publications.

Rostov, R. L., & Rosenthal, R. (1984). *Understanding behavioral science.* New York: McGraw Hill.

Schneider, E. H., & Cady, H. L. (1967). Evaluation and synthesis of research studies relating to music education: 1930–62. *Bulletin of the Council for Research in Music Education, 9*(Spring), 3–16.

Standley, J. M. (1996). A meta-analysis on the effects of music as reinforcement for education/therapy objectives. *Journal of Research in Music Education, 44*(2), 105–133.

Taylor, R. G. (Ed.). (1981). *The documentary report of the Ann Arbor Symposium.* Reston, VA: Music Educators National Conference.

Thompson, B. (1996). AERA editorial policies regarding statistical significance testing: Three suggested reforms. *Educational Researcher, 25*(2), 26–30.

Tunks, T. (1978). The use of omega squared in interpreting statistical significance. *Bulletin of the Council for Research in Music Education, 57*(Winter), 28–34.

Yarbrough, C. (1984). A content analysis of the *Journal of Research in Music Education,* 1953–83. *Journal of Research in Music Education, 32*(Winter), 213–222.

Yarbrough, C. (1996). The future of scholarly inquiry in music education: 1996 senior researcher award acceptance address. *Journal of Research in Music Education, 44*(3), 190–203.

Transforming Research in
Music Education History

3

GORDON COX

The question "What is history?" is the subject of fierce debate: History is a science that discovers; it is an art that creates; historical narratives are constructions governed by the same rules and constraints as literature; "history with purpose" can realize some grand metaphysical theme; history has ended. Historians today are being forced to rethink, in the light of postmodernist criticism, the categories and assumptions that have underpinned their work (see Evans, 1997; Munslow, 2000).

Research in music education history cannot remain immune from this debate (see McCarthy, 2003). Indeed, I base this chapter on the premise that music education history is, like the history of education, "a contested and changing terrain" (Aldrich, 2000, p. 63). The challenge of facing up to contest and change was acknowledged by Heller and Wilson (1992) in their chapter in the first *Handbook of Research on Music Teaching and Learning*. They called for "new interpretations of old subjects" (p. 102). More specifically, they detailed the following research needs: revision of existing studies, application of new techniques, and cooperation with fields outside music education. Heller and Wilson's suggestions comprise the kernel of this chapter. However, while they focused on the detail of researching music education history in the American context, I shall present a critical review of historical accounts with a general emphasis on Anglo-American literature, but including an international dimension.

The purposes of this chapter are fourfold: to offer a critique of the classic approaches to music education history; to generate suggestions for transforming the scope of music education history; to explore selected areas of study that illustrate possibilities for this broadening of horizons; to suggest ideas for research, based on the notion of "a usable past" (Hansot & Tyack, 1982).

Classic Approaches to Historical Research in Music Education

Judged by the quantity of dissertations, articles, and books on the subject, there is evidence of a continuing interest in music education history. In American universities, there has been a steady stream of dissertations on the history of music education (see Humphreys, Bess, & Bergee, 1996–97). For 20 years, researchers have been nurtured by the pioneering efforts of George Heller, the founding editor of *The Bulletin of Historical Research in Music Education* (see McCarthy, 1999b). In 2000, the *Bulletin* was renamed the *Journal of Historical Research in Music Education,* and it was edited by Jere Humphreys from 1999–2003, and since then by Mark Fonder. Outside the United States, moreover, a number of significant books have been published since 1990 that have sought to uncover and reconstruct the history of music teaching and learning in different countries, including Canada (Green & Vogan, 1991), Germany (Gruhn, 1993), Great Britain (Cox, 1993; Cox, 2002; Pitts, 2000) and Ireland (McCarthy, 1999a).

This recent research activity has its roots in a substantial corpus of classic histories of music education published during the 20th century in the United Kingdom (see Scholes, 1947; Simpson, 1976; Rainbow, 1967, 1989, 1990), and in the United States (see Birge, 1928; Britton, 1950, 1989; Sunderman, 1971; Tellstrom, 1971; Mark, 1978; Keene, 1982; Mark & Gary, 1992). In spite of such achievements, however, the work has tended to be marginalized by education historians both in the United Kingdom (see Cox, 1999, p. 449) and the United States (see Heller & Wilson, 1992, p. 105).

What are the broad characteristics of this research? I shall focus critically on the work of Rainbow in the United Kingdom, and on the critiques by American music education historians of the classic histories of American music education. My purpose is to deal with the assessment of previous work in the light of new insights and perspectives, bearing in mind that all historians are restricted by the sources available to them, and are influenced by their own worldview and value system.

In the United Kingdom, Bernarr Rainbow (1914–1998) almost single-handedly kept the flame of historical research in music education alight, from the publication of *The Land Without Music* (1967) to *Music in Educational Thought and Practice* (1989). *The Land Without Music* is a landmark study in its detailed and scholarly investigation of musical education in England between 1800 and 1860, and its continental antecedents. Rainbow wrote out of pedagogical concerns: He wanted to find out why English achievements in the teaching of singing at sight came to be supplanted by continental methods until the arrival of John Curwen, who synthesized the different strands.

On closer examination it can be argued that the book was a justification for Rainbow's aesthetic, political, and educational outlook. It was essentially whiggish, it emphasized the heroes (notably John Curwen), and praised successful revolutions (specifically the tonic sol-fa movement). However, Rainbow looked back to a golden age of sight-singing and hand signs that in reality probably never existed. In effect, he treated sight-singing texts like master plans: It was taken for granted that the development of an effective method would reap untold benefits on popular music education. Furthermore, there is little detail from Rainbow's account of the teachers or pupils who used these instructional texts. Moreover, the indigenous vernacular musical culture is portrayed as deprived in some way, and problematic for formal instructional methods.

In the United States, the classic histories of music education represent major contributions to music education scholarship. Livingston (1997) has highlighted their achievements: Birge's (1928) remarkable detail and attention to the political aspects of music education; Tellstrom's (1971) investigation of the relationship of music education to the development of major educational movements; Keene's (1982) breadth of interest in dealing with various historical and philosophical tendencies; Mark's (1978) thorough treatment of the contemporary period; Mark and Gary's (1992) comprehensive account that attempts to include contributions to music education in the United States from traditions other than European.

The critique of such work focuses on the issues of the relative coverage of men and women (Livingston, 1997), geographic representation (Humphreys, 1997), and the concentration on white Eurocentric traditions (Volk, 1993). Humphreys (1998) helpfully compares and contrasts the contributions of Birge and Allen Britton. He views Birge as a talented amateur who tended not to validate his sources and who skewed his research to his own region of residence. Britton's (1950, 1989) work, by contrast, was rigorous and document driven with at least some emphasis placed on validation. He became the most prominent and influential American historian of music education, and trained several dozen historians who still constitute the nucleus of the cadre of American music education historians. Nevertheless, Humphreys critically observes that Britton's students exhibit a certain homogeneity in their approach to music education history, with an emphasis on leading individuals, programs, and institutions at the expense of rank-and-file music education, formal and institutionalized music education at the expense of other types, and a bias toward certain regions, men, and European-style musical practices.

Howe (1998) sums up the position succinctly:

> The extant scholarly publications on the history of music education, written by white male authors, are chronological with an emphasis on white male educators in public school music. They also have emphasized the music teaching of white educators teaching the music of North European countries. New approaches, different primary sources, and different research methods could produce a comprehensive history of music education. (pp. 97–98)

More specifically, Howe argues that alternative perspectives of the history of music education in the United States could include those of African Americans and women in music education. Research methodology might draw on techniques derived from oral history, sociology, and ethnomusicology. The purpose of all this would be to assemble a more comprehensive, richer, and fuller history of music education. Howe's mention of new approaches, different primary sources, and different research methods helpfully prompts us to consider the wider dimensions of the history of education.

Broadening Horizons

The history of education as a field of enquiry has had its ups and downs, but it has long moved away from a concentration on "the great educators," the history of institutions and administration (acts and facts), and a celebration of state-sponsored education since the 19th century (see McCulloch & Richardson, 2000, pp. 40–51; Richardson, 1999). From the late 1960s, it has achieved much in its embrace of a whole raft of approaches that Cohen (1999) has detailed, including social control and social conflict, urban history, family history, history of women, history of people of color, history of religious minorities, and history "from the bottom up." Even this is not an exhaustive list, however. Other significant influences have included functionalism, Marxism, and poststructuralism.

Lee (1991) takes up some of these issues in his discussion of research in music education history. He argues that in order to professionalize the field, we need to know and be aware of what the specialized content is. His definition of music education is encouragingly inclusive: It comprises all deliberate efforts to pass music from one generation to another. This means investigating both formal and informal instruction, state-sponsored music education, and music education outside the aegis of the state, the learning and teaching of music by ordinary people in unstructured settings, as well as that undertaken by specialists in structured settings. Essentially, the focus is on the act of learning or teaching some aspect of music.

Lee's list of areas to be explored is illuminating, and includes: a wider contextual consideration; an intensified interest in the philosophy of history and of historiography; an exploration of the implications of the newer historical research (outlined by Cohen above); an engagement with international and comparative perspectives; an exploration of newer techniques (including statistics, demography); and oral history.

All of this has considerable potential for researchers in the field, which Cohen (1999) expands on in his discussion of the new cultural history of education. He argues that they should: attempt to cross disciplinary boundaries; read history into any cultural artifact, whether "elite" or popular; regard any cultural artifact as text in history. Such attempts may bring researchers to postmodernist history, which in Evans's (1997) judgment has encouraged historians to look more closely at the documents, to think about texts and narratives in fresh ways, and has opened up many new areas and subjects for research.

I argue in the rest of this chapter that historians of music education should focus on the following concerns: research should be responsive to the social, historical, ideological, and cultural contexts in which the teaching and learning of music take place; due attention should be paid to the actual teaching and learning of music; and that music education is a broad area encompassing both formal and informal settings. To illustrate something of the potential riches of the interactions between these concerns I turn to three areas of interest: first, the relationship between music education, national, and cultural identity; second, curriculum change and conflict; and third, historical perspectives of music educators working in public schools and studios.

Music Education, and National and Cultural Identity

The relationships and interactions between music and the formation of national and cultural identity through formal and informal instruction contain fruitful possibilities for music education historians. I shall focus on three examples of research that deal with the very different contexts of music education in Ireland, Barbados, and India. These three distinct countries are, however, linked through their relationship as former colonized territories of Great Britain. Finally, in this section, I shall indicate briefly the potential of a related field, that of missionary endeavor.

McCarthy's (1999a) study of music education in 19th- and 20th-century Ireland explores the relationship between musical and cultural development through an investigation of the music transmission process. Underlying it is the notion of national identity, supported by a view of music as the embodiment of a set of values and beliefs that are inextricably linked to power structures and ideologies. Ireland provides a valuable site for such an investigation, shaped as it has been by the two political ideologies of colonialism and nationalism. The institutions and communities, which contributed to the sense of statehood, were frequently associated with musical participation, and this participation in McCarthy's eyes served as both a maker and marker of identity.

The central conflict between traditional Irish musical culture and the conventions of the Western Classical style in the mid-19th century found its most extreme manifestation within formal schooling, in particular the normal schools (teachers colleges), in which the musical diet was based on the Hullah Method of singing at sight. McCarthy views this practice as culturally discontinuous with the experience of the majority of young people the system sought to educate. In contrast were the informal flowerings of Irish musical culture, including temperance bands, the Irish Ballad associated with the Young Ireland movement, and traditional music and dance activity.

It becomes clear, as McCarthy concludes, that the strongest and most successful traditions in the transmission of music in Irish culture have developed outside of the formal systems. She identifies three causes of the primary weakness of music education in formal institutions in Ireland: cultural fragmentation produced by colonialism; dependence on a weak economy; and the dominant role of competing political ideologies in providing the raison d'être for music as a subject in the curriculum. In comparison, the hope for the future is for an agenda based on democracy, diversity, and inclusiveness.

McCarthy's work, through its engagement with the wider horizons of colonialism and nationalism, resonates with experiences in different parts of the world. I have selected two tightly focused studies of aspects of music education in Barbados and India in order to pursue this notion of musical colonialism.

The Barbados educational system provides the backdrop for Cameron McCarthy's (1999) research on the British influence on the school song genre of Barbadian public schools. These songs emerged in the late 19th century; they are "part of the lineaments . . . of a borrowed or imposed tradition of English school ritual that thrives in Barbadian schools today in the postcolonial era" (1999, p. 156). On one level, the songs serve the purpose of fostering school solidarity, consensus, and group identity, but they also contain complex symbolic messages.

According to McCarthy's analysis of songs from 24 Barbadian high schools, the elite, middle-class grammar school songs situate the Barbadian child as an autonomous agent of empire with the promise of a better social future. They help reflect the tradition that education in Barbados was committed to producing a black intellectual elite, a middle-class that was positioned with the British and the empire, and between the lower classes and the national white planter-mercantile elites. The songs fabricate the class divide, which has underpinned the Barbadian education system (derived from British imperialism).

This divide is evident in the school songs of the Barbadian primary and comprehensive schools, which, according to McCarthy, are regarded as inferior to the grammar schools. Their songs "have a different ring to them" (1999, p. 166); they emphasize industry and hard work for the black working-class youth. The school songs of Barbadian high schools thus draw lines between manual and mental labor, desire for "cultivation," and the desire for doing the "tasks at hand." McCarthy's conclusion is that the songs embody paradoxes that go beyond a constructed loyalty to empire, and develop ideas of ownership of knowledge, ownership of fate, and emancipation through learning.

The complexity of cultural dualism is taken up by Farrell (1997) in his exploration of the place of Indian music within the context of colonialism. One of Farrell's investigations concerns the promulgation of staff notation as an aid to musical literacy. The Bengali musicologist Tagore (1840–1914) was a tireless music educator who had an intense interest in the creation of a national music and a belief in the purity of Hindu music as handed down in Sanskrit sources. He wanted to find the most appropriate notations for Indian music, and to establish institutionalized music education. The question of how Indian music should be written down for educational purposes became the center of a fierce debate in the 1870s between Tagore and Charles Baron Clark, inspector of schools in Bengal. Clark believed staff notation would be the best medium for instruction. Intriguingly, Tagore and the nationalists fought the British on their own ground, and tried to match with a Hindu version of staff notation. As Farrell observes, the parameters of the struggle were always defined by the colonizer rather than the colonized. Staff notation in this context became ideological: It was "the musical tool par excellence for spreading the structures and paradigms of Western musical systems" (1997, p. 67).

Farrell's study, however, hints at the paradoxes contained within the colonial context. For example, S. W. Fallon, a British Raj official, was inspector of schools in Bihar, North India, and wrote a report to the Bengal government in 1873, requesting funds for the introduction of song materials he had collected into the music education system of Indian schools. Fallon wanted to relay back to Indians in schools authentic aspects of their own culture, rather than imposing an artificial idea of Indian classical music derived from classical sources. His plans were wide-ranging and based on an in-depth knowledge of local culture. Although it is not known whether or not his populist scheme came to fruition, it was one of several initiatives to institutionalize music education in India. Farrell points out that the forms these institutions took functioned paradoxically as symbols of both Indian nationalism and loyalty to the British authorities.

Finally, in this discussion of music education and national and cultural identity, there is one related area of research, inextricably linked with colonialism, which contains rich possibilities as a further field of investigation: the relationship between missionary endeavors, native peoples, and music education. A selection of extant work hints at the cultural and historical potential of such an approach: the musical instruction of Native Americans by the Jesuits in Latin America (De Couve, Dal Pino, & Frega, 1997), the musical influences of the Moravians on the Labrador Coast Inuit (Lutz, 1982), the educational impact of British missionaries on music in the schools of Kenya (Agak, 1998), the development of *The Cherokee Song Book* by the dedicated New England evangelicals Lowell Mason and Samuel A. Worcester (Lee, 1997), and the role of brass bands in the hands of British missionaries as a replacement/antidote for "uncivilized" native practices (see Herbert & Sarkissian, 1997).

The studies that I have reviewed in this section demonstrate some of the potential that is to be found in locating music education within the wider parameters of power structures, including those of colonialism and nationalism. More specifically, postcolonial theory has the potential to generate new and ongoing debates among historians of education concerning the ethical issues involved in reclaiming the past from the privileged position of "whiteness," and increasing our curiosity about racial, cultural, and gender divisions (Goodman & Martin, 2000).

We need more research that will illuminate our understanding of music education's function in fostering a sense of identities that have to be constantly invented, transformed, and recovered. The result of such investigation should serve to encourage music educators to question aspects of their own music education tradition that they may take for granted.

The Music Curriculum: Change and Conflict

If music is so bound up with social and cultural identity, it is hardly surprising that its place in the school curriculum should be fiercely contested and surrounded by controversy. We require some historical compass in order to make sense of it all.

It is the argument of Goodson and Marsh (1996) that curriculum theorists have developed amnesia concerning the historical past. But the recovery of a historical perspective could make all the difference to our understanding of the school curriculum and the positioning of subjects within it. The problem is that the curriculum generally is regarded as a given by the majority of teachers, children, and parents, something natural and immutable. But Goodson and Marsh maintain that it is a social artifact, an archetype of "the division and fragmentation of knowledge within our societies" (1996, p. 150). By studying the history of school subjects, we come to realize that they are "the most quintessential of social and political constructions" (1996, p. 1). In the discussion that follows, I focus on three pieces of research that examine the music curriculum as a heavily contested area in the United States, Australia, and the United Kingdom.

The entrance of music into the American public schools, according to Eaklor (1985), highlighted the uniquely American ambivalence between musical and extramusical considerations. She places early public school music within the context of New England psalmody and contemporary social thought, and notes the conflict between music's function as a moral or social art, and its cultivation as art. This tension was to be exemplified in the later history of the singing schools, which had originally been founded in 18th-century America to improve music in public worship. On the one hand, the urban singing school was transformed into an institute for training singers, while, on the other hand, the country singing school retained its social and religious functions.

In the postrevolution era, there was a repudiation of traditional American hymnody, fuguing tunes, and shape notes in favor of new European techniques concentrating on correctness and simplicity. But Eaklor also notes the tussle at the heart of the public school system itself: It was regarded both as an agent of change and as a conservative sanctuary of rural and traditional values. The musical dilemma was that the rejection of the indigenous shape notes had been achieved in favor of European methods: A method of educating the masses was overturned through using methods for teaching the few. Eaklor's conclusion is that the adoption of European notation and Pestalozzianism was inconsistent with the ostensibly nationalist goals of the school system.

In 19th-century Australia, according to Weiss (1995), the arts entered the public schools at worst by default, through an uneasy alliance of the aesthetic and the moral in justifying music's place on the curriculum. The multiplicity of intentions ascribed to singing were later developed by Inspector W. J. McBride in 1906 into six justifications: Pleasure, Ethical Reasons, Discipline, Patriotism, the Physical, and the Intellectual. Attempting to serve these multifarious purposes might result in satisfying none of them.

Weiss warns against thinking that educational progress is inevitable, or indeed uniform across all subjects in the curriculum. Three examples illustrate the gist of her argument. First, the humble and quite cheap private venture schools that existed before state schools offered more choice in the curriculum—including music. Second, although progressive education (child-centered rather than teacher- and subject-centered) established itself between the 1910s and 1930s, it did not have an automatic impact on music. It might have been thought that the arts lent themselves quite obviously to the aims of progressive education, but music expanded less than the visual arts during this period. The new educational discourse might stress individual expression, but opportunities for "free expression" in music were still hedged about by teacher direction. Moreover, the ideas of progressive educationists had virtually no impact on communal musical events such as the popular demonstrations of massed singing by children at the annual Decoration Concerts. Weiss warns that we should not be misled into believing that the discourse of the time represents totally the practice. In other words, the rhetorical curriculum might well be different from the enacted curriculum; there was a gulf between theory and practice. Third, the variety of educational contexts adds to the complexity of the music education historian's task. For example, music in Australian private and Catholic schools inhabited different musical worlds from the public schools, and from each other.

Weiss's conclusion is that the process of change never ceases. Two factors, she argues, may affect future attitudes to music in schools: The arts are still "fads and frills"; and the growing importance of the federal government in educational policy will increasingly determine the purpose and direction of public education, with a stress on the basics, and a view of the arts as being of secondary importance. The significance of Weiss's article is that it does not regard the history of music education in schools as a story of continuing improvement but is, rather, a vessel buffeted in different directions by political and educational pressures.

Finally, the pressures of more recent political concerns and pressures on the music curriculum are best exemplified in the United Kingdom by the work of Shepherd and Vulliamy (1994) in their ostensibly sociological study of the introduction of a national music curriculum. They frame their analysis by a historical discussion of the rise of the "new sociology of education," which in Britain had its roots in cultural relativism. Central to their argument was that the alienation of children from school music, apparent both in the United Kingdom and Canada, was caused by the music curriculum being based on criteria abstracted from the tradition of the established Western canon. Shepherd and Vulliamy believed that popular music should be introduced according to the criteria associated with those who created and appreciated the music. This sociohistorical context provided the basis of their fundamental disagreement with the Conservative government's proposals for a curriculum based on the Western canon. These proposals were countered by the more radical ideas put forward by the Music National Curriculum Working Party, which reflected the musically pluralist nature of contemporary society. Such notions, however, did not represent the monocultural image of England that Margaret Thatcher's Conservatives had in mind. The ensuing battle was appropriately described by Shepherd and Vulliamy as "The Struggle for Culture."

All this research concerning change and conflict in the music curriculum emphasizes the importance for historians of analyzing the preactive definitions of music before it enters the classrooms, because such definitions come to be seen as natural and unquestioned, and result in the curriculum tensions that have been explored in this section: in the United States, the ambivalence between the musical and the extramusical; in Australia, the uneasy alliance between the moral and the aesthetic; and, in the United Kingdom, the assumption that the music curriculum should be based on the established Western canon.

One of the problematic areas for music education historians researching the curriculum is tackling the historical context of genres that are unfamiliar to them because of their training but are central to the lives of young people, such as popular music, jazz, and the music of different cultures. A start has been made with Elliott's (1985) study of the origins and development of jazz education in Canada, Brehony's (1998) sociohistorical study of representations of schooling in rock and pop music, Livingston's (2001) examination of the historical labels of country music, and Volk's (1998) substantial historical perspective concerning multiculturalism in American music education. Investigating the history of these crucially significant musics in educational contexts is a priority because they encapsulate many of the conflicts and contestations concerning music's rightful place as a curriculum subject.

Music Educators

Music teachers are central to the effective implementation of the school curriculum, yet, as we observed in the opening discussion of classic approaches to music education history, we know little about them. Because of this neglect, I shall focus on mainstream research, which has investigated the contributions of leading figures in public school music education rather than grassroots teachers. I shall do this, however, within a framework that will hopefully suggest new possibilities for greater inclusiveness. I shall follow my discussion of public school music educators with a consideration of studio music educators.

Public School Music Educators   In her insightful discussion of the uses of biography in the study of educational history, Finkelstein (1998) makes a comparison:

> Biography is to history what the telescope is to the stars . . . biography provides a unique lens through which one can assess the relative power of political, economic, cultural, social and generational processes on the life chances of individuals, and the general revelatory power of historical sensemaking. (p. 45)

Finkelstein asserts that biography provides four indispensable entrées into the study of history through its relationship with the origin of new ideas, as a window on social possibility, as an aperture through which to view the relationship between educational practice and social change, and as a form of mythic overhaul.

Many of the traditional biographies of great music educators focus on Finkelstein's first entrée, the origin of new ideas. Howe's (1997) biography of the American music educator, Luther Whiting Mason (1818–1896) lies in this category. We might describe Mason's big idea as the promulgation of an internationalist view of music education. He worked toward this first through synthesizing ideas from many places into the *National Music Course* (1870), which was the first school music textbook series in America. Howe traces the international network of connections Mason later developed through his endeavors, particularly in Germany and Japan. Mason's purpose was ambitious: to construct a worldwide system of music education. His activities were prodigious: He headed the committee in Germany that published his *Neue Gesangschule* based on his *National Music Course;* he was employed in Japan in the Meiji period to teach young pupils, to participate in teacher training, to perform and to create music materials; he exerted strong influence on the official Japanese three-volume song collection for schools. Moreover, Mason had ideas for developing an international textbook, although this remained a dream. Howe provides, through her judicious handling of a rich variety of primary sources, a highly detailed picture of music education innovations in the United States, Germany, and Japan during the 19th century. It helps us escape something of the parochialism that can bedevil research in this field.

The discovery of social possibility, the second of Finkelstein's suggested relationships between history and biography, is characterized in the story of Charles Faulkner Bryan (1911–1955), particularly in relation to his career in the Works Progress Administration (WPA) (Livingston, 2003). The WPA had been introduced by President Roosevelt to provide jobs in the 1930s, and to help the country recover from the Great Depression. Music education programs were introduced that were innovative, daring, and often successful.

In his role as supervisor of the Tennessee WPA program, Bryan, who was a Roosevelt supporter, wanted to widen music education access by providing model concert bands and by enabling children to receive free instrumental lessons. He organized a statewide training institute for WPA teachers in Tennessee based on topics such as class piano, folk music, and music education. Lessons were provided in a multiplicity of settings: settlement houses, government housing projects, and churches. The program was extended to all races. Bryan's booklet on the class piano was one way he envisaged of fulfilling the project's democratic aims: He advised teachers to employ an informal, nonthreatening manner with their students, and to be sure to make room for students with lesser abilities. Bryan insisted on a new egalitarianism and the integration of music into everyday life. One of his priorities was to establish new music organizations in the growing towns and cities located near army camps and munitions factories. In Livingston's account we are provided with an inclusive vision of music education through the work of an influential music educator, who possessed a deep sense of conviction about the social possibilities contained within music during a period of intensive educational reconstruction.

Finkelstein's third entrée for biographical studies into the study of history enables researchers to view relationships between educational processes and social change. In this respect, there has been a historical silence concerning the contributions and achievements of female music educators. There are encouraging signs that this silence is starting to be addressed (see Howe, 1993, 1994, 1998, 1999; Stevens, 2000), but the work is fragmentary, and generally unrelated to the concerns of feminist scholarship.

However, the biography of Ruth Crawford Seeger (1901–1953) by Judith Tick (1997) does provide a possible model for such work. The account focuses on the multiple and divided selves of Crawford Seeger. She is remembered as a composer for her modernist works written between 1930 and 1932. Around 1932 she lost her psychic equilibrium, according to Tick, and burned her score of the Sonata for Violin and Piano. After that, she virtually ceased composing. Tick alludes to "a terrible inner crisis about which no further information survives" (1997, p. 200).

For the rest of her life, Crawford Seeger became identified as a tireless worker for the urban folk revival movement, as well as the "matriarch" of one of its best-known families. She also made a substantial contribution to music education. As a female musician, she was clearly affected by the changing political and social upheavals of the Depression years, as well as by her marriage to the radical musicologist Charles Seeger. In her move toward the left, she became "a politically committed artist" (Tick, 1997, p. 190). The couple moved to Washington, DC, in 1935, in order for Charles to take up a full-time post with the Resettlement Administration, which involved training and placing professional musicians in communities of displaced and homeless people. Crawford Seeger hurled herself thereafter into motherhood, teaching, and folk music. Her work in a Washington cooperative nursery school between 1941 and 1943 launched her career as a music consultant in early education, which culminated in the publication of the highly influential collection of *American Folk Songs for Children* (1948).

Tick describes how Crawford Seeger meshed the values of progressive education with those of the urban folk revival movement. She shifted the emphasis in the classroom away from individual creativity toward group participation, and through the "folk movement" of mothers' cooperatives "she centered the revival into the world of women and women's work" (1997, p. 290). Ruth Crawford Seeger may have been the "liver of too many lives at once" (1997, p. x), but her achievement was that she acted out the inevitable tensions and paradoxes within herself. The importance of this biography for music education historians is that it demonstrates the possibilities of developing links between gender, music, politics, and the experience of education within an exploration of the life of a significant female music educator in 20th-century America.

Finally in the consideration of Finkelstein's categories, we come to "mythic overhaul," what we might call the challenging of stereotypes. Sang (1991) investigated the status of Lowell Mason as "the father of music education in America," by examining in some detail the relative contributions of William Woodbridge, who had been impressed by the musical work of Nageli and Pfeiffer and introduced their musical adaptations of Pestalozzian ideas to music educators in America, and Elam Ives, Jr., who translated their work and was probably the first American singing teacher to employ their principles into his singing teaching. While Sang argues for a greater recognition of Ives's contribution, he nevertheless concludes that Mason should still retain his role as one of the leading figures in introducing music into the American public school curriculum. The significance of Sang's article lies in its reassessment of the accounts provided by some of the classic histories, and in its detailed catalogue of misunderstandings regarding the contributions of this trio of American music educators.

In her content analysis of the first 20 volumes of the *Bulletin of Historical Research in Music Education*, McCarthy (1999b) notes that biographical studies comprise the largest single category of papers, with a clear emphasis on men. There is little work that attempts to define, analyze, and interpret the typical activities of music teachers and their students in schools. The research tradition is still dominated by the great music educators.

The Studio Teacher   A second strand of research focusing on music educators is concerned with the studio, or private music teacher. We move away here from the narrowly biographical approach, and encounter a wider range of sources and methods. Of particular significance is the innovative work on music teachers in 18th-century England by Richard Leppert, who in *Music and Image* (1988) devotes a chapter to "Music Education as Praxis." As evidence, he uses images of the teaching of music to upper-class amateurs in England during the period found in paintings, drawings, and prints.

In England, foreigners, particularly Italians, were prized as music teachers. As a result of his analysis of the visual portrayal of music teachers, Leppert concludes that they were ambivalent creatures, proud yet deferential, both servants and entrepreneurs, tradesmen and professionals. An abiding concern on behalf of the parents, which arises through Leppert's reading of his visual evidence, was the effect of the music teacher on the female student. The ideal music teacher was a male gender version of the girl's mother: good-tempered, genteel, no vulgarity, no physical constraints, softness of voice.

In an earlier related study, Leppert (1985) concerned himself with the lives of music masters who ministered to the children of the upper class. He wanted to indicate the kinds of social conventions at play, and to illuminate the general relation between musical life in 18th-century England and the social forces that in part controlled it. Through exploring the lives and financial conditions of well-known music teachers, including Burney and Herschel, Leppert observes that metropolitan teachers were able to live "a genteel but restricted life" (1985, pp. 157–158), but the job was not easy with its long hours and stiff competition for students. In the provinces, such teachers remained poor all their lives, and had to put up with satire, cope with mediocrity for much of the time, and deal with pupils who were proud dabblers expecting to receive compliments.

Leppert's work is innovative in using visual representation as evidence, and in its focus on the teacher within a historical treatment of an ideology of music anchored in practice. An exploration of 20th-century images of music teachers in schools and studios as featured in the movies is a fertile area for future investigation (see Brand & Hunt, 1997).

In contrast to this is work that considers the problematic history of the profession of studio music teaching. Roske (1987) focused on the growth of private music teaching in 19th-century Germany. For his methodology, he utilized social statistics. Roske located a systematic index of private music teachers in the directories of the North German town Altona (now part of Hamburg), and was thus able to trace the professionalization of music instruction through a period of 50 years. In 1802, the town had only two music teachers but, by 1845, 45 music teachers were listed. The picture of employment, however, was somewhat complex. Roske delineated three work situations for such teachers: full-time music teachers, music teachers with additional music-related employment, and music teachers with additional employment in nonmusic fields. This complexity was compounded by a good deal of mobility within the profession. Nearly one third of Roske's sample were not engaged in private music teaching in the town for longer than 5 years.

Another key theme in the study was the place of female studio teachers. There was a steady rate of growth in their numbers: by 1849 they comprised 35.9% of the town's studio music teachers. In particular, piano teaching became the domain of (mostly married) women. Roske draws attention to a trend in his study toward a gradual feminization of the entire music teaching profession. However, females had a less steady status within the profession than males.

Studio music teachers are characterized in this selection of research as being somewhat marginal figures. The contrasting research techniques based on visual images and social statistics illustrate something of the methodological possibilities that are available. A key area for future research is understanding and perhaps countering this marginality by investigating attempts to gain professional status for this group of music educators (see Ehrlich, 1985).

Toward a Usable Past for Music Educators

Within the current educational climate in the United Kingdom, there are constant pleas for research to improve the quality of educational practice in schools, and to solve practical problems (see McCulloch, 2000, pp. 5–6). In the United States some years ago, Heller and Wilson (1982) insisted that historical research in music education "must treat questions that contemporary practitioners are concerned about" (1982, p. 14).

How can this be done? How can researchers move away from Rainbow's rose-tinted view of the educational past, into an engagement with the present? McCulloch (1994) is helpful in his argument that establishing the dynamic connections between past, present, and future implies an educational history that is present-minded, seeking to provide an understanding of the problems and possibilities of the present. Through such an approach, it is possible to construct "a usable past" (Hansot & Tyack, 1982), in which the problems and limitations of past traditions can be delineated, with the intention of evaluating current educational policies (for a fiercely opposed view, however, see Cohen, 1999, pp. 24–29).

I will suggest five possibilities for the development of "a usable past" for music educators. As examples, I shall select research that predominantly relates to the United Kingdom context, but that nevertheless has much wider implications.

First, an engagement with contemporary policy: Historical studies that confront policy making decisions create a dialogue between research and practice. Gammon (1999), for example, treats the cultural politics of the English National Music Curriculum between 1991 and 1992 as just one aspect of government policy that involved:

> disregarding and "distressing" professionals, the destruction of institutions and the centralisation of power whilst at the same time the denial of such centralisation through the rhetoric of increased choice and the improvement of standards. (Gammon, 1999, p. 131)

Such research serves as a salutary reminder to music educators of Reese's (1986) observation that the power to influence the curriculum, to select textbooks, to inaugurate innovative programs depends ultimately on political strength.

Second, the development of a curriculum history that disentangles the complexities, constraints, and disappointments of curriculum reform. In my own research (Cox, 2001) on the influence of two major curriculum development projects in music sponsored by the Schools Council in the 1970s, I point to the deep division they came to represent between those educators who believed that children's music should comprise children creating their own music, and others who were more concerned with children recreating other people's music. The point of such work is that it enables curriculum developers in music to visit "a whole storehouse of old solutions that are regularly and often unwittingly recycled to meet familiar problems" (Hansot & Tyack, 1982, p. 16).

Third, addressing what Rousmaniere (1997) refers to as "the historical silence on teachers' work" (p. 5). By not attending to teachers' accounts of their experience, historians have misread the actual conditions of teachers' work, and have underestimated their ability to shape schooling in many different ways (see Altenbaugh, 1997; Finkelstein, 1989). Life history research provides a method of rescuing this silent history, and illuminating present-day concerns. For example, Morgan's (1998) study of the life histories of instrumental teachers focuses upon upbringing, perspectives, and beliefs about music education, learning experiences, and critical events. In particular, Morgan confronts the feelings of marginalization that many of these instrumental teachers reported. Research in this tradition articulates the voices of teachers and brings them out of the shadows (see Sparkes, 1994). It has implications for the training, recruitment, retention, and the continuing professional development of music teachers.

Fourth, to encourage and enable music teachers to engage with a range of ideas from the past and the present and so begin to construct a philosophical basis for classroom practice, with the intention of helping them gain a depth of understanding that could enhance their teaching. In *A Century of Change in Music Education* (2000), Stephanie Pitts identifies a body of key texts in music education with the intention that, through reading them, music educators will be prompted to ask fundamental questions about the music curriculum, and then to generate their own answers. Through this process, Pitts envisages that music teachers might capture or recapture an enthusiasm for music education.

Finally, to establish international connections across and between cultures, (see McCarthy's history of the International Society for Music Education (2004) which will eventually result in historically grounded comparative work (for example, an international study of the history of formal schooling in music, which might act as a counterpoint to Campbell's [1991] cross-cultural guide to music teaching and learning with its emphasis on traditional music learning). As a result, music educators working in a variety of countries and cultures can be encouraged to question what they take for granted in their practice.

Conclusion

I have attempted to uncover some of the ideas and assumptions that have underpinned the orthodoxy of research in the history of music education and then to survey some rather scattered pieces of research, which have suggested fresh approaches and methods. In this review of the classic histories of music education I was anxious to counter tendencies, which, with the benefit of hindsight, might be regarded as myopic and narrow. One way of countering such tendencies, I have suggested, is for music education historians to learn from the insights of social scientists, while at the same time remaining rooted in pedagogical concerns (what might be regarded in the case of education history and social history as "two parallel strands of research overlapping at many points" [Cunningham, 1989, p. 79]). It is in facing up to the tension between the social and the pedagogical traditions that the future of historical research in music education lies.

In pursuing this idea, and in the subsequent process of rethinking the categories and assumptions of music education history, I have found the notion of "the enlarging vision" (McCulloch & Richardson, 2000, pp. 68–78) helpful. It relates to the major impact of the social sciences on historical research in education since the 1980s. Historians of education are increasingly drawing on aspects of sociology, cultural studies, and anthropology in their research. This, in turn, influences the scope of their interpretative perspectives to encompass such crucial areas of concern as gender, race, and social class. In order to glimpse the possibilities of an "enlarging vision," researchers are being encouraged to incorporate the following key processes into their work: engagement in a critical and skeptical dialogue with theory; exploration of the potential of methodological pluralism (also see Humphreys, 1996, 1997) and the new technologies as research tools (see Crook, 2000).

The development of an "enlarging vision" by music education historians could well be strengthened by a commitment to the three central concerns that have formed the nub of this chapter: Research should be responsive to the social, historical, ideological, and cultural contexts in which the learning and teaching of music take place; due attention should be paid to the actual teaching and learning of music; and music education should be viewed as an essentially broad area of activity, encompassing both formal and informal settings. Furthermore, this commitment could be underpinned by a deeper involvement on the part of researchers with the history of education as a field of study, and with the varieties of historical traditions in the teaching and learning of music across different cultures. All this could transform research in music education history and thus offer a greatly extended understanding of the historical richness of music teaching and learning in all its diversity. As a result of such rethinking, music education historians might not only be able to imagine the past but also might play a powerful role in the crucial debates about the present and the future of music education.

REFERENCES

Agak, H. O. (1998). Gender in school music in the Kenyan history of music education. In C. v. Niekerk (Ed.), *ISME '98 Proceedings* (pp. 1–21). Pretoria: ISME.

Aldrich, R. (2000). A contested and changing terrain: History of education in the twenty-first century. In D. Crook & R. Aldrich (Eds.), *History of education for the twenty-first century* (pp. 63–79). London: University of London Institute of Education. Bedford Way Papers.

Birge, E. B. (1928). *A history of public school music in the United States.* Philadelphia: Oliver Ditson. (Reprinted 1966 Reston, VA: MENC).

Brand, M., & K. Hunt (1997). The celluloid music teacher: An examination of cinematic portrayals of music teaching and music education in films. In R. Rideout (Ed.), *On the sociology of music education* (pp. 138–142). Norman: University of Oklahoma School of Music.

Brehony, K. J. (1998). "I used to get mad at my school": Representations of schooling in rock and pop music. *British Journal of Sociology of Education, 19*(1), 113–134.

Britton, A. (1950). *Theoretical introductions in American tune-books to 1800.* Unpublished doctoral dissertation, University of Michigan, Ann Arbor.

Britton, A. (1989). The how and why of teaching singing schools in eighteenth-century America. *Bulletin of the Council of Research in Music Education, 99*, 23–41.

Campbell, P. S. (1991). *Lessons from the world: A cross-cultural guide to music teaching and learning.* New York: Schirmer.

Cohen, S. (1999). *Challenging orthodoxies: Toward a new cultural history of education.* New York: Peter Lang.

Cox, G. (1993). *A history of music education in England 1872–1928.* Aldershot: Scolar.

Cox, G. (1999). Towards a usable past for music educators. *History of Education, 28*(4), 449–458.

Cox, G. (2001). "A house divided": Music education in the United Kingdom during the Schools Council Era of the 1970s. *Journal of Historical Research in Music Education, 22*, 160–175.

Cox, G. (2002). *Living music in schools 1923–1999: Studies in the history of music education in England.* Aldershot, UK: Ashgate.

Crook, D., & R. Aldrich. (2000). *History of education for the twenty-first century.* London: University of London Institute of Education. Bedford Way Papers.

Crook, D. (2000). Net gains? The Internet as a research tool for historians of education. In D. Crook & R. Aldrich (Eds.), *History of education for the twenty-first century* (pp. 36–49). London: University of London Institute of Education. Bedford Way Papers.

Cunningham, P. (1989). Educational history and educational change: The past decade of English historiography. *History of Education Quarterly, 29*(1), 77–94.

De Couve, A. C., Dal Pino, C., & Frega, A. L. (1997). An approach to the history of music education in Latin America. *Bulletin of Historical Research in Music Education, 19*(1), 10–39.

Eaklor, V. L. (1985). The roots of an ambivalent culture: Music, education, and music education in antebellum America. *Journal of Research in Music Education, 33*(2), 87–99.

Ehrlich, C. (1985). *The music profession in Britain since the eighteenth century: A social history.* Oxford: Clarendon Press.

Elliott, D. (1985). Jazz education in Canada: Origins and development. *Bulletin of Historical Research in Music Education, 6,* 17–28.

Evans, R. J. (1997) *In defence of history.* London: Granta Books.

Farrell, G. (1997). *Indian music and the West.* Oxford: Clarendon Press.

Finkelstein, B. (1989). *Governing the young: Teacher behavior in popular primary schools in nineteenth-century United States.* London: Falmer.

Finkelstein, B. (1998). Revealing human agency: The uses of biography in the study of educational history. In C. Kridel (Ed.), *Writing educational biography: Explorations in qualitative research* (pp. 45–49). New York: Garland.

Gammon, V. (1999). Cultural politics of the English national curriculum for music, 1991–1992. *Journal of Educational Administration and History, 31*(2), 130–147.

Goodman, J., & Martin, J. (2000). Breaking boundaries: Gender, politics, and the experience of education. *History of Education, 29*(5), 383–388.

Goodson, I. F., & Marsh, C. J. (1996). *Studying school subjects: A guide.* London: Falmer.

Green, J. P., & Vogan, N. (1991). *Music education in Canada: A historical account.* Toronto: University of Toronto.

Gruhn, W. (1993). *Geschichte der Musikerziehung.* Hofheim: Wolke Verlag.

Hansot, E., & Tyack, D. (1982). A usable past: Using history in educational policy. In A. Lieberman & M. W. McLaughlin (Eds.), *Policy making in education: Eighty-first yearbook of the National Society for the Study of Education, Part One* (pp. 1–22). Chicago: NSSE.

Heller, G. N., & Wilson, B. D. (1982). Historical research in music education: A prolegomenon. *Bulletin of the Council for Research in Music Education, 69,* 1–20.

Heller, G. N., & Wilson, B. D. (1992). Historical research. In R. Colwell (Ed.), *Handbook of research on music teaching and learning.* New York: Schirmer.

Herbert, T., & Sarkissian, M. (1997). Victorian bands and their dissemination in the colonies. *Popular Music, 16*(2), 165–179.

Howe, S. (1997). *Luther Whiting Mason: International music educator.* Warren, MI: Harmonie Park Press.

Howe, S. (1998). Reconstructing the history of music education from a feminist perspective. *Philosophy of Music Education Review, 6*(2), 96–106.

Howe, S. (1999). Leadership in MENC: The female tradition. *Bulletin of the Council of Research in Music Education, 141,* 59–65.

Howe, S. W. (1993/4). Women music educators in Japan during the Meiji period. *Bulletin of the Council for Research in Music Education, 119,* 101–109.

Humphreys, J. T. (1996/7). Expanding the horizons of music education history and sociology. *Quarterly Journal of Music Teaching and Learning, 7,* 5–19.

Humphreys, J. T. (1997). Sex and geographic representation in two music education history books. *Bulletin of the Council for Research in Music Education, 131,* 67–86.

Humphreys, J. T. (1998). The content of music education history? It's a philosophical question, really. *Philosophy of Music Education Review,* 6(2), 90–95.

Humphreys, J. T., Bess, D. M., & Bergee, M. J. (1996–7). Doctoral dissertations on the history of music education and music therapy. *Quarterly Journal of Music Teaching and Learning,* 7, 112–124.

Keene, J. A. (1982). *A history of music education in the United States.* Hanover, NH: University Press of New England.

Lee, W. (1991). Toward the Morphological Dimensions of Research in the History of Music Education. In M. McCarthy & B. D. Wilson (Eds.), *Music in American schools 1838–1988* (pp. 114–117). College Park: University of Maryland.

Lee, W. (1997). Lowell Mason, Samuel A. Worcester, and *The Cherokee singing book. Chronicles of Oklahoma,* 75(1), 32–51.

Leppert, R. D. (1985). Music teachers of upper-class amateur musicians in eighteenth-century England. In A. W. Atlas (Ed.), *Music in the classic period: Essays in honor of Barry S. Brook* (pp. 133–158). New York: Pendragon.

Leppert, R. D. (1988). *Music and image: Domesticity, ideology and socio-cultural formation in eighteenth-century England.* Cambridge: Cambridge University Press.

Livingston, C. (1997). Women in music education in the United States: Names mentioned in history books. *Journal of Research in Music Education,* 45(1), 130–144.

Livingston, C. (2001) Naming country music: Meanings behind labels. *Philosophy of Music Education Review,* 9, 19–29.

Livingston, C. (2003). *Charles Faulkner Bryan: His life and music.* Knoxville: University of Tennessee Press.

Lutz, M. M. (1982). *Musical traditions of the Labrador Coast Inuit.* Ottawa: National Museums of Canada. (Canadian Ethnology Service Paper No. 79)

Mark, M. L. (1978). *Contemporary music education.* New York: Schirmer.

Mark, M. L., & Gary, C. L. (1992). *A history of American music education.* New York: Schirmer. (Second edition 1999 Reston, VA: MENC)

Mason, L. W. (1870). *The national music course.* Boston: Ginn.

McCarthy, C. (1999). Narrating imperialism: The British influence in Barbadian public school song. In C. McCarthy, G. Hudak, S. Miklaucic, & P. Saukko (Eds.), *Sound identities: Popular music and the cultural politics of education* (pp. 153–173). New York: Peter Lang.

McCarthy, M. (1999a). *Passing it on: The transmission of music in Irish culture.* Cork, Ireland: Cork University Press.

McCarthy, M. (1999b). *The Bulletin of Historical Research* in music education: A content analysis of articles in the first twenty volumes. *Bulletin of Historical Research in Music Education,* 20(3), 181–202.

McCarthy, M. (2003) The past in the present: Revitalising history in music education. *British Journal of Music Education,* 20(2), 121–134.

McCarthy, M. (2004). *Toward a global community: The International Society for Music Education 1953–2003.* Nedlands, Australia: International Society for Music Education.

McCarthy, M., & Wilson, B. D. (Eds.). (1991). *Music in American schools 1838–1988.* College Park: University of Maryland.

McCulloch, G. (1994). *Educational reconstruction: The 1944 education act and the twenty-first century.* London: Woburn Press.

McCulloch, G. (2000). Publicizing the educational past. In D. Crook & R. Aldrich (Eds.), *History of education for the twenty-first century* (pp. 1–16). London: University of London Institute of Education. Bedford Way Papers.

McCulloch, G., & Richardson, W. (2000). *Historical research in educational settings*. Buckingham, UK: Open University.

Morgan, C. (1998). *Instrumental music teaching and learning: A life history approach*. Unpublished doctoral thesis, University of Exeter, UK.

Munslow, A. (2000). *The Routledge companion to historical studies*. London: Routledge.

Pitts, S. (2000). *A century of change in music education: Historical perspectives on contemporary practice in British secondary school music*. Aldershot, England: Ashgate.

Rainbow, B. (1967). *The land without music: Musical education in England 1800–1860 and its continental antecedents*. London: Novello.

Rainbow, B. (1989). *Music in educational thought and practice: A survey from 800 BC*. Aberystwyth, Wales: Boethius Press.

Rainbow, B. (1990). *Music and the English public school*. Aberystwyth: Boethius.

Richardson, W. (1999). Historians and educationists: The history of education as a field of study in post-war England—Part 1: 1945–72. *History of Education, 28*(1), 1–30.

Roske, M. (1987). The professionalism of private music teaching in the 19th century: A study with social statistics. *Bulletin of the Council for Research in Music Education, 91*, 143–148.

Rousmaniere, K. (1997). *City teachers: Teaching and school reform in historical perspective*. New York: Teachers College Press, Columbia University.

Sang, R. C. (1991). Woodbridge, Mason, Ives, and Pestalozzianism: A perspective on misunderstanding and controversy. In M. McCarthy & B. D. Wilson (Eds.), *Music in American schools 1838–1988* (pp. 66–70). College Park: University of Maryland.

Scholes, P. (1947). *The mirror of music 1844–1944: A century of musical life in Britain as reflected in the pages of the* Musical Times. London: Novello and Oxford University Press.

Seeger, R. C. (1948). *American folk songs for children*. Garden City, NY: Doubleday.

Shepherd, J. & Vulliamy, G. (1994). The struggle for culture: A sociological case study of the development of a national music curriculum. *British Journal of Sociology of Education, 15*(1), 27–40.

Simpson, K. (Ed.). (1976). *Some great music educators: A collection of essays*. London: Novello.

Stevens, R. (2000). Emily Patton: An Australian pioneer of tonic sol-fa in Japan. *Research Studies in Music Education, 14*, 40–49.

Sunderman, L. F. (1971). *Historical foundations of music education in the United States*. Metuchen, NJ: Scarecrow Press.

Tellstrom, A. T. (1971). *Music in American education, past and present*. New York: Holt, Rinehart & Winston.

Tick, J. (1997). *Ruth Crawford Seeger: A composer's search for American music*. New York: Oxford University Press.

Volk, T. (1993). The history and development of multicultural music education as evidenced in the *Music Educators Journal 1967–1992. Journal of Research in Music Education, 41*(2), 137–155.

Volk, T. M. (1998). *Music, education, and multiculturalism: Foundations and principles.* New York: Oxford University Press.

Weiss, S. (1995). Fundamental or frill? Music education in Australian schools since the 1880s. *Research Studies in Music Education, 5,* 55–65.

Quantitative Analysis

4

EDWARD P. ASMUS

RUDOLF E. RADOCY

Research is a systematic process by which investigators gather information, organize it in a meaningful way, and analyze and interpret it. Much information is expressible as quantities or numeric judgments. Researchers may combine and manipulate numbers in a myriad of ways to gain insights and reach conclusions regarding their problems, questions, and hypotheses. After briefly overviewing quantification and measurement, this chapter presents univariate and multivariate statistical techniques for the analysis of research data. The chapter is not a statistical treatise or a critique of the state of the quantitative art in music education research. It is intended to guide the reader in understanding, questioning, and applying basic aspects of quantitative techniques.

Quantification

Quantitative methods greatly enhance the study of musical processes by providing the accuracy and rigor required to produce conclusions upon which the researcher and others can rely (Lehman, 1968). Phelps (1986) points out that researchers who develop their research in a manner that produces quantitative data are in a better initial position to produce research that is significant to the field of music education.

Quantification is the assignment of a number to represent an amount or a perceived degree of something. That is, the association of numbers with behaviors, objects, or events. The units of weight necessary to balance a scale quantify a person's body weight. The height of an enclosed column of mercury quantifies the thermal activity in air. An adjudicator's rating quantifies the apparent quality of a musical performance. Virtually anything is quantifiable, whether in terms of some logical counting unit or some sensory impression. The degree of objectivity varies with the method of quantification. Such variance is a matter of measurement theory in general, and validity in particular.

Quantification has met considerable resistance in music education. The general outlook is that music is so complex and deals with aesthetic elements that are so far beyond tangible matters that it is impossible to quantify musical behaviors, objects, or events. Whybrew (1971, p. 3) has claimed that the precision and objectivity of quantification appear to some as "antithetical" to the aesthetic nature of music. Nevertheless, a significant body of knowledge about musical phenomena has arisen through the use of quantitative methods. The application of quantitative methods to music has been strongly supported at least since the 1930s. In 1936 Carl Seashore wrote the following:

> Musical performance as a form of behavior lends itself surprisingly well to objective study and measurement. However, it requires a rather cataclysmic readjustment in attitude to pass from the traditional introspectional and emotional attitude of the musician to the laboratory attitude of exact measurement and painstaking analysis. (p. 7)

Today, music educators commonly use quantitative methods for such tasks as grading, student evaluation, contest and festival ratings, auditioning students for ensembles, and assigning chairs in an ensemble.

Why Quantitative Research Techniques?

Research is a multifaceted enterprise, and there are many ways to investigate a problem. Numerical expression enhances the precision and specificity of phenomena under investigation. Numbers enable a researcher to describe in specific terms the subject matter under investigation and the results of the investigation. Furthermore, with the aid of statistical techniques, numbers and the resulting quantifications are important tools for framing and answering precise questions.

Quantitative methods have evolved for assigning numeric values to virtually all aspects of music and for the thorough, robust analysis of these values. As Madsen and Madsen (1978, p. 50) have pointed out, "It is the quantification of specific responses and subsequent logical methods of analysis that provide the background for experimental research."

Measurement: The Source of Quantities

The foundation of quantitative methods in research is measurement (Wilks, 1961). Measurement increases the precision and objectivity of observations whose results may be analyzed through statistical methods (Leonhard, 1958). It is the basic means humankind has used for understanding the universe (Finkelstein, 1982). This section discusses measurement because it is the source of quantities, and it imposes certain constraints on the manipulation of the quantities produced.

Definition

S. S. Stevens (1975, pp. 46–47), defined *measurement* as "the assignment of numbers to objects or events according to rule." Payne (1982, p. 1182) stresses that measurement must be more than counting; it must allow "the comparison of something with a unit or standard or quantity of that same thing, in order to represent the magnitude of the variable being measured." Boyle and Radocy (1987, p. 6) simply refer to measurement as quantifying data. Obviously, some observed object or event is expressed numerically. Fortunately for music education research, measurement does not always require using standard counting units, for example, centimeters, hertz, points, lengths of the king's foot. Impressions, judgments, and sensations may be quantified (Radocy, 1986; Stevens, 1975).

Stevens (1959, p. 18) described measurement as "the business of pinning numbers on things." Initially, only physical measurements were made by science, which resulted in classical measurement theory being based on additive quantities. Modern measurement theory is predicated on the "correspondence between a set of manifestations of a property and the relations between them and a set of numbers and the relations between them" (Finkelstein, 1982, p. 5).

Good measurement must (1) be operationally defined, (2) be reproducible, and (3) produce valid results. The goal of measurement is to assign numbers in an objective, empirical manner to objects, behaviors, or events for the purpose of their accurate description (Finkelstein, 1982). Care during the measurement process is essential to research, as it forms the foundation for all quantitative methods.

Levels of Measurement

The rules that are applied in the measurement of an object, behavior, or event yield numeric values with specific characteristics. On the basis of these characteristics, a set of numeric values can be placed into different levels of measurement. The levels of measurement, ordered from lowest to highest, are nominal, ordinal, interval, and ratio levels.

At the *nominal level* of measurement the numbers are labels for identifying some classification, as in coding all male subjects as "1" and all female subjects as "2." These numbers provide a means for placing objects or events into particular categories (Moore, 1988). Examples of nominal variables are gender, social security numbers, the numbers on players' football jerseys, and the numbering of individual musicians in a marching band.

The *ordinal level* indicates the position of an item in a set of items ordered from smallest to largest. Ordinal measurement provides no indication of how much more or less one object or event has than another object or event. A common illustration in music is the seating in a band or orchestra, where the principal in a given section presumably plays better than the other section members, but there is no specification of how much better.

The *interval level* of measurement describes the degree to which one unit may differ from another unit on a particular property. Examples of interval variables are scores on music aptitude tests, the number of members in various bands, and scores on music achievement tests.

An interval measure has some arbitrary zero point and a unit interval of constant size. A score of zero on an achievement test and zero degrees on a Fahrenheit or Celsius thermometer exemplify arbitrary zero points: A student who could answer no questions correctly might know something about the subject matter, and the temperature can fall "below zero." Test points and degrees of temperature exemplify measurement units that are presumed to be psychologically or physically equal: It is just as far from a score of 10 to 12 as it is from 55 to 57, and the number of degrees separating Fahrenheit temperatures of 21° and 27° is equal to the number of degrees separating 73° and 79°. It is not legitimate to say that a test score of 50 represents a performance that is "twice as good" as a test score of 25, or that a temperature of 80° is "twice as hot" as a temperature of 40°. Ratio comparisons such as these require a zero point that is a genuine absence of the property in question.

The *ratio level* of measurement describes a unit on the basis of the ratio of the unit's possession of a property in relation to another unit. That is, it describes a unit in terms of its having so many times as much of the property as another unit. Examples of ratio variables are loudness, the proportion of students in a class who passed an examination, and pupil–teacher ratio.

An "absolute" zero is found in ratio measurement. A temperature of 200° on the Kelvin scale is "twice as hot" physically as a temperature of 100°; 0° here is the theoretical absence of heat, a point at which molecular motion ceases. A measure of sound power where no sound results in a power measurement of zero is an example of a ratio scale.

Each succeeding level in the ordered levels of measurement must contain the basic empirical operations of all previous levels (Table 4-1) (Stevens, 1959). Knowing the numbered seat assignment of a member of a hundred-voice choir does not allow the determination of the individual's score on a music achievement test. However, knowing that student's music achievement score will allow the assignment of the student's rank in the class, which may then result in the student's placement into a particular numbered seat. From this, it can be noticed that some data can be expressed at different levels of measurement (Stevens, 1959). For example, the members of a choir may be numbered for identity and ease in keeping records of robe assignments—a nominal level of measurement. This choir may be the first-place choir at a contest where the choirs were ranked—an ordinal level of measurement. The choir may also have received a 99 out of a possible 100 score at the contest—an interval level of measurement. Finally, the choir may also be said to have received a score twice as good as that for their previous performance—a ratio measurement.

There is a relationship between the level of measurement and applicable statistics. In general, the lower the level of measurement, the more limited is the number of available statistical procedures. Asher (1976) has argued that educational researchers should strive for the interval level of measurement because of the variety of analyses available and the ability to test higher-order relationships between variables. However, advances in nonparametric statistics and multivariate analysis have allowed a much greater breadth of analysis than available a few decades ago. Indeed, a significant body of literature in music education has resulted from research that has utilized only nominal and ordinal scales. The complexity inherent in music learning suggests that the researcher should strive for interval measurement because, in comparison with nominal and ordinal data, interval data are more precise and allow use of a wider variety of statistical techniques.

TABLE 4-1. Characteristics of Various Levels of Measurement

Scale	Basic Empirical Operations	Example	Measures of Location	Measures of Dispersion	Correlation	Significance Test
Nominal	Determination of equality	Numbering of players—1, 2, 3, . . .	Mode	—	Contingency correlation	Chi-square
Ordinal	Determination of greater or less	Ranking in music competitions	Median	Percentiles	Rank-order correlation	Sign test Run test
Interval	Determination of the equality of intervals of differences	Score on musical aptitude test	Arithmetic mean	Standard deviation	Correlation ratio	t test F test
Ratio	Determination of the equality of ratios	Loudness in sones	Geometric or harmonic mean	Percent	Variation	

Note: Patterned after S. S. Stevens (1959).

Precision in an Imprecise Enterprise

Music has been said to be a very subjective enterprise. *Subjectivity* implies that there are personal biases and prejudices in operation that may have significant influence on the obtained data. The music researcher should strive for as much objectivity as possible because this will yield data that are the most consistent and sound. The researcher selecting the most appropriate measurement method is involved in evaluating the issues related to reliability and validity.

Reliability   In simple terms, reliability is the consistency with which a measuring technique measures. More specifically, as Stanley's (1971) authoritative treatise makes clear, reliability is the portion of variance in the measured property that is attributable to differences in the property itself, rather than to differences in the application of the technique on different occasions, or to other diverse sources of variance due to "error." Reliability affects the precision of measurement as well as the credence that a researcher may give results, so reporting reliability estimates is an important part of presenting the results of quantitative research.

There are several ways to estimate reliability, based on observed consistency across time or within a set of items or observers. Stanley (1971) reviews the "classic" techniques, and Boyle and Radocy (1987) refer to ways appropriate for performance measures. Music education researchers need to be cognizant that reliability is not limited to paper-and-pencil tests.

Reliability is usually estimated by determining the level of agreement between tests or among observers (Asher, 1976, pp. 93–94). The level of agreement can be determined statistically by the *correlation ratio*. The correlation ratio is a value ranging from −1 to +1 where 0 indicates no relationship, −1 indicates a perfect negative relationship, and +1 indicates a perfect positive relationship. To calculate a correlation ratio, two matched sets of values are necessary. It is through the type of values the two sets contain that different methods for estimating reliability are derived. *Equivalence* is the agreement between two tests that measure the same attribute. *Internal consistency* is obtained from different subsets of items contained within a measure. Reliability, in its pure sense, is the stability of the measure across time, which may be ascertained by determining the agreement between two different administrations of the same test at some time interval.

Validity   Validity refers to the extent to which a measurement technique measures what it is supposed to measure. According to Asher (1976, p. 97), validity is an indication of how effective, truthful, and genuine a measurement is. The validity of a measure may be determined from three primary perspectives: content validity, criterion-related validity, and construct validity.

Content validity is the test's effectiveness in providing a substantive measure of what the test is supposed to measure. *Criterion-related validity* is the level of agreement between a particular test and another indicator known to measure the particular trait of interest. Criterion-related validity may be considered further as *concurrent validity*, when the criterion measure is administered at nearly the same time as the test in question, or *predictive validity*, when the criterion is some future performance, such as eventual classroom or musical achievement. *Construct validity* is the effectiveness of a test to measure specific traits underlying the test (Ebel and Frisbie, 1986). Cronbach (1971, p. 462) indicates that the word *concepts* could be substituted for *constructs*, but constructs is more indicative "that the categories are deliberate creations chosen to organize experience into general statements." This has led some to suggest that construct validity is essentially concerned with the scientific variables measured by a test (Asher, 1976).

Music teachers concerned with whether a standardized test truly measures the objectives of their teaching are involved in establishing content validity. A researcher who wishes to determine if a test of auditory acuity is as effective at measuring pitch discrimination as the *Seashore Measures of Musical Talents* (Seashore, Lewis, & Saetveit, 1939/1960) pitch subtest is concerned with criterion-related validity. A researcher who wishes to determine whether a melodic perception test is also measuring rhythm and tonal memory is concerned with construct validity.

Subjectivity   Subjectivity is inevitable in measurement and research because people are making judgments regarding what to measure, how to measure, and what the measures mean. Although a multiple-choice achievement test that has high reliability and empirical evidence of validity is more "objective" than a judge assigning ratings at a music festival, there is also subjectivity in writing the test items and in interpreting what the scores mean. The objective-subjective aspect of measurement is a continuum of various degrees: It is not a dichotomy.

Indirect Measurement   A measure is conceptually direct when a property is measured in terms in itself. Measuring length in terms of length, as in measuring the length of one side of a room with a carpenter's rule, is an example. In contrast, measuring rhythm perception by judging the precision with which a student claps a pattern after hearing it exemplifies *indirect measurement*. Indirect measures are inevitable in quantifying musical behavior because much behavior is covert, and overt behavior often is interpreted as evidence of some knowledge or attitude. Indirect measures abound and include written tests, judgment procedures, and electrical and mechanical measures.

Measurement Types in Music

There are many ways to classify types of measurement applicable to quantitative research in music education. Boyle's (1974) classification of musical test behaviors into performance, reading/writing, listening, and "other cognitive" is useful, as is 'the Johnson and Hess (1970) grouping of subjects' response behaviors and ways to elicit their responses. Another particularly useful classification scheme for conceptualizing music education research possibilities is the division of measurements into psychomusic tests and mechanized measures.

Psychomusic tests examine some psychomusical construct or psychoacoustical property as it is observed through some indicator created by a subject's conscious efforts, such as a test score or a performance. Psychomusic tests include measures of achievement in general music, musical performance skill, pitch discrimination, musical aptitude, attitude toward music, and sight singing.

Mechanized measurement, which includes electronic measures, employs one or more devices to obtain data from a subject; it does not require that a subject actively complete a form or report, or perform. Examples include monitoring physiological aspects, such as heartbeat and blood pressure, employing stroboscopic devices to monitor a subject's intonation during performance, analyzing a complex tone's frequency components and relative intensities and phases, and studying a room's reverberant properties.

Presumably, mechanized measurement is more reliable and "objective" than most psychomusical measures. A series of stroboscopic readings may be more consistent and easier to "read" than a series of subjective human judgments regarding a performer's intonation. Mechanized measurement avoids inherent problems of error that may be induced in the recording of a subject's response. For instance, a subject may mismark an answer sheet by simply responding to item 5 in the location of item 6. This is avoided by mechanical systems. The greater the error in a measurement, the lower the reliability (Lord & Novick, 1968).

Statistical Principles

Strictly speaking, one may quantify without employing statistics, but most quantitative research needs to describe characteristics and draw inferences. Statistical treatments must be appropriate for the research questions and the data. This section reviews basic principles regarding descriptive and inferential statistics, hypothesis testing, and specific properties of statistics.

Descriptive Versus Inferential Statistics

The primary difference between descriptive and inferential statistics is the use to which the statistics will be put. If the purpose is to describe the data, then *descriptive statistics* are used (Borg and Gall, 1979, p. 406). If the purpose is to make inferences about a population of individuals from data gathered from a sample of this population, then *inferential statistics* are used (Best and Kahn, 1989, p. 222). Practically, most research studies begin with descriptive statistics and then, once overall characteristics of the data are known, inferential statistics are applied to determine the characteristics of the population. In some cases, after inferential statistics have been applied, interesting phenomena are noted for particular samples whose data are then treated with descriptive statistics to determine the characteristics of these samples.

The purpose of descriptive statistics is to describe and summarize relatively large amounts of data (Sax, 1979, p. 370), thus reducing the data to a few statistics that simplify interpretation (Borg and Gall, 1979, p. 406). They often describe central tendencies and variability in the data, as well as simply relate how much of what exists. Analysis of the results of a classroom achievement test, a listing of the numbers of students enrolled in particular music classes, grade point averages for all members of a student body, and demographic data exemplify some uses of descriptive statistics.

Inferential statistics are employed to make judgments about some group beyond those subjects who contribute data. A general music class may be considered representative of other general music classes; a set of trumpet mouthpieces may be considered representative of available mouthpieces. On the basis of probabilities and known or surmised properties of the particular sample, a researcher infers characteristics of the larger group. In short, one "draws an inference."

A *statistic* is a numerical characteristic obtained from a sample. A *parameter* is a numerical characteristic obtained from a population. It is the role of inferential statistics to estimate the parameters of a population on the basis of observations derived from a sample (Best and Kahn, 1989, pp. 222–223).

Usually samples are drawn from a population utilizing random sampling techniques. The purpose of random sampling is to produce values for which margins of error can be determined statistically when the sampled values are generalized to a larger population (Borg and Gall, 1979, p. 182). Random sampling provides the most efficient means of providing data that can be generalized to the larger population from which the sample was drawn.

The Elements of Statistics

Populations   All members of a particular group of interest comprise the population. Fifth-grade instrumental music students in a city's schools, clarinet reeds available in a music store, learning-disabled students in music classes, string students taught by a Suzuki-based method, or virtually any logical group are populations. Populations may be huge, as in the population of all 6-year-olds, or tiny, as in the population of all students in one school who have absolute pitch. Generalization to a population is implicit in much music education research. In order for researchers to generalize to a specific population, all members of the population need a relatively equal chance to contribute to the data from which the inferences are drawn.

Samples   A sample is a subset of a population. A group of voters carefully chosen from "representative" precincts by a polling organization is a sample of a population of voters. The subjects of research in which inferences are to be made are a sample of the population of interest.

Ideally, a sample is obtained in a way that gives each and every member of the population an equal chance of being selected. This is a *random sample*. Selecting subjects on the basis of random number tables, computerized random number generators, tossing fair dice, or drawing numbered slips of paper from a thoroughly mixed set are legitimate applications of randomization. Merely scanning a list of names or looking over a set of objects and in effect saying, "Let's take this one, and that one; we'll eliminate that one . . ." is not a random process. A random sample of sufficient number allows a researcher to generalize results to the population with confidence.

Truly random samples are almost always impossible to obtain. Some reasons include the necessity to work with volunteer subjects, a need to use intact classrooms or ensembles rather than mix subjects across groups, proscriptions caused by informed-consent aspects of using human subjects, and selective loss of subjects. Many samples employed in quantitative research thus are ersatz random samples: samples chosen on the basis of who is available, but deemed to be representative or like the members of some larger population. Researchers must use their training and experience to make an informed decision as to the representativeness of the sample. Many applications of inferential statistics proceed as if the sample were random.

Samples could be obviously nonrandom to a degree where there is no point in claiming that they are representative of a population in any way. Using the first 15 students one meets on campus as somehow representative of the student body clearly is using a nonrandom sample. So is a researcher's employing a group of the general population to answer questions about specific musical phenomena because they are available, without the researcher's having any knowledge of their musical backgrounds.

Sample Size   One somewhat controversial issue is sample size. In general, the larger the size of a representative sample, the more stable and representative are the results of the inference. Classical statistical texts (e.g., Li, 1964) clearly show that larger sample sizes enhance the probability of finding a difference between experimental treatments when one "truly" exists in the population. They restrict the range within which some "true" value is likely to fall. Of course, with sufficiently large samples, even population differences that lack any "practical" significance will be statistically significant (Heller and Radocy, 1983).

How large is large enough? Kirk (1982, p. 8) indicates that adequate sample size is a function of experimental effects and the number of treatments, error variance in the population from which the sample comes, and the probability of making a false judgment about the outcome of a statistical test. Since some of these properties are not always known in advance, Kirk also presents procedures for estimating certain sample sizes. Consistent rules of thumb are hard to find. The Bruning and Kintz (1977) statistical "cook-book" recommends 10 to 15 subjects per experimental group. Cohen's (1988) treatise provides various means for estimating minimal sample sizes.

Drawing Inferences

Das and Giri (1986) identify three main characteristics of the inferential process: (1) the inferences are made with observations that are not exact but that are subject to variation making them probabilistic in nature, (2) methods are specified for the appropriate collection of data so that the assumptions for particular statistical methods are satisfied, and (3) techniques for the proper interpretation of the statistical results are devised.

Null Hypotheses   Inferences are drawn on the basis of the outcomes of statistical tests. What is tested is a statement of no cause and effect, or no relationship, a *null hypothesis*. The null hypothesis results from a *hypothesis*, a tentative statement of cause and effect or relationship. In turn, the hypothesis is implied by questions that the researcher is trying to answer. Research questions, hypotheses, and null hypotheses are not always stated explicitly in a research report, but are implied by what the researcher investigates and how. Questions are implied in the form of, "What is the effect of _____ on _____?"

Hypotheses lead to deliberate statements of no cause and effect, or no relationship. These null hypotheses are directly testable through techniques of inferential statistics. An example of a null hypothesis statement is "There is no difference in students' knowledge of excerpts between the beginning of the music appreciation course and the end."

Conceptually, a researcher tests a null hypothesis by judging whether an observed outcome of a statistical test is sufficiently likely to belong to a distribution of events—a distribution that will occur if the null hypothesis is true; that is, there "really" is no difference or relationship in the population. If the observed outcome is not too extreme, in accordance with statistical probabilities, it is deemed to belong to the distribution that exists if the null hypothesis is true. If the observed outcome is too extreme, it is considered to be too unlikely to belong to that distribution—it probably belongs to another, and the null hypothesis probably is false. Just what is "too extreme" is a matter of judgment of just how far from the center of a hypothesized distribution the outcome is.

Statistical Significance   The necessary degree of extremity is a matter of statistical significance. Essentially, *statistical significance* is the likelihood that the observed result occurred by chance alone. To say that an outcome is significant at or beyond a certain level is to specify the odds. A researcher claiming statistical significance at the .05 level ($p \leq 5.05$) is saying that the null hypothesis will be rejected 95 times out of 100. Although some researchers have claimed that results are significant at the .10 level ($p \leq .10$) or even at the .20 level ($p \leq .20$), it is rare that a researcher claims statistical significance unless the .05 level ($p \leq .05$) is attained. If the outcome of an experiment may cause a major revision to existing instructional procedures or lead to considerable reallocation of resources, the researcher may require a greater significance level, such as the .01 level or the .001 level.

Statistically significant occurrences are deemed unlikely to have occurred by chance alone, in accordance with a set of statistical probabilities and a researcher's interpretative judgment. Practical significance does not necessarily follow. Large samples, for instance, are prone to produce small but statistically significant differences that have no practical importance. Basically, practical significance comes down to "So what?" (Heller and Radocy, 1983).

Correct Decision Versus Error   Although statistical techniques are powerful tools for assessing population characteristics in accordance with sample characteristics, they are not infallible. The correct decision versus error issue may be conceptualized as an interaction of two dimensions. One dimension is reality; that is, whether the null hypothesis is in fact true or false. The other dimension is the researcher's decision to retain or reject the null hypothesis. If the researcher retains a null hypothesis that is in fact true *or* rejects a null hypothesis that is in fact false, that researcher makes a correct decision. If the researcher rejects a null hypothesis that is in fact true, that researcher commits a Type I or alpha error. The researcher who fails to reject a null hypothesis that is in fact false commits a Type II or beta error. Establishing a more stringent criterion for statistical significance, which essentially reduces the number of outcomes that will be deemed too extreme to occur by chance alone, reduces the likelihood of Type I error. Increasing the sample size reduces the likelihood of Type II error.

Parametric Versus Nonparametric Statistics

Parameters are values such as means and variances of some population. *Parametric statistics* are based on distributions of possible outcomes with known parameters. *Nonparametric statistics,* also called "distribution-free" statistics, are based on distributions with unknown parameters. Parametric statistics are applicable to data with at least an interval level of measurement, and nonparametric statistics are applicable to data with nominal and ordinal levels of measurement (Best, 1981, p. 221). Parametric statistics are more numerous and tend to be more powerful and more frequently used. Nonparametric statistics do not require the same number of assumptions about the underlying population as are required by parametric statistics.

Parametric statistics make a greater number of assumptions about the population parameters. First, the data are at least at the interval level of measurement. Second, the data of the population are normally distributed. Third, the distribution of the data for the various samples is generally the same. To be normally distributed means that the data, when graphed, create the well-known well-shaped curve of the normal distribution (Figure 4-1). When the distributions of the various samples are approximately equal, the samples are said to have the characteristic of homogeneity of variance.

Nonparametric statistics require that observations are independent and that measurement is at the nominal or ordinal levels (Madsen and Madsen, 1978, p. 78). Nonparametric tests do not assume that the population is normally distributed, and they do not assume homogeneity of variance in the samples (Rainbow and Froehlich, 1987, p. 230). Siegel and Castellan (1988, p. xv) cite four advantages of using nonparametric statistics: (1) the tests are distribution-free in that they do not assume that the data are normally distributed, (2) they can employ ordinal data that are simply ranks, (3) these statistics are simple to calculate, and (4) they are appropriate in the study of small samples.

Puri and Sen (1971, p. 1) point out that researchers seldom know the underlying distribution of a population and that the use of parametric statistics in situations where the underlying distribution is not normal is highly suspect. However, Borg and Gall (1979, p. 464) recommend the use of parametric statistics when the researcher has interval scores but has neither normally distributed scores nor homogeneity of variance among the samples because (1) the outcome of a parametric technique is affected very little by moderate departure from the technique's theoretical assumptions, (2) nonparametric statistics are generally less powerful, and (3) for many educational research problems, suitable nonparametric tests are not available.

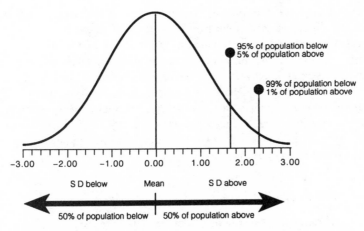

Figure 4.1. The normal curve with reference of population percentages.

The decision to employ parametric or nonparametric methods depends on the data as well as a researcher's beliefs. Nominal or ordinal data of small sample sizes may be handled more appropriately with nonparametric methods. A researcher who is satisfied that there is no reason to question the propriety of parametric statistics in a particular situation should employ parametric statistics. Assuredly, the researcher should not do both: The researcher either believes that the conditions for parametric statistics are satisfied or does not believe it.

Variables

A *variable*, in the broad sense, is something that does not remain the same under all conditions; that is, it varies. Variables are characterized according to the functions they serve in the research design and in the applicable statistical tests.

Independent Variables

In quantitative research, researchers often compare two or more levels of an *independent variable* on a dependent variable. For example, the effects of two or more instructional approaches could be compared. When investigators are free to decide what will be done and when, they are able to "manipulate" an independent variable. In cases where they must accept previously existing conditions, such as subjects' gender or ethnicity, the independent variable is labeled as an "assigned" variable. The reader should be aware that other labels do exist.

Dependent Variables

Dependent variables presumably "depend" on the effect of independent variables. Changes between pretest and posttest scores exemplify dependent variables. If a researcher is studying the effects of instruction, different forms of instruction constitute an independent variable, and some measure of the result of instruction constitutes a dependent variable. Many quantitative studies contain just one dependent variable, in which case the use of univariate statistics is appropriate. Other studies, especially many contemporary ones, feature simultaneous investigation of the effects of independent variables on more than one dependent variable. In those studies, multivariate statistical techniques are mandatory.

Statistical Conceptualization

In cases where changes in the dependent variable are conceived as resulting from the manipulation of an independent variable, as when attitudes might change as a result of exposure to music across time, or where they are conceived as resulting from a "natural" or assigned independent variable, as when differences in musical taste might be due to gender, there is an underlying *factorial model:* An independent variable clearly is a causal agent or factor that determines what happens to a dependent variable.

In cases where the variables are conceived as a set of relationships—as, for example, where one might relate scores on a measure of musical ability with scores on a test of academic achievement—there is an underlying regression model. Here, depending on the research question, either variable could be "independent" or "dependent." The conception is of related variables, or predictor and criterion variables. For example, Hedden (1982) related a set of predictor variables—attitude toward music, self-concept in music, musical background, academic achievement, and gender—to a criterion variable of musical achievement.

"Other" Variables

Many variables exist that are neither independent nor dependent; most of them are irrelevant. Most research in music education need not be concerned with changing conditions of cosmic ray penetration, eye color, shoe size, hair length, position or rate of the Humboldt current, or subjects' prior exposure to Boolean algebra, for example. However, nuisance or confounding variables could influence a dependent variable. An example would be home musical background in a study of contrasting approaches to teaching instrumental music. Nuisance variables can be controlled by statistical techniques, random selection of subjects, or changing an experimental design and its associated statistical treatment to incorporate a nuisance variable as another independent variable.

Univariate Versus Multivariate Statistics

The distinction between univariate and multivariate statistics varies somewhat from author to author, but the generally distinguishing feature is that *univariate statistics* are used in analyzing the characteristics of one dependent variable (Hair, Anderson, Tatham, and Grablowsky, 1984, p. 5; Harris, 1985, p. 5; Kachigan, 1986, pp. 4–5). *Multivariate statistics*, on the other hand, are used in simultaneously analyzing a number of dependent variables. Multivariate statistics frequently provide a simplification of the data by summarizing the data with relatively few parameters (Chatfield and Collins, 1980, pp. 6–7). Not only do these procedures allow for the testing of hypotheses, but a number are exploratory in nature and can generate hypotheses as well as test hypotheses.

The study of musical processes usually involves multiple variables that could be expected to be affected by some factor. For instance, a 10-week experimental treatment in which fourth-grade students received a particular music-teaching method for 30 minutes each day might be expected to affect both rhythm and pitch skills. With traditional statistical procedures used in music research, separate analyses would be performed on each of these skills to determine if the skills had been positively influenced by the treatment. Analyzing each skill separately involves the application of univariate statistics. Unfortunately, the use of separate univariate statistics in such cases increases the possibility of producing a significant result that is actually due to chance (Harris, 1985, pp. 6–7). Thus the research is subject to Type I error. Multivariate statistics provides a means around such problems by providing an overall test to determine whether the experimental treatment actually produced a significant effect on both skills and, if so, subanalyses can be performed to determine if the significant effect occurred for each of the skills separately.

Multivariate statistics are an assortment of descriptive and inferential procedures for analyzing the simultaneous effects of phenomena on a number of variables. There exists a multivariate analogue of virtually every univariate procedure. Most research in music will become increasingly involved in the application of multivariate procedures because of the complex nature of music processes. This is most appropriate because multivariate statistics have been claimed to produce more interesting results and to be more scientifically productive (Kachigan, 1986, p. 5). To avoid the use of multivariate statistics will result in research with a greater probability of error and research that does not provide the full range of insights that multivariate statistics provide. Harris (1985, p. 5) has stated that "if researchers were sufficiently narrow-minded or theories and research techniques so well developed or nature so simple as to dictate a single independent variable and a single outcome measure as appropriate in each study, there would be no need for multivariate techniques."

As with univariate statistics, there are both parametric and nonparametric multivariate statistical procedures. For the parametric case, the distribution that forms the foundation for multivariate statistics is the multivariate normal distribution (Muirhead, 1982, p. 1). This distribution is an extension of the normal distribution to more than one variable. As in the univariate case, most sampled measurements tend to be normally distributed.

Univariate Tests: One Independent Variable

Chi-Square Tests

The family of chi-square tests essentially compares an observed classification of frequencies with an expected classification. For example, in a study of elementary students tempo perceptions, Kuhn and Booth (1988) used chi-square to determine whether the numbers of subjects who classified musical examples as going slower, staying the same, or going faster were significantly different from a chance distribution of the three tempo change classifications.

The assumptions of chi-square include independence of each observation from each other observation, placement of any observation in one and only one cell in the table formed by the classifications of observed and expected, and a sufficiently large sample size (Hays, 1988, p. 772). According to Wike (1971), if the total number of observations exceeds the total number of subjects, some subjects are contributing to more than one observation, and the independence criterion is violated. Sufficient sample size is controversial, but Wike suggests that the total sample size should exceed 20 and the expected frequency in any classification should be at least 5. There are various adaptations for smaller numbers and for situations where subjects contribute more than one observation; the Siegel (1956) treatise and Wike's book are good sources of additional information.

t Tests

A widely applicable set of parametric statistical tests is based on a family of statistical distributions called the t distributions. Essentially, the researcher compares an observed t value with a hypothesized t value of zero; if the observed outcome is too far away from zero in accordance with the probabilities of the hypothesized t distribution, the null hypothesis is rejected. In using a t test, one assumes that all samples are drawn randomly from normally distributed populations with equivalent variances. In practice, these assumptions often are violated.

An *"independent"* t test compares two samples that are not matched in any way. The two groups represent two levels of an independent variable, and the t value is computed from the measures of the dependent variable. For example, Darrow, Haack, and Kuribayashi (1987) used independent t tests in comparing preferences for particular musical examples of two groups of subjects who differed in musical experience.

A *"related measures"* t test compares two matched groups. Often, the groups are "matched" because they are two sets of scores from the same group of people, as in a comparison of pretest and posttest scores. Price and Swanson (1990) used this type of related measures (matched, dependent, paired) t test in comparing their subjects' pretest and posttest scores on cognitive knowledge, attitudes, and preferences.

A less commonly applied t test is a test to compare an observed sample mean with a hypothesized population mean. An investigator might compare a mean score on a standardized musical achievement test administered in his or her school with a hypothesized mean equivalent to a published norm to see if the school's mean was "better" or "worse" than a hypothesized national mean.

A multiplicity of t tests that are testing a series of null hypotheses with data obtained in the same study may be unwise, not only from the standpoint of efficiency but because of increasing the probability of Type I or alpha error. Fortunately, the t test is a special case of a large family of more efficient statistical techniques known as analysis of variance.

Analysis of Variance

The family of t distributions is mathematically related to another family of statistical distributions, the F distributions. Mathematicians can show that $t^2 = F$. Therefore, a t test may be conceived as a special case of analysis of variance, which relies on the F distribution, where there are only two sets of measures to compare. The *analysis of variance* (ANOVA) is much more flexible because it can account for more than two levels of an independent variable and be extended to account for more than one independent variable simultaneously, and, through multivariate techniques, even more than one dependent variable simultaneously.

The assumptions of the analysis of variance are that the samples are obtained randomly from normally distributed populations, with equivalent variances. In practice, the randomization is critical; the other criteria may be "bent" a little (Li, 1964).

Types of ANOVA   An ANOVA may be employed to analyze the difference between separate groups and repeated measures of the same group. If a subject can be in one and only one group, the comparison is between separate groups, each of which represents a level of an independent variable. If the same subjects experience different levels of an independent variable, there are *repeated measures* involved. A *mixed design* is one in which any particular subject experiences just one level of one (or more) independent variable(s) while simultaneously experiencing all levels of one (or more) other independent variable(s). For example, in a music preference study, all students in a junior high school can listen to each of five musical styles; the style variable is a repeated measure. If the investigator is interested in differential effects of gender, the gender variable is an independent variable where each subject can be at just one level.

The analysis of variance indicates via one or more F tests whether there is a significant difference between or among the levels of the independent variable. When two or more independent variables are studied simultaneously, F tests also are applied to any possible interaction(s); these are discussed later in the context of factorial designs. The original F tests do not indicate where the significance lies. If there are only two levels, the location of any significant difference is obvious. Otherwise, further testing is necessary.

Post-ANOVA Comparisons   Opinions differ regarding multiple comparison tests to follow a significant F value. Kirk (1982) distinguishes between orthogonal and nonorthogonal comparisons and between a priori (planned) comparisons and a posteriori (data snooping) comparisons. Orthogonal comparisons use nonoverlapping information. In general, if there are k levels of the independent variable, there are $k - 1$ orthogonal comparisons. With four groups, for example, the possible comparisons for significant differences between two levels involve the differences between groups 1 and 2, 1 and 3, 1 and 4, 2 and 3, 2 and 4, 3 and 4. Three pairwise comparisons—the difference between 1 and 2 as compared with the difference between 3 and 4, the difference between 1 and 3 as compared with the difference between 2 and 4, and the difference between 1 and 4 as compared with the difference between 2 and 3—are orthogonal. The other possible comparisons are non-orthogonal; for example, comparing the difference between group 1 and group 2 as compared with the difference between group 1 and group 3 involves group 1 in each difference, so it is nonorthogonal. *Planned comparisons* are hypothesized before the experiment. *A posteriori comparisons* emerge from the data.

To reduce the likelihood that some comparisons will be significant by chance alone, various adjustments to the significance level may be necessary, so statisticians have created a family of multiple comparison measures. Kirk describes four situations. When comparisons are limited to planned orthogonal comparisons, a modified form of the t test that incorporates part of the analysis of variance summary (the mean square for error variance) is appropriate. Dunn's test is appropriate for all planned comparisons, whether or not they are orthogonal. For a posteriori comparisons and mixtures of planned and unplanned comparisons, possibilities include Fisher's LSD (least significant difference) test, Tukey's HSD (honestly significant difference) test, Scheffé's test, the Newman-Keuls test, Duncan's new multiple range test, and Dunnett's test. In general, planned orthogonal comparisons are more powerful than the others. Computational procedures differ, and some tests are more versatile regarding the possibility of comparing combinations of levels within an independent variable.

An ANOVA Example   The results of an ANOVA are presented in a *source table*. Gfeller, Darrow, and Hedden (1990), in a study of mainstreaming status among music educators, presented a fully documented source table, which appears here as Table 4-2. The grouping variable, or factor, of music education type contained three levels: instrumental, vocal, and general mu-

TABLE 4-2. ANOVA Source Table of Gfeller, Darrow, and Hedden (1990)

Source of Variance	Sum of Squares	df	Mean Squares	F	p
Between groups	186.43	2	93.21	4.84	.010
Within groups	1,327.57	69	19.24		
Total	1,514.00	71			

TABLE 4-3. Newman Keuls Multiple Range Test of Gfeller, Darrow, and Hedden (1990)

Elementary Music Educators	Vocal Music Educators	Instrumental Music Educators
20.60	22.26	24.81

Note: Rule under values indicates nonsignificance. All other comparisons significant ($p < .01$).

sic educator. The dependent variable was the teachers' perception of the instructional support they were receiving. In the source table, the mean squares are obtained by dividing the sum of squares by the corresponding degrees of freedom. The F value is obtained by dividing the between-groups mean squares with the within-groups mean squares. Note that there was a significant difference at the .01 level between the types of teachers as indicated by p in the table. The post hoc analysis was performed using the Newman Keuls Multiple Range Test (Table 4-3). This analysis indicates that the instrumental music educators have a higher opinion of the instructional support they receive for mainstreaming than do the other music educators.

Analysis of Covariance

A research design may not always control for effects of extraneous or "nuisance" variables. For example, in a study comparing the relative efficacies of two methods of teaching beginning instrumentalists, the two groups might differ significantly in their initial music aptitude, despite randomization. In a study where the researcher must necessarily work with intact groups, the students in one classroom may have some inherent advantage, such as parents who encourage and support private music lessons. Aptitude and parental support variables occasionally may be built into the experimental design as additional independent variables, but when that is not feasible, statistical control may be attained via *analysis of covariance,* where the additional variable functions as a *covariate.* The covariate varies along with the other variables, and its effects are mathematically; in effect, the researcher is able to indicate the effects of the independent variable with any effects of the covariate under statistical control. Analysis of covariance may be extended to factorial designs with more than one independent variable and/or covariate and to multivariate designs with more than one independent variable, dependent variable, and/or covariate.

Univariate Tests: Two or More Independent Variables

Factorial Design Concepts

The number of independent variables or factors and their associated levels determine which ANOVA model is appropriate. The model extends the partitioning of the total sums of squares beyond the within-treatments and between-treatments sums of squares done by the one-way ANOVA. The F value is still the ratio of the sums of squares of interest divided by the sums of squares within treatments now designated as *error* (Edwards, 1968, p. 120).

Figure 4-2 presents three different experiments that all use musical achievement as the dependent variable. In the first experiment, it is desired to determine the effect of three levels of musical aptitude, the single independent variable or factor, on musical achievement. This experimental design would require a *one-way ANOVA*. The second experiment is designed with a two-level factor of gender and a three-level factor of musical aptitude level. This experimental design, because it involves two factors, requires a *two-way ANOVA*. The third experiment extends the second by including a third factor of grade level, which requires a *three-way ANOVA*. ANOVAs with more than one factor may also be referred to by the number of levels of

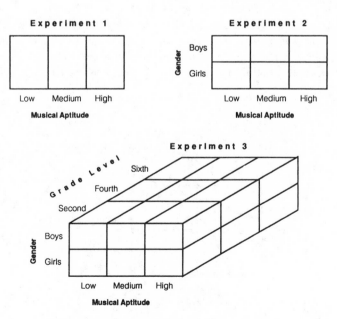

Figure 4.2. Three experimental designs in music.

each factor. The second experiment would be referred to as a 2 × 3 ANOVA, and the third experiment would be referred to as a 2 × 3 × 3 ANOVA.

The two-way ANOVA required by the second experiment in Figure 4-2 can further partition the between-treatment sums of squares into the *main effects* for each of the factors of gender and musical aptitude as well as for the interaction of these two factors. In this case, the partitioning of the treatment sums of squares yields sums of squares for the gender main effect, the musical aptitude main effect, and the gender x musical aptitude (gender by musical aptitude) *interaction*. An *F* ratio can be produced for each partition by dividing with the appropriate error team. The error term in this case is the within-treatment sums of squares. Thus, tests can be applied to determine if a significant difference exists in musical achievement attributable to gender, musical aptitude, or the interaction between gender and musical aptitude.

A significant interaction in a multiway ANOVA indicates that the effect of the various levels of the factors involved is not uniform. In the case of the second experiment in Figure 4-2, a significant gender x musical aptitude interaction might indicate that girls of high aptitude achieve more than boys of high aptitude while girls of low aptitude achieve less than boys of low aptitude. The opposite also could be true. It would be necessary to plot the means for the cells of the interaction, as in Figure 4-3 (p. 116) to determine the nature of the significant interaction. In this case, our initial supposition is indicated by the graph of the interaction. In general, a plot of significant interaction will reveal prominent nonparallel lines, although the lines may not always intersect.

The concepts presented for the second example can be extended for other multiway ANOVAs. Consider the characteristics of the three-way ANOVA of the third experiment in Figure 4-2. The between-treatments sums of squares can be partitioned into three main effects: gender, musical aptitude, and grade level. In addition, the following combinations of factors produce

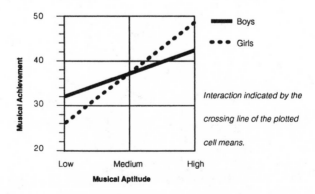

Figure 4.3. Hypothetical interaction effects for Experiment 2.

interactions that can be tested: gender x musical aptitude, gender x grade level, musical aptitude x grade level (two-way interactions), and gender x musical aptitude x grade level (three-way interaction).

Simple Effects

In the example provided by Experiment 2, we may find that there are significant differences due to the main effects of both gender and musical aptitude. For the main effect of gender, there are only two means: one for the boys and one for the girls. Thus, the gender main effect states that the girls and boys performed significantly differently from each other on musical achievement, the dependent variable. For the main effect of musical aptitude, there are three means, one for each of the three musical aptitude levels. A number of methods are available to determine how these means differ through both post hoc and a priori methods. The multiple comparisons that are required to account for the differences among all the means have come to be called *simple effects*.

Simple effects are of two types: planned and unplanned (Kachigan, 1986, p. 306). Comparisons planned prior to data analysis are also known as *a priori comparisons*. Comparisons determined after the completion of an ANOVA where significant differences for the main and interaction effects have been noted are unplanned comparisons, also known as *post hoc comparisons*.

A Priori Comparisons   The most accepted method for analyzing simple effects that are preplanned is through the testing of *orthogonal comparisons* (Kachigan, 1986, p. 306). Orthogonal comparisons are established by the assignment of weights to the means so that the sum of all the weights is equal to zero. For instance, in Experiment 2 of Figure 4-2, we might have obtained a significant musical aptitude main effect. This effect has three means. To compare the low aptitude mean $(\overline{x}_l)$ with the medium aptitude mean $(\overline{x}_m)$, we would subtract the second mean from the first mean. This in mathematical formulation would be:

$$\overline{x}_l - \overline{x}_m$$

which is equivalent to

$$(+1)\, \overline{x}_l + (-1)\, \overline{x}_m.$$

Removing the mean symbols leaves the two weights

$$+1 \text{ and } -1,$$

which also sum to zero. Orthogonal contrasts are created in just this manner. They also provide the ability to compare, say, the high musical aptitude mean ($\bar{x}_h$) against the average of the low and medium level musical aptitude means. This comparison would be mathematically displayed as

$$\bar{x}_h - \frac{\bar{x}_l + \bar{x}_m}{2} = \bar{x}_h - \frac{\bar{x}_l}{2} - \frac{\bar{x}_m}{2},$$

which would have the weights of

$$+1 \quad -\frac{1}{2} \quad -\frac{1}{2},$$

which also sum to zero.

Two contrasts, to be orthogonal to each other, must have the products of their respective coefficient weights sum to zero. The number of possible orthogonal contrasts is one less than the number of levels in the ANOVA effect of interest. For our musical aptitude effect of Experiment 2, there are three levels, which means that two orthogonal comparisons are possible. It is possible, however, to create a number of different sets of orthogonal comparisons. Table 4-4 presents a number of possibilities for the musical aptitude effect. Note that constants have been used in some of the contrasts to avoid fractions.

The test of the significance of an orthogonal contrast is done by testing whether the sum of the products of each weight times its respective mean is equal to zero. The test requires that the sum (W) of all the Weight (w) $\times$ Mean ($\bar{x}$) products is calculated as

$$W = w_1 \bar{x}_1 + w_2 \bar{x}_2 + \ldots + w_k \bar{x}_k.$$

The standard error (S_w) for the sum of all the Weight $\times$ Mean products is then calculated as

$$s_w = s \sqrt{\sum \frac{w_i^2}{n_i}},$$

where

TABLE 4-4. Possible Orthogonal Contrasts for Musical Aptitude

Contrast	Low Mean	Medium Mean	High Mean
1	2	-1	-1
2	0	1	-1
1	-1	-1	2
2	1	-1	0

s = square root of the within-treatment or error mean square,

w^2_i = squared weight in a contrast, and

n_i = the sample size for a mean in the contrast.

The test is distributed as t with the same degrees of freedom as for the within-treatment sums of squares and an alpha twice that selected for the original ANOVA.

$$t = \frac{W}{s_w}.$$

An equivalent interval to test this value is

$$W \pm (\alpha/2^t\ df)(s_w)$$

where

$1 - \alpha/2^t\ df$ = critical value of t for a particular confidence level with the same degrees of freedom as for the within—treatment sum of squares.

The value of using orthogonal contrasts is that both the significance levels of each comparison and the entire set of comparisons are known (Kachigan, 1986, p. 310). If for each of our musical aptitude comparisons we use a significance level of .05, the probability for the entire set is $.95 \times .95 = .85$ that the set is without a Type 1 error, or the probability of one Type I error in the set is .15 (1 − .85). For post hoc—that is, unplanned comparisons— the probability in the set of comparisons is not known.

Post Hoc Comparisons   Duncan's (1955) multiple range test provides one method for the post hoc determination of which of the differences of the means are significant. Use of post hoc methods assumes that there were no hypothesized differences prior to the implementation of the experiment. The method involves ordering all the means from lowest to highest in a table and calculating the standard error of the mean. A statistical table is then employed to find a multiplier value based on the degrees of freedom for the within-treatment partitioning of the sums of squares. Multipliers are found for two through to the total number of levels. The standard error of the mean and the multipliers are then multiplied. This forms the *shortest significant ranges*. The lowest mean is then subtracted from the highest mean. If this value is larger than the shortest significant range for the spread of levels covered by the lowest to the highest mean, then a significant difference between means has been identified. This process continues comparing the next smallest mean to the highest mean until no difference is noted. A line is drawn under the means from the highest mean to the point where no difference occurs. This entire procedure is then repeated, comparing the next highest mean to the smallest values and so on until all significant mean differences have been identified.

Scheffé (1953) proposed another post hoc method for testing any and all comparisons of a set of means. In this procedure a table of all comparisons of interest is created. For the musical aptitude levels of Experiment 2 in Figure 4-2, a table similar to Table 4-5 might result. In the first row of Table 4-5, the low mean is compared to the medium mean by using the weights 1 and -1, respectively, while 0 is assigned to the high-aptitude level as it is not being considered in this contrast. The sum of the squared weights is obtained by squaring each of the weights in the row and adding them together. To test a particular contrast, the difference between the sum of the scores for one compared treatment group is subtracted from the sum of the other, and this result is squared. The squared difference between the group sums is then divided by the sum of the squared weights from the table. The resulting value is divided by the error mean square from the analysis of variance producing F. To determine the significance of this F, the number of means minus one is used as the degrees of freedom for the numerator and the within-treatment degrees of freedom is used for the denominator degrees of freedom. With these values, the tabled value for a desired significance level is identified. This value is then multiplied by the number of means minus one to produce F'. To be significant, F must be greater than or equal to F'.

Symbolically, the Scheffé test amounts to:

$$MS_{D_i} = \frac{D_i^2}{n \sum w_i^2}$$

$$F = \frac{MS_{D_i}}{s^2}$$

$$F' = (k - 1)F_{(k - 1),dfw},$$

where

D_i^2 = squared difference of the sum of scores for the contrasted means,

$\sum w_i^2$ = sum of the squared weights for the contrast,

TABLE 4-5. Scheffé Contrast Vectors for Comparing Means in Experiment 2

Comparison	Means			Sum of Squared Weights
	Low	Medium	High	
Low vs. medium	1	-1	0	2
Low vs. high	1	0	-1	2
Medium vs. high	0	1	-1	2
Low vs. medium + high	2	-1	-1	6
High vs. low + medium	-1	-1	2	6

n = number of subjects in a treatment level,

k = total number of treatment levels, and

dfw = within-treatment or error mean square degrees of freedom.

Cell Size

The power of an analysis of variance is predicated on the number of subjects that are contained within each of the cells of the experimental design. All things being equal, the greater the number of individuals within a cell, the greater the power. This is related to the assumptions of homogeneity of variance and the measured values being normally distributed. The larger the sample for each cell, the greater the probability that the sampled values for the cell will have these characteristics. The researcher must be cautioned about including too many independent variables within an analysis as the sample size within the cells may become very small. This usually occurs when a researcher decides on a particular analysis of variance after the data are collected rather than before. To avoid such problems, the experiment should be planned carefully in advance to ensure that the number of subjects in each cell will be as equal as possible and as large as feasible. Practically, factorial experiments with fewer than 10 subjects in each cell should be avoided.

Randomized Block Designs

The full factorial designs considered thus far take the total sample of subjects and randomly assign each subject to one of the treatment level combinations. If one of the treatment, or condition, levels is related to the dependent variable, then a *randomized block design* could be formed. The benefit of the randomized block design is that the error variance—that is, the denominator in the ratio—is reduced, which makes it more likely that a significant ratio will be obtained (Kachigan, 1986, p. 299).

In the randomized block design, blocks are formed of subjects with similar characteristics on a trait. The number of subjects in the block must be equal to the number of treatments, and all subjects in a block must have homogeneous characteristics on the trait related to the dependent variable. Consider an experiment where the dependent variable was rhythm learning after a 10-week instructional period. Five different treatments were used: (1) Orff method, (2) Kodály method, (3) Education through Music method, (4) Gordon method, and (5) no-contact control group. The experimenters were interested in the relative effectiveness of these methods in teaching rhythm and, in addition, were interested in determining if a differential effect occurred for various musical aptitude levels. Musical aptitude should be related to rhythm achievement. Therefore, blocks could be formed of high, medium, and low musical aptitude. Because the number of subjects in a block is equal to the number of treatments, there would be five students in each of the three blocks, requiring a total of 15 students. The blocks would be formed by ranking the students according to musical aptitude and placing the first five in the high block, the second five in the medium block, and the last five in the low block. The subjects within each block would be randomly assigned to one of the five treatment conditions.

The statistical treatment of such data is summarized in Table 4-6. The variance in the data is partitioned into total, treatment, blocks, and block x treatment. The block x treatment is used as the error term in the ratios for treatment and block main effects. The fictitious results of this experiment indicate a significant effect for treatment and a significant effect for aptitude. Further analysis for simple effects would be necessary to identify exactly where the differences between means lie.

Repeated Measures Designs

It often occurs that an experiment is designed in which the subjects are measured more than once during the course of an experiment. This may occur if all the sampled subjects are provided each of the various treatments

TABLE 4-6. A Fictitious Example of a Randomized Block Design

	Treatment					Block Means
	Orff	Kodály	ETM	Gordon	Control	
Block Musical Aptitude						
Low	22.00	19.00	14.00	26.00	14.00	19.00
Medium	34.00	24.00	19.00	37.00	11.00	25.00
High	39.00	33.00	28.00	42.00	23.00	33.00
Treatment means	31.67	25.33	20.33	35.00	16.00	25.67

Source	SS	df	MS	F	$p <$
Treatment	735.33	4	183.83	6.66	0.012
Block (musical aptitude)	493.33	2	246.67	8.94	0.002
Treatment × Block	220.67	8	27.58		
Total	1449.33	14			

General Form

Source	SS	df	MS	F
t Treatments	$\sum_{nj} (\bar{x}_{.j} - \bar{x}..)^2$	$t - 1$	SS_t / df_t	MS_t / MS_c
b Blocks	$\sum_{ni} (\bar{x}_{.i} - \bar{x}..)^2$	$b - 1$	SS_b / df_b	MS_b / MS_c
$t \times b$ Error	$SS_{total} - SS_t - SS_b$	$(t - 1)(b - 1)$	$SS_{t \times b} / df_{t \times b}$	
Total	$\sum\sum_{(xy} - \bar{x}_.)$	$tb - 1$		

$\bar{x}.$ = grand mean $\qquad$ x_{ij} = a cell value
$\bar{x}_j$ = a treatment mean $\qquad$ $n_{.j}$ = number of cells for a treatment
$\bar{x}_i$ = a block mean $\qquad$ n_j = number of cells for a block

or when the researcher desires to determine the effects of a treatment a number of times during the experiment. The appropriate analysis of this form of experiment is called repeated measures ANOVA.

Repeated measures ANOVA is a special case of the randomized block design in which each block is a subject. In repeated measures situations, the subject is not randomly assigned to a treatment, but rather is subjected to all treatments. Consider an experiment in which it is desired to know the effects of extraneous sound on an individual's ability to do simple math problems. Four sound conditions exist: (1) silence, (2) sedative music, (3) stimulative music, (4) random pitch durations. In this experiment 10 subjects are tested doing simple math problems during each of the sound conditions.

Data for such an experiment are presented in Table 4-7. Note that the only ratio of interest is the main effect for sound condition. A between-subjects main effect also can be tested using the within-subjects mean square as the denominator in the ratio. Note that the formulas used in deriving the condition's main effect are the same as that used in determining the treat-

TABLE 4-7. A Fictitious Example of a Repeated Measures Design

	Sound Condition				Subject Means
	Silence	Sedative	Stimulative	Random	
Subject					
1	15.00	14.00	8.00	17.00	13.50
2	7.00	9.00	5.00	11.00	8.00
3	12.00	10.00	9.00	15.00	11.50
4	19.00	17.00	10.00	22.00	17.00
5	13.00	14.00	7.00	15.00	12.25
Condition means	13.20	12.80	7.80	16.00	12.45

Source	SS	df	MS	F	$p <$
Between subjects	170.20	4	42.55	18.11	0.001
Within subjects	202.75	15	13.52		
Sound conditions	174.55	3	58.18	24.76	0.001
Error	28.20	12	2.35		
Total	372.95	19			

General Form

Source	SS	df	MS	F
Between n subjects	$\sum_{ni} (\bar{x}_{i.} - \bar{x}_{..})^2$	$n - 1$	SS_b / df_b	MS_b / MS_c
Within subjects	$\sum\sum x_{ij} - \bar{x}_{i.})$	$n(t - 1)$	SS_w / df_w	
t Treatments	$\sum_{n.j}(\bar{x}_{.f} - \bar{x}_{..})^2$	$t - 1$	SS_t / df_t	MS_t / MS_t
Error	$SS_{total} - SS_t - SS_b$	$(t- 1)(n - 1)$	$SS_{t \times b} / df_{t \times b}$	
Total	$\sum\sum(x_{ij} - \bar{x}_{..})$	$tn - 1$		

$\bar{x}_{..}$ = grand mean $\quad\quad\quad\quad\quad x_{ij}$ = a cell value
$\bar{x}_{j}$ = a treatment mean $\quad\quad\quad n_{.j}$ = number of cells for a treatment
$\bar{x}_{i}$ = a subject's mean $\quad\quad\quad n_{i}$ = number of cells for a subject

ment main effects in the fictitious randomized block design example. To identify exactly where the means differed between the conditions, simple effects would have to be tested.

Other Designs

Analysis of variance provides a very flexible means for analyzing data from virtually all types of experiments and is treated much more extensively in texts by Glass and Hopkins (1984), Hays (1988), Winer (1971), and Winkler and Hays. (1975). Full factorial models, randomized blocks, and repeated-measures designs have common applications in music research. Other designs, such as the *nested designs*, where a grouping variable such as type of ensemble, band, or chorus may be nested under school, require different variance partitioning than previously described designs. It is also possible to have various combinations of the types of models presented here, which are known as mixed models. The researcher should consult one of the texts cited for detailed descriptions of how to analyze data from such models.

Multivariate Factorial Designs

Fundamental Concepts

Frequently a researcher is interested in more than one dependent variable within an experimental design. Referring back to the experiments in Figure 4-2, you may recall these designs all have musical achievement as the one dependent variable. This made univariate ANOVA models the most appropriate for these designs. If the researcher now desired to include two different measures of musical achievement, one being knowledge of musical concepts and the other musical performance skill, the univariate ANOVA would no longer be appropriate. The family of statistical models most appropriate for this new situation would be *multivariate analysis of variance* (MANOVA).

It has been common practice to analyze data from situations such as those just described with two separate univariate ANOVAs. This, however, leads to the great probability of obtaining a significant difference due simply to chance. MANOVA protects from this possibility by first simultaneously testing to determine whether there are any differences across the various dependent variables. MANOVA has the additional benefit of not only providing tests of significance about the dependent variables of interest but also being able to provide an indication of the pattern of relationships between the dependent variables (Sheth, 1984).

Manova

One-way and multiway experimental designs with more than one dependent variable can be analyzed with MANOVA. The overall null hypothesis is tested by reducing the number of measures to a single value by applying a linear combining rule (Harris, 1985, p. 19). The weights of the combining rule are applied in such a way as to produce the largest possible value. It is this value that tests the overall null hypothesis. This set of weights is the discriminant function, which is discussed later in the "Discriminant Analysis" section.

Overall Test   A number of overall tests of MANOVA results exist. Wilks's lambda is the most commonly employed: Harris (1985, p. 169) identifies four reasons for this: (1) historical precedence, (2) it provides a fairly good approximation to the distribution of *F*, (3) it is a more powerful test under certain circumstances, and (4) the discriminant functions on which Wilks's lambda is based are easier to compute than are characteristic roots. In addition, Harris notes that Wilks's lambda has been shown to be more robust against violations of the multivariate normal and homogeneity of variance assumptions of MANOVA than is the greatest characteristic root criterion (p. 170). Many computer programs, such as SPSS^x MANOVA (SPSS, 1988), provide these statistics along with their approximations in the output.

Subanalyses   Once a significant overall test has been identified, it is common to then look at the univariate subanalyses of variance in which each dependent variable is analyzed separately. This allows the researcher to identify which of the dependent variables is producing significant differences for the particular effect. Computer programs that compute MANOVA generally provide this output whether the overall test is significant or not. In addition to separate, independent univariate subanalyses, some programs provide step-down subanalyses in which the variance of preceding variables to have been analyzed with ANOVA is removed from the following variables yet to be analyzed. In this manner, the effect of a theoretical ordering of variables on following variables can be determined. For instance, in our Experiment 2 example with the two dependent variables of music knowledge and music skill, it might be desirable to determine if overall differences of the musical aptitude main effect are independent between knowledge and performance. The analysis could be arranged so that the performance subanalysis ANOVA occurred first, with the knowledge subanalysis last. The step-down process would first test the separate, independent ANOVA for performance and remove the performance-related variance from the data prior to testing the final knowledge ANOVA. If the knowledge step-down ANOVA was not significant but the separate performance ANOVA was, it could be concluded that musical aptitude has a profound effect on musical performance achievement. In addition, musical performance achievement is shown to be strongly related to the acquisition of musical knowledge. This is because when the variance of musical aptitude and performance is removed prior to testing musical knowledge, musical knowledge is no longer significant. Of course, this is a hypothetical example, but it does show MANOVA's capacity to provide the researcher with a wealth of information about not only the effects of interest also but the relationships between the dependent variables.

MANOVA Example   As part of a study on the effectiveness of two forms of instruction on aural and instrumental performance skills, Kendall (1988) reported a MANOVA. The 3 × 2 factorial design included three levels of musical aptitude (above average, average, and below average) and two types of treatment (comprehensive and modeling). The analysis included four dependent variables: Instrumental Eye-to-Hand Coordination Test (IETHCT), Verbal Association Test (VAT), Instrumental Performance Test (IPT), and the Melodic/Rhythmic Sight-Reading Test (MRSRT). An extended source table that includes the multivariate and the univariate ANOVAs for the significant multivariate effect is presented in Table 4-8. As can be seen, there was one significant multivariate main effect for treatment—the type of instruction received. The subanalyses indicate that the effects were attributable to the Verbal Association Test and the Melodic/Rhythmic Sight-Reading Test. Kendall found through inspection of the means that the comprehensive treatment was more effective on these two dependent variables than the modeling treatment.

Mancova

As in the univariate case, there is a multivariate analog to the analysis of covariance, the *multivariate analysis of covariance* or MANCOVA. The need for MANCOVA is to provide statistical control for factors that might influence the set of dependent variables of interest. For instance, achievement has been found to be influenced by socioeconomic status. This relationship could be applied to the Experiment 2 of Figure 4.2, where there were two forms

TABLE 4-8. MANOVA and Subanalyses from Kendal (1988)

Source	Wilks's Lambda	Hypothesis Mean Square	Error Mean Square	F	p <
Treatment	.425			22.65	.001
IETHCT		314.07	864.74	0.36	NS
VAT		1,433.93	320.32	4.48	.030
IPT		220.11	718.61	0.31	NS
MRSRT		16,869.63	219.40	76.89	1.001
Music aptitude level	.825			1.69	NS
Treatment × Music Aptitude Level	.934			0.58	NS

Note: The degrees of freedom were not completely reported so are not included here.
Abbreviations: IETHCT = Instrumental Eye-to-Hand Coordination Test; VAT = Verbal Association Test; IPT = Instrumental Performance Test; MRSRT = Melodic/Rhythmic Sight-Reading Test.

of musical achievement measured: knowledge and performance. The influence of socioeconomic status can be removed from the dependent variables prior to testing for main and interaction effects of gender and musical aptitude. This is done by removing the variance that overlaps between the two achievement dependent variables and socioeconomic status, the *covariate*. The result is a clearer picture of the true effects of gender and musical aptitude on the two dependent variables.

MANCOVA can be extended further to include more than one covariate. For instance, a researcher may desire to remove the effect not only of socioeconomic status but also of home music environment prior to testing the gender and musical aptitude effects. Such procedures allow a great deal of statistical control over the data analysis. However, it is the researcher's responsibility to assure that the initial design is not flawed in some manner that would introduce systematic bias. When the research situation does not allow for early design control of experimental bias, then MANCOVA provides a means for reducing this bias in the data analysis.

Computing Resources

Most major statistical computer packages now provide programs or subroutines for performing complex MANOVA and MANCOVA analyses. Such programs may come under the title of *general linear model*. The choice of computer programs is dependent on the availability of programs to the researcher, the researcher's knowledge of the particular statistical package, the particular procedures that the researcher desires to apply, and the output the program produces. Today's powerful computing environments make the extreme calculating complexity of multivariate statistics no more difficult or time-consuming than simple univariate statistics. The researcher, however, should not choose to use a particular statistical procedure and then design a research study. Rather, the research study should be designed and then the appropriate statistical procedures should be selected.

Correlation

In addition to studying the effects of independent variables on dependent variables and describing populations in various ways, researchers may wish to show relationships among variables or sets of variables. Correlation techniques facilitate quantification of relationships.

In simple terms, a *correlation coefficient,* which may range from -1.00 to $+1.00$, shows the size and direction of a relationship between two sets of scores. The larger the absolute value of the number, the stronger the relationship, whether it be positive or negative. The most common type of correlation, the one most researchers would assume another researcher is talking about without any further qualification, is the Pearson product-moment correlation. The two variables must be measured at at least the interval level, and homoscedasticity is assumed. *Homoscedasticity* essentially means that if all of the scores on one variable are categorized into classes in terms of the other variable, the scores within the classes are normally distributed and the variances of the scores within the various categories are equal. Furthermore, the observations are assumed to be independent, and the underlying relationship is assumed to be linear. In a linear relationship, as one variable changes, the other changes in such a way that a straight line describes the relationship. In a curvilinear relationship, the changes must be described by a curved line or series of line segments that alternate in direction. For a visual depiction of both linear and curvilinear relationships, see the graphing section later in this chapter.

Two sets of ranks (ordinal measures) may be described by *rank-order correlation,* also known as Spearman's rho. Two sets of dichotomies may be related through *tetrachoric correlation;* one dichotomy and a continuous variable featuring interval measurement may be related through *point-biserial correlation.* Point-biserial correlation is commonly used in psychometrics to express the relationship between answering a particular single item correctly, a dichotomy, and overall test score, the continuous variable.

The relationships between a number of variables can be depicted in a correlation matrix. The correlation matrix is a diagonal matrix in that the values of the lower left portion of the matrix are replicated in the upper right. Hedden (1982), in a study of the predictors of musical achievement for general music students, reported a correlation matrix for one of the participating schools composed of the major variables of the study: Attitude toward Music Scale (ATMS), Self-Concept in Music Scale (SCIM), Music Background Scale (MB), Iowa Test of Basic Skills (ITBS), students' gender, and Music Achievement Test (MAT). This correlation matrix is reproduced as a complete diagonal matrix in Table 4-9. The lower-left portion of the matrix is not filled in because the correlation for any one variable, say, gender, with another variable, say, MAT, is the same as the correlation for MAT with gender.

TABLE 4-9. Full Diagonal Correlation Matrix from Hedden (1982)

Variable	ATMS	SCIM	MB	ITBS	Gender	MAT
ATMS	1.000	.642	.461	.226	.373	.352
SCIM		1.000	.603	.400	.085	.472
MB			1.000	.535	.159	.450
ITBS				1.000	−.040	.505
Gender					1.000	.034
MAT						1.000

Abbreviations: ATMS = Attitude Toward Music Scale; SCIM = Self-Concept in Music Scale; MB = Music Background Scale; ITBS = Iowa Test of Basic Skills; MAT = Music Achievement Test.

Extensions of Correlation

The concept of the interrelationship among a set of variables has produced a great number of valuable statistical tools. These tools all utilize the variance shared between variables and the variance unique to particular variables to further the understanding of the relationships between the variables and to provide tests of hypotheses about these relationships.

Partial Correlation

It can happen that a researcher wants to know the degree of relationship between variables when the effect of a third variable is removed. In such situations, the researcher is interested in the *partial correlation*. The partial correlation is the correlation between two variables when the common variance of one or more variables is removed. This provides another form of statistical control by removing unwanted variance to allow a clearer view of the relationship between two variables.

The *partial correlation coefficient* can be mathematically defined as

$$r_{12.3} = \frac{r_{12} - r_{13}\,r_{23}}{\sqrt{(1 - r_{13}^2)(1 - r_{23}^2)}},$$

where

r_{12} = correlation between variables 1 and 2,

r_{13} = correlation between variables 1 and 3, and

r_{23} = correlation between variables 2 and 3.

This partial correlation indicates the relationship between the variables 1 and 2 with the effect of variable 3 removed. Figure 4-4 presents a graphic means of showing this relationship using a Venn diagram. It should be noted that the complete pattern of relationships within the Venn diagram can be

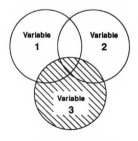

Figure 4.4. Partial correlation between Variables 1 and 2 controlling for 3.

determined from such procedures and that these procedures can be extended to indicate the relationship between two variables with the effect of any number of variables removed.

Kendall (1988) provides correlations for three variables related to aural perception and instrumental performance: a measure of student ability to perform on an instrument heard melodic patterns, a measure of student ability to respond in solfège to heard melodic patterns, and a measure of instrumental performance (Table 4-10). A research question could be, "What is the relationship between ability to perform heard melodic patterns and solfège response ability when the variance associated with instrumental performance ability is removed from the relationship?" To answer this question, a partial correlation coefficient would be appropriate. The results of this analysis in Table 4-10 indicate that the partial correlation drops to .59 from the original bivariate correlation of .63 when the variance associated with instrumental performance ability is removed. The difference between the variances (r^2) of the bivariate correlation and the partial correlation indicates that the variance associated with instrumental performance ability in the relationship between the ability to perform heard melodic patterns and the ability to solfège heard melodic patterns is approximately 5 percent.

Multiple Regression

Multiple regression is the extension of a correlation between two variables to the case where there are a number of variables being related to a single variable. In multiple regression, the set of variables being related to a single variable are known as the *predictor variables*. The single variable to which the independent variables are being related is the *criterion variable*.

Multiple regression extends the bivariate regression

$$y = a + bx,$$

where y is predicted by a value of the predictor variable x multiplied by a weight and added to a constant, the y *intercept* in which only one variable x is involved, to

TABLE 4-10. Example of Partial Correlation Using the Data of Kendal (1988)

	Correlation Matrix					r	r^2
	Heard/ Played	Heard/ Solfege	Instrumental Performance				
Heard/Played (P)	1.00			Bivariate$_{(rPS)}$		0.63	0.40
Heard/Solfège (S)	0.63	1.00		Partial$_{(r_tP.S)}$		0.59	0.35
Instrumental Performance (I)	0.40	0.28	1.00	Difference			0.05

$$y = a + b_1x_1 + b_2x_2 + \ldots + b_kx_k,$$

where for a number of k variables there are corresponding weights. Thus, a single variable is predicted by a number of other variables.

The results of multiple regression produce a statistic of the degree of relationship between the predictor variables and the criterion variable, the multiple correlation coefficient (R). This statistic ranges from -1 to $+1$ and is interpreted in a manner similar to that used to interpret the simple bivariate correlation. As with the bivariate correlation, when R is squared (R^2), the proportion of variance in the criterion variable accounted for by the predictor variables is revealed. This variance can be tested with an F test. In addition, *beta weights*, the coefficients of the standardized predictor variables, are provided that indicate the relative importance of the predictor variables in predicting the dependent variable. The absolute values of the betas indicate the order of importance of the predictor variables for predicting the criterion. However, these values indicate only the relative importance of the predictor variables and not their absolute contributions to the prediction because their importance depends on other variables included in the analysis. This is because beta weights are related to partial correlation coefficients in that their value is a function not only of the correlation between the criterion variable and the particular predictor variable but also of the correlations between all of the predictor variables.

The set of independent, or predictor, variables for a particular criterion variable can be analyzed in a number of different ways. The most obvious is to have all predictor variables simultaneously regressed on the criterion variable. Another method is to start with just one predictor variable and the criterion variable, after which another predictor variable is added, and another, until all predictor variables are included. The order of predictor variable entry can be determined on theoretical grounds, or it can be determined statistically. In either case, the amount of variance by which the prediction of the criterion variable is increased (or decreased) with the addition of a predictor variable can be tested. The testing of variance can be used as one basis for selecting which predictor variable should next enter the prediction equation. The variable that is the next largest contributor to the explained variance in the relationship of the predictor variables to the criterion could be selected.

The addition of predictor variables to the regression equation is called *forward stepping. Backward stepping* is also possible where the analysis begins with all predictor variables included in the regression equation and succeeding variables are removed from the equation on the basis of the smallest contribution to the prediction of the criterion variable or on some theoretical basis. A variety of other methods are available, and combinations of these methods are possible. The researcher must select the method that provides the analysis appropriate to the particular research study.

In a study of the factors that contribute to various aspects of work performed in first-year college theory courses, Harrison (1990a) reported a series of multiple regressions using the various aspects of the theory work as the dependent variables. Harrison used a forward-stepping procedure that determined "the best linear combination of statistically significant predictor variables ($p < .05$)" (p. 180). Table 4-11 contains the multiple regression analysis for the written work criterion variable for first-semester college students. In the table, Harrison provides a thorough compilation of the important statistics available for multiple regression. For this variable, the math score on the *Scholastic Aptitude Test* (SAT) is the most important predictor variable, which accounts for 19 percent of the variance (R^2 change), followed in order by high school grade-point average, accounting for an additional 6 percent of the variance, and whether the student was an instrumentalist, accounting for an additional 2 percent of the variance. The total amount of variance in theory written work grade accounted for by these three variables is 27 percent (R^2).

Multiple regression is a very flexible analytical procedure. It can be used not only to identify the degree of relationship between a set of predictor variables and a criterion variable but also to produce analyses of variance. Researchers who are interested in such uses and a more detailed discussion should consult the text by Kerlinger and Pedhazur (1982).

Discriminant Analysis

Discriminant analysis is used to study the case where there is a set of continuous independent variables predicting a single discrete grouping variable (Goodstein, 1987). For instance, a researcher may be interested in predicting the beginning band instrument on which students would be the most successful from a set of independent variables such as motivation, preferred sound quality, pitch acuity, parental desire, musical aptitude, physical capabilities, and parental support. This situation would require the use of discriminant analysis.

The particular variables used as independent variables are selected because they are believed to have some relationship with the single categorical dependent variable (Kachigan, 1986, p. 360). This parallels the process that would be used for the selection of the predictor variables for multiple re-

TABLE 4-11. Multiple Regression Predicting First-Semester Written Theory Work Grade from Harrison (1990a)

Variables	r	R	R^2	R^2 Change	F Change	$p <$	B	Beta Weights
SAT math	.43	.43	.19	.19	36.37	.001	.01	.32
HS GPA	.41	.50	.25	.06	12.41	.001	1.92	.26
Instrument	−.15	.52*	.27	.02	5.43	.022	−1.05	−.16

* = ..0001 level.

gression. Whereas the calculation of the multiple-regression model centered on the determination of the set of weights for the predictor variables, discriminant analysis involves the determination of the discriminant function. The *discriminant function* is a set of weighted predictor variables for classifying a person or object into one of the groups of the dependent variable. The discriminant function is calculated in such a way as to minimize the classification error. It would hold that the larger the difference between the groups of the dependent variable on the measured independent variables, the fewer classification errors will be made.

The number of discriminant functions necessary to fully characterize the model will be equal to the number of groups in the dependent variable minus one. The process of calculating each of the discriminant functions is based first on determining the discriminant function that will have the greatest success in classifying the persons or objects into one of the dependent groups. Then, the next most successful function is calculated, and so on until all discriminant functions have been calculated. Each discriminant function, then, contains the set of weights that maximally separates persons or objects into one of the dependent variable's groups. Note that the reason for needing only one discriminant function less than the number of groups is that in the two-group case, if we know the person or persons classified into one group, all people left are classified into the other group—the fundamental principle of *degrees of freedom*.

Discriminant functions can be tested for their significance in differentiating the dependent variable groups beyond that expected by chance. The multivariate indicators of this significance are the same as frequently produced by the output of MANOVA: Mahalanobis D^2, Wilks Lambda, and Rao V. This is not surprising since a MANOVA determines the significant differences between groups on continuous variables. Indeed, Tatsuoka and Lohnes (1988, p. 210) have indicated that discriminant analysis is now used more in determining differences between groups than in its original use of classifying persons or objects into groups. This important relationship allows the researcher to gain additional insight into the group relationships of a MANOVA.

An additional method of evaluating the quality of the discriminant functions is to determine their accuracy of classification. The predicted and actual group memberships of a dependent variable can be compared. This process yields the proportion of people or objects correctly classified and the proportion misclassified.

As with multiple regression, the squared standardized discriminant function coefficients or beta weights can be analyzed to determine the relative importance of each independent variable in the classification of the persons or objects into a particular dependent group. The analysis of these weights provides significant insights about the independent variables and the groups of the dependent variable.

May (1985) studied the effects of grade level, gender, and race on first-, second-, and third-graders' musical preferences. As a follow-up to a MAN-

OVA, May presented a table of discriminant analyses for each of these grouping variables. Table 4-12 presents the primary discriminant information for the grade-level effect. As can be seen, only function 1 was significant at $p < .05$ and accounted for 63 percent of the variance in the analysis.

Canonical Correlation

Canonical correlation provides a means of analyzing the relationship between two sets of continuous variables. Usually, one set of variables is considered to be the independent or predictor variables of the other set of dependent or criterion variables. The process can be conceived as an extension of multiple regression where there are two sets of weighted combinations of variables, one for the predictor variables and one for the criterion variables. The canonical correlation is the correlation between the derived predictor variables and the derived criterion variables. The derived variables are called *canonical variates.* In a manner similar to the calculation of the beta weights of multiple regression, *canonical weights* are derived that maximize the canonical correlation. The number of sets of possible canonical variates is equal to the number of variables in the smaller set of variables minus one.

The squared canonical correlation is the amount of variance shared by the derived canonical-variates. The canonical correlation coefficients can be tested for significance. The squared canonical weights show the relative contribution of the individual variables to a derived variable in a manner parallel to the squared standardized regression weights of multiple regression. The amount of variance accounted for by a weighted combination of the original predictor variables in the opposite weighted combination of original criterion variables is not symmetrical. That is, the proportion of variance accounted for in the criterion variables by the predictor variables does not have to be equal. The predictor variables may account for more or less of the variance in the criterion variables than the criterion variables may account for in the predictor variables. This is because we are dealing with the original variables and not the derived canonical variates. The canonical cor-

TABLE 4-12. Discriminant Function Subanalysis for Grade Level from May (1985)

	Function 1	Function 2
Eigenvalue	.101	.060
Percent of variance	62.91	37.09
Canonical correlation	.303	.267
Wilks lambda	.857	.944
Chi-square	86.651	32.397
df	48	23
p	< .0005	< .0902

relation is based on the derived canonical variates, so its square indicates the proportion of variance accounted for by the canonical variates symmetrically. For a detailed example of canonical correlation, see May (1985).

Factor Analysis

Factor analysis is a family of techniques that can be used to study the underlying relationships between a large number of variables. The raw material for factor analysis is the correlation matrix or covariance matrix, which indicates the bivariate interrelationships of a variable set. Three primary techniques are under the factor analysis umbrella: principle components analysis, common factor analysis, and maximum likelihood factor analysis. Principle components analysis creates underlying components that accommodate all the variance within a correlation matrix. Common factor analysis produces underlying factors that are based on the common or shared variance of the variables. Maximum likelihood factor analysis estimates the population parameters from sample statistics and can provide statistical tests of factor models.

Factor analysis can be used in a wide variety of research activities; including identifying underlying traits within a data set, developing theory, testing hypotheses, and data set reduction, among others. Having such wide applicability in the research process makes it a very powerful tool.

The various methods for performing factor analysis all attempt to define a smaller set of derived variables extracted from the data submitted for analysis. These derived variables are called factors or components depending on the type of factoring method used. The factors can be interpreted on the basis of the weight of each measured variable on each of the factors. Scores for each subject can be calculated for each factor based on the obtained weights. These *factor scores* may be used for further statistical analysis.

The steps involved in performing a factor analysis are as follows: (1) determine the substantive reasons for performing a factor analysis, (2) obtain data with sufficient sample size to assure stability of the intercorrelation matrix between all the variables to be factored, (3) select the appropriate factoring method, (4) determine the appropriate number of factors to represent the data, (5) select the appropriate method of factor rotation to derive the weights upon which the interpretations will be based, (6) interpret the derived factors, and (7) compute the factor scores, if desired.

Principal Components   Principal components analysis uses all the variance associated with the variables without partitioning the variance into constituent parts. The resulting components contain the variance unique to each variable, the variance each variable has in common with the other variables, and variance attributable to error (Asmus, 1989a). The principal components model is most appropriate when the variables being analyzed are believed to be quite different from each other and are considered to have large amounts of unique variance. The principal components model is useful for data reduction purposes when it is desired to have the reduced set of derived variables account for the greatest amount of variance in the calculated factor scores.

Common Factor Analysis Common factor analysis explains the interrelationships between a set of variables by using only the variance that the variables have in common. Unlike the principal components model, this requires considerably fewer factors than the number of variables (Cureton and D'Agostino, 1983, p. 2). The common factor model partitions the variance associated with a variable into that which is common among the variables, that which is unique to the particular variable, and that which is associated with error. The common factor model is most appropriate when the variables being analyzed are similar to each other, as in a set of items to evaluate musical performance.

Maximum Likelihood Factor Analysis Maximum likelihood factor analysis uses sample statistics to estimate the population parameters of the factoring results. The procedure involves finding the population parameter values that are most likely to have produced the data (Harnett, 1982, p. 333; Lunneborg and Abbot, 1983, p. 222). Gorsuch (1983, p. 127) indicates that as the sample size increases toward that of the population, the maximum likelihood estimate will converge to the population parameter, and that across samples the parameter estimates will be the most consistent possible. The maximum likelihood method allows testing hypotheses about the factors extracted through the use of chi-square tests. When the number of factors in an analysis are tested, a significant chi-square indicates that there is still significant covariance in the residual matrix (Gorsuch, 1983, p. 129). That is, too few factors have been extracted to this point. Maximum likelihood factor analysis has been developed for use only with large samples. The maximum likelihood model is most appropriate where it is desired to draw conclusions about a population from a large representative sampling of members of that population.

Confirmatory factor analysis extends the maximum likelihood model to allow the testing of a number of hypotheses beyond the number of factors. The most prominent applications have been in testing hypothesized factor structure, in testing the validity of a test or battery of tests, and in causal path analysis (Gorsuch, 1983, pp. 133–140).

Computing a Factor Analysis A factor analysis is based on a correlation matrix. It is imperative that the correlation matrix be as stable as possible, which is to say that the sample size on which the correlation matrix is based should be as large as possible. The subject to variable ratio should never be less than 3:1 and should exceed 5:1 (Asmus, 1989a, p. 4). Sample sizes in excess of 250 tend to produce stable correlation matrices because of the relatively small error term for correlations with samples larger than this value. The measure of sampling adequacy, an indicator available in some computer packages, should never be lower than .5 (Kaiser and Rice, 1974).

Duke and Prickett (1987), as part of a study of applied music instruction, presented a correlation matrix that included the 10 items of a music teaching evaluation form used by 143 observers. This correlation matrix will be factor analyzed to show the steps involved in the factor analytic process. Duke and Prickett's correlation matrix has a subject to variable ratio of 14.3:1 and yields a measure of sampling adequacy of .847. These figures indicate that the correlation matrix has sufficient sample size to warrant factor analysis.

The items of the Duke and Prickett measure were adapted from Moore's (1976) evaluative instrument. All the items were selected to assess important aspects of the domain of music teaching in a private applied music setting. Because of this, it could be expected that there would be considerable variance shared between the items. This suggests that common factor analysis would be the most appropriate factor model for these data. The reason for factoring these data is not only to provide and exemplify the factor analysis process but also to provide some indication of the underlying constructs that are evaluated by the measure. Thus, because of the large common variance expected and because of the exploratory nature of the analysis, common factor analysis will be applied.

One of the most difficult decisions in performing a factor analysis is to determine how many factors best represent the data. Such decisions are usually based on previous research or theory, the eigenvalue-of-one criterion, a scree test in common factor analysis, and interpretation of the resulting factors (Asmus, 1989a, pp. 13–14). In Moore's (1976) original evaluation instrument, the items were divided into three categories: teacher interaction, musicianship, and creativity. In the table overlaying the scree test in Figure 4-5, it can be seen that three factors are indicated by eigenvalues of one or greater. The scree test of Figure 4-5 does not indicate any significant drop in the plotted line between the eigenvalues after the second eigenvalue so it yields little assistance in determining the number of factors. However, because of Moore's division of items into three categories and the eigenvalue-of-one criterion's indicating three potential factors, the number of factors in the analysis was constrained to three, which accounted for 65.5 percent of the variance in the correlation matrix.

The next decision in the factoring process is to determine the appropriate form of rotation to obtain simple structure. Simple structure maximizes the loading of a variable on one factor while minimizing the variable's loadings on the other factors (Asmus, 1989a, p. 19). Two major forms of rotation are available: orthogonal and oblique. Orthogonal rotation keeps the factors independent of each other and is most appropriate when it is believed that the resulting factors will indeed be independent or when it is desired to have the final factors maximally separated. Oblique rotation allows the factors to

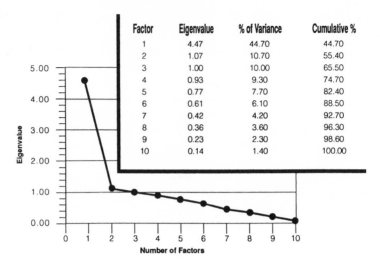

Factor	Eigenvalue	% of Variance	Cumulative %
1	4.47	44.70	44.70
2	1.07	10.70	55.40
3	1.00	10.00	65.50
4	0.93	9.30	74.70
5	0.77	7.70	82.40
6	0.61	6.10	88.50
7	0.42	4.20	92.70
8	0.36	3.60	96.30
9	0.23	2.30	98.60
10	0.14	1.40	100.00

Figure 4.5. Scree test of Duke and Prickett (1987) data.

be related to each other. In the case of the Duke and Prickett data, the resulting factors logically should be related to each other because the items were selected to evaluate the single concept of music teaching. Many types of orthogonal and oblique rotations are available. In a practical sense, the researcher is usually limited to those available in the computer statistical package being used. In the present case, SPSS* (SPSS, 1988) was the statistical package that provided oblimin oblique rotation for the analysis (Table 4-13). For a capsulated description of the major rotations, see Asmus (1989a).

The *factor pattern matrix* provides the relative weights for the variables on each of the derived factors. Interpretation of the factors is made in light of these weights along with the correlations of the variables with the factor that are presented in the *factor structure matrix*. The absolute values of the pattern weights are usually used to develop the initial conceptualization of a factor. Note that student participation and student attitude have relatively strong weights on the first factor and low weights on the other factors. This factor was labeled "Student Involvement." The second factor had strong weights on items that were interpreted to represent "Teacher Approach with Students." The final factor was interpreted as "Technical Aspects of Instruction."

A few items have relatively strong loadings on more than one factor; that is, the items *cross load*. Overall lesson effectiveness, for instance, has fairly strong loadings on all factors. Logically a good lesson not only would involve the teacher's approach with students, the factor upon which this item loads most heavily, but also would incorporate significant student involvement and good technical aspects of instruction. Similarly, it is logical that

TABLE 4-13. Factor Results of Duke and Prickett Data

Variables	Student Involvement	Teacher Approach With Students	Technical Aspects of Instruction
Pattern matrix			
Student participation (StPar)	0.747	−0.169	0.076
Student's attitude (StAtt)	0.588	−0.204	0.042
Quality of instruction (Instr)	0.044	−0.293	−0.001
Overall lesson effectiveness (OvEff)	0.280	−0.469	0.308
Attitude toward students (T-Att)	0.031	−0.849	0.041
Reinforcement effectiveness (Reinf)	−0.041	−1.004	−0.055
Lesson organization (Org)	0.141	0.045	0.931
Teacher's musicianship (Qual)	0.321	−0.087	0.432
Clarity of presentation (Clar)	−0.134	−0.082	0.281
Teacher's creativity (Creat)	0.113	0.008	0.199
Structure matrix			
Student participation (StPar)	0.843	−0.522	0.430
Student's attitude (StAtt)	0.687	−0.472	0.362
Quality of instruction (Instr)	0.165	−0.310	0.184
Overall lesson effectiveness (OvEff)	0.580	−0.764	0.677
Attitude toward students (T-Att)	0.397	−0.886	0.545
Reinforcement effectiveness (Reinf)	0.356	−0.956	0.515
Lesson organization (Org)	0.441	−0.554	0.953
Teacher's musicianship (Qual)	0.505	−0.471	0.592
Clarity of presentation (Clar)	−0.004	−0.189	0.283
Teacher's creativity (Creat)	0.178	−0.154	0.233
Factor Correlation Matrix			
Student involvement	1.000		
Teacher approach with students	−0.414	1.000	
Technical aspects of instruction	0.342	−0.581	1.000

the teacher's musicianship not only would load on the technical aspects of instruction but also would influence student involvement—a fact long claimed by music teachers.

The factor structure matrix reveals many strong correlations of the items across the factors. This indicates that the derived factors are strongly related. As can be seen in the factor correlation matrix, the factors are indeed related to a considerable degree. Teacher approach, because of its negative weights, is inversely related to student involvement and the technical aspects of instruction. Student involvement, on the other hand, has a fairly substantial relationship with the technical aspects of teaching.

Statistical Based Modeling

Modeling

The conceptualization of theory generally produces a mental model of the interrelationships between the variables accommodated by the theory (Hanneman, 1988). Visual representations of the model help clarify the theory further. Such models can be evaluated statistically and, through modern computer systems, can be represented and manipulated in graphic form (Asmus, 1989b). The development of theory in music education has been a concern of many in the profession. The statistical methods available for evaluating theoretical models provide powerful tools for the testing and refinement of such theory.

The foundation of statistical based modeling is causation implied in the interrelationships between variables described by a theoretical model. The statistical correlation of variables provides the basis for explaining this causation. Although scientists and philosophers have debated the efficacy of such a position, several authors have clearly articulated the rationale for using intercorrelations to establish causation (Simon, 1985; Wright, 1921).

Statistical based modeling can be used to both test and develop theory. When theory is being tested, a formal model is established and then the causal links within the model are statistically tested. When theory is being developed, a formal model is evaluated statistically. Then, casual links are added or deleted until a model evolves that has satisfactory statistical and conceptual prowess. Two major types of statistical based modeling are available to researchers: *measured variable modeling* and *latent trait modeling*. In the former, variables that have been measured from a sample are used to form a model. In the latter, the underlying constructs of variables are used as the basis for the model.

Measured Variable Modeling

There are two forms of measured variable modeling: *causal analysis* and *path analysis*. Both are based on multiple regression of real-world data. That is, a variable identified as being caused by other variables in a theoretical model becomes the criterion variable in a multiple regression. The variables that cause the criterion variable are the predictor variables in this regression. The difference between causal and path analyses is that causal analysis uses the unstandardized regression coefficients or beta (b) weights to indicate the contribution of a causal variable to a dependent variable while path analysis uses the standardized regression coefficients or Beta (β) weights to indicate this contribution (Blalock, 1985).

Figure 4-6 presents a path model developed from a correlation matrix of variables extracted from a larger matrix presented by Harrison (1990b) in

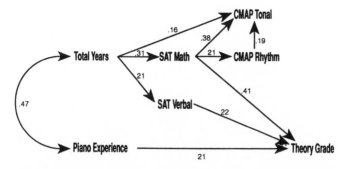

Figure 4.6. Path analysis of selected variables from Harrison (1990b). (CMAP = College Musical Aptitude Profile; SAT = Scholastic Aptitude Test)

a study of music theory grade prediction. Harrison calculated the matrix from 121 first-year college music majors. Two types of variables exist within the system. *Exogenous variables*, caused by variables outside the system and linked with the curved line, are represented by total years of experience on musical instruments and whether or not the student had piano experience. *Endogenous variables* are caused by variables inside the system and are linked by the straight lines. The values in the figure are the path coefficients or β weights from the multiple regressions of a variable and its linked causal variables (Table 4-14).

TABLE 4-14. Path Analysis Multiple Regressions of Harrison's (1990b) Data.

Paths To	From	Beta	t	$p <$	R	R^2	df	F	$p <$
Theory Grade									
SAT	Math	0.41	4.80	0.00	0.62	0.38	3,117	23.75	0.01
SAT	Vrbl	0.22	2.68	0.01					
Piano	Exp	0.21	2.82	0.01					
CMAPT	Tonal								
SAT	Math	0.38	4.55	0.00	0.53	0.28	3,117	15.42	0.01
	Rhy	0.19	2.31	0.02					
CMAP									
Totl	Yr	0.16	1.99	0.05					
CMAP	Rhy								
SAT	Math	0.21	2.34	0.02	0.21	0.04	1,119	5.49	0.02
SAT	Math								
Totl	Yr	0.31	3.56	0.00	0.31	0.10	1,119	12.65	0.01
SAT	Vrbl								
Tot	Yr	0.21	2.34	0.02	0.21	0.04	1,119	5.49	0.02

Abbreviations: SAT = Scholastic Aptitude Test; CMAP = College Musical Aptitude Profile.

The model was developed by placing the variables in their time ordering. Total years and piano experience would have been primarily determined prior to a student's having taken the SAT in late high school; the SAT would have been taken before the College Musical Aptitude Profile (CMAP; Schleuter, 1978), and the theory grade was assigned after the students had taken the CMAP. As Harrison found, music theory grade has no linkages from the two CMAP variables. Music theory grade is significantly predicted by the two SAT scores and whether or not the student had piano experience. These variables account for 38 percent of the theory grade. The strongest of the linkages is that between SAT math and the theory grade, as indicated by the path coefficient of .41. In the model, two variables play a pivotal role: SAT math and total years of experience. SAT math has substantial linkages with the CMAP variables and the theory grade, while total years of experience has strong linkages with the SAT variables and the CMAP tonal variable. Does participation in music influence overall academic achievement? This model suggests that this is so.

Latent Trait Modeling

Measuring the Unmeasurable   Many in the field of music have claimed that a variety of important musical concepts are simply unmeasurable. *Latent trait modeling* provides a means of accounting for these "unmeasurable" concepts in complex systems. As with the measured variable modeling described earlier, latent trait modeling begins with a conceptual model that is depicted graphically. Then, through appropriate specification, the model can be tested using maximum likelihood principles.

A *latent trait* or *latent variable* is estimated from one or more indicators of the hypothetical factor (Cooley, 1978; Jöreskog, 1979). Latent traits are underlying variables that can be conceived as the factors produced by factor analysis. Indeed, latent trait modeling can be considered a blend of multiple regression and factor analysis (Ecob and Cuttance, 1987). The procedure involves the development of structural equations that incorporate latent variables. A general computer program named LISREL (Jöreskog and Sörbom, 1989; SPSS, 1988) provides estimates of the coefficients in these structural equations (Jöreskog, 1982).

There are considerable benefits for the use of latent traits in music education research. Latent traits provide a means for accommodating concepts that are difficult to measure. Many variables in music education research contain considerable measurement error. Latent traits provide a means for compensating for this error (Jöreskog, 1979). Latent trait modeling also provides much greater information about the variables that have been measured, their interrelationships, error, and the theoretical model being investigated.

A Latent Trait Model of Theoretical Understanding   The selected subset of Harrison's (1990b) correlation matrix used in demonstrating the concepts of measured variable modeling can be applied in demonstrating latent trait modeling. The model tested is presented in Figure 4-7. The figure follows the conventions that latent traits are indicated by ovals and measured variables are indicated by rectangles. In the model, three latent variables predict the dependent latent variable of theoretical understanding. The three independent latent variables are musical background, scholastic achievement, and musical aptitude. Note that the measured variables' paths do not point toward their associated latent variable. Rather, the opposite is true. This indicates that the latent variables are underlying causes of the observed variables or are intervening variables in a causal chain (Jöreskog, 1982, pp. 83–84). In the present model, the arrows from outside the model pointing toward variables or traits in the model indicate measurement error. The various symbology used in latent trait modeling as it is implemented in LISREL is defined in Table 4-15.

The relationship between latent trait modeling and factor analysis is evident in the results of a maximum likelihood factor analysis with oblimin rotation of Harrison's data (Table 4-16). Note that the three factors, which account for 69.9 percent of the variance, are musical background, musical aptitude, and scholastic achievement. These are the same independent latent traits used in the latent trait model. Theory grade loads with the scholastic achievement variables as would be expected from the previous path analysis of these variables.

The overall goodness of fit for the latent trait model is tested with chi-square. In this case, the fit is quite good ($x^2 = 8.91$, $df = 9$, p $p > .445$). The model accounts for 52 percent of the variance in the latent trait of theoretical understanding. The model indicates that scholastic achievement

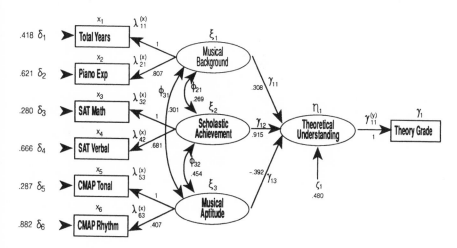

Figure 4.7. Latent trait model of theoretical understanding from Harrison's (1990b) data.

TABLE 4-15. LISREL Symbol Glossary

Symbol	Character	Description
η	eta	Vector of latent dependent variables
ξ	xi	Vector of latent independent variables
ζ	zetz	Vector of residuals (errors—random disturbances)
β	Beta	Matrix of the direct effects of latent dependent variables on other latent dependent variables
γ	Gamma	Direct effects of latent independent variables on the latent dependent variables
ε	epsilon	Vector of error terms
δ	delta	Vector of error terms
y		Observed dependent variable
x		Observed independent variable
Φ	Phi	Covariance matrix of the latent independent variables
ψ	Psi	Covariance matrix of the residuals
θ_ε	Theta$_\varepsilon$	Covariance matrix of the ε error terms
θ_ε	Theta$_\delta$	Covariance matrix of the δ error terms
$\lambda_{bi}^{(x)}$	lambda$_{bi}$	Path arrow from ξ_i to x_b
$\lambda_{ag}^{(y)}$	lambda$_{ag}$	Path arrow from η_g to y_a
β_{gh}	beta$_{gh}$	Path arrow from η_h to η_g
γ_{gi}	gamma$_{gi}$	Path arrow from ξ_i to η_g
ϕ_{ij}	phi$_{ij}$	Path arrow from ξ_j to ξ_i
ψ_{gh}	psi$_{gh}$	Path arrow from ζ_h to ζ_g
$\theta_{ab}^{(\delta)}$	theta$_{ab}^{(\delta)}$	Path arrow from δ_b to δ_a
$\theta_{cd}^{(\varepsilon)}$	theta$_{cd}^{(\varepsilon)}$	Path arrow from ε_d to ε_c

has significant impact upon theoretical understanding, musical background has considerably less influence, and musical aptitude is inversely related to theoretical understanding of first-year college music majors. Note that a number of the measured independent variables have error terms that are quite large. The ability of latent trait modeling to compensate for this error is demonstrated, as the model does statistically fit the data and accounts for a significant proportion of the variance in theoretical understanding.

Multidimensional Scaling

Scaling Concepts

Multidimensional scaling refers to a number of methods that provide spatial representations of the relationships between variables on a map (Green, Car-

TABLE 4-16. Maximum Likelihood Factor Analysis of Harrison's (1990b) Data

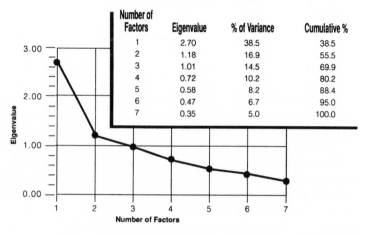

Scree Test of Harrison Data

Number of Factors	Eigenvalue	% of Variance	Cumulative %
1	2.70	38.5	38.5
2	1.18	16.9	55.5
3	1.01	14.5	69.9
4	0.72	10.2	80.2
5	0.58	8.2	88.4
6	0.47	6.7	95.0
7	0.35	5.0	100.0

	Pattern Matrix			Structure Matrix		
	Musical Background	Musical Aptitude	Scholastic Achievement	Musical Background	Musical Aptitude	Scholastic Achievement
Piano Experience	1.03	−0.22	−0.09	0.99	0.22	0.19
Total Years	0.41	0.14	0.17	0.50	0.34	0.36
SAT Verbal	−0.10	0.03	0.63	0.24	0.55	0.79
SAT Math	−0.02	0.22	0.69	0.09	0.31	0.62
Theory Grade	0.16	−0.11	0.73	0.34	0.29	0.72
CMAP Tonal	0.02	0.98	−0.09	0.27	0.94	0.39
CMAP Rhythm	0.02	0.28	0.07	0.11	0.31	0.20
Factor Correlation Matrix						
Musical Background	1.00					
Scholastic Achievement	0.28	1.00				
Musical Aptitude	0.29	0.49	1.00			

Abbreviations: CMAP = College Musical Aptitude Profile; SAT = Scholastic Achievement Test.

145

mone, and Smith, 1989; Kruskal and Wish, 1978). The map's geometric representation of the data, usually in a Euclidean space of few dimensions, provides a visual means of interpreting the interrelationships of the variables and the variables' dimensionality (Young, 1987). The same mathematical models as employed by factor and discriminant analysis form the basis of multidimensional scaling (Nunnally, 1978). However, multidimensional scaling emphasizes the visual analysis of the variables in a space that reflects the variables' perceived similarities (Miller, 1989, p. 62).

Multidimensional scaling methods employ proximities of variables as input (Kruskal and Wish, 1978). The *proximities* are numbers that represent perceived similarities or differences among the variables. Typically, data are obtained by asking subjects to judge the similarity between two psychological objects. Computational methods are available that allow the use of data reflecting most levels of measurement. However, ordinal data tend to be most commonly employed. Correlations can be considered proximities as they may be conceived as indices of similarity or differences and are appropriate for analysis with multidimensional scaling (Kruskal and Wish, 1978, pp. 10–11).

Miller (1989) cites a number of advantages for multidimensional scaling: It has enormous data reduction power, subjects can easily make the similarity judgments often used for multidimensional scaling, it is easier to visualize and interpret than factor analysis, the dimensions do not require specification prior to the analysis, in more complex stimulus domains it may sort out those attributes that are not important in making the required judgments, data of ordinal and nominal levels can be analyzed, and the data need not be related linearly.

An Application of Multidimensional Scaling

Larson (1977) presented the results of an investigation into undergraduate music majors' aural skills of melodic error detection, melodic dictation, and melodic sight singing in diatonic, chromatic, and atonal pitch categories. As part of his results, Larson presented a matrix of intercorrelations among the various aural tasks. An application of multidimensional scaling can be demonstrated by using Larson's correlations as proximity indices because they do indicate the similarity of the various aural tasks. The purpose of scaling these data will be (1) to determine the similarities of the nine aural task combinations and (2) to identify the major dimensions characterized by the scaling procedures.

Figure 4-8 presents the variables as points in the two-dimensional Euclidean space of a solution that accounts for 99.1 percent of the variance in the scaled data. The center vertical and horizontal axes represent the two dimensions of the solution. The vertical dimension was interpreted as "task" while the horizontal dimension was interpreted as "pitch assurity." These interpretations were based on the variables' location along the two center

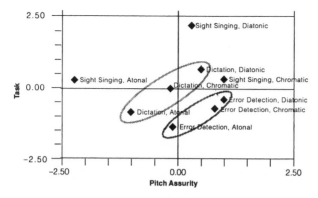

Figure 4.8. Multidimensional scaling solution of Larson's (1977) data.

axes. The error detection variables cluster along a diagonal plane, as do the dictation variables, and, with the exception of chromatic sight singing, the sight-singing variables do as well. The tasks appear to be ordered from easy to difficult, with sight singing being the easiest and error detection being the most difficult. Another grouping of the variables can also be made. The atonal variables form a grouping in a diagonal plane opposite to those marked in the figure. The diatonic variables also group well in a similar diagonal plane. With the exception of chromatic sight singing, the chromatic variables form along this diagonal plane. As in the diagonal task planes, the pitch variables appear to be ordered from easy to difficult, with diatonic pitch tasks being the easiest and atonal pitch tasks being the most difficult. The chromatic sight-singing variable defies the overall logic of the map presented here. It could be that sight singing, a production task, interacts differently with pitch structure than the listening tasks of dictation and error detection.

Nonparametric Statistics

Fundamental Concepts

Nonparametric statistical tests have great value in music education, as they are based on much less stringent assumptions than parametric statistics described to this point. The primary assumptions of nonparametric statistics are that the observations are independent and that there is underlying continuity to the variable in some cases (Conover, 1980; Gibbons, 1985; Siegel and Castellan, 1988). No assumption is made about the underlying distribution of the population from which the sample was drawn. Nonparametric statistics require only nominal or ordinal data. Parametric statistics, by contrast, require interval or ratio level data, make assumptions about the specific population distribution, and make inferences about population parameters.

Gibbons (1985, p. 29) suggests that nonparametric statistics should be chosen over parametric statistics when the assumptions required by parametric statistics are not satisfied by the data, when the fewest number of assumptions are met by the data, when sample size is small, and when a particular nonparametric test will provide a more adequate test of the null hypothesis. The mathematical simplicity of nonparametric tests adds to their attractiveness in that not only is their calculation simpler but also it is more likely that the user will understand and apply the tests appropriately (Conover, 1980).

Nonparametric Statistical Tests

Selection of the appropriate nonparametric statistical test depends on the particular null hypothesis being tested and the data's level of measurement. There are fewer nonparametric statistical tests than parametric tests. However, statistics are available for most situations involving traditional experimental designs. The nonparametric tests described here focus on tests relating to a single sample, related samples, independent samples, and measures of association. Single-sample tests are for those situations where only one group of subjects has been measured. Related samples are for when two samples have been measured but the samples are related in some way such as the same group being measured twice. Independent samples are two or more measured samples that are not related in any systematic way. Measures of association provide a means for determining the similarity or difference between two measures. For an easy-to-follow description of how to calculate the majority of statistics described here, the reader is directed to the work of Moore in the text by Madsen and Moore (1978) *Experimental Research in Music: Workbook in Design and Statistical Tests*.

One-Sample Tests   In the case of research in which the entire set of observations on a variable are to be analyzed, the family of nonparametric one-sample tests may be appropriate.

Chi-Square Goodness-of-Fit Test   The chi-square goodness-of-fit test determines whether an observed number of cases in each of a number of categories is the same as that expected by some theory. The procedure requires independent observations of a variable with the observations grouped into categories. The statistic assumes that the sample is random and that the variable has at least nominal level of measurement.

Suppose an elementary music teacher had taught a unit on tempo. The instructional goal was to have at least 70 percent of the 100 students able to identify a change to faster when it occurred in music. The teacher assumed that 15 percent of the remaining group would not be able to detect any change and that the other 15 percent would indicate that the piece went slower when it indeed went faster. The teacher gave a single-item exam to determine the students' attainment. The data of this fictitious situation are presented in Table 4-17.

Note that in Table 4-17 the chi-square value has degrees of freedom equal to the number of categories minus one. The significance level in our fictitious sample is .075; this is larger than the .05 value of significance traditionally used as the lower bound of significance. Therefore, the statistic indicates no significant difference between the data's observed distribution and the expected distribution. The teacher's assumption that 70 percent of the students would be able to correctly identify an increase of tempo, with 15 percent not being able to detect a tempo change and 15 percent wrongly identifying a decrease in tempo, is supported by the chi-square goodness-of-fit test.

Kolmogorov Goodness-of-Fit Test   Goodness-of-fit tests determine if a random sample of some population matches an expected distribution. That is, goodness-of-fit tests test the null hypothesis that the unknown distribution of the sample is indeed known (Conover, 1980, p. 344). The example cited for the chi-square goodness-of-fit test actually tested the teacher's belief (hypothesis) that 70 percent of the class would be able to correctly identify increases in tempo, 15 percent would be unable to detect any change, and 15 percent would detect a decrease in tempo (a known distribution).

The Kolmogorov goodness-of-fit test provides a means for determining goodness of fit with ordinal data and provides a means for establishing a confidence region for the unknown distribution function. This test has benefits over the chi-square test when sample size is small and appears to be a more powerful test in general. The Kolmogorov test assumes that the data were drawn from a random sample and have some unknown distribution.

Suppose, for example, that a band director gave the 72 band students in the band a test to measure their knowledge of the historical aspects of the music that was being studied. A random sampling of 11 students' scores was taken to determine if the scores were distributed evenly between the minimum score of the class (50) and the maximum score of the class (100).

TABLE 4-17. Chi-Square Goodness-of-Fit Test on Fictitious Data

Category	Observed	Expected	Residual
Faster	78	70.00	8.00
No Change	15	15.00	.00
Slower	7	15.00	−8.00
Total	100		

	Chi-Square	D.F.	Significance
	5.181	2	.075

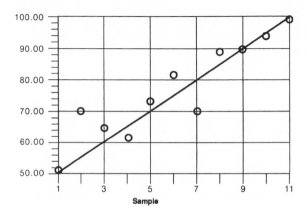

Figure 4.9. Fictitious random sampling of 11 scores for a band history test.

Figure 4-9 presents the data for the 11 randomly selected students with the hypothesized distribution of the scores plotted as a solid line. Note that distributions that are spread in such a manner are known as uniform distributions. The Kolmogorov goodness-of-fit test for this sample was .494 with an alpha level of .967. Thus, the band director can be statistically certain that the distribution of scores is uniform between the minimum and maximum of this test as based on this sample.

Binomial Test   The binomial test is used with dichotomous data, that is, data having each individual data point in one of only two categories. For instance, a question is answered either right or wrong, a student listens to the music or does not, or a trumpet student knows the fingerings or does not. Such data are tested with the binomial distribution, which indicates the probability p that the first of two possible events will occur and that the opposite event will occur with probability $q = 1 - p$. The binomial test has great versatility and can be applied in a considerable number of situations (Conover, 1980, p. 96).

The data for the binomial test are the outcomes of a number of trials where the result can be only one thing or another such as right or wrong, good or bad. Each of the trials is assumed to be independent of the others. The outcome of a trial is assumed to have the same probability for each and every trial.

Kuhn and Booth (1988) presented the results of a study on the influence of ornamented or plain melodic activity on tempo perception. In a series of tables they presented binomial comparisons of 95 elementary students' responses to various test items. The items required the students to listen to two musical examples and respond by indicating whether the second example was faster or slower than the first example or whether the tempos were the same (pp. 143–144). To demonstrate the use of binomial comparisons, the data of test item 2 will be used. Students' responses for this item, in which there was no change in the second example, were 18 indicating slower, 53 indicating no change, and 24 indicating faster.

Figure 4-10 presents the various possible binomial comparisons for these data where the comparisons were tested for an even distribution of students in each of the two possible categories. That is, the test proportion was .50 or 50:50. Note that both the comparisons made with the correct no-change category are significantly different ($p > .05$) from being the expected proportion of .50. The comparison between the incorrect categories of faster and slower are not significantly different from the expected 50:50 proportion. The fourth pie chart was not contained in the Kuhn and Booth tables but demonstrates a practical application of this test for music classroom situations. Consider a situation where it was desired that 70 percent of all the elementary students taking a tempo perception test would correctly identify that no change had occurred to the Kuhn and Booth item. After the number of students answering incorrectly either faster or slower were added together, the resulting value could be tested with the number of students answering the item correctly to determine whether the students had attained the 70 percent criterion. As can be seen, the number of correct responses does not achieve the 70 percent criterion level as indicated by the probability value p being less than .05.

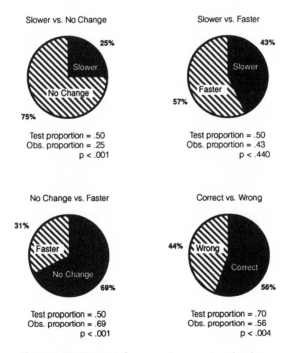

Figure 4.10. Binomial comparisons using the data of Kuhn and Booth (1988).

Contingency Tables   A contingency table is a matrix of frequency data representing two or more categorical variables. Consider the situation where a high school music program wishes to know the makeup of their students by sex (male or female) and primary ensemble participation (band, chorus, orchestra). The data could be displayed in a matrix such as the following, with sex across the rows of the matrix and ensemble type down the columns of the matrix:

	Band	Chorus	Orchestra
Male	34	30	12
Female	42	67	29

Contingency tables are usually described by their number of rows and number of columns; this is a 2×3 contingency table. As can easily be noted, contingency tables display a large amount of information based on nominal data. Additional information could be displayed in such a table, including various percentages based on the number in the rows, the number in the columns, or the total number contained in the table.

Chi-Square Test for Independence   Statistics are also available to determine various characteristics of a contingency table. Chief among these is the chi-square test for independence. The statistic assumes that the sample has been drawn at random and that each observation can be categorized into only one of the cells in the matrix. The hypothesis tested by this statistic is that the two categorical variables that make up the table are independent of each other.

Flowers and Dunne-Sousa (1990) reported a study of 93 preschool "children's abilities to echo short pitch patterns in relation to maintenance of a tonal center in self-chosen and taught songs" (p. 102). Within the report, a 3×3 contingency table is presented of students' age by self-chosen song category: modulating, somewhat modulating, and not modulating from the tonal center. Data presented in this table are used to provide an example of the results from a common computer program (CROSSTABS from SPSS[x], 1988) that demonstrates the amount of information that can be obtained from such frequency counts (Table 4–18). The table is an exact copy of the output from the SPSS[x] computer program. Note that the area at the top left of the display describes the content of each of the cells. The top-most value in each cell is the frequency for that particular combination of age and self-chosen song. The reader is encouraged to compare the table presented in the excellent article by Flowers and Dunne-Sousa with the computer output presented here. The authors reported the chi-square test for independence for this contingency table, which is contained at the bottom of Table 4–18. Note the significant chi-square value indicating that the two categorical variables are not independent. Rather, age is related to the ability to sing a self-chosen song on the tonal center. This led Flowers and Dunne-Sousa to conclude that

TABLE 4-18. 3 × 3 Contingency Table Using the Data of Flowers and Dunne-Sousa (1990): Age (Preschool Students Age) by SONG (Type of Song Selected)

AGE	Count Row % Column % Total %	Modulating 1	Somewhat Modulating 2	Not Modulating 3	Row Total
3 years old	3	13	5	1	19
		68.4	26.3	5.3	21.1
		31.0	14.7	7.1	
		14.4	5.6	1.1	
4 years old	4	10	11	9	30
		33.3	36.7	30.0	33.3
		23.8	32.4	64.3	
		11.1	12.2	10.0	
5 years old	5	19	18	4	41
		46.3	43.9	9.8	45.6
		45.2	52.9	28.6	
		21.1	20.0	4.4	
	Column Total	42 46.7	34 37.8	14 15.6	90 100.0

Chi-Square	Value	DF	Significance
Pearson	10.35247	4	.03489

"as would be expected, 3-year-olds comprised the largest proportion of modulating singers" (p. 107).

Measures of Association for Contingency Tables   The smallest form of contingency tables to which the chi-square test of independence can be applied is the 2 × 2 table. When a researcher wishes to establish the degree of association or relationship between the two categorical variables that define the contingency table, the *phi coefficient* is the most appropriate. This coefficient is a special case of the Pearson product-moment correlation (Conover, 1980). It is normally calculated from the chi-square value, which will always be positive. Therefore, the phi coefficient is a value that ranges from 0, independence or no association, to +1, dependence or perfect association.

For tables larger than 2 × 2, *Cramer's V* provides an appropriate statistic. It is a slightly modified form of the phi coefficient that accounts for a greater number of rows or columns. Cramer's V, because it is usually calculated from the phi coefficient, will also have a value that ranges from 0, independence, to +1, dependence. Cramer's V obtained from Flowers and Dunne-Sousa's (1990) data is .24.

The contingency coefficient provides another index of association. Its lowest value is 0, but its maximum value varies with the size of the table. The larger the table, the larger the potential maximum value (Gibbons,

1985). It is most appropriate when both nominal variables have the same number of categories. A contingency coefficient of .32 was obtained for the Flowers and Dunne-Sousa (1990) data. Note that there is a discrepancy between the Cramer's V and the contingency coefficient. In the Flowers and Dunne-Sousa case, Cramer's V is the more conservative.

Whereas the measures of association described here are those most commonly employed, a considerable number of other measures of association are available for analysis of contingency tables. These statistics all serve different functions in the analysis of the degree of association between the two categorical variables that comprise the contingency table. For further information, the reader is directed to statistical texts that emphasize contingency table analysis.

Tests For Two Related Samples

Sign Test   The sign test compares the differences between pairs of variables by using the sign of the difference between each pair. That is, if the second value of a pair is larger, a plus (+) is assigned; if the second value is smaller, a minus (−) is assigned; and a tie is not counted. The data pairs must have some natural relationship to each other, the data must be at least at the ordinal level of measurement, and the two variables should be mutually independent.

The data from 20 randomly selected high school band students who were measured on their preference for a band piece prior to rehearsing it and then measured again 6 weeks later just prior to the concert performance of this piece will be used to demonstrate the sign test (Asmus, 1987). The sign test will be used to determine whether the students' preference for the band work changed after the 6-week rehearsal period. The results of the analysis are presented in Table 4–19. From the table, we note that 15 students' preferences actually declined while five of the students' preference increased. There were no ties. A significant difference ($p < .05$) between the first and second preference assessments is indicated. In other words, the students' preference for the band work did change significantly in a negative direction.

TABLE 4-19. Sign Test for Differences in Preference before and after Rehearsal

Category	Students
− Differences (Preference 2 < Preference 1)	15
+ Differences (Preference 2 < Preference 1)	5
Ties	0
Total	20
2-Tailed $p < .04$	

Wilcoxon Signed Ranks Test   The Wilcoxon signed ranks test is used to evaluate matched pairs of data from fairly small samples. The test assumes that the data are of at least the ordinal level of measurement and that the pairs are mutually independent.

Price (1988) used the Wilcoxon signed ranks test to determine if a music appreciation class affects the number of times a traditional composer is mentioned by students when "asked to list and rank their favorite composers" (p. 37). Price provides a thorough listing of these data in his Table 2. The results of the Wilcoxon signed ranks test on Price's data are presented here in Table 4-20.

The Price (1988) data analyzed with the Wilcoxon matched-pairs test produces a significant difference, as indicated by the probability of $p <$ .0008 for the test statistic Z. That is, there is a significant effect of the music appreciation class on the number of times formal traditional composers are mentioned by students who have completed the course. As the mean ranks in the table indicate, the students are likely to mention more formal, traditional composers after the course than before.

Cochran Q Test   The Cochran Q Test is used to test the effect of a number of treatments when the effect of the treatment forms a dichotomous variable such as "success" or "failure." The data must be independent for each subject, the effects of the treatments are measured in the same manner for each treatment, and the subjects are assumed to have been randomly selected from the population. The Cochran Q test tests the contention that all the treatments are equally as effective.

Three adjudicators' ratings of 16 marching bands participating in a contest will be used to demonstrate an application of the Cochran Q test. The bands were rated in the categories of music performance, marching and maneuvering, and percussion by an adjudicator assigned to each category. The success ratings were assigned by giving those bands with scores greater than the average in that category a success rating and those bands at or below the average in that category an unsuccessful rating. Table 4-21 presents the results of the Cochran Q test on the successful-unsuccessful data

TABLE 4-20. Wilcoxon Matched-Pairs Signed Ranks Test of Price (1988) Data

	Mean Rank	Cases
− Ranks (postcourse < precourse)	13.93	14
+ Ranks (postcourse > precourse)	25.90	29
Ties (postcourse = precourse)		7
Total		50
$Z = -3.3568$	2-Tailed $p < .0008$	

TABLE 4-21. Cochran Q Test of Three Adjudicators' Success Ratings of 16 Marching Bands

	Unsuccessful	Successful
Music adjudicator	10	6
M and M Adjudicator	9	6
Percussion adjudicator	9	7

Number of Bands	Cochran Q	DF	$p<$
16	.4000	2	.8187

Abbreviations: M & M = marching and maneuvering.

to determine if the judges rated the bands in a similar manner. As the probability figure indicates, there were no significant differences between the ways the judges rated the bands.

Friedman Test   The Friedman test is employed in the situation where each subject ranks two or more items on some continuum. The test assumes that each subject's ranking is independent of all the other subjects, that each subject is ranking the same items, and that all subjects rank the items along the same continuum. The Friedman test evaluates the contention that the ranked items are distributed evenly across the continuum on which they were ranked.

LeBlanc, Colman, McCrary, Sherrill, and Malin (1988) presented the results of a study of the effect of tempo variation on the preferences of six age groups for traditional jazz. As part of the study, the authors presented the results of Friedman tests for each age group to determine if tempo affected the preference rating for music. Table 4–22 presents the relevant data taken from the tables and text of the research report. Note that there are

TABLE 4-22. Means and Friedman Tests of Tempo Effect on Preference From LeBlanc et al. (1988)

Grade Level	Slow	Moderately Slow	Moderately Fast	Fast	Chi-square	df	p <
3	2.99	3.24	3.92	3.99	150.76	3	.01
5	2.47	2.58	3.23	3.50	186.10	3	.01
7	1.91	2.07	2.52	2.64	144.66	3	.01
9,10	2.07	2.40	2.82	2.88	164.38	3	.01
11,12	2.15	2.37	2.83	3.08	213.18	3	.01
College	2.88	3.18	3.51	3.58	91.54	3	.01

Note: The preference ratings had a possible range of 1 to 7.

significant differences for each of the age groups. An inspection of the means led the authors to conclude that increasingly faster tempos brought increasingly higher preference ratings.

Independent Samples

Median Test   The median test is conducted in situations where there are a number of samples measured on the same variable. The test does not require that the number of subjects in each sample be equal. The test does assume that each sample has been drawn at random, that the samples are independent of each other, and that the measurement scale of the variable is at least at the ordinal level. The median test is used to test the contention that all the populations from which the samples were drawn have the same median.

Consider the hypothetical case where a choral music teacher wanted to know if different forms of vocal warm-up would affect vocal performance. The teacher used three different classes: One received no warm-up (control group); another received a warm-up using staccato "ha" on a series of scales, rhythmic patterns, and arpeggios; the final class received a warm-up on "mah-may-mee-moh-moo" on a comparable series of scales, rhythmic patterns, and arpeggios. After the warm-up, each student was tested as to vocal quality and flexibility using a performance assessment instrument the choral teacher had devised. Because the classes were intact, there was unequal sample size across the classes. The median test was applied to the vocal scores to determine whether the medians were different between the groups. As the results of this analysis indicate (Table 4–23), there was a significant difference between the medians. The table indicates that the control group had more scores below the median than any other group. The distribution of scores above and below the median was evenly split for the "mah-may . . ." warm-up group while the "ha" warm-up group had the majority of scores above the median. It could be concluded that the "ha" warm-up procedure was more effective in this fictitious example.

Mann-Whitney U   The Mann-Whitney U test is used in situations similar to those of the median test, except that it is used when there are only two

TABLE 4-23. Median Test of Hypothetical Choral Data

	Control Group	Warm-up "ha"	Warm-up "mah-may . . ."
Scores greater than the median	3	11	9
Scores less than the median	15	3	9

Cases	Median	Chi-Square	DF	Significance
50	27.0	12.3303	2	.0021

samples. The test is considered more powerful than the median test because it uses rankings of each sample in its calculation. There is an assumption with this statistic that the samples have been drawn at random from their populations, that the measurement scale of the variable is at least ordinal, and that the two samples are independent of each other. The Mann-Whitney U tests the contention that the two groups have been drawn from the same population.

Flowers (1988) used the Mann-Whitney U test to determine differences between two groups of elementary education majors on their pretest–posttest differences of rated preference for four symphonic works. One of the two groups received music appreciation lessons on the symphonic works while the other group taught the music to elementary school students. The analysis performed on the posttest gain scores led Flowers to conclude that "although both groups had increased their preference ratings, there was no significant difference between the groups in amount of gain ($z = -1.45$, $p = .15$)" (p. 25).

Kolmogorov-Smirnov Two-Sample Test   The Kolmogorov-Smirnov two-sample test is used to test the contention that the scores in two independent samples are distributed in the same manner. The assumptions of this test are that the samples have been drawn at random, that the samples are mutually independent of each other, and that the data are at least at the ordinal level of measurement.

The data from a marching band contest will be used to demonstrate the Kolmogorov-Smirnov two-sample test. In the contest, bands competed in one of two divisions: Class A and Open Class. Class A bands tended to be smaller and not as advanced musically or in their presentation as the Open Class bands. The total scores five adjudicators assigned in the areas of music performance, marching and maneuvering, general effect, percussion, and auxiliary groups are used as data. The Kolmogorov-Smirnov test is applied to determine if the two distributions of total scores were the same for Class A bands as for Open Class bands. The results appear in Table 4–24 and

TABLE 4-24. Kolmogorov-Smimov 2-Sample Test of Marching Band Contest Scores

Band Level	n
Class A	12
Open Class	4
Total	16
K-SZ	2-Tailed $p <$
1.732	.005

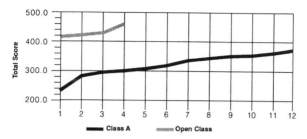

Figure 4.11. Distributions of sorted marching band scores.

Figure 4-11. A significant difference is detected between the score distributions of the Class A bands and the Open Class bands. As can be seen in Figure 4–11, Open Class bands not only had higher total scores than Class A bands, but the distribution of scores has a different shape.

Kruskal-Wallis Analysis of Variance   The Kruskal-Wallis ANOVA is used in the situation where there are more than two independent samples. The statistic is based upon a ranking of the entire set of data to test the contention that all of the population distributions represented by the samples are identical. The assumptions are that the samples are drawn from their respective populations at random, that the samples are mutually independent, and that the variable upon which all subjects were assessed is at least at the ordinal level of measurement.

Flowers (1983), in a study of vocabulary and listening instruction on nonmusicians' descriptions of changes in music, used the Kruskal-Wallis ANOVA to test for differences between four experimental groups on pre-post verbal description gain scores. The verbal description scores were obtained by counting the number of references to elements of music made in response to changes heard in a musical excerpt. The four experimental groups included a contact control group, which received no instruction in vocabulary or listening experiences; a vocabulary group, which received instruction in music vocabulary; a listening group, which was provided with music listening experiences; and a vocabulary plus listening group, which received both vocabulary instruction and listening experiences. The Kruskal-Wallis test indicated a significant difference in the mean rankings of the gain scores for each of the four groups ($H = 17.25$, $df = 3$, $p < .001$).

Dunn's Multiple Comparison Procedure   Following a significant Kruskal-Wallis one-way analysis of variance, Dunn's multiple-comparison procedure can be applied to determine the exact location of the mean rank differences. This allows the researcher to determine which of the populations included in the Kruskal-Wallis analysis significantly differ from each other. Flowers (1983), in the study just described, followed the significant Kruskal-Wallis analysis of variance with Dunn's multiple-comparison procedure on the four groups in her study. She found that "vocabulary plus listening produced significantly higher verbal descriptive scores than vocabulary only or contact control conditions, but not significantly different from listening only" (p. 184). Table 4–25 duplicates that provided by Flowers to support her conclusion.

Graphic Data Analysis Methods

For most individuals, especially those with little familiarity with statistics, graphic displays of research data provide the most easily grasped methods for understanding the data. The advent of small, yet powerful microcomputers with graphic capabilities has created a wealth of systems for the graphing of research data. Graphic methods can be as simple as a display of the number of people within a certain category through the use of bar graph or pie chart or as complex as the interaction of data through real-time display of data in multidimensional space.

Graphic methods of data analysis are expanding daily. Graphic methods no longer entail only the display of data; graphic interfaces can be used to cause the calculation of various statistics. An example of this was provided in this chapter's section on path analysis. As a whole, graphic methods help the researcher better conceptualize the research and thus allow a better understanding of the variables involved and the nature of the research study than is possible through purely numerical methods. Graphic methods have the additional benefit of utilizing less of the researcher's time in analysis of the data because of the relative ease of interpreting graphic data displays over numeric data displays, though graphic data displays do use a much greater proportion of computer time.

Throughout this chapter, various forms of graphic displays have been provided to assist the reader in understanding the various concepts being discussed. This section presents some of the major graphic methods in greater detail. The methods surveyed only skim the surface of the tremendous number of graphic analysis methods available.

TABLE 4-25. Mean Ranks of Pre-Posttest Differences Described by Flowers (1983)

Contact Control	Vocabulary Only	Listening Only	Vocabulary Plus Listening
46.44	54.37	67.50	81.69

Note: Table is duplicated from Flowers (1983). Underlines represent no differences at the .05 level. Those means not connected are significantly different.

Graphing Frequencies

One-Dimensional Frequency Plots   The graphing of frequencies is often needed when the characteristics of a population or phenomenon are required. The graphing of frequencies can be done through the use of bar graphs or pie charts. Figure 4-12 presents a pie chart that displays the proportion of responses teachers made in the final rating of an inservice workshop experience. Note that out of the four possible categories in the rating scale, 84 percent were either "excellent" or "good." The "fair" portion of the pie chart has been exploded to emphasize the 16 percent of the teachers who may not have had the level of experience that they had actually desired.

Three-Dimensional Frequency Plots   An extension of the single-dimension frequency plot is the three-dimensional frequency plot. Consider the data of Austin (1988), where, in a study of elementary band students' music motivation, he provided the number of responses in the attribution categories of "Luck," "Task Difficulty," "Ability," and "Effort" for each of the recipients of four different division ratings: I, II, III, and IV. The frequency data were converted to percentages and are graphically displayed in Figure 4-13. This display is a three-dimensional bar graph where the vertical dimension represents the frequency of response and the other two dimensions represent the various categories involved. It can be seen in the figure that the most-used attribution category by the elementary students for all the division categories was "Effort." The least used was "Task Difficulty." Note, however, that there seems to be a slight increase in the use of Luck attributions with lower performance ratings.

Describing the Distribution of Interval Data

Frequency Polygon   The frequency polygon displays data in line graph form with the vertical or *y*-axis representing the frequency with which the particular score occurred. The horizontal or *x*-axis of the frequency polygon is

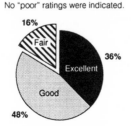

Figure 4.12. Teacher ratings about the quality of an in-service workshop.

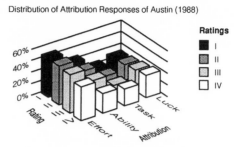

Figure 4.13. Proportion of attributions for different division ratings.

the range of interval scores for the variable under analysis. Figure 4-14 presents a frequency polygon of the scores participants in a summer music workshop made on a 12-item knowledge test. The figure shows that the most commonly occurring score was 9 and that moving away from this score the frequency of the scores declines. If the sample size approached infinity, we would expect the frequency polygon to resemble the normal curve.

Frequency Histogram   The frequency histogram is similar to the frequency polygon, but rather than having the information displayed as a line graph, a bar graph format is used. The x-axis remains the range of scores, and the y-axis is the frequency of occurrence of the particular scores. Figure 4–15 presents, among other information, the frequency histograms for two different sets of marching band contest scores. The sets of scores are for the same bands at the same contest in two different years. On top of each histogram, the normal curve has been plotted for the data with the same mean and representing the overall distribution of the scores. As can be seen, neither set of scores is distributed normally. Most of the scores tend to be below the mean.

Box Plots   Above each frequency histogram in Figure 4–15 is a box plot that also characterizes the distribution of the respective set of marching band

Figure 4.14. Frequency polygon of scores on a summer music workshop knowledge test.

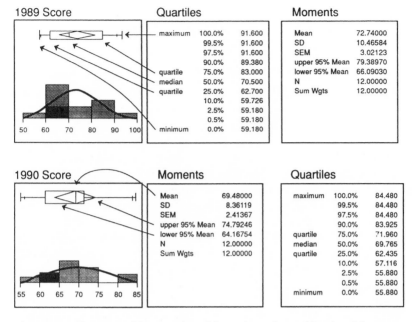

Figure 4.15. Frequency histograms and box plots of marching bands' contest scores for two different years.

scores. The arrows indicate what each of the different points on the box plot represents. If the scores were normally distributed, the median line would be in the center of the box and the box would be centered on the line representing the range of scores from the minimum to the maximum. The small vertical tick mark at the extremes of the range line presents the tenth and ninetieth percentiles respectively. Had the distribution been more normal, the other percentiles in the quartiles table would have been displayed. The diamond characterizes the distribution's mean and the 95 percent confidence intervals for the mean. If the distribution were normal, the median line would appear in the exact center of the diamond.

Figure 4-15 also characterizes the growing trend for graphics analysis programs to provide a wide variety of statistical information. The figure is a slightly modified form of the output from the graphics analysis package JMP (SAS, 1989). The modifications were necessary so that the arrows could be added to define the various points in the box plots.

Plots of Means

Plotting the means for various subgroups on a variable or plotting the means on a number of different variables for a particular sample is a common practice in the analysis and reporting of data. Such plots help determine particular trends inherent in the data or allow the researcher to determine relationships between the groups of variables of interest. In most cases, the vertical *y*-axis characterizes the value of the mean while the *x*-axis characterizes the particular subgroups or variables of interest.

One-Dimensional Mean Plots   One of the most common forms of mean plots are those created after an analysis of variance that produced a significant interaction. The means for the various groups involved in the interaction are plotted with the vertical *y*-axis representing the magnitude of the mean and the horizontal *x*-axis representing the grouping variable's categories. Kantorski (1986), as part of a study on the effects of accompaniment intervals and register on string instrumentalists' intonation, provided a graph of the significant register by accompaniment interaction that he obtained. Figure 4-16 is a copy of that graph. The crossed lines indicate the interaction. It can be noted that the upper register tends to be further from tempered intonation for all intervals but the unison. For the case of unison intervals, the upper register more closely approximates tempered intonation than the lower register.

LeBlanc et al. (1988, p. 156) presented the results of a study on "the effect of four levels of tempo on the self-reported preferences of six different age-groups for traditional jazz music listening examples." In their report, the authors presented a figure that plotted the preference means across all tempos for each of the age groups. The values reported by the authors were used to replicate this graph in Figure 4-17. The original graph of LeBlanc and colleagues included only the linked squares. As can be seen, the means have a decidedly curvilinear form, with the preference for traditional jazz dropping to its lowest point for the grade 7 group. This version of the graph has utilized the capabilities of the graphing program to overlay a curvilinear

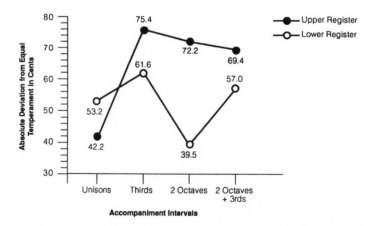

Figure 4.16. Plot of two-way ANOVA interaction of register and accompaniment intervals duplicated from Kantorski (1986).

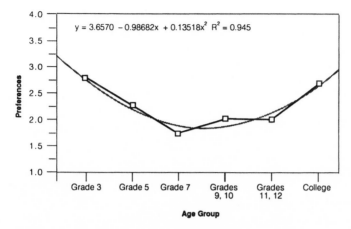

Figure 4.17. Plot of jazz preference means from LeBlanc et al. (1988).

trend line and its associated statistics. The fit of the curved line is extremely good with these data. This is verified by the R^2 value, which indicates that 94.5 percent of the variance in the means is accounted for the curved line. This represents an R value of .972, indicating a very substantial fit.

Two-Dimensional Mean Plots   The plots of means in which there are two grouping variables of interest are often best handled by plotting the data in three-dimensional space: one dimension representing the magnitude of the means and the other two dimensions representing the two categories of interest. The data of LeBlanc et al. (1988) described above will be utilized to demonstrate this application. The effect of the grade level and tempo categories are characterized in a single graph in Figure 4-18. The curvilinear relationship between grade level and preference for traditional jazz noted earlier is clearly seen in this three-dimensional plot. The effect, as shown by

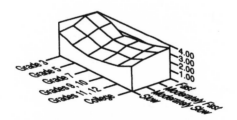

Figure 4.18. Three-dimensional plot of the effect of grade level and tempo on means for traditional jazz obtained by LeBlanc et al. (1988).

this plot, is most pronounced for slow pieces, though there appears to be a steeper slope for the lower grades at faster tempos. The figure also indicates a tendency in all age groups for preference to rise as the tempo becomes faster. This effect is lowest for the grade 7 group, which has the overall lowest preference for traditional jazz.

Plotting Relationships

Scattergrams   Scattergrams are the plotting of each individual data point by indicating the point's relative magnitude on two variables. One variable's magnitude is characterized by the vertical *y*-axis, and the other variable's magnitude is characterized by the horizontal *x*-axis. The marching band contest data for two consecutive years will be utilized to provide an example of the scattergram. Figure 4-19 displays the location of the juncture of each participating band's 1989 contest score with their 1990 contest score. It can be seen that the scores are distributed in a diagonal form moving from lower left to upper right. This ascending diagonal form is characteristic of variables that have a positive relationship. Variables with a negative relationship distribute the scores in a diagonal from upper left to lower right. No relationship would be indicated by a random spread of the points on the graph.

Figure 4-19 has the linear trend line plotted on the graph. The tabular information indicates that the two sets of scores have 70 percent of their

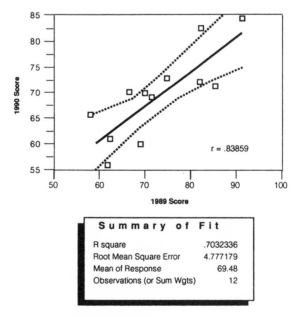

Figure 4.19. Plot of the marching band scores for two consecutive years.

variance in common. The dotted lines represent the 95 percent confidence intervals for scores predicted with the displayed regression information.

Multidimensional Graphing   Multidimensional graphing is possible today in real time. This form of graphing allows items to be plotted as in a scattergram with an additional one or more dimensions added. Usually multidimensional graphing limits the plots to three-dimensional space, as this is all that can be easily handled on a computer screen. Each dimension of the space represents another interval or ratio level variable. The interesting aspect of multidimensional graphing is that the data can be "spun" in space so that the relationship between the three variables can be viewed from any possible angle.

Semantic differential data collected from high school students in response to two different musical excerpts provide an excellent example of multidimensional graphing. Semantic scales are bipolar adjectives, such as beautiful-ugly, separated by a seven-point continuum. Subjects respond to an object or event by checking the point along the continuum that best reflects their assessment of the object or event on the bipolar adjective scale. Semantic scales typically form three groupings: activity, evaluation, and potency. In the present data, a fourth grouping reflective of preference was added. The pattern weights from a three-dimension, common factor analysis of the data with oblique rotation were plotted using a graphing program with multidimensional capabilities. The plot was rotated in space until the formulation contained in Figure 4-20 was obtained.

The display of Figure 4–20 was created by having lines drawn from the central point of the plot to each of the variable points within the graph.

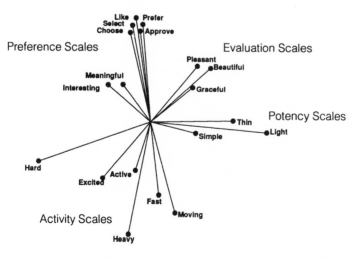

Figure 4.20. Three-dimensional plot of four sets of semantic differential scales.

This is frequently a useful aid in identifying clusters of variables. The four groups of semantic scales are apparent in Figure 4–20. The figure reveals that the semantic scale hard-soft is across from the potency scales to which it belongs. This is because the scale should have been recoded to soft-hard; this would move it to within the cluster of potency scales. Note also that the interesting and meaningful scales cluster together slightly apart from the evaluation and preference groupings. However, these scales are in the same general region as preference and evaluation. The heavy-light scale is interesting in that it is clearly located within the region of the activity scales, but it is typically found in other studies within the potency scales.

When to Use What Statistic

Selecting the most appropriate statistic to use in a particular situation must be tempered by theoretical and practical considerations. Theoretically, the selection of the statistic should be based on the purpose of the research as specifically described in a research question or null hypothesis. In addition, the characteristics of the data collected will reduce the number of statistical possibilities and aid greatly in the selection of the most appropriate statistic. Practically, researchers will be limited by the computing resources available and their knowledge of statistics. The hope is that the latter limitations have been lessened somewhat by this chapter, as lack of knowledge is the weakest excuse for the application of inappropriate statistics.

The initial decision is to use either parametric or nonparametric statistics. Elsewhere in this chapter, various facets of this issue have been discussed at length. After the calculation of descriptive statistics and, possibly, the production of frequency histograms and/or box plots, the decision can be made if the sample size is sufficient and the distribution is approximately normal. In general, if these conditions are met, then parametric statistics should be applied. If not, nonparametric statistics should be applied.

The next decision is to determine the type of statistic to apply. This decision is based on the particular research question or null hypothesis that has been established to guide the research process. The choices for parametric statistics are somewhat greater than for nonparametric statistics, as can be seen in Figure 4-21.

The actual statistical procedure that is applied must be determined from both the particular null hypothesis and the type of data collected. For instance, a researcher may wish to predict from five variables, known to be normally distributed, which musical experience a student will have in high school: band, chorus, general music, orchestra. Because there is more than one predictor variable, one of two multivariate relational procedures could be applied: multiple regression or discriminant analysis. Because the dependent variable is a categorical variable that describes the group to which a person belongs, discriminant analysis would be the statistic of choice.

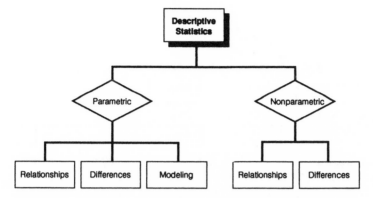

Figure 4.21. Flow chart leading to major type of statistic to be applied.

A flow chart describing the various categories of parametric statistics is contained in Figure 4-22, and a flow chart describing the various categories of nonparametric statistics is contained in Figure 4-23. These flow charts do not include all existing statistics but do cover those that have been discussed in this chapter. These statistics, the authors believe, are those that have found the greatest applicability in music education.

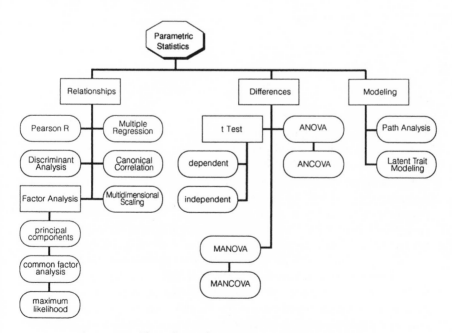

Figure 4.22. Flow chart of parametric statistic categories.

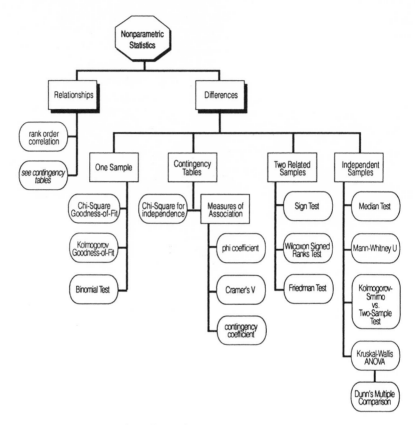

Figure 4.23. Flow chart of nonparametric statistic categories.

Conclusion

This chapter has attempted to describe quantitative methods applicable in music education. It is hoped that, by description and example, the reader has become acquainted with the variety of available quantitative and statistical procedures that can provide significant insight into musical processes. Although they are not the entirety of available quantitative methods, the procedures described here are those frequently applied in music education research, evaluation, and assessment or are those that, in the authors' belief, have significant potential to enhance knowledge about musical processes.

Today the reader need not be discouraged by the mathematical complexity of some of the procedures described here. Rather, if the researcher has selected the appropriate statistic, understands the assumptions that the statistic makes, and can interpret the results produced by the statistical procedure, modern computing power takes care of the mathematical details. This frees researchers from the tedium of the mathematics of the statistic and allows them to spend more time conceptualizing the research and understanding the implications of the results.

REFERENCES

Asher, J. W. (1976). *Educational research and evaluation methods*. Boston: Little, Brown.

Asmus, E. P. (1987). *The effects of rehearsing a musical work on the aesthetic perceptions of band students: A pilot study*. Paper presented at the Western Divisional Meeting of the Music Educators National Conference, Sacramento, April 1987.

Asmus, E. P. (1989a). Factor analysis: A look at the technique through the data of Rainbow. *Bulletin of the Council for Research in Music Education, 101,* 1–29.

Asmus, E. P. (1989b). Computer-based modeling of music concepts for testing, evaluating, and refining theory. *Psychomusicology, 8,* 171–182.

Austin, J. R. (1988). The effect of music contest format on self-concept, motivation, achievement, and attitude of elementary band students. *Journal of Research in Music Education, 36,* 95–107.

Best, J. W. (1981). *Research in education* (4th ed.). Englewood Cliffs NJ:, Prentice-Hall.

Best, J. W., & Kahn, J. V. (1989). *Research in education* (6th ed.). Englewood Cliffs, NJ: Prentice-Hall.

Blalock, H. M. (Ed.). (1985). *Casual models in the social sciences* (2nd ed.). New York: Aldine.

Borg, W. R., & Gall, M. D. (1979). *Educational research: An introduction*. New York: Longman.

Boyle, J. D. (1974). Overview. In J. D. Boyle (Comp.), *Instructional objectives in music* (pp. 79–82). Vienna: Music Educators National Conference.

Boyle, J. D., & Radocy, R. E. (1987). *Measurement and evaluation of musical experiences*. New York: Schirmer.

Bruning, J. L., & Kintz, B. L. (1977). *Computational handbook of statistics* (3rd ed.). Glenview, IL: Scott, Foresman.

Chatfield, C., & Collins, A. J. (1980). *Introduction to multivariate analysis*. London: Chapman and Hall.

Cohen, J. (1988). *Statistical power analysis for the behavioral sciences* (2nd ed.). Hillsdale, NJ: Lawrence Erlbaum.

Conover, W. J. (1980). *Practical nonparametric statistics* (2nd ed.). New York: John Wiley.

Cooley, W. W. (1978). Explanatory observational studies. *Educational Reserarcher, 7* (9), 9–15.

Cronbach, L. J. (1971). Test validation. In R. L. Thorndike (Ed.), *Educational measurement* (pp. 443–507). Washington, DC: American Council on Education.

Cureton, E. E., & D'Agostino, R. B. (1983). *Factor analysis: An applied approach*. Hillsdale, NJ: Lawrence Erlbaum.

Darrow, A., Haack, P., & Kuribayashi, F. (1987). Descriptors and preferences for Eastern and Western music by Japanese and American nonmusic majors. *Journal of Research in Music Education, 35,* 237–248.

Das, M. N., & Giri, N. C. (1986). *Design and analysis of experiments* (2nd ed.). New York: John Wiley.

Duke, R. A., & Prickett, C. A. (1987). The effect of differentially focused observation on evaluation of instruction. *Journal of Research in Music Education, 35,* 27–37.

Duncan, D. B. (1955). Multiple range and multiple F tests. *Biometrics, 11,* 1–42.

Ebel, R. L., & Frisbie, D. A. (1986). *Essentials of educational measurement* (4th ed.). Englewood Cliffs, NJ: Prentice-Hall.

Ecob, R., & Cuttance, P. (1987). An overview of structural equation modeling. In P. Cuttance & R. Ecob (Eds.), *Structural modeling by example* (pp. 9–23). Cambridge: Cambridge University Press.

Edwards, A. L. (1968). *Experimental design in psychological research* (3rd ed.). New York: Holt, Rinehart, Winston.

Finkelstein, L. (1982). Theory and philosophy of measurement. In P. H. Sydenham (Ed.), *Handbook of measurement science* (Vol. 1) (pp. 1–30); New York: John Wiley.

Flowers, P. J. (1983). The effect of instruction in vocabulary and listening on nonmusicians' descriptions of changes in music. *Journal of Research in Music Education, 31,* 179–189.

Flowers, P. J. (1988). The effects of teaching and learning experiences, tempo, and mode on undergraduates, and children's symphonic music preferences. *Journal of Research in Music Education, 36,* 19–34.

Flowers, P. J., & Dunne-Sousa, D. (1990). Pitch-pattern accuracy, tonality, and vocal range in preschool children's singing. *Journal of Research in Music Education, 38,* 102–114.

Gfeller, K., Darrow, A., & Hedden, S. K. (1990). Perceived effectiveness of mainstreaming in Iowa and Kansas schools. *Journal of Research in Music Education, 38,* 90–101.

Gibbons, J. D. (1985). *Nonparametric methods for quantitative analysis* (2nd ed.). Columbus, OH: American Science Press.

Glass, G. V., & Hopkins, K. D. (1984). *Statistical methods in education and psychology.* Englewood Cliffs, NJ: Prentice-Hall.

Goodstein, R. E. (1987). An introduction to discriminant analysis. *Journal of Research in Music Education, 35,* 7–11.

Gorsuch, R. L. (1983). *Factor analysis* (2nd ed.). Hillsdale, NJ: Lawrence Erlbaum.

Green, P. E., Carmone, Jr., F. J., & Smith, S. M. (1989). *Multidimensional scaling: Concepts and applications.* Boston: Allyn and Bacon.

Hair, J. F., Anderson, R. E., Tatham, R. L., & Grablowsky, B. J. (1984). *Multivariate data analysis with readings.* New York: Macmillan.

Hanneman, R. (1988). *Computer-assisted theory building: Modeling dynamic social systems.* Newbury Park, CA: Sage.

Harnett, D. L. (1982). *Statistical methods* (3rd ed.). Reading, MA: Addison-Wesley.

Harris, R. J. (1985). *A primer of multivariate statistics.* Orlando, FL: Academic Press.

Harrison, C. S. (1990a). Relationships between grades in the components of freshman music theory and selected background variables. *Journal of Research in Music Education, 38,* 175–186.

Harrison, C. S. (1990b). Predicting music theory grades: The relative efficiency of academic ability, music experience, and musical aptitude. *Journal of Research in Music Education, 38,* 124–137.

Hays, W. L. (1988). *Statistics* (4th ed.). New York: Holt, Rinehart, and Winston.

Hedden, S. K. (1982). Prediction of musical achievement in the elementary school. *Journal of Research in Music Education, 30,* 61–68.

Heller, G. N., & Radocy, R. E. (1983). On the significance: Addressing a basic problem in research. *Bulletin of the Council for Research in Music Education, 73,* 50–58.

Johnson, T. J., & Hess, R. J. (1970). *Tests in the arts.* St. Charles, IL: Central Midwestern Regional Educational Laboratory.

Jöreskog, K. G. (1979). Structural equation models in the social sciences: Specification, estimation and testing. In K. Jöreskog & D. Sörbom (Eds.), *Advances in factor analysis and structural equation models* (pp. 105–127). Cambridge: Abt.

Jöreskog, K. G. (1982). The LISREL approach to causal model-building in the social sciences. In K. G. Jöreskog & H. Wold (Eds.), *Systems under indirect observation: Casuality—structure—prediction* (pp. 81–99). Amsterdam: North-Holland.

Jöreskog, K. G., & Sörbom, D. (1989), LISREL 7.0 [Computer program]. Lincolnwood, IL: Scientific Software.

Kachigan, S. K. (1986). *Statistical analysis: An interdisciplinary introduction to univariate and multivariate methods.* New York: Radius.

Kaiser, H. F., & Rice, J. (1974). Little Jiffy, Mark IV. *Educational and Psychological Measurement, 34,* 111–117.

Kantorski, V. J. (1986). String instrument intonation in upper and lower registers: The effects of accompaniment. *Journal of Research in Music Education, 34,* 200–210.

Kendall, M. J. (1988). Two instructional approaches to the development of aural and instrumental performance skills: *Journal of Research in Music Education, 36,* 205–219.

Kerlinger, F. N., & Pedhazur, E. J. (1982). *Multiple regression in behavioral research: Explanation and prediction* (2nd ed.). New York: Holt, Rinehart, and Winston.

Kirk, R. E. (1982). *Experimental design: Procedures for the behavioral sciences* (2nd ed.). Monterey, CA: Brooks/Cole.

Kruskal, J. B., & Wish, M. (1978). *Multidimensional scaling.* Beverly Hills, CA: Sage.

Kuhn, T. L., & Booth, G. D. (1988). The effect of melodic activity, tempo change, and audible beat on tempo perception of elementary school students. *Journal of Research in Music Education, 36,* 140–155.

Larson, R. C. (1977). Relationships between melodic error detection, melodic dictation, and melodic sightsinging. *Journal of Research in Music Education, 25,* 264–271.

LeBlanc, A., Colman, J., McCrary, J., Sherrill, C., & Malin, S. (1988). Tempo preferences of different age music listeners. *Journal of Research in Music Education, 36,* 156–168.

Lehman, P. R. (1968). *Tests and measurements in music.* Englewood Cliffs, NJ: Prentice-Hall.

Leonhard, C. (1958). Evaluation in music education. In N. B. Henry (Ed.), *Basic concepts in music education* (The 57th year book of the National Society for the Study of Education). Chicago: University of Chicago Press.

Li, J.C.R. (1964). *Statistical inference I.* Ann Arbor, MI: Edwards Brothers.

Lord, F., & Novick, R. L. (1968). *Statistical theories of mental test scores.* Reading, MA: Addison-Wesley.

Lunneborg, C. E., & Abbot, R. D. (1983). *Elementary multivariate analysis for the behavioral sciences.* New York: North-Holland.

Madsen, C. K., & Madsen, C. H. (1978). *Experimental research in music.* Raleigh, NC: Contemporary.

Madsen, C. K., & Moore, R. S. (1978). *Experimental research in music: Workbook in design and statistical tests.* Raleigh, NC: Contemporary.

May, W. V. (1985). Musical style preferences and aural discrimination skills of primary grade school children. *Journal of Research in Music Education, 32,* 7–22.

Miller, R. (1989). An introduction to multidimensional scaling for the study of musical perception. *Bulletin of the Council for Research in Music Education, 102,* 60–73.

Moore, D. S. (1988). *Statistics: Concepts and controversies* (2nd ed.). New York: W. H. Freeman.

Moore, R. S. (1976). The effects of videotaped feedback and self-evaluation forms on teaching skills, musicianship and creativity of prospective elementary teachers. *Bulletin of the Council for Research in Music Education, 47,* 1–7.

Muirhead, R. J. (1982). *Aspects of multivariate statistical theory.* New York: John Wiley.

Nunnally, J. C. (1978). *Psychometric theory* (2nd ed.). New York: McGraw-Hill.

Payne, D. A. (1982). Measurement in education. In H. E. Mitzel (Ed.) *Encyclopedia of educational research* (5th ed.; Vol. 3). New York: Free Press.

Phelps, R. P. (1986). *A guide to research in music education* (3rd ed.). Metuchen, NJ: Scarecrow.

Price, H. E. (1988). The effect of a music appreciation course on students' verbally expressed preferences for composers. *Journal of Research in Music Education, 36,* 35–46.

Price, H. E., & Swanson, P. (1990). Changes in musical attitudes, opinions, and knowledge of music appreciation students. *Journal of Research in Music Education, 38,* 39–48.

Puri, M. L., & Sen, P. K. (1971). Nonparametric methods in multivariate analysis. New York: John Wiley.

Radocy, R. E. (1986). On quantifying the uncountable in musical behavior. *Bulletin of the Council for Research in Music Education, 88,* 22–31.

Rainbow, E. L., & Froehlich, H. C. (1987). Research in music education. New York: Schirmer Books

SAS Institute. (1989). *JMP: Software for statistical visualization* [Computer program]. Cary NC: SAS Institute.

Sax, G. (1979). *Foundations of educational research.* Englewood Cliffs, NJ: Prentice-Hall.

Scheffé, H. A. (1953). A method for judging all contrasts in the analysis of variance. *Biometrika, 40,* 87–104.

Seashore, C. E. (1936). The objective recording and analysis of musical performance. In C. E. Seashore (Ed.), *Objective analysis of musical performance* (pp. 5–11). Iowa City: *University* Press.

Seashore, C. E., Lewis, D., & Saetveit, J. (1960). *Seashore measures of musical talents*. New York: Psychological Corporation. (Original publication in 1939)

Sheth, J. N. (1984). How to get the most out of multivariate methods. In J. F. Hair, R. E. Anderson, R. L. Tatham, & B. J. Grablowsky (Eds.), *Multivariate data analysis with readings* (pp. 19–29). New York: Macmillan.

Siegel, S. (1956). *Nonparametric statistics for the behavioral sciences*. New York: McGraw-Hill.

Siegel, S., & Castellan, N. J. (1988). *Nonparametric statistics for the behavioral sciences* (2nd ed.). New York: McGraw-Hill.

Simon, H. A. (1985). Spurious correlation: A causal interpretation. In H. M. Blalock (Ed.), *Causal models in the social sciences* (2nd ed., pp. 7–21). New York: Aldine.

SPSS. (1988). *SPSS^x user's guide* (3rd ed.). Chicago: SPSS.

Stanley, J. C. (1971). Reliability. In R. L. Thorndike (Ed.), *Educational measurement* (2nd ed.). Washington, DC: American Council on Education.

Stevens, S. S. (1959). Measurement, psychophysics, and utility. In C. W. Churchman & P. Ratoosh (Eds.), *Measurement definitions and theories* (pp. 18–63). New York: John Wiley.

Stevens, S. S. (1975). *Psychophysics*. New York: John Wiley.

Tatsuoka, M. M., & Lohnes, P. R. (1988). *Multivariate analysis: Techniques for educational and psychological research* (2nd ed.). New York: Macmillan.

Whybrew, W. E. (1971). *Measurement and evaluation in music*. Dubuque, 10: Wm. C. Brown.

Wike, E. L. (1971). *Data analysts*. Chicago: Aldine-Atherton.

Wilks, S. S. (1961). Some aspects of quantification in science. In H. Woolf (Ed.), *Quantification: A history of the measurement in the natural and social sciences (pp. 5–12)*. Indianapolis: Bobbs-Merrill.

Winer, B. J. (1971). *Statistical principles in experimental design* (2nd ed.). New York: McGraw-Hill.

Winkler, R. L., & Hays, W. L. (1975). *Statistics: Probability, inference and decision* (2nd ed.). New York: Holt, Rinehart and Winston.

Wright, S. (1921). Correlation and causation. *Journal of Agricultural Research, 20,* 557–585.

Young, F. W. (1987). *Multidimensional scaling: History, theory, and applications*. Hillsdale, NJ: Lawrence Erlbaum.

On Philosophical Method

ESTELLE R. JORGENSEN

The doing of philosophy is characterized by certain features or conditions that can be recognized despite differences in individual style, rigor, or orientation.[1] These features are described in terms of how philosophy functions, and I call them "symptoms of the philosophical" because they constitute a profile of aspects that are present to a greater or lesser degree and indicate that philosophy is taking place.[2]

Each of these symptoms will be sketched in turn, with examples cited from the philosophical literatures in aesthetics, education, and music education—literatures from which philosophy of music education properly draws.[3] Some methodological differences between philosophers will then be outlined, followed by remarks on the implications of the analysis for doing philosophy in music education.

Symptoms of the Philosophical

Among other things, philosophy clarifies its terms, exposes and evaluates underlying assumptions, relates its parts as a systematized theory that connects with other ideas and systems of thought, and addresses questions that are characteristically philosophical.

Philosophy Clarifies Its Terms

The philosopher is vitally concerned with the meaning of words because words are the vehicles for communicating ideas. To select the right words is to clarify meaning and sharpen and refine the ideas being expressed. Although ambiguity, vagueness, and figurative language are common features of discourse, the philosopher works to ensure the greatest possible precision in meaning by clarifying the denotation and significance of words used. Without vigilance, ideas in any system of thought are cluttered and untidy, their meaning unnecessarily vague and ambiguous, making it difficult to compare ideas and systems of thought because one is uncertain of what is being compared. The philosopher's function is to ensure that the house of ideas is tidy.

Questions such as What is the nature of music? What is the nature of education? What is the nature of music education? are important to music education because clarifying terms illuminate interrelationships and connections between ideas. For example, if two studies of musical appreciation are compared, unless one has a basis for believing that the expression *musical appreciation* means the same in each case, the comparison does not make sense; the two studies may be about different things.

Clarifying terms also enables one to critique ideas. Such a critique is ineffective unless the meanings of the terms used are as clear as the language permits. Where ambiguities exist (and Scheffler [1979] reminds us that they play an important part in discourse), the philosopher may simply acknowledge and clarify ambiguities qua ambiguities, and explore the richness they may offer. Having clarified one's terms, one can compare one's ideas with those of another, see points of similarity and difference, weakness and strength, and thereby critique both sets of ideas. Critical dialogue not only illumines one's thinking through sharpening and focusing the meaning attributed to a given term, but it enables careful adjudication of the ideas of others about this term. Through continued criticism, terms used within the field of discourse become more precise in their meaning, understandings become more widely shared, and justifications for positions held are better defended.

To return to our example of musical appreciation, a critique of Scholes's (1935), Wing's (1968), or Crickmore's (1968) concepts of musical appreciation is possible only to the extent that each writer clarifies what musical appreciation means, and that the critic's own concept of music appreciation is clear. Normal usage may constitute a basis on which a term comes to have meaning, as is certainly the case with the notion of musical appreciation. The philosopher, however, is not content to let the matter rest here and asks such questions as: What ambiguities are present in normal usage of the term *music appreciation*? What do Scholes, Wing, and Crickmore understand by musical appreciation? What weaknesses and strengths characterize their ideas? How do their concepts of musical appreciation stand up to scrutiny in relation to philosophical literature about the nature of musical experience? What specific features ought to characterize musical appreciation? How does such a philosophical view of musical appreciation illumine the common practical usage of the term? What does the philosophical or the common usage concept of musical appreciation imply for instructional practice, for measurement of musical appreciation, and for the identification of factors that might denote it?

Clarifying one's terms enables studies to be devised that utilize these ideas in research and apply them in practice. Not only can the ideas be critiqued, but so, too, can the research methods that purport to measure or use them and the applications that ostensibly follow from them. Here, one can move beyond questions of reliability to those of validity and achieve a penetrating critique of the significance of a particular study or the appropriateness of a given practical application.

For example, tests of musical appreciation such as those developed by Wing (1968) and Crickmore (1968) can be compared with a given concept of musical appreciation and evaluated not only with respect to the reliability of the measurement scales but also with respect to their validity—that is, whether these tests are in fact measuring musical appreciation or something else. Also, courses that purport to develop musical appreciation can be compared with the concept of musical appreciation, and judgments made as to whether they are accomplishing what they should in terms of the denotation of musical appreciation.

Philosophers often make taxonomies or classifications of the various phenomena they are studying. They do this in order to make distinctions and show similarities and differences not only between different things but within a particular thing. Several examples may be cited. Meyer (1956) distinguishes between various apposed views of the location and character of musical meaning. By way of showing the "morphology" of the musical symbol, Epperson (1967) posits a hierarchy of four orders of musical abstraction in western classical music, the first being the easiest to access and the most particular, the fourth and most abstract being the most difficult to access and most universal. Kivy (1984) develops a taxonomy of musical representations running from the most clearly recognized to the most abstract. And Howard (1982) differentiates various kinds of teacher talk and action involved in communicating to students how to perform music.

Although at first glance some distinctions may seem to be quite fine and of minor significance, upon reflection their importance becomes apparent. For example, Kivy (1980) distinguishes between music as *expressive of* and *as an expression of* emotions, holding that western classical music is expressive of emotion. This distinction is crucial in clarifying various points of view about emotion's specific role in Western classical music and other world musics, and evaluating respective philosophical positions. That Kivy makes this distinction and argues the merits of his position enables subsequent philosophical discussion that further illumines the nature of musical meaning.

The rigor of distinction making has been less evident in music education than it should be. For example, his important work in bringing philosophy and advocacy to the attention of the music education community notwithstanding. Reimer (1989) uncritically borrows Meyer's (1956) taxonomy of musical meaning and Langer's (1942, 1953) view of artistic symbolism, thereby failing to take sufficient account of the social context in which individuals are socialized into particular understandings of music. His philosophy, therefore, has restricted application to Western school music and does not adequately address artistic aspects of music making, the plethora of world musical traditions, and matters relating to music education conceived of as lifelong experience, ranging from the most elemental to advanced levels of musical instruction. Also, in the absence of further elaboration, Reimer's discussion of the ideas of various philosophers as representative philosophical "schools" tends to caricature their positions rather than clarify differences and similarities between them.[4] Philosophers in music education need to better clarify the meaning of the concepts they employ, and make more penetrating distinctions than they have in the past.

Similarly, descriptive and experimental research in music education could benefit from considerable work in clarifying terms. In much music education research, definitional issues are hastily worked through and concepts borrowed from other fields such as psychology without sufficient consideration as to their meaning. Factor analysis and other statistical techniques are frequently relied upon to clarify the meaning of terms that are then applied within empirical studies. For example, while his efforts in grappling with conceptual and empirical issues are important, in his essay on musical appreciation Crickmore (1968) hurries past a host of philosophical problems implied within the concept of musical appreciation to develop a test to measure something that still remains unclear. If one were now to use Crickmore's musical appreciation test in an empirical study to compare children's musical appreciation in terms of such variables as socioeconomic status, age level, and gender, one would further compound the problem. This is precisely the way in which much descriptive and experimental work in music education is conducted. Statistical analysis cannot substitute for philosophical critique. The function of statistics is to *test* hypotheses, not to *generate* them; that is the work of philosophy. As Goodman (1976, p. 264) reminds us, empirical evidence is a matter of goodness of "fit": fit of the model to the evidence, and the evidence to the model. Without a clearly articulated model to test, a piece of descriptive or experimental research, no matter how cleverly designed, is unscientific and invalid (cf. Gibboney, 1989).

Philosophy Exposes and Evaluates Underlying Assumptions

Assumptions predicate and underlie action. They consist of beliefs held to be true, taken for granted and acted on. All action is predicated on assumptive sets that may be more or less implicit or explicit. In the process of exposing and evaluating underlying assumptions, the philosopher makes explicit that which otherwise may remain implicit, and clarifies aspects that are prior to and deeper than the actions to which they give rise. As a physician seeks to treat an illness' underlying causes rather than only its symptoms, so the philosopher explicates and exposes the root causes, reasons, and presuppositions of action rather than only its manifestations.

Translating assumptions into practice is difficult. Explicit or implicit assumptions are sometimes highly general and may be transposed into a variety of specific actions, each of which may imply differing and sometimes conflicting specific assumptive sets. In the course of translating theory into practice, one must frequently reconcile desired alternatives with possible or practical alternatives in a particular set of circumstances. This involves bringing together things that are in tension—a process that may not be easy to achieve—so that theory and practice may not have a one-to-one correspondence. Schwab (1971) denotes this complex process whereby one reconciles the variety of potential visions of a particular situation, each of which implies a correspondingly varied assortment of practical implications, as the "arts of eclectic."

To expose implicit or unclear underlying assumptions, one utilizes critical and analytical thinking in reasoning from effect to cause. Critical thinking involves the capacity to judge the relative worth of actions and ideas. Analytical thinking entails the ability to take a situation or an idea apart much as a mechanic takes an engine apart. One separates its constituent elements, makes judgments about the significance of those elements, and speculates about the various causes that might have led to a particular thing. This kind of speculative thinking is not undisciplined but is guided by logical and moral rules. Logical rules enable consistency within the analysis itself, whereas moral rules provide consistency of the analysis with the mores of the society or social group. Assumptions lie beneath the surface at various levels like the levels in an archeological dig, and one comes to an understanding of them rationally, intuitively, and imaginatively. Once they have been grasped, though, one can systematically engage in a penetrating critique of each model and deduce those implications that necessarily follow from the analysis. One can then see how they compare, which features are better or worse than others, and how aspects of each may be melded with others.

Evaluating underlying assumptions requires criteria by which these assumptions may be judged. Appeals to precedent, weight of authority, logic, moral claims, realism of expectations, ease of application, and aesthetic appeal are among the criteria by which the worth of assumptions may be adjudicated.

Exposing and evaluating underlying assumptions within music education serve some important purposes. Clarifying that which is implicit or unclear facilitates a more penetrating analysis than would be possible without such clarification. Suppose that a school district plans to adopt a particular course in musical appreciation for children aged 12 to 15 years. Beyond considerations of the material's age-appropriateness and the measurement of learning gain that may result from taking the course are basic questions about the course's underlying assumptions: What is the author's concept of musical appreciation? On what philosophical grounds is its author's concept defensible? What does the course assume about the ways in which its author believes musical appreciation can be taught and learned? On what grounds can one justify the author's chosen methods? These, among other questions, go beyond an analysis of the course content and its measured effects to look at the factors prior to and behind it, and in so doing reveal the central issues of causation and motivation, offering the tools to answer such questions as Why is this position being taken? Should it be endorsed?

Explicating assumptions assists in deciding between alternatives. Because education involves selecting alternatives in the worlds of ideas and practice that are ultimately defended philosophically as well as practically, the alternatives must be as clear as possible. For example, one might ask, Is the goal of school music education the development of musical appreciation, composition, or performance? Which is the most desirable alternative? If all are desirable, how are the competing claims of the alternatives to be reconciled? How does one music appreciation curriculum compare with another? The answers to these questions are predicated upon an exposition and evaluation of the underlying assumptions.

Various examples of philosophers exposing and evaluating underlying assumptions may be cited. Dewey (1916, 1938/1963) clarifies the assumptions underlying two approaches to education: a traditional conservative approach rooted in the past and a progressive forward-looking approach utilizing new and different educational methods. Scheffler (1973, pp. 67–81) analyzes the assumptions underlying three philosophical models of teaching based on the ideas of John Locke, St. Augustine, and Immanual Kant. And Alperson (1991) outlines the assumptions underlying three alternative strategies for developing a philosophy of music education and systematically critiques each position.

There has been little analysis of this sort in music education. While some of the suggested approaches to music education have a relatively articulated philosophical basis (e.g., Suzuki, 1969; Kodály, 1974; Jaques-Dalcroze, 1921/1976), their development has arisen from, and discussions of their merit turn principally on, practical issues rather than the assumptions on which they are based. Such debate as has occurred has seldom benefited from incisive philosophical analysis of underlying assumptions. Teachers have defended their chosen method(s) on the basis of personally held opinions rather than dispassionately reasoned arguments. Many believe that a combination of methods will automatically yield a wider and superior view of music education than just one method, despite the fact that the assumptions on which the methods rest may be contradictory (Jorgensen, 1990).

Were the underlying assumptions of these methods to be systematically explicated, not only would they be better articulated and defended than they are now, but conflicting assumption sets would be exposed and teachers would better understand which methods can or should be combined in given circumstances, and why. Descriptive and experimental researchers would also benefit from such clarification by having access to theories in which methods are carefully described and philosophically grounded.

Philosophy Relates Its Parts as a Systematized Theory That Connects With Other Ideas and Systems of Thought

Philosophers seek to construct a body of thought that coheres as a whole yet is structurally organized. Their observations are not isolated phenomena but constitute a systematically analyzed whole. All the parts are present that are needed to form the whole. Every part is necessary and relevant to the whole, and no part is extraneous. Each part is logically consistent with every other part. As such, this body of thought is like a work of art. It is like Langer's (1953) concept of the work of art as a "highly articulated" object, in that its parts seem to fuse to form a whole and yet have a separate existence, so that one understands the whole as well as the constituent parts.

As a systematized theory, the body of thought that the philosopher constructs is intended to have explanatory value. It is purposeful in its clarification of terms and exposition and evaluation of underlying assumptions. Further, it is systematic in its attempt to order that which may otherwise be chaotic. The analogy of the philosopher as the architect of the house, the designer of the ideas that account for a given phenomenon in a meaningful way, suggests that the philosopher articulates the frames of reference within which one sees the world or one's version of it. Through a methodical and careful explication, the philosopher clarifies ideas that may be ambiguous and in disarray, and designs a conceptual framework that is not only ordered but insightful.

Moreover, this system of thought is not isolated but integrated within, or related to, other systems of thought in ways that are clarified by the philosopher. As such, it connects or corresponds to these other systems, be they ideas or phenomena in the empirical world. The evidence of this correspondence may be of varying kinds, including logical argument, appeals to authority, precedent, example, or analogy. In the scientific worldview, empirical data constitute the most persuasive evidence. In the philosophical worldview, however, other nonscientific ways of knowing may be equally or more persuasive, and the philosopher admits as evidence that which the scientist may exclude.

Philosophers are inveterate gatherers and cites of examples. Although they differ about the roles examples serve, as we shall see later, philosophers agree that examples are essential to illustrate and test their ideas. Kivy's attempt to clarify the nature of musical expression and representation, to show that musical meaning is found within and without the musical piece, is grounded in examples. In *The Corded Shell* (1980), one encounters Lilian, the St. Bernard dog; and in *Music Alone* (1990), the cast of characters from E. M. Forster's *Howard's End*—Mrs. Munt, Helen, Margaret, and Tibby. These serve not only as examplars but also as analogies of, or metaphors for, aspects of musical experience. Likewise, Goodman (1976) makes extensive use of examples in his *Languages of Art*. In distinguishing exemplification as a symbol function, for example, he uses a swatch of cloth, the centaur, Pickwick, Don Quixote, and Pegasus, and metaphors (e.g., "Metaphor, it seems, is a matter of teaching an old word new tricks," p. 69) to make his points. When he speaks of gestures, Goodman cites the example of the orchestra conductor whose gestures "denote sounds to be produced but are not themselves sounds" (p. 61).

Creating a systematized theory that relates to other systems of thought connects the various ways of knowing, be they scientific, artistic, religious, philosophical, or otherwise. Establishing these connections achieves a broader perspective on the world. The scientific way of knowing is only one of a plethora of ways in which we understand ourselves and our world. As we relate these ways of knowing to each other, we come to understand that the realities they address are different, complementary, and intersecting. Restricting one's vision to a particular way of knowing results in a limited view of one's self and the world.

Moreover, such a systematized theory serves to explain why things are as they are, or as they appear to be, in terms of a philosophical worldview. Philosophers' explanations help to illumine the nature of self and the world, one manifestation of the human tendency to reflect on one's place in the world. These philosophical explanations have their own validity, quite apart from questions of how well they interface with other scientific, artistic, or religious explanations: They ultimately are judged in their own terms.

The implications for a philosophy of music education are profound. Not only should it exemplify the characteristics of a systematic theory that relates to other systems of thought (educational, artistic, religious, scientific, or otherwise), but also it should ultimately be judged in philosophical, not scientific terms. Science may *enhance* philosophy, but it cannot constitute the *ultimate test* of it. Many philosophical propositions lie outside science's purview and are justified in nonscientific ways. This is not to say that science is unimportant in the study of music education. Quite the contrary. Philosophy draws on science and science on philosophy; each illumines the other. However, one is not judged in terms of the other. Science ultimately judges science; and philosophy, philosophy. Consequently, explanation in music education is understood to be multifaceted rather than monolithic: As nonscientific ways of knowing complement scientific ways of knowing, so music education is properly studied scientifically and nonscientifically. Philosophy thus assumes a central place alongside science in music education research. Such a position requires rethinking the methods of inquiry appropriate to the study of music education and philosophy's place in music education research.

Various examples of philosophers constructing theories that connect with other systems of ideas exist. Schelling (in translation, 1989) proposes a grand schema (to show that the arts, sciences, and social phenomena are emanations of a single absolute) that moves from general principles to specific aspects of the various arts. He follows in the tradition of Plato and Kant, and his ideas relate particularly to those of other German writers such as Schopenhauer (in translation, 1969) and Hegel (in translation, 1975). Langer (1967, 1972, 1982) develops not only a theory of art but also, importantly, a theory of the mind. She constructs an argument within the framework of such ideas as the nature, meaning, and significance of artistic symbols; the virtuality of time and space in artistic apprehension; and the nature of feeling as the basis for artistic cognition. Her work is in the tradition of Kant, Ludwig Wittgenstein, and Ernst Cassirer, and relates especially to the ideas of Dewey (1934/1979) and Meyer (1956), among others. Adorno (1984) elaborates a theory that examines the relevance of aesthetic categories such as form, beauty, truth, content, and objectification and places the arts within the context of society. His aesthetic theory is opposed to those of Plato, Kant, and Sigmund Freud, among others, and his ideas relate especially to the work of such musicians and philosophers as Busoni (1911/1962) and Bloch (in translation, 1985). Goodman (1976) articulates a theory of symbols in which the arts function as symbol systems or ways of world making. Throughout, he compares his ideas to those of such writers as René Descartes, Jerome Bruner, Émile Jaques-Dalcroze, and Joseph Margolis; and his theory-as-a-whole can be related to the work of various philosophers involved in the study of musical semiotics (see Rantala, Rowell, and Tarasti, 1986; Margolis 1986). Although traditions of documentation vary from one philosopher to another, all place themselves in the context of a philosophical tradition. Even if they specify little about that tradition, an inspection of their ideas and the writers to whom they refer indicates something of the particular traditions from which they draw and to which they contribute.

Relatively few systematic theories of music education have emerged in the twentieth century. Among these, a noteworthy study appears in Small's *Music-Society-Education* (1980). Drawing from two historical paradigms of music and society (the traditional Western and "potential" worldviews), Small derives implications for music education and proposes that music education's task is to *reconstruct* culture as well as *transmit* it. His reconceptualist (see Pinar, 1975) view of the music curriculum resonates with work in ethnomusicology, musical anthropology, and sociology by such writers as Merriam (1964), Blacking (1976), Shepherd, Virden, Vulliamy, and Wishart, (1977), Frith (1978), and Nettl (1985). Following a discussion of the assumptions underlying the potential society that he believes music prophesies and to which he suggests music educators should aspire. Small develops a model of music education that features an international, inclusive, cooperative, and egalitarian approach to music making within the context of world musics that contrasts with the parochial, exclusive, competitive, and hierarchical approach to music making in the Western classical tradition.

Music education would benefit from the development of paradigms that reflect the variety of world musics, the international pervasiveness of music education, its multidisciplinary nature, its relevance to the entire life cycle, under the auspices of the various social institutions that carry it forward. Historically, music educators in search of the boundaries of their field have settled for a definition that is pragmatically rather than philosophically grounded. Music education has been construed mainly as musical instruction in Western-style elementary and secondary schools, simply because this is what many music educators do. This limited definition excludes much that properly concerns the interrelationship of music and education.

A more inclusive view suggests that music education is both music in education and education in music, a fusion of two essential elements in a synthesis or integrated whole.[5] The philosopher's challenge is to balance alternative emphases on music and education. An accent on music may devote insufficient attention to the process whereby musical understanding is educed and to music's place in the larger educational enterprise. A focus on education may place inadequate stress on musical knowledge and education's place in the larger musical enterprise. However, a recognition of music education as both education in music and music in education affords a balanced yet broad understanding of the interrelationship of music and education.

Philosophy Addresses Questions That Are Characteristically Philosophical

As a way of understanding, philosophy addresses questions that differ from those of other ways of knowing, be they artistic, scientific, religious, or otherwise. These questions make up a profile of interests and concerns that are typically philosophical.

Ontological questions have to do with the nature of being and reality. For example, When does music occur? Is it the idea in the composer's head, the notes in the score, the musical performance at a given place and time, or the listener's sensations of sound? What is the nature of the musical experience? What is the nature of the educational experience? For example, Kivy (1990) posits various types of musical experience in the listener to Western instrumental classical music, arguing that there is a quantitative rather than a qualitative difference in the experience from the most elemental to advanced levels of training. Sessions (1950/1962) describes three different types of musical experience—those of the composer, performer, and listener. Dewey (1916, 1938/1963) depicts educational experience as potentially educative or miseducative, as the reconciliation of various tensions (doing and undergoing, taking advantage of present desire while also envisioning future possibilities, interfacing person and subject matter, focusing on means and ends, resolving freedom and control, reconciling tradition and change, and balancing the individual's needs with those of the group).

Epistemological questions relate to the nature of knowing and understanding.[6] For example, How does one come to know music? What is the nature of the knowledge implied in understanding music? How is learning educed? Bruner (1963) posits that an understanding of the structure of any subject (whereby one experientially grasps the underlying assumptions, conceptual framework, and methods of inquiry in the subject matter) enables one to gain meaningful knowledge of the material. Like Eisner (1985) and others, Bruner (1979, 1986) holds that the arts provide ways of knowing that contrast with those of the sciences, and constitute distinct forms of knowledge and perspectives on the world that are uniquely aesthetic or artistic. With Shepherd and others (Shepherd et al., 1977), Bruner (1973, 1986) sees all the symbol systems on which education is based—those of language, music, art, drama, religion, among others—as culturally mediated, and interpreted in corporate or collective as well as individual or personal ways. Although various composers and philosophers agree that music is understood in its own terms in ways that are characteristically musical, there is considerable philosophical disagreement over the precise nature of musical meaning (whether propositional or otherwise), and its location (within or outside the music itself).

Axiological questions regard matters of valuation. For example, Is Western classical music "better" than other Western genres? Are the arts a necessary part of education or just nice to have (see Broudy, 1979)? Which musical skills are of greatest importance? For example, on musical values, Blacking (1976), Shepherd et al. (1977), Small (1980), Fletcher (1987), Frith (1987), and Swanwick (1988) argue that because the values underlying Western classical music do not apply universally to all world musics, music education today must incorporate a variety of musics within the classroom, thereby offering various sets of artistic or aesthetic value systems. Budd (1985) suggests that a new theory of musical valuation is needed. Such a theory would assist teachers in choosing examples for study from a wide array of world musics. The plethora of educational values concerning the arts is illustrated in the contrasting positions of Aristotle (*Works of Aristotle*, 1921), for whom the arts need have no use other than that they enable people to enjoy their lives, and Locke (in a 1913 edition), who is determined that every educational aspect shall have a particular vocational use, thereby marginalizing the arts or excluding them altogether.

Ethical questions refer to the underlying social mores and rules of a given society or social group. For example, When is an elitist system of music education preferable to a universalistic one? How should teachers relate to students? Several examples will illustrate. Peters (1966) grapples with such issues as the concept of education as initiation into a way of life that society's members believe to be worthwhile, the nature of education's ethical foundations and the justifications invoked, and problems of social control. Arguments linking music as one of the arts to "the good" as an educational end go back to antiquity. Plato (*Collected Dialogues of Plato*, 1961) believes that a particular moral quality is associated with any given piece of music. Kant (in translation, 1952) holds that beauty functions as a symbol of the good, and thereby refers to it. Schiller (in translation, 1967) posits that the arts constitute the means whereby the good can be implied before it is understood conceptually, and the way by which the person who has yet to attain full moral development imaginatively or intuitively grasps the idea of the good. Beardsmore (1971) argues that the arts provide an understanding of what the good is. While it is not the artist's intention to moralize, the work of art nevertheless illumines the nature of the good.

Logical questions relate to the rules for reasoning, be they deductive, inductive, analogical, or however conceived. For example, Is this particular justification for music education well taken? Are there logical flaws in this argument? Is this musical curriculum consistent with the theoretical principles it purports to espouse? In their analyses of Kant's aesthetic theory, such writers as Crawford (1974) and McCloskey (1987) expose the logical problems and point to evident strengths they see in Kant's argument. Scheffler (1973) outlines the role of logic in educational decision making, and his analysis of Schwab's curriculum theory constitutes a useful model for examining logical and other aspects of an argument. Budd (1985) exposes some of the logical flaws in arguments about the relationship of music and the emotions by Schopenhauer, Langer, Meyer, and others.

Political questions have to do with issues of governance and social order. For example, How can this theoretical model be applied in practice? How should democratic principles translate into the music classroom? Who should control music education? We see political questions exemplified in the work of Dewey (1916, 1927) and Read (1958), for whom education constitutes the means of preparing citizens for the democracy and the arts the key to its preservation. Notwithstanding its detractions, Dewey holds, democracy illustrates principles of freedom and social control that should be upheld within the classroom. Read argues that the arts are central to the educational process: Only as people are artists will they be fully actualized and productive and cooperative members of society. Discussions of the interface of the arts and politics are also found in the work of such writers as Fischer (1963), Barzun (1974), Taylor (1978), Attali (1985), and Eagleton (1990).

Aesthetic or artistic questions refer to considerations of what is beautiful and how beauty is to be adjudicated. For example, What is a work of art? How does one relate to it? Are there universal aesthetic criteria? What is the nature of artistry? Among the philosophers to explore these sorts of problems, Hanslick (in translation, 1986) examines the nature and basis of beauty in music, Prall (1929, 1936) investigates the nature of aesthetic judgment and analysis, Beardsley (1981) grapples with problems in the philosophy of art criticism, Dahlhaus (1982, 1985) discusses aspects of musical aesthetics as evidenced in the history of Western classical music and the nature of nineteenth-century aesthetic realism, and Ecker and her colleagues (Ecker, 1985) articulate aspects of a feminist aesthetic. Although most philosophers focus on aesthetic apprehension, studies by Howard (1982) and Wolterstorff (1986) are among a comparatively few philosophical studies of the work of musical artists.[7]

These philosophical question sets address a wide range of issues in music education. Their common point of reference is their challenge to the validity of extant ideas and practices: They systematically ask whether these ideas and practices are well grounded. They bypass the peripheral and trivial issues, going to the core of *why* things are as they seem to be and where they seem to be going. As such, they address central questions relating to music education and challenge its very reason for being. That such question sets are already philosophically well established enables philosophers to clarify their terms, expose and evaluate assumptions, and develop systematic bodies of thought that connect with other ideas in respect to a wide range of issues touching on music education.

Differences in Approaches

I have sketched symptoms of the philosophical that more or less exemplify the work of philosophy. Philosophers disagree about aspects of how philosophy should be done. To illustrate, I shall briefly outline three interrelated and overlapping sets of contrasting positions—phenomenology/positivism, deduction/induction, and synopsis/analysis—reflecting differences in epistemological stance, perspectives on reasoning, and purposes of doing philosophy, respectively.

Phenomenology and Positivism

Reese (1980, p. 428) succinctly describes *phenomenology*, from the Greek *phainomenon* ("appearance") and *logos* ("knowledge of"), as "an approach to philosophy centering on analysis of the phenomena that flood [human] awareness." One of the principal architects of twentieth-century phenomenology is Husserl (in translation, 1931; see Sokolowski, 1988), who regards consciousness as an integral part of reality rather than as "a given," and holds that one cannot describe what one perceives without also describing one's consciousness of what one experiences as one perceives. One therefore intuitively engages in introspection about one's experience of the empirical world with a view to gaining knowledge of self and the world.

Several philosophical studies of music from a phenomenological perspective may be cited, including those by Pike (1970), Schutz (1976), and Smith (1979). Although there are few phenomenologically oriented philosophical studies of music education, a notable example is provided by Bartholomew (1991).

Reese (1980, p. 450) characterizes *positivism* as a related group of philosophies that take an "extremely positive" view of science and scientific method. To the logical positivist (see Hanfling, 1981; Smith, 1986), inference by means of empirical evidence constitutes the predominant means of gathering knowledge, and one bases one's judgments on logic and reason rather than on intuition. The scientific method constitutes the primary means whereby phenomena in the natural world are studied.

The groundwork for educational positivism in the twentieth century was laid by Dewey's (1933) endorsement of the scientific method as the primary source of knowledge and his emphasis on educational experimentation using the scientific method. Subsequently, the ideas of B. F. Skinner and J. Wolpe on operant conditioning and counterconditioning, respectively, building on earlier work by Ivan Pavlov, E. L. Thorndike, and G. B. Watson, among others, gave rise to procedures such as those used in behavior modification, and behavioral models of learning applied in mastery learning and direct instruction, exemplified in teaching/discipline strategies and competency-based music education advocated in Madsen and Madsen (1974) and Madsen and Yarbrough (1980), respectively.

Although phenomenology and positivism are contrasting positions, the lines are less clear in practice: (1) Both make observations and collect empirical data. (2) Philosophers hold positions that have both positivistic and phenomenological elements. For example, while he endorses the importance of reason, Dewey (1916, 1933) also underscores the role of intuition and imagination in the learning process. (3) The excessively narrow interpretation of scientific method that excluded intuitive, emotive, and imaginational aspects of cognition has been challenged by philosophers of science, and the range of acceptable scientific research methods broadened accordingly. (4) Phenomenological research methods such as participant observation and case study approaches have benefited from the insights of positivism in drawing attention to the importance of logic, reason, rigor, and inference in discovering knowledge.

The impact of positivism on music education research in recent decades has downgraded the importance of philosophical research and detrimentally affected the quality of philosophy of music education teaching and research. The popularity of scientific studies of music and education, the superficiality of philosophical teaching, and the lack of emphasis on philosophical research have resulted in somewhat of a hiatus of serious philosophical research in music education.[8] Fortunately, prominent music education researchers now realize that theory building enhances descriptive, experimental, and historical research; philosophy can make an important contribution to music education research; and both positivistic and phenomenological insights can benefit music education research.

Deduction and Induction

Reese (1980, p. 120) describes *deduction* (from the Latin *de*, "from," and *ducere*, "to lead") as reasoning in which the conclusion follows necessarily from the premises, whether from the general to the general, from the general to the particular, or from the particular to the particular. Deduction has its roots in logical rules that establish the conditions under which it can and should proceed (see Carnap, 1958; Langer, 1967; Simpson, 1988).

For example, in his *Critique of Judgment*, Kant (in translation, 1952) lays out a classic deductive argument that establishes a kind of reason he denotes as "judgment" (rooted in aesthetic and teleological concerns) that links pure and applied reason and establishes a trilogy of interconnected species of reasoned thought. In Kant's argument, each point follows logically and necessarily from the previous one until the paradigm is complete. Similarly, in *Languages of Art*, Goodman (1976) derives a theory of symbols deductively by establishing the theoretical categories of symbol function, analyzing the specific semantic and syntactic features of various arts, and deducing shared functional qualities that comprise "symptoms of the aesthetic." As with Kant, if any of his assumptions fail to convince, or if his logic is flawed, the argument falls or must be bolstered by other means.

Induction is distinguished from deduction mainly on the basis of "probable" rather than "necessary inference." As Reese (1980, p. 251) observes, induction and deduction are incorrectly distinguished on the basis of whether the inference moves from "specific facts to general conclusions" (induction) or from "general premises to specific conclusions" (deduction) because such a distinction only compares one sort of induction with one sort of deduction. Indeed, Carnap (1952) posits various species of induction by which a judgment of the probable truth of a particular inference is made. On the basis of evidence, be it example, analogy, predictive quality, or the like, one accepts or rejects a given proposition. Although X does not follow *necessarily* (on the basis of logical rules) from Y, nevertheless, on the basis of certain evidence, one infers that X *probably* follows from Y.

For example, in *Sound and Semblance* (1984), *Sound Sentiment* (1989), and *Music Alone* (1990), Kivy develops an analysis that is pervasively inductive, drawing particularly on example and analogy. He admits that his differences with Goodman include a disagreement over how one should do philosophy. Where Goodman logically derives general propositions, which may then be tested with reference to specific examples, Kivy draws conclusions from various specific examples. Not only do his various characters such as Lilian and Tibby serve as examples, analogies, and metaphors for aspects of musical experience, but Kivy derives his analysis out of an examination of musical examples. Honegger's *Pacific 231* serves, in Kivy's words, as a "paradigm" of "representational" music, and he leans on excerpts from Monteverdi's *Arianna*, Handel's *Messiah*, Beethoven's *Ninth Symphony*, Bach's *Cantata No. 78* ("*Jesu, der du meine Seele*"), Earl Robinson's *The Lonesome Train*, and Haydn's *Missa in Tempore Belle*, among others, to derive as well as illustrate ideas regarding aspects of musical expressiveness.

Seldom is the work of one philosopher entirely either deductive or inductive. In practice, philosophers typically combine approaches. For example, in the First Moment of Kant's *Critique of Aesthetic Judgment*, we see the palace, a Rousseau, the Iroquois sachem, and the uninhabited island as Kant elaborates the particular quality of delight that a work of art provides, and a dish of food, Canary wine, among other examples he uses to distinguish between the beautiful and the good. He obviously draws ideas from the examples he considers. Similarly, Kivy lays out his argument in a logical fashion in which deduction forms an integral part. Viewed as a whole, Kivy's analysis is also deductive in the sense that one statement leads to the next that follows necessarily from it, even though each statement is established inductively rather than deductively. One may logically follow the arguments in *Sound Sentiment, Sound and Semblance,* and *Music Alone* from beginning to end as Kivy systematically builds the case for his thesis.

Music educators historically have focused on the inductive development of theories based on empirical evidence, at least to the extent that theory development is of any concern. In so doing, they have followed the predominant research methodologies in education and music. As noted elsewhere (Jorgensen, 1980, 1981), music education would benefit from complementary deductive approaches.

Synopsis and Analysis

Synopsis (in the sense in which I am using the term here) involves constructing a comprehensive paradigm that elaborates one's own philosophical perspective while building on the views of other philosophers. One's objective is not so much to critique other points of view (although critique is included) as to utilize them in explicating elements of one's own philosophy for purposes of *verification rather than refutation.* Such synoptic philosophies are often conceived at a high level of generalization; witness Kant's philosophy of reason, Schelling's philosophy of art, Langer's theory of mind, and Dewey's philosophy of experience.

Analysis, as Reese (1980, p. 13) notes, "from the Greek *analytikos,* derived from the verb *analyein,* 'to resolve into its elements,' " involves the breaking down of a thing into its various parts. Analytic philosophers such as Scheffler, Kivy, and Budd approach the ideas of other philosophers critically and use evidence for purposes of *refutation rather than verification.* An important element in their analysis is the clarification of language. Analytic philosophies tend to focus on more specific problems than do synoptic philosophies.

In illustrating the difference between synoptic and analytic approaches to aesthetics, one might cite Goodman (1976) and Collingwood (1938) as examples of a synoptic approach and Kivy (1989) and Budd (1985) as examples of an analytic approach. What Kivy and Budd attempt to do (and Urmson, 1989, p. 26, suggests that neither Goodman nor Collingwood is primarily concerned with this) is to explicate ideas, often implicit in everyday language, as material to be elucidated rather than as propositions to be critiqued. The former are architects and builders of the house; the latter are its inspectors and appraisers. This is not to say that some analysis does not go on in the midst of synopsis and vice versa. Rather, the focus of philosophical endeavor differs significantly between these approaches.

In music education, philosophical thought has been predominantly synoptic; witness the work of Reimer (1989) and Swanwick (1981, 1988). While there has been relatively little analytic philosophy, useful models include Howard (1982), Alperson (1991), and Elliott (1995).

Coda

Doing philosophy in music education may sometimes be disturbing, uncomfortable, and even painful. To challenge the myths and assumptions that have been held as "received wisdom" is to invite criticism from those for whom a different way of seeing things is provocative and unsettling. We may remember Plato's allegory in which the inhabitants of the cave go so far as to seek to kill the one who brings a different perspective to bear on their situation. So, in music education, to challenge the status quo is to invite hostility or rejection from those with a vested interest in seeing things remain as they are.

Yet despite the potential difficulties of following such a path, the philosopher relentlessly pursues truth, variously understood, however elusive. Whereas Plato finishes his allegory of the cave on a desperate note, a more optimistic story would have concluded with at least some of the cave's inhabitants coming out with their prophet into the sunlight. The critique that philosophy brings and the vision that it offers may be destructive of complacency, yet they appeal to seekers for wisdom and understanding. The disciplined reflection that philosophy demands may fall on some deaf ears, yet it is welcomed by those people who wish to understand what the interrelationship between music and education can and should be. For these persons, philosophy ultimately benefits scholarship and practice in music education.

NOTES

1. Each essay is a product of its time. This piece, written at the outset of the 1990s, came before a burst of philosophical writing in music education internationally. The Anglo American literature includes Walker (1990), Swanwick (1994), Elliott (1995), Jorgensen (1997), Bowman (1998), Swanwick (1999), Tillman (2000), Jorgensen (2003), Koza (2003), Reimer (2003), Woodford (2005), and 12 volumes of *The Philosophy of Music Education Review* (with an index to the first 10 volumes in volume 11, no. 1). Philosophical research was fostered by five international symposia in the philosophy of music education held in Bloomington, Indiana (1990); Toronto, Canada (1994); Los Angeles, California (1997); Birmingham, United Kingdom (2000); and Lake Forest, Illinois (2003), culminating in the formation of the International Society for the Philosophy of Music Education (*www.ispme.org*) in 2004. Besides essays published in Colwell and (1992) and Colwell and Richardson (2002), other literature on philosophical method includes Phelps, Ferrara, and Goolsby (1993, chap. 3) and Reichling (1996), and ideas in this essay are extended in Jorgensen (2001).

2. The term *symptom* is borrowed from Goodman (1976) although here not used narrowly to indicate only the symbolic features of a particular way of understanding.

3. For introductions to the philosophical literatures in music, aesthetics, and education, respectively, see Alperson (1986), Margolis (1987), and Peters (1967). For additional philosophical studies of education see Hirst and Peters (1970), Hirst (1974), Passmore (1980), and Broudy (1988).

4. This is especially true, Bowman 1991 argues, of Reimer's treatment of the contributions of the "formalists" to aesthetic understanding. See Reimer (2003) for a further amplification of his views on aesthetic education.

5. Envisaging music education in this way enables the perspectives of philosophical thought in education as well as music to be brought to bear on music education.

6. Scheffler (1965, p. 1) defines the task of epistemology as "the logical analysis of knowledge."

7. This will doubtless change given the praxialist emphasis in the philosophy of music, evident in the work of Sparshott, among others (see Alperson, 1986).

8. During this time, while various journals such as *The Journal of Aesthetic Education* have published philosophical articles on music and music education, these have been outside the mainstream of music education research.

REFERENCES

Adorno, T. (1984). *Aesthetic theory* (Trans. C. Lenhardt; Ed. G. Adorno & R. Tiedemann). London and New York: Routledge and Kegan Paul.

Alperson, P. (Ed.) (1986). *What is music? An introduction to the philosophy of music*. New York: Haven.

Alperson, P. (1991). What should one expect from a philosophy of music education? *Journal of Aesthetic Education, 25*(3), 215–242.

Attali, J. (1985). *Noise: The political economy of music*. (Trans. B. Massumi). Minneapolis: University of Minnesota Press.

Bartholomew, D. (1991). Whole/part relations in music: An exploratory Study. *Journal of Aesthetic Education, 25*(3), 175–191.

Barzun, J. (1974). *The use and abuse of art*. Princeton and London: Princeton University Press.

Beardsley, M. (1981). *Aesthetics: Problems in the philosophy of criticism* (2nd. ed). Indianapolis and Cambridge: Hackett.

Beardsmore, R. W. (1971). *Art and morality*. London and Basingstoke: Macmillan.

Blacking, J. (1976). *How musical is man?* London: Faber and Faber.

Bloch, E. (1985). *Essays on the philosophy of music* (Trans. P. Palmer; intro., D. Drew). Cambridge: Cambridge University Press.

Bowman, W. (1991). The values of musical formalism. *Journal of Aesthetic Education, 25*(3), 41–59.

Bowman, W. (1998). *Philosophical perspectives on music*. New York: Oxford University Press.

Broudy, H. S. (1979). Arts education: Necessary or just nice? *Phi Delta Kappan, 60*, 347–350.

Broudy, H. S. (1988). *The uses of schooling*. New York: Routledge, Chapman and Hall.

Bruner, J. (1963). *The process of education*. New York: Vintage Books.

Bruner, J. (1973). *The relevance of education* (Ed. A. Gill). New York: W. W. Norton.

Bruner, J. (1979). *On knowing: Essays for the left hand* (expanded ed.). Cambridge: Harvard University Press.

Bruner, J. (1986). *Actual minds, possible worlds.* Cambridge: Harvard University Press.

Budd, M. (1985). *Music and the emotions: The philosophical theories.* London: Routledge and Kegan Paul.

Busoni, F. (1962). Sketch of a new esthetic of music. In *Three classics in the aesthetic of music.* New York: Dover. (Original work published 1911)

Carnap, R. (1952). *The continuum of inductive methods.* Chicago: University of Chicago Press.

Carnap, R. (1958). *Introduction to symbolic logic and its application* (Trans. W. H. Meyer and J. Wilkinson). New York: Dover.

The collected dialogues of Plato including the letters (1961). (Ed. E. Hamilton & H. Cairns). New York: Pantheon Books.

Collingwood, R. G. (1938). *The principles of art.* Oxford: Oxford University Press.

Colwell, R., ed. (1992). *Handbook of research on music teaching and learning: A project of the Music Educators National Conference.* New York: Schirmer.

Colwell, R., & Richardson, C., eds. (2002). *The new handbook of research on music teaching and learning.* New York: Oxford University Press.

Crawford, D. W. (1974). *Kant's aesthetic theory.* Madison: University of Wisconsin Press.

Crickmore, L. (1968). An approach to the measurement of musical appreciation (1). *Journal of Research in Music Education, 16,* 239–253.

Dahlhaus, C. (1982). *Esthetics of music* (Trans. W. Austin). Cambridge: Cambridge University Press.

Dahlhaus, C. (1985). *Realism in nineteenth-century music* (Trans. M. Whittall). Cambridge: Cambridge University Press.

Dewey, J. (1916). *Democracy and education: An introduction to the philosophy of education.* New York: Macmillan.

Dewey, J. (1933). *How we think: A restatement of the relation of reflective thinking to the educative process* (rev. ed.). Boston: D. C. Heath.

Dewey, J. (1927). *The public and its problems.* Denver: Alan Swallow.

Dewey, J. (1979). *Art as experience.* New York: G. P. Putnam's Sons. (Original work published 1934).

Dewey, J. (1963). *Experience and education.* New York: Collier Books. (Original work published 1938).

Eagleton, T. (1990). *The ideology of the aesthetic.* Cambridge: Basil Blackwell.

Ecker, G. (Ed.). (1985). *Feminist aesthetics* (Trans. H. Anderson). Boston: Beacon Press.

Eisner, E. W. (Ed.) (1985). *Learning and teaching the ways of knowing.* Chicago: National Society for the Study of Education, 84th Yearbook, pt. 2.

Elliott, D. (1991). Music as knowledge. *Journal of Aesthetic Education, 25*(3), 21–40.

Elliott, D. (1995). *Music matters: A new philosophy of music education.* New York: Oxford University Press.

Epperson, G. (1967). *The musical symbol: A study of the philosophic theory of music.* Ames: Iowa State University Press.

Fischer, E. (1963). *The necessity of art: A Marxist approach* (Trans. A. Bostock). Harmondsworth: Penguin.

Fletcher, P. (1987). *Music and education.* Oxford: Oxford University Press.

Frith, S. (1978). *The sociology of rock.* London: Constable.

Frith, S. (1978). Towards an aesthetic of popular music. In R. Leppert & S. McClary (Eds.), *Music and society: The politics of composition, performance and reception* (pp. 133–149). Cambridge: Cambridge University Press.

Gibboney, R. A. (1989). The unscientific character of educational research, *Phi Delta Kappan, 71,* 225–227.

Goodman, N. (1976). *Languages of art: An approach to a theory of symbols.* Indianapolis: Hackett.

Goodman, N. (1978). *Ways of worldmaking.* Indianapolis: Hackett.

Hanfling, O. (1981). *Essential readings in logical positivism.* Oxford: Basil Blackwell.

Hanslick, E. (1986). *On the musically beautiful* (Trans. G. Payzant). Indianapolis: Hackett.

Hegel, G. W. F. (1975). *Aesthetics* (Trans. A. J. Ellis). Oxford: Clarendon Press.

Hindemith, P. (1952). *A composer's world: Horizons and limitations.* Cambridge: Harvard University Press.

Hirst, P. H. (1974). *Knowledge and the curriculum: A collection of philosophical papers.* London: Routledge and Kegan Paul.

Hirst, P. H., and Peters, R. S. (1970). *The logic of education.* London: Routledge and Kegan Paul.

Howard, V. (1982). *Artistry: The work of artists.* Indianapolis: Hackett.

Husserl, E. (1931). *Ideas: General introduction to pure phenomenology* (Trans. W. R. Boyce Gibson). London: Collier Books.

Jaques-Dalcroze, É. (1976). *Rhythm, music and education* (Trans. H. F. Rubinstein). New York: Arno Press. (Original work published 1921).

Jorgensen, E. R. (1980). On the development of a theory of musical instruction. *Psychology of Music, 8*(2), 25–30.

Jorgensen, E. R. (1981). On a choice-based instructional typology in music. *Journal of Research in Music Education, 29,* 97–102.

Jorgensen, E. R. (1990). Philosophy and the music teacher: Challenging the way we think. *Music Educators Journal, 76*(5), 17–23.

Jorgensen, E. (1997). *In search of music education.* Urbana: University of Illinois Press.

Jorgensen, E. (2001). What are the roles of philosophy in music education? *Research Studies in Music Education, 17,* 19–31.

Jorgensen, E. (2003). *Transforming music education.* Bloomington and Indianapolis: Indiana University Press.

Kant, I. (1952). *The critique of judgement* (Trans., with analytical indexes, J. C. Meredith). Oxford: Oxford University Press.

Kivy, P. (1980). *The corded shell: Reflections on musical expression.* Princeton: Princeton University Press.

Kivy, P. (1984). *Sound and semblance: Reflections on musical representation.* Princeton: Princeton University Press.

Kivy, P. (1989). *Sound sentiment: An essay on the musical emotions including the complete text of "The Corded Shell."* Philadelphia: Temple University Press.

Kivy, P. (1990). *Music alone: Philosophical reflections on the purely musical experience.* Ithaca: Cornell University Press.

Kodály, Z. (1974). *The selected writings of Zoltan Kodaly* (Ed. F. Bonis; Trans. L. Halapy & F. Macnicol). London: Boosey and Hawkes.

Koza, J. (2003). *Stepping across: Four interdisciplinary studies on education and cultural politics.* New York: Peter Lang.

Langer, S. K. (1942). *Philosophy in a new key: A study of the symbolism of reason, rite, and art.* Cambridge: Harvard University Press.

Langer, S. K. (1953). *Feeling and form: A theory of art developed from "Philosophy in a New Key."* London: Routledge and Kegan Paul.

Langer, S. K. (1967). *An introduction of symbolic logic* (3rd. rev. ed.). New York: Dover Publications.

Langer, S. K. (1967, 1972, 1982). *Mind: An essay on human feeling* (3 vols.). Baltimore: Johns Hopkins University Press.

Locke, J. (1913). *Some thoughts concerning education.* Cambridge: Cambridge University Press.

Madsen, C. H., & Madsen, C. K. (1974). *Teaching/Discipline: A positive approach for educational development* (2nd. ed). Boston: Allyn and Bacon.

Madsen, C. K., & Yarbrough, C. (1980). *Competency-based music education.* Englewood Cliffs: Prentice-Hall.

Margolis, J. (Ed.). (1987). *Philosophy looks at the arts: Contemporary readings in aesthetics* (3rd ed.). Philadelphia: Temple University Press.

Margolis, J. (Ed.). (1986). On the semiotics of music. In P. Alperson (Ed.), *What is music? An introduction to the philosophy of music.* New York: Haven.

McCloskey, M. A. (1987). *Kant's aesthetic.* Albany: State University of New York Press.

Merriam, A. P. (1964). *The anthropology of music.* Evanston: Northwestern University Press.

Meyer, L. (1956). *Emotion and meaning in music.* Chicago: University of Chicago Press.

Nettl, B. (1985). *The western impact on world music: Change, adaptation, and survival.* New York: Schirmer Books.

Passmore, J. (1980). *The philosophy of teaching.* Cambridge: Harvard University Press.

Peters, R. S. (1966). *Ethics and education.* London: George Allen and Unwin.

Peters, R. S. (Ed.). (1967). *The concept of education.* London: Routledge and Kegan Paul.

Phelps, R., Ferrara, L., & Goolsby, T. (1993). *A guide to research in music education,* 4th ed. Metuchen, NJ: Scarecrow.

Pike, A. (1970). *A phenomenological analysis of musical experience and other essays.* New York: St. John's Press.

Pinar, W. (Ed.). (1975). *Curriculum theorizing: The reconceptualists.* Berkeley: McCutchan.

Prall, D. W. (1929). *Aesthetic judgment.* New York: Thomas Y. Crowell.

Prall, D. W. (1936). *Aesthetic analysis.* New York: Thomas Y. Crowell.

Rantala, V., Rowell, L., & Tarasti, E. (Eds.). (1986). Essays on the philosophy of music. *Acta Philosophica Fennica. 43,* part 1.

Read, H. (1958). *Education through art* (3rd. ed.). London: Faber and Faber.

Reese, W. L. (1980). *Dictionary of philosophy and religion: Eastern and Western thought.* Atlantic Highlands: Humanities Press.

Reichling, M. (1996). On the question of method in philosophical research. *Philosophy of Music Education Review, 4*(2), 117–127.

Reimer, B. (1989). *A philosophy of music education* (2nd. ed.). Englewood Cliffs: Prentice-Hall.

Reimer, B. (1991). Essential and non-essential characteristics of aesthetic education. *Journal of Aesthetic Education, 25*(3), 193–214.

Reimer, B. (2003). *A philosophy of music education: Advancing the vision.* Upper Saddle River, NJ: Prentice Hall.

Ross, W. O. (1921). *The works of Aristotle.* London: Oxford University Press.

Scheffler, I. (1965). *Conditions of knowledge: An introduction to epistemology and education.* Chicago: University of Chicago Press.

Scheffler, I. (1973). *Reason and teaching.* Indianapolis: Bobbs-Merrill.

Scheffler, I. (1979). *Beyond the letter: A philosophical inquiry into ambiguity, vagueness and metaphor in language.* London: Routledge and Kegan Paul.

Scheffler, I. (1985). *Of human potential: An essay in the philosophy of education.* Boston: Routledge and Kegan Paul.

Scheffler, I. (1986). *Inquiries: Philosophical studies of language, science, and learning.* Indianapolis: Hackett.

Schelling, F. W. J. (1989). *The philosophy of art* (Ed., Trans., & Intro. D. W. Stott). Minneapolis: University of Minnesota Press.

Schiller, F. (1967). *On the aesthetic education of man in a series of letters* (Ed. and Trans. E. M. Wilkinson & L. A. Willoughby). Oxford: Clarendon Press.

Scholes, P. (1935). *Music, the child and the masterpiece: A comprehensive handbook of aims and methods in all that is usually called "musical appreciation."* London: Oxford University Press.

Schopenhauer, A. (1969). *The world as will and representation* (Trans. E.F.J. Payne). New York: Dover.

Schutz, A. (1976). Fragments of a phenomenology of music. *Music and man, 11,* 6–71.

Schwab, J. (1971). The practical: Arts of eclectic. *School Review, 79,* 493–542.

Sessions, R. (1962). *The musical experience of composer, performer, listener.* New York: Atheneum. (Original work published 1950)

Shepherd, J., Virden, P., Vulliamy, G., & Wishart, T. (1977). *Whose music: A sociology of musical languages.* London: Latimer.

Simpson, R. L. (1988). *Essentials of symbolic logic.* London: Routledge.

Small, C. (1980). *Music-society-education* (2nd. ed.). London: John Calder.

Smith, F. J. (1979). *The experiencing of musical sound: Prelude to a phenomenology of music.* New York: Gordon and Breach.

Smith, L. D. (1986). *Behaviorism and logical positivism: A reassessment of the alliance.* Stanford: Stanford University Press.

Sokolowski, R. (Ed.) (1988). *Edmund Husserl and the phenomenological tradition: Essays in phenomenology.* Washington: Catholic University of America Press.

Suzuki, S. (1969). *Nurtured by love: A new approach to education* (Trans. W. Suzuki). New York: Exposition Press.

Swanwick, K. (1981). *A basis for music education.* Windsor: NFER-Nelson.

Swanwick, K. (1988). *Music, mind and education.* London: Routledge.

Swanwick, K. (1994). *Musical knowledge: Intuition, analysis, and music education.* London: Routledge.

Swanwick, K. (1999). *Teaching music musically.* London: Routledge.

Taylor, R. L. (1978). *Art, an enemy of the people.* Atlantic Highlands: Humanities Press.

Tillman, J. (2000). *Constructing musical healing: The wounds that heal*. London: Jessica Kingsley.

Umson, J. O. (1989). The methods of esthetics. In R. Shusterman (Ed.), *Analytic aesthetics*. London: Basil Blackwell.

Walker, R. (1990). *Musical beliefs: Psychoacoustic, mythical, and educational*. New York: Teachers College Press.

Wing, H. (1968). *Tests of musical ability and appreciation* (2nd. ed.). Cambridge: Cambridge University Press.

Wolterstorff, N. (1986). The work of making a work of music. In P. Alperson (Ed.), *What is music? An introduction to the philosophy of music*. New York: Haven.

Woodford, P. (2005). *Democracy and music education: Liberalism, ethics, and the politics of practice*. Bloomington and Indianapolis: Indiana University Press.

Assessment's Potential in
Music Education

RICHARD COLWELL

An entire section of the first *Handbook of Research on Music Teaching and Learning* was devoted to assessment. Those authors successfully summarized the history of assessment in music with chapters on assessment in five areas: teaching, creativity, program, general, and attitude. What is most surprising is the limited research and scholarship devoted to assessment in music over the past several decades. This chapter is an update on a few of the issues raised in the first *Handbook*.

In the 21st century, assessment has become one of the more important issues in education. State departments of education are especially active, which also increases the state's influence on the curriculum. The priority of education in the United States has risen, and now education outweighs almost all other domestic social issues—immigration, the homeless, welfare, national defense, medical benefits—and even foreign policy. Evaluation's importance is portrayed by its use in the struggle for power over the curriculum. The struggle centers on whether assessment resources are to be used to improve instruction or to make educators and education institutions more accountable. Although there is overlap, the processes to attain these two objectives differ in substantial ways. One clue to assessment thinking at the federal level is the change on July 7, 2004, in the name of an important government agency (the GAO) from the "General Accounting Office" to the "Government Accountability Office." A second clue is passage of the elementary and secondary act of 2001 (or No Child Left Behind, NCLB) with its complex accountability provisions. Cibulka has suggested that much of the Washington language is built on faith rather than foundation, offering policies designed without solid evidence that any of the approaches will help failing schools (2003, p. 267). Assessment data seldom are definitive with respect to educational policy; policies in education and in the arts are made more subjectively than objectively. Present assessment with respect to policy is focused on arts organizations, artists, and their employment, rather than on public school students. The Educational Testing Service argues for assessment, asserting that the United States has forfeited nearly a quarter of a trillion dollars every year from its GNP as a result of failure to educate Hispanics and African Americans (Smith, 2004, p. 33). With such data, it is likely this population will receive priority in the allocation of resources.

A major objective of this chapter is to caution music educators about what outcomes music instruction can attain with a reasonable allocation of resources. Music and education are wide-ranging, complex subjects. Few music educators are sufficiently educated to adapt strategies and instruments from other disciplines, including the discipline of education, and fewer still are equipped to construct viable measures for the most formidable objectives. Too often these well-meaning music educators adopt new goals and objectives for the profession because these can be assessed with tools similar to those used in other subjects with outcomes that are likely to be positive. A description of a few of these outcomes is provided later in this chapter. Recommendations for major programmatic changes are inappropriate in that neither the objectives nor the assessments of music programs have been publicly criticized.

Arts advocates welcome positive assessments, some of which are relatively marginal in value. In fact, Jennifer Chowning, arts education coordinator for Americans for the Arts, comments, "There is little incentive to offer the arts when it's not tested, especially since arts education is expensive and requires a long-term commitment and special facilities (Ashford, 2004, p. 23). The high public interest and greatly expanded funding for education, preschool through college, has brought to the playing field two assessment issues, standards and accountability. The definition of a performance standard is a description of how well or at what level a student is expected to perform, and accountability is the avenue for ascertaining that value for resources expended is attained. A few individuals have questioned whether assessment as the single means of establishing value is appropriate (Broadfoot, 2000). High-stakes evaluation has become the subject of educational and political debates, often so emotional as to complicate the resolution of the accompanying assessment issues. The arguments for and against high-stakes tests are not addressed in this chapter. High-stakes tests seldom distort information about the general performance level of students (Greene, Winter, and Forster, 2004). Further, results from 3,300 language arts students, comparing multiple-choice with open-ended, on-demand writing tasks, showed little difference (Heck and Crislip, 2001, p. 275). The U.S. Office for Civil Rights has entered the fray, publishing in December 2000 *The Use of Tests When Making High-Stakes Decisions for Students*. John Fremer (2000) suggests that the level of public debate about testing needs to be raised, as there is "so much uninformed and wrong-headed commentary." Assessment literature in the arts is equally marginal. Good assessments provide data on the extent of success and failure but only hint at causes. Our well-accepted music contest rating scales provide only the most limited information on why the performance was exemplary; a community (as well as the school board) has almost no causal information on why their music ensembles have been rated outstanding for the past decade or so. Assessment, of course, has always been part of teaching and learning; what is new is its uses. One type of assessment, program evaluation, has become a major discipline that provides data on programs as diverse as welfare, the military, and education. These programs have clear objectives, such as reducing dropouts, stopping smoking, and similar objectives that can be easily measured. In education, assessment is used to portray the success of society in enabling all students to attain high standards in multiple areas, with the additional role of determining the value of funding for administration, programs, and facilities—these in addition to its continued role in aiding teaching and learning.

The focus of the chapter is a description of selected recent developments in assessment in education and in music teaching and learning. It is written for the individual who already has a basic grasp of the principles of assessment. Not much space is devoted to such important admonitions as the following:

1. There must be a direct match between the curriculum and what the student is expected to know and do in the assessment. (Note: a major section is devoted to research in taxonomies, which is intended to assure a close relationship between the curriculum and any assessment.)
2. On-demand assessments should address important outcomes, not trivial items selected for ease of measurement.
3. Allowing students to answer three out of five question is inappropriate on high-stakes tests. All questions should be important; all questions must be answered to determine minimal competency.

The statement that what is tested is what is taught (often used pejoratively) does not indicate a fault of the assessment system; it arises when teachers and curriculum writers are insecure about the importance and priority of the goals of instruction. Assessors have a range of excellent devices to provide data on a variety of educational procedures and products, but in the hands of the inept one or more of these tools can be counterproductive to attaining the goals of schooling.

Overview

Research and evaluation remain separate disciplines, although the boundaries are a bit fuzzy when the two disciplines have similar concerns as to the fundamental purpose of education for all students. Passage of the NCLB Act has, however, brought research and evaluation closer because both fields must appraise the worth of evaluation devices. Researchers are concerned when a single test is used to assess the worth of an intervention. The evaluation community believes that interpretation of data from any single measure does not constitute a valid assessment. Thus, both fields have concerns about the accountability requirements of NCLB. Evaluators have pointed out measurement problems in documenting annual yearly progress (Linn, 2003a), problems that are even more pronounced in music because of variables in music classes that include not only teaching and learning resources but also student interest, motivation, and previous school and out-of-school experiences. Little research has been conducted on yearly progress, but Petzold's conclusion from the 1960s that a minimum of 2 years of instruction is necessary to show measurable change seems reasonable. Further, determining the outcomes for which the schools are responsible is a developing topic, including the question of whether *every* student must be competent in algebra or have played a musical instrument, a question relevant to any discussion of accountability.

Evaluation uses research methods, but evaluation includes a process for identifying content and performance goals (as well as opportunity to learn standards) and a means to interpret and analyze results against these goals. The overly ambitious goals in NCLB and the music portion of National Assessment of Educational Progress (NAEP) should not discourage music educators from using evaluation to improve teaching and learning. A rule of thumb in evaluation suggests that when only 10 percent of the students are successful at a task, the objectives (NAEP test questions) need to be revised. Research studies should provide a window on assessment tools, as research usually "tests" the results of an educational intervention. Unfortunately, the results of research studies in music education are not very helpful, for little attention has been paid to the dependent variable. Investigators make up their own, providing vague descriptions of competency or relying on a single observation, although lack of objectivity has not discouraged some from applying the most sophisticated statistical procedures on crude measures such as grades in music class or in band. (In 2003, 46.6 percent of students had an A average [McGinn, 2005, p. 26]—one can only imagine the grade average in music classes.)

Arguments in education over constructivism do not materially affect assessment in music education, as the breadth of the 1994 voluntary national standards requires every teaching format. It seems, however, that music educators and arts advocates who are attempting to provide data on the value of music instruction need to have, at least dimly, a vision of the purpose of the schools for all children. "The public good" is a broad objective, along with "long-term good for children" (not their current interests), accompanied by the most current instructional objectives available (Meier, 2000, p. 218). Deborah Meier believes that students have to have dispositions and habits of heart and intellect that make caring, competent citizens (cited in Goodlad, Mantle-Bromley, and Goodlad, 2004, p. 99). John Goodlad's interviews with teacher educators found that not one came even close to suggesting that the schools were to serve a democratic mission (Goodlad, 2004, p. 308). Goodlad concluded that we need to start by asking teachers to think about characteristics of the world we live in, rather than the disciplines educators have developed to interpret these characteristics, an integrated approach (p. 325). Fullan (2003) also found little attention to the purpose of schooling in the education of educators (p. x). Nel Noddings argues for the importance of happiness in life and that education is to prepare one for life (Noddings, 2003). Foshay suggests schooling is to develop a sense of self that includes the principal attributes of humanness (Foshay, 2000, p. xvii). Shulman's table of learning suggests six way stations: engagement and motivation, knowledge and understanding, performance and action, reflection and critique, judgment and design, and commitment and identity (Shulman, 2002, p. 38). With such broad objectives, Bryan, an early-20th-century music educator, was in tune with today when he suggested that music makes six contributions: enhancement of happiness, development of minds that rise about the obvious and literal, opening the door to one's heritage, developing social consciousness, placing all students on an equal level of response, and exposing an individual to new values (Cox, 2004; Livingston, 2004). Thus, some music teachers primarily promote social learning—self-control, social awareness, participation, cooperation, making decisions, enthusiasm, solving problems, use of strategies, the new, student enjoyment, energy, beliefs, motivation, preference, values, interest, honesty, civility, civic responsibility, willingness to volunteer, courage, justice, temperance, transcendence, imagination, and intuition. Sedlacek's (2004) noncognitive variables that affect outcomes (positive self-concept, realistic self-appraisal, successfully handling the system, preference for long-term goals, availability of a strong support person, leadership experience, community involvement, and knowledge acquired in a field, p. 7) support the importance of social outcomes. Measures of emotional engagement are usually self-report measures. As helpful as noncognitive variables might be, they are notoriously unreliable, and Goodlad reports that the significant lesson for researchers is that the validity of self-assessments is untrustworthy (Goodlad, 2004, p. 269). The present spokesman for democracy in music education is Paul Woodford (2005).

The argument for process rather than product continues in the education community on the basis that education is a quest and that inquiry does not have specific outcomes; rather, inquiry seeks knowledge and understanding (Delandshere, 2003, p. 1477). Her argument is to move the discussion about knowledge to knowing and suggesting that structure of knowledge, its complexity, and its processing cannot be discerned and used in evaluation. Such an argument would mean that the evaluation for accountability and the formative evaluation in the classroom are one and the same (p. 1466). These arguments touch on the role of reflection, what it means to think, and the extent to which thinking can be taught.

One can devote assessment resources to these outcomes—the issue is whether they are the most essential outcomes of good music instruction. (The complexity of assessing a few of these outcomes is addressed later in this chapter.) A supporting argument is that to avoid absolutes, music teachers do claim to teach for life-long learning and a willingness to engage the subject. It seems obvious that a student can participate socially in music, gain much, but never wrestle with the musical meaning that is also present in these experiences. Evaluators should want to know what a student does when he or she really understands music and how this differs from the "doing" of one who does not really understand.

Although advocates often promote social or fringe outcomes, an extensive study by Winner and Hetland (2000) found little evidence that music instruction was "causal" in student attainment of social outcomes or improved outcomes in other school subjects. Since 2000, a few doctoral students in music education have sought confirming data on nonmusical outcomes, but these studies are flawed by selectivity and inability to control feasible alternative explanations. Neither advocates nor music educators have been concerned about the validity of assessments.

Educational standards, content, performance, opportunity to learn, assessment, and teacher education are designed to provide a framework for accountability and to answer the question, Are the schools performing adequately for the dollars invested? But what kind of accountability? Linda Darling-Hammond suggests that accountability has become political, legal, bureaucratic, professional, and market oriented (2004, p. 1050). If the arts are unique and have their own habits of mind, as Sam Hope believes (2004, p. 93), music and the other arts need some level of protection from the external forces of accountability, which include economic, religious, and academic forces, along with student apathy and lack of basic consequences. Once the accountability question is decided, focus turns to the definition of standards. Bennett Reimer and Elliot Eisner differ in their writings about standards because Reimer focuses on content standards that have served to broaden the definition of what constitutes music education, and Eisner discusses standards in terms of how well students should perform (Reimer, 2005, p. 113). Paul Lehman (2004), in an interview in *Teaching Music*, suggests that the success of the standards rests in large part on their role in advocacy. Lehman did not respond to the interviewer's question as to whether achievement levels have risen, which points up the differences in interpreting the role of the standards. Anthony Palmer argues that the music standards are not feasible because they rise out of reductionist, positivist, and objectivist features of assessing knowledge and understanding and that they must be written to apply to everyone (2002, p. 106). In a rebuttal, Christine Brown, arts consultant for the state of Iowa, suggests that standards are at the heart of school reform and have been adopted carefully and thoroughly with the interests of students in mind (2000, p. 118). The fact that all states are attempting to conform to NCLB indicates that the states are taking the accountability portion of the reform movement seriously, that some aspects of standards are seem as permanent, and that assessment issues will grow rather than wither away. Standards-referenced testing adds a new dimension, as tests are no longer either norm- or criterion-referenced with respect to interpretation. The major change in assessment related to standards is that with standards-referenced tests, one must establish cut scores to accommodate basic, proficient, and advanced levels (Cizek, Bunch, and Koons, 2004). Considerable care is required to identify the cutoff between basic and proficient and several methods have been advanced, the most common being Bookmark and Angoff.

Popham (2004) writes that we have far too many curricular aims in most state recommendations (p. 31) and that we would be in a better position if we isolated a small number of items that can be described clearly, are genuinely teachable, and coalesce the most important of the state's existing curricular aims (p. 33). On the other hand, to select aims for a valid education too narrowly may result in the overemphasis of some goals at the expense of others (Linn, 2003b, p. 3). Linn goes on to suggest that objectives mandated by the accountability system should be ambitious, but also should be realistically obtainable with sufficient effort. Standards, however, cannot be used to directly inform assessment. Goals, aims, and objectives based on the standards must be formulated so that they provide the guidance for selecting instruction and assessment. Elmore (2004, p. 44), believes that standards-based reform represents a fundamental shift in the relationship between policy and institutional practice. He would like assessment to concentrate on what goes on *inside* schools—a reasonable approach but one that would challenge evaluators in music, where so much learning occurs outside the classroom. To follow Elmore, music, educators would need to adopt a laserlike focus on instructional objectives, objectives that may be causal for any general outcomes.

State standards in music have not received much attention. One doctoral dissertation reviewed standards in Texas (Milner, 2000) and one in New Jersey (Frankel, 2002). Such evaluations cannot be expected to have any impact on arts policy: First, policy makers are interested in overall effect; second, to combine the results from assessing the nine music standards is a formidable task in terms of both validity and reliability.

A number of smaller issues cloud discussions about assessment. *High-stakes assessment* is the focus of wrangling about the value and use of assessments in education. The definition of *high-stakes* is not firm; it generally refers to situations where the assessment determines whether a student passes a grade level, graduates from secondary or tertiary school, is licensed to teach, or is denied renewal of licensure of accreditation based upon an assessment. An audition or interview can be high-stakes (for example, failure to qualify for the Boston Marathon), the height of the stake depending upon the importance placed on the task by the individual or the culture. Concern intensifies when a single assessment is used in these high-stakes events, although the definition of single assessment is also controversial. Does a battery of tests that encompasses many competencies constitute a single assessment? When one has several opportunities to pass an assessment, is this a "single assessment"? There are few, if any, high-stakes assessments in the pre-K–12 school music program, although selection for the madrigals may seem high-stakes to the auditioning singers. Arts advocates champion music as a basic subject without realizing that basic subjects are those subjects of sufficient importance to society that a high-stakes test may be required. Language arts and mathematical competence are the most common high-stakes subjects. High-stakes testing is a component of the standards movement, with most states developing such assessment in conjunction with their standards. The literature and discussion of high-stakes assessment are useful to music educators to the extent that improvements in its use aid development of better measures in music.

Evaluation and *assessment* are used interchangeably in this chapter. *Measurement* has traditionally referred to a single test, a test being the smallest unit in assessment. Individuals are measured in terms of height or weight but not in terms of personal characteristics. *Evaluation* is distinguished by the making of judgments based on the data derived from measurements and other procedures, while *assessment* refers to a considerable body of data that has the potential to diagnose and provide clues to causes. Assessment is then used to improve or judge instruction or do both.

Little distinction is made in this chapter between achievement and ability; the term *aptitude* is today seldom used in education and is not used here. *Achievement* customarily refers to short-term learning, *ability* to more long-term outcomes. No priority is assigned to the relative importance of facts, knowledge, concepts, principles, understandings, creativity, critical thinking, metacognition, strategic knowledge, procedural knowledge, performance, and other worthwhile outcomes. Each outcome is appropriate at times. Also, no priority is assigned to types of assessments: auditions, rubrics, portfolios, videos, narratives, observations, demonstrations, exhibitions, fill-in-the-blanks, performances, interviews, essays, classroom discussion, research papers, and multiple-choice tests; each is situationally appropriate depending upon the task to be assessed and how instruction has been conducted. Even checklists, when repeated, can provide valid data (University of Western Michigan: The Evaluation Center).

Confusion occurs when one investigator uses the term *musical ability* and another the term *music aptitude* for the same competence (Hallam and Shaw, 2002). Much ability in music is not "natural" and depends on an intervention or an experience. The postmodern idea is to believe that ability, including aptitude, is constructed and that single tests are invalid predictive measures of success. Thus, there is interest in identifying unique skills that might constitute music ability (aptitude). McPherson's list of these skills is sight reading, performing rehearsed music, playing from memory, playing by ear, and improvising (1996). Hallam's list of skills is aural, cognitive, technical, musicianship, performance, and listening (1998). The research on "ability" is not as sophisticated as the development of an "aptitude" test, such as those constructed by Gordon and Karma. Determining ability usually consists of interviews, questionnaires, and observations. Hallam and Prince (2003) posed the question, Musical ability is? to more than 400 individuals, including 129 musicians. Only 39 percent of the musicians (28% of total sample) identified aural skills in their definition. Reynolds and Hyun (2004), who conducted a similar study with teachers but administered the Gordon aptitude test along with the questionnaire, confirmed that teachers define *ability* more broadly than the Gordon test.

Authentic assessment as a descriptor is avoided, as it is seldom related to assessment in music education. Almost all assessment in music is authentic. The more important concern is transfer of what has been learned. Criteria must be met for an assessment task to be considered authentic. McTighe and Wiggins (1999) argue that the following characteristics must be present: realistic; requires judgments and innovation; requires the students "to do" the task; replicates or simulates the context in which adults are tested in the workplace, community, or home; assesses a student's ability to efficiently and effectively use a repertoire of knowledge and skills to negotiate a *complex* (italics mine) task; and allows appropriate opportunities to rehearse, practice, consult resources, obtain feedback, and refine (p. 318). Others agree that for a task to be authentic the student must interpret, synthesize, and evaluate complex information; consider divergent information; show understanding of core ideas (content and concepts); demonstrate methods and procedures used by experts; present their explanations and conclusions in oral, written, and symbolic fashion; and argue that similar problems are encountered out of school (Newman, Marks, and Gamran, 1996, cited by Grant, Gradwell, and Cimbricz, 2004, p. 318). Almost everyone agrees that demonstrated performance has a place in evaluation. Drivers' examinations, adjudicated music contests, scouting merit badges, and trouble shooting by mechanics are the demonstration examples recommended by Theodore Sizer (2004), but they may not be authentic. The idea of demonstration works only with some of the music standards—those that have been most traditional and focus on performance. The emphasis on performance is probably overrated because any task performed only once has a sizable measurement error. Performing music of a different style could also result in a different evaluation.

Critical reflection and self-assessment are also not addressed in depth, despite their presence in the education literature. More than a few music educators have argued that a desired outcome of instruction is critical thinking and problem solving. Jorgensen (2004, p. 204) argues that developing critical thinking is not something that can be assessed; it is the essence of education. What most teachers mean by critical thinking is analytical thinking (Sternberg, 2003, p. 5). Analytical thinking requires students to analyze, critique, judge, compare and contrast, evaluate, and assess. Critical thinking means that students have the ability to attribute, sequence, prioritize, analyze for bias, infer the cause, and know when to act upon information. Beyer's 1988 definition is the ability to distinguish between verifiable facts and value statements, distinguish relevant from irrelevant observations or reasons, determine the factual accuracy of a statement, determine the credibility of a source, identify ambiguous statements, identify unstated assumptions, detect bias, identify logical fallacies, recognize logical inconsistencies in a line of reasoning, and determine the overall strength of an argument or conclusion (p. 136).

Music instruction would seldom have these outcomes. Creative thinking is, of course, the ability to invent, discover, imagine, suppose, predict—not just compose music in the classroom, with or without a computer. The authors of the 1997 NAEP in music have naively argued that assessing students' creative and/or expressive abilities is just as important as assessing technical and historical knowledge ("Developing an arts assessment," 2004, p. 24). It was probably a small step to suggest that creativity in musical compositions could be assessed by use of Flow as described by M. Csikszentmihalyi (Byrne, MacDonald, and Carlton, 2003, p. 277; Custodero, 1999, pp. 79–80.)

Critical reflection and self-assessment are also not addressed despite their presence in the educational literature. Self-assessment, especially of skills, is more complex than most realize; its importance is instructional. Reflection is also important. Experiencing music, however, is more important than talking *about* music, and an emphasis on reflection as an assessment technique could influence the objectives of instruction, an influence that should be avoided.

Rubrics is another hazy term; it refers to a tool for evaluation of performance in the areas of teaching, composing, conducting, improvising, singing, and playing. Such rubrics have seldom been subjected to the rigor required in assessment, and their misuse is potentially damaging to the assessment profession. They are most useful on items about which there is general consensus as to what constitutes excellence.

Organization

Eight areas have been selected as topics for the chapter. First, "Dependent Variables in Research" and "Recently Published Tests" describe the published research that relates to assessment since the publication of the first *Handbook* in 1992. Second, "Unpublished Measures" describes unpublished instruments that were systematically developed. Third is a brief discussion of the criteria for a rubric to be used as an assessment device and the rubric's limitations. Fourth, there is a brief description of the potential of program evaluation in music. Fifth, the various types of validity are defined; sixth, recent developments in educational taxonomies are outlined. Here the intent is to emphasize the importance of connecting instructional objectives and procedures with assessment. Seventh and eighth are the chapter's two concluding sections, one on the potential of technology in assessment, the other on what the future of assessment *may* be should the current reform movement result in systemic change in education. As the extent of change in education or in the music program is hypothetical, the future of assessment can be based only on current premises.

Assessment in Music Education

To achieve high standards for everyone requires an extensive assessment program to chart progress and to facilitate learning in a multitude of areas: facts, skills, understandings, self-esteem, metacognition, and interest in continuing to learn. Past assessment measures have not provided satisfactory answers; if those measures had been adequate, education would not be so impoverished, with many of the traditional assessment measures completely inadequate for any high-stakes evaluation. Any assessment needs to provide an improved understanding of how and why interventions do and do not work. As indicated, a rating scale or an observation may be reliable but not provide critical information as to why the individual or the intervention was successful. Educators and others have criticized assessment devices and procedures for not being valid, for being poorly connected to the competencies expected of students, and for failing to provide data needed for change. Validity is not a property of a test, despite the general use of the term, but rather a property of the specific uses and interpretations that are made of test scores, which explains why one can have "consequential" validity (Baker and Linn, 2004, p. 50). Assessment, for example, an audition, however, is not an exact science; there will always be a certain amount of error, providing an opportunity not only for the politicization of assessment but also, more important, for the voicing of many viewpoints and interpretations. Assessment does mobilize commitment, energy, and knowledge on a topic. Effective evaluation probably requires external norms. Assessment will always be needed because description tends to focus on symptoms rather than the cause.

It is difficult to suggest just how important assessment is to music education in the 21st century, as music education is not connected to education in the same manner as mathematics, language arts, science, or even social studies. Music education is not one of the subjects criticized for its lack of effectiveness; music's public issue has been an inadequate amount of instructional time due to its low priority in the eyes of most educational administrators, at the local and/or state level. Program evaluation is hampered by the existence of two (or more) independent music programs: required music education and elective music education, each with variations. It is not clear that valid music education "programs" exist except at the collegiate level. Individual teachers have undoubtedly developed their own focused, sequential program in general music. Variations of required music programs include integrated course work, enhancement of other subjects, and recreation. Elective music—band, orchestra, choir, guitar, group piano, advanced placement theory, and more—is focused on skill development, and these experiences, traditionally defined, have few common outcomes. With such diversity, development of assessments of student competency in music has been impeded due to multiple *satisfactory* outcomes. It is likely, although not certain, that music would command higher priority on the school's resources if a music assessment were high-stakes—and high-stakes at every grade level. Any judgment about the importance of assessment must wrestle with the initial question of whether the purpose of assessment is aiding progress toward achieving "standards" or toward accountability, an important difference. The accountability movement currently appears to have more support than the standards movement. Use of assessment to improve instruction remains relevant.

Music educators may decide that their outcomes are not high-stakes and take a lower road toward assessment, but if so there will still be a need to rethink the role of assessment and music's relationship to basic subjects. Further, new curricula, new ways of teaching, new priorities require new forms of assessment. Ratings at contests and festivals and student satisfaction have been the primary assessment indicators in music; these do not reveal current program strengths and weaknesses and provide only partial answers in any assessment endeavor.

Evidence from learning psychology reveals that assessment properly conducted makes a major difference in student learning and, when incorrectly used, a corresponding negative effect. The current hype, however, has not produced much action in music education in the United States, Canada, or Great Britain. To many music educators, assessment is so much a part of instruction—especially in achieving goals in performance—that they do not believe more is needed. Other music educators believe that any assessment is inappropriate as either too quantitative or too mechanical. The literature commonly divides assessment by its purpose, summative assessment indicating degree of worth of the finished product, formative assessment indicating only feedback obtained in the process of moving toward the final goal or outcome. Assessment when embedded in music instruction is formative evaluation because its primary purpose is to improve the performance and, one would hope, the learning. Despite the desire of arts advocacy groups to have "hard" data on music learning, there has been little interest in summative evaluation of learning in required music instruction and only slightly more interest in outcomes of elective music experiences. The expensive 1997 arts assessment by NAEP (National Assessment of Educational Progress) had little effect on teaching priorities, and few teachers can relate the results or describe their programs in relation to these national outcomes. Whereas the first national assessment was designed to provide useful data for curriculum writers, the 1997 version conformed more to the concerns of the chief state school officers, who insisted that NAEP be designed so there was nothing objectionable (Lagemann, 2000, p. 192). As a consequence, the 1997 NAEP was an *indirect* measure of student learning, revealing more of what students had not learned than what they had. NAEP provided no feedback to students or schools; it thus had no effect on learning. Pockets of interested officials, such as SCASS (State Collaborative on Assessment and Student Standards), are pondering arts assessment issues, but any connection with extant programs is unknown. Arguing that the arts are basic, several state and major school districts have been funded to construct assessments for their arts programs. More can be expected. At this writing, New York has invested the most in arts assessment but with only initial, approximate norms. FairTest, a nonprofit organization based in Cambridge, Massachusetts, is a national player in criticizing tests and how they are used. It looks for issues of equity in the instruments. Educational Testing Service, however, has promoted the use of evaluation devices for half a century and tends to be the natural target for barbs from FairTest. FairTest is not against all assessment (although its publications give that impression), tending to approve of portfolio assessments without addressing their equity or validity. The public generally accepts the idea of assessment as a source of data on teaching and learning, aware of its importance in describing outcomes in science and medicine. Licensing tests are accepted as routine, ranging from a license to operate a motor vehicle to a license to operate in a hospital whether with knives, machines, or on-the-couch questions. The testing of teachers prior to awarding a license has become accepted practice in 41 states, and the public currently supports an assessment to determine whether students deserve to graduate or even pass from one grade to another.

Dependent Variables in Research

With assessment in music consisting mainly of formative evaluation, a primary resource to identify devices used to assess outcomes is the body of research in the field. All research has independent and dependent variables (although those two sometimes hide under different names). The discussion that follows is a result of scrutinizing the 1990–2005 issues of the major relevant publications in the field: *Psychology of Music, Psychomusicology, Journal of Research in Music Education,* the *Bulletin of the Council for Research in Music Education, Research Studies in Music Education, Music Education Research,* the *British Journal of Music Education, and Dissertation Abstracts International.* The studies cited were selected to indicate *types* of assessment used, with no judgment of their appropriateness. Many of the studies have serious flaws in the research design or in the interpretation of results and would not be cited in a chapter on research. Most evaluations in music do not control well enough for prior knowledge, which has the greatest influence on posttest tasks. The focus of teachers has been on how any results will be used rather than on improving the measures. Although the jury is still out, mandated assessment appears to be improving teaching and learning, as illustrated by clear evidence in Maryland, Kentucky, and Massachusetts (Lane, Parke, and Stone, 2002).

Continuous Response Digital Interface

The paucity of use of valid and reliable measures as dependent variables is surprising, as is the frequent use of observation or description, these latter procedures unaccompanied by a description of their systematic development. A Continuous Response Digital Interface (CRDI) developed at Florida State University was the dependent measure in a large number of studies (Blocker, Greenwood, & Shellahamer, 1997; Brittin, 1996; Brittin & Duke, 1997; Brittin & Sheldon, 1995; Byrnes, 1997; Davis, 1998; DeNardo & Kantorski, 1995, 1998; W. Fredrickson, 1994, 1995, 1997, 1999, 2001; Geringer, 1995; Gregory, 1994; Johnson, 1996; Lychner, 1998; Madsen, 1997a, 1997b, 1998; Madsen, Brittin, & Capprella-Sheldon, 1993; Madsen & Coggiola, 2001; Rentz, 1992; Sheldon, 1994; Sheldon & Gregory, 1997; Siebenaler, 1997; Skadsem, 1997). Initially this device was used only to report on one dimension of a subject's response to musical stimuli; by the end of the decade the device was sufficiently more sophisticated so that it could provide a reading on two responses. The reading is displayed on a dial, connected to a computer. The connection with the computer provides multiple readings per second and thus provides data that are reliable. The validity of the data remains unknown. The premise for its use is that there is a match between aesthetic response, the dial reading, and the place in the score at which the reading was taken. Should *reflection* be necessary to respond, the CRDI would measure an important *preaesthetic* point. The chief developer of the CRDI reports that the same information is obtained that one obtains from a paper-and-pencil test, a finding that is supportive of its concurrent validity (Madsen, 1997a, p. 64). A current criticism of assessments throughout education is that they are not authentic; that the evaluation is not "real-world" but an artificial, multiple-choice assessment. Authenticity is not a major issue in music research, as nearly every dependent variable involves some type of music performance. Assessment critics would fault the CRDI because manipulating a dial is artificial to the same extent as a multiple-choice test is. In defense of its partial authenticity, the CRDI has been used with recordings of accepted great music similar to the requirement of many multiple-choice tests.

Along with authentic assessment, reflection is promoted as an assessment tool. Requiring students to describe musical meaning and understanding is troublesome. Students with equal understanding are not equally verbal. Even the terms *higher* and *lower* are confusing to young music students (Hair, 1997); thus attempts to measure student reflections when the experience entails far more complex musical concepts calls into question the potential of student verbalization as an important assessment tool.

Observation

The most common dependent variable in the research studies examined was simple observation of student and teacher performance, either live or videotaped. No observation schedule provided data on its validity or reliability, whether a Likert scale or a professional description of the observation was used. A common study was one that modeled the observation form used in earlier research by Madsen and Yarbrough, but no statements were made that concerned the rigor of the form's development or the adaptation (Elkholm, 2000). An encouraging trend is an increase in the number of points on the Likert scales used, often 7 or 9; Yarbrough's observation of teaching videos used 10 criteria (Effective Teaching Response Form, [Yarbrough & Henley, 1999]). Curiously, no criteria for excellence in teaching exist. To avoid establishing criteria, Goolsby (1996) identified three levels of teaching: student teachers, first-year teachers, and experienced teachers, rough categories if teaching excellence is the research criterion.

The misconceptions about the validity of many of the dependent variables indicate the present naïveté of much music education research. The use of observation as a valid assessment tool is one of the most flagrant flaws. Observation is an extremely crude method of determining the extent of learning in music, as a little serious thought will reveal. Yet teachers are often evaluated solely on the basis of observation, a process that does not reveal their teaching capabilities and gives only minimal evidence of student learning that occurs as a result of the teaching intervention. A student performance, live or recorded, is perhaps a better assessment device, but any single performance provides only an approximation of musicianship, musical understanding, attitude toward learning music, knowledge of and about music, or ability to discriminate. A seminal article on the weaknesses of observation in music (Froehlich, 1995) pointed up that observer agreement and precision of agreement reveal little about the validity and reliability of assessing the behavior of the teacher. Froehlich argues that valid observations require: (1) that they be derived from a specific instructional theory; (2) that, once collected, they are examined within the context of that theory; and (3) accuracy, which depends upon not only the construct of interest to the researcher but also on the participants' agreement that what was observed reflected their own interpretation of the behavior under study (p. 188). Froehlich's arguments begin to address the complexities of observing teaching and learning and the minimal requirements for generalizability, transfer, and assumption of task and attribute relationship. As in all research and evaluation, estimation of error is important, and without well-designed investigative procedures predicting the amount of error is extremely difficult.

Teacher Evaluation

Ingram, Louis, and Schroeder (2004) found that about half of the teachers and administrators judged teacher effectiveness and school effectiveness by other indicators than student achievement, thus limiting the possibility that this means of teacher evaluation will be readily accepted by the profession (p. 1273). Pullin (2004) has outlined the legal challenges facing the state and federal agencies that are attempting to influence the preparation of teachers. Steiner reports that teacher education programs are not well aligned with the expected competencies of teachers, further complicating the development of assessment measures prior to induction into the profession. And Gray (2004) reminds us that it is quite difficult—indeed, nearly impossible—to flunk out of most colleges these days, thus eliminating this approach to the improvement of teaching. Reinforcing these conclusions and with additional data, Hess, Rotherham, and Walsh (2004) conclude that teacher preparation programs are not teaching important skills or working to weed out unsuitable candidates (pp. 279–284). The National Board for Professional Teaching Competency tasks have received little attention from the research community beyond asking teachers their opinion of the experience (Standerfer, 2003). A significant part of the process is in describing, analyzing, and then reflecting on one's teaching, although there is also a 3-hour formal examination. INTASC (Interstate New Teacher Assessment and Support Consortium) has 13 standards by which to measure competency, with those for music specialists and classroom teachers based generally on the voluntary national standards. Without any research or assessment data on these teacher standards, the pass rate on standardized and state teacher certification tests approaches 90 percent. Similarly, in teacher evaluations principals give unsatisfactory marks to only 1 percent of their teachers. Under these circumstances, the pressures for developing assessment tools for teachers will be political and based on very limited data—at present, Tennessee is the primary source for such data. Consensus seems to be forming around the development of measures that focus on the following: basic scholarship, a knowledge of teaching and learning, a knowledge of collegiality, knowledge of educational context, management of the change process, a sense of moral purpose and a willingness for continuing learning (Lieberman and Miller, 2004, p. 25).

Other Measures

On the few occasions where the semantic differential was used as an assessment measure, there was a consistent lack of the expected rigor, that is, of establishing the viability of the semantic differential, and a statement of the extent to which the three constructs that are the usual outcomes—evaluation, potency, and activity—related to the research question.

Music education researchers did use a few dependent measures from outside the field to assess basic knowledge, personality, or teacher competencies; those that were used were rarely employed more than once during the past decade. Those measures emphasized an affective component—Gregorc's *Style Delineator*, Eysenck's tests, and the Dunn, Dunn, and Price *Learning Indicator*. The competence devices used more than once included the *Wechsler PreSchool Test*, the *Developing Cognitive Abilities Test*, the *Watkins-Farnum Performance Scale*, the Ohio and Australian proficiency examination, the Asmus attitude scale (unpublished), and Gordon's *Primary Measures of Music Audiation*.

Summary

Inspection of the dependent variables in published research and doctoral dissertations reveals little change from past practice, that is, teacher/researcher/panel of judges determining treatment effect. Interjudge reliability is generally high except in judging musical compositions. This interjudge reliability is a correlation among judges, *not* between judge and dependent variable. Limited use was made of researcher-constructed instruments, only one of which was examined for reliability except as noted in "Recently Published Tests," later in this chapter. Researchers appeared to believe there was no need to determine reliability or validity of interviews, observations, and especially Likert scales.

Recently Published Tests

Edwin Gordon's Readiness Test

Only one new test was published during the past decade—Edwin Gordon's *Harmonic Improvisation Readiness Record* and *Rhythm Improvisation Readiness Record* (1998)—which is actually two tests, as the scores of the two parts are not combined. As the title suggests, this readiness test was not developed as an achievement test but more as a needs-assessment measure. Its use to measure improvisational competence has not been established, nor does the author suggest this as a use. These tests are important as they continue to emphasize Gordon's primary contribution to music education, which is the centrality of the *mental conception* of music, an ability he has termed audiation. One wonders why there has not been more emphasis placed on teaching audiation in music classrooms, as this competency is essential to attaining many of the goals of the complete musician. It may be that teachers relate audiation only to creating and improvising and believe, as Gordon states in the test manual, "neither improvisation nor creativity . . . can be taught" (p. 8). The test results are of interest, as the scores for students in third-grade general music do not differ significantly from those of high school students in selective ensembles. One of the author's explanations for the lack of difference is that little instructional effort has been exerted to attain the needed competencies.

Gordon describes three ways one can improvise (possible dependent variables): One may perform a variation of a melody, without giving attention to the underlying existent or implied harmony (p. 8); a melody may be performed over a series of harmonic patterns (harmonic progressions); and harmonic patterns may be improvised to an old or new melody (p. 9).

Technical Considerations   The manual has numerous typographical errors, making it difficult to be confident of any critique. The sample size used to establish the norms is more than 15,000 students, Grades 3–12 (p. 48); the Ns for Grades 3–6, 7–8, and 9–12 are not provided. The number of students by grade level is established, however, based on a study conducted in Gilbert, South Carolina (pp. 58–59), where the total N was 918. In a second study, a clever strategy to establish validity was to have 95 fourth- and fifth-grade students in a parochial school listen to six recorded unfamiliar songs, performed twice, and ask the students to "sing a response that sounded like the song but was not an imitation of the song."

Gordon concludes that the harmony and rhythm tests are independent and that the rhythm test is more basic (p. 76). He asserts that students with scores of 22 and above are "ready." As a score of 20 can be obtained by chance (40 items with response of "same" or "not same"), additional research is necessary. Researchers interested in test development should study Tables 7 and 8 (pp. 52–53), Item Difficulty and Item Discrimination for Grades 3–12, as both indices are nearly the same for all 86 items for Grades 3–6, 7–8, and 9–12, one of the most impressive examples of item stability for any test battery.

Nonstandard Published Measures

One test published only on the computer, John Flohr's *Contemporary Rhythm Skills Assessment* (2000), is computer-administered. It is designed to assess steady beat and rhythm pattern competence of students ages 4–12. It can be accurate to a millisecond. Part 1 consists of a folk song played at five different tempi; the task is to supply the beat. In part 2, the testee must listen to and repeat 20 rhythm patterns by tapping on the computer's space bar. A critique is not possible due to the fact that the results from students of nine different age groups, 4–12, are combined, making the data difficult to interpret.

James Froseth and Molly Weaver published *Music Teacher Self-Assessment* (1996), but this is not an assessment tool. Its purpose is to train teachers in observation techniques. The authors made no attempt to establish any validity or reliability for the observation scales or to argue that the observations are focused on important teaching ventures. It is also not based on any observational research. The use of the word *assessment* in the title is misleading.

Unpublished Measures

Instrumental Music Assessment

Gary McPherson (1995, 2005) developed a five-part assessment for instrumental music as his doctoral dissertation and has since continued its development. McPherson's work is important because he addresses concerns of teachers—practice, technique, and improvisation. His test is appropriate for Australian music education, where there is more emphasis on aural skills, musicology, theory, listening, appraising music, and composing, a much broader program than found in instrumental music instruction in the United States. The current tentative movement toward teaching more *music* in the rehearsal indicates the importance of a careful review of McPherson's assessment research. His contribution is more a think piece to the literature in assessment than a rigorously developed assessment instrument. McPherson's concern was instructional; the tests were his way of attempting to identify strategies that students use in performing. In a search for learning strategies, McPherson provides an excellent description of the process of learning to play an instrument, enabling the reader to make a decision on the content- and criterion-related validity of the assessment measures. McPherson's term is *convergent* validity. Test reliability is not addressed; data on the reliability of the judges are provided, but this reliability number is not informative about the tests themselves, their coverage, length, and other qualities that would be important should the test be considered as a high-stakes measure. McPherson's primary concern was assessment of the student's musical memory and ability to play by ear. His sample consisted of 101 clarinet and trumpet students who lived in New South Wales, Australia, and were preparing to take the Australian Music Examinations Board (AMEB), which assesses a student's ability to perform a repertoire of rehearsal music. As his interest was in high school students, he divided his sample into students 12–15 years of age and those 15–18. (Often test developers seek a disparate group, as reliability may be enhanced when students vary.) McPherson used the *Watkins-Farnum Performance Scale* as a measure of sight-reading and data from the 12-point rating scale of performance from the AMEB test. He then created three additional measures, one assessing the ability to perform from memory, one the ability to play by ear, and a third to improvise. McPherson established pitch, rhythm, and phrasing as the criteria and asked three judges to rate the performance on a 6-point scale: no attempt, very poor, fair, good, reasonably accurate, and no errors.

Playing by ear was defined as the ability to perform a melody shortly after hearing it, perform a piece held in long-term memory that was learned aurally, and transpose a piece learned under one of the two methods. It was necessary for McPherson to identify two well-known songs for which his subjects had never seen the notation.

McPherson constructed a two-part test, the first part requiring the students to play "Happy Birthday" in two keys, F and G, and "For He's a Jolly Good Fellow" in F and C. Part 2 consisted of four short melodies played by the same instrument as that of the student. The melodies were played four times, with a one-measure rest between each playing. After each melody, the subject was asked to play the melody twice in the original key and twice in the transposed key. The evaluation was, again, on a 6-point scale for both renditions.

The third test, on ability to improvise, consisted of seven items. Items 1 and 2 required the student to formulate an answering phrase to a four-measure musical question. Item 3 required a rhythmic improvisation to a melody that used only the durations of a given rhythm pattern. Items 4 and 5 provided an opening phrase for an improvisation. In Item 6, students were given a recorded piano accompaniment and asked to improvise a melody. Item 7 was a free improvisation in any style.

Having an instrumental music test available other than the Watkins-Farnum may encourage teaching the competencies McPherson investigated. McPherson's interpretation of his results suggests that the study of piano is important; beginning instruction at a young age helps, as well as the more obviously important mental rehearsal and envisioning how one would perform a song or improvisation on one's instrument. The requirement for judges makes the test inconvenient to administer.

Cognitive-Affective Measure

Lee Bartel (1992) aided the research community by providing research data on the robustness of the semantic differential to provide a measure of cognitive and affective responses to music. His tool was appropriately named the Cognitive-Affective Response Test; it consisted of 18 semantic differential scales, 9 for each dimension. His premise is that meaning in music can be assessed using the ideas of Charles Osgood (1957) in measuring meaning in language. Bartel emphasized the importance of minimizing the *evaluative* component of the semantic differential (while retaining the cognitive and affective components) when listening to music—should meaning have a relationship to the evaluation component it would be a separate construct.

Bartel's research results indicate that careful selection of the adjectives is required before the semantic differential can be trusted as an assessment measure. If one is constructing a semantic tool (questionnaire, Likert-type scale, etc.), pilot studies are necessary. Reliability and validity are critical and must be reported. Bartel's task was to identify adjectives meaningful both to the music and to the cognitive and affective dimensions of linguistics. Bartel drew upon the philosophical position of Peter Kivy (1984), who had provided a tripartite framework of adjectives to describe music. Bartel's task was to use different musical styles (he began with classical and gospel) that loaded on his two constructs of *cognitive* and *affective* when subjected to factor analysis, as his goal was to construct a test that provided a single score of meaning. The test has not been published; this is unfortunate, as it and a study by Robert Miller (1979) are seminal works in multidimensional scaling and should be related to responses from the CRDI.

Computerized Adaptive Technology

In view of the widespread reliance on observation and professional judgment for the assessment of objectives in music, it is not surprising that little attention has been paid to capitalizing on advances in the field of measurement. Walter Vispoel (1992), an educational psychologist, applied computerized adaptive technology (CAT) to extant music aptitude tests, using item response theory (IRT). With IRT (CAT) the computer selects the next appropriate question based on the correctness of the last response. The difficulty level of the questions in the computer's item data bank must be known or estimated, as the task of the computer is to advance the competent student quickly to more demanding items (it selects easier items when a response is incorrect). Testing is begun with a question of average difficulty, and the computer takes over until the desired reliability criterion is met. The use of a computer adaptive test is particularly appealing for situations where students must listen acutely, and fatigue is an issue in obtaining reliable and valid scores. Vispoel's use of only 30 college students means that the results are tentative and considerable additional research is needed. He used the tonal memory section of Seashore's *Measures of Musical Talents*, and the musical memory subtest from the second edition of the Drake *Musical Aptitude Tests*, finding that 9 items were as reliable as 30; he estimated concurrent validity based upon student self-reports on measures used by Drake a half-century ago. As neither the Seashore nor the Drake is currently in use, Vispoel's research teases us to identify important outcomes and to construct IRT measures that cover a broad range of outcomes, including mastery, diagnostic, and grade-specific tools.

Auditory Skills and Other Efforts

Louise Buttsworth, Gerald Fogarty, and Peter Rorkle (1993) developed a test for tertiary students to replace individual auditions, using as the criterion a battery of tests given at the end of one semester of aural training. Fourteen tests were constructed, all dealing with auditory skills, most with low reliability. Their work, too complex to be summarized, is an excellent example of the difficulty of constructing even a skills assessment.

One doctoral student (McCurry, 1998) constructed a test battery based on the Voluntary National Standards to document the value of using hand chimes in fourth- and fifth-grade general music. She used 80 students divided into four groups: choral, instrumental, general music, and hand chime. Her dependent variable, a measure of achievement on the nine standards, is of interest, as it illustrates the perspective of a classroom teacher on appropriate tasks at this grade level.

Other research that involved test construction, but less rigorous, includes doctoral dissertations by Diane Hardy, The Construction and Validation of an Original Sight-Playing Test for Elementary Piano Students (1995); Claude Masear, The Development and Field Test of a Model for Evaluating Elementary String Programs (1999); Henry Mikle, The Development of an Individual Sight-Reading Inventory (1999); and Hong Wei, Development of a Melodic Achievement Test for Fourth Grades Taught by a Specific Music

Learning Methodology (1995). There has been little interest in reestablishing the validity of extant tests, the one exception being a doctoral dissertation by Charles Norris (1998), who explored the relationship of the aural tonal memory section of aptitude tests to a student's ability to vocally reproduce short tonal patterns. With a (small) sample of 210 students across eight grade levels (5–12) he found a stable relationship and a correlation of .66 with the Seashore measures.

Building on her doctoral dissertation, Sheila Scott (2000) experimented with 7 students to determine if it was possible to obtain a measure of a student's understanding of the characteristics of melody through oral explanations that she called think alouds and whether the student's understanding matched 1980s learning outcomes (Biggs & Collis, 1982). Scott found the task extremely time-consuming; to create the test materials, she wrote 26 melodies that portrayed 13 different characteristics of melody. Students responded inconsistently, ranging from understanding Level 2 to Level 5 on her test. Understanding at Level 5 did not indicate understanding at Levels 1–4, raising validity and sequencing issues.

A Published but Unavailable Test

The major assessment effort of the decade was the music portion of the NAEP that assessed students in Grade 8 (Persky, Sandene, & Askew, 1998). The contribution of this assessment (other than elevating the status of music among school subjects) was the construction and scoring of open-response tasks. Students were asked to perform, to improvise, and to create, providing a comparison of student achievement on these tasks with the 1970 national assessment. The new assessment raised as many questions as it answered; for example, the final report says that no consistent pattern was found between frequency of instruction and student scores (p. 145).

Rubrics

Development and Definition

Because rubrics have become almost a separate assessment technique, a definition and a short discussion of them seem appropriate. As used for assessment, a rubric is generally a well-defined rule, guide, or standard. Teachers of composition often offer carefully worded rubrics as their sole assessment device for a classroom experience, the scoring of which is enormously time-consuming and subjective (Hickey, 1999). Rubrics are often associated with authentic assessment devices but in fact lead to standardization of responses rather than to divergent and original thought. However, rubrics can clarify performance objectives, as the student is able to understand in rather precise terms what is expected. Rubrics are highly effective in focusing student effort (narrowing it) and serve well as external motivation. The greatest use of rubrics has been in language arts, and it is clear that students can and will "write to the rubric." The appropriate research process in rubric development is to have a panel of judges evaluate a large number of musical compositions, place these in four or five categories according to worth, and then formulate rubrics that best describe the compositional attributes that distinguish each group. Once adequate research has been completed, additional student compositions can be evaluated against these rubrics.

The intent of those who believe in rubrics is to obtain a single score, often for use in high-stakes assessment. Unless the rubric becomes as detailed as a checklist, it is difficult to imagine a rubric providing feedback that would be helpful. Thomas Newkirk (2000) believes that the use of rubrics indicates a resurgence of "mechanized instruction" in writing (p. 41). He argues (in the case of English composition) that rubrics conceal or mystify the process of writing when process may be one of the objectives. Linda Mabry (1999) in an excellent treatment of rubrics and their effect on teaching argues that rubrics overwhelm the writing curriculum and that writing to the rubric is more powerful than teaching to the test. The use of rubrics has not only standardized scoring but also standardized writing. Rubric construction in music has not had any rigorous scrutiny and at present is usually an inappropriate evaluation measure. Rubrics have to meet rigorous criteria to be of any value. As is evident from other fields, students become very adept at writing to the rubric but that knowledge limits student creativity. With rubrics, students are weak in judging self-expressive and individualistic tasks; it is therefore surprising that rubrics are frequently used to judge student compositions. Peer assessment is often recommended, but this procedure is more difficult than most presume. Third-year undergraduate students assessing performance found that the breadth of music across a diverse range of musical styles on a wide range of instruments made the task both daunting and difficult (Blom and Poole, 2004, p. 123). The assessment of compositions by youthful, untrained students can be little more than a teaching device. Performance standards are the most difficult to implement with rubrics: They limit the variability of scores, they fail to detect what a student really can do, and they are not useful for high stakes testing, and the prompts are difficult, if not impossible, to construct in advance. Those who have attempted to assess creativity have found it feasible (Beston, 2004, p. 37). Cantwell and Jeanneret (2004, p. 10) investigated the relationship of part to whole, as is required with rubrics, and found it necessary to use Snow's cognitive and conative structures in learning in determining detail, main ideas, and themes. Assessing composition needs to consider originality, improvement, development of personal style, expression, the conveying of ideas, aesthetics, technical skill, expressiveness, effective use of form, effective use of the elements, and the development of previously used ideas—a lot to consider. Acceptance in assessment has been based on the power of the descriptions and whether these descriptions appear to differentiate quality in products and tasks.

Use in Portfolios

Our understanding of rubrics in portfolios stems from research in language arts. Aschbacher (1999) conducted an extensive project with establishing rubrics for middle school language arts, beginning with six descriptor scales: type of assignment, type of content knowledge used, type of student response, type of choice students were given, grading dimensions used, and types of feedback provided, plus five 4-point evaluative scales: cognitive demands of the task, clarity of grading, alignment of the task with learning goals, alignment of grading criteria with learning goals, and overall task quality. The alignment between grading with rubrics and student learning was .65, not high. Teachers not only volunteered but also were paid to be interviewed and to allow the investigator to look at student work. Even experienced teachers have had insufficient preparation to use rubrics. The relationship between overall rating and grading clarity was .14, with goals/task .16 and with goals/grading .24 at the elementary school level, slightly higher for middle school. Teachers had difficulty articulating their goals for the students and had only a vague notion of the criteria they used in grading student work. Seldom were students given assignments that were both coherent and intellectually challenging, and one-third or less of the reading comprehension, draft writing, and project assignments provided any intellectual rigor. No assessment method can be successful unless there is excellent instruction.

Program Evaluation

Importance of Program Evaluation

Few examples can be found of program evaluation in music. Indeed, in the entire area of teacher education little attention is given to program evaluation. Why then is it the subject of discussion here? The answer lies in the fact that if music is to be considered as an equal subject, educators and the public will focus on the adequacy of the *program,* not the test scores of individual students enrolled in the program or the competence of ensembles. The few evaluators who have assessed music "programs" have assessed ad hoc activities such as those of composers and artists in the schools, opera organizations, and interested groups, and activities sponsored by orchestras. Constance Gee's (1994) evaluation of the artist in the classroom accurately portrays a valid assessment of a partial program. Despite an additional decade of these ad hoc music programs by artists in the schools, there are no additional data on their effectiveness. Program evaluators, often advocates, have seldom looked at typical school programs and, when they have, have neglected to give consideration to the goals of the program.

At present, program evaluation is the dominant form of assessment in all areas affected by the federal government (and what area is today not affected by the federal government?). The Government Performance and Results Act of 1993 called for the use of performance measurement in virtually all federal agencies by the year 2000. This act has provided a major impetus to assessment of the large-scale social (and other) programs funded by the federal government (Richardson, 1992). Assessments have been conducted, for example, of programs designed to reduce smoking and alcohol use among adolescents, programs to eliminate drug usage, and programs to educate school-age children about sexually transmitted diseases. Other programs evaluated are those that concern toxic waste, catastrophic illness, air safety, deterring insider trading, terrorism, health care costs, nuclear hazards, AIDS, industry competitiveness, the trade imbalance, the social underclass, and employment for welfare mothers. There are also program assessments of those after-school and extended-day programs that receive federal money.

Music education needs to establish its place in the nation's educational priorities, but it lacks quantitative data necessary for comparison purposes or for use by efficiency experts. The major difficulty with seeking teaching or learning guidance from program evaluation continues to be the absence of experiences planned to constitute a program that have sufficient clarity and consensus on outcomes. Secondary school experiences are planned, nonsequentially, around performances Elementary school music experiences are much too varied (although often excellent) even within a single school district to fairly assess for comparative purposes. The last major effort to establish a music "program" was some 20 years ago with a series of music texts published by Silver-Burdett under the leadership of Bennett Reimer, Beth Crook, and David Walker (1974–1985). The profession does need to give increased attention to program integrity. Mike Blakeslee (2004) of the National Association for Music Education suggests that the field is clouded by less than rigorous thinking about what systems contribute to learning and that music classes often lack defined learning outcomes (p. 32). He argues that it is time for arts education to develop the same clear goals for student achievement that we expect for other areas of the wider curriculum (p. 34). Milner (2000) attempted to assess music "programs" in Texas in relationship to the Texas Essential Knowledge and Skills examination but found it necessary to separately assess Kodaly, Orff, standard, and eclectic programs. Government leaders use program evaluation to make decisions, especially when the data match their beliefs. Resources are allocated on the basis of program evaluations. Program evaluations are conducted for a variety of purposes: to back up beliefs, monitor public opinion, obtain a sense of what occurs in a program, show the program's importance, and affect the power structure. Arts advocates appear to have a better sense of the potential use of program evaluation data than do music teachers. Advocates sense that the reform movement is a power struggle over the curriculum, and in that struggle data from program evaluation are important, especially when standards are used for program justification. The federal government has actively supported the standards movement and has initiated program assessment on the effectiveness of curricula in most basic subjects.

Philosophies of Program Evaluation

Several differing evaluation philosophies exist, arising from the varying possible political colors of program assessment. The sheer quantity of material—citing one point of view or the other—makes fair treatment of program assessment nearly impossible. Most people in the field agree that the text by Shadish, Cook, and Leviton (1991) is the basic source. This volume, titled *Foundations of Program Evaluation: Theories of Practice,* consists of the ideas of seven leading program evaluators, followed by a critique of the strengths and weaknesses of each. Each of these seven, plus others in the field, has named his own assessment technique, making it necessary for any discussant to wade through differences among adaptive, realistic, discrepancy, cost-benefit, utilitarian, connoisseurial, planned variation cross-validation, justice, pluralistic, program theory, goal-free, and many more program evaluation models.

Purpose

In defining the purpose of evaluation, Ernest R. House (1994) cites Michael Scriven, determining the merit or worth of something according to a set of criteria, with those criteria often (but not always) explicated and justified (p. 14). House suggests that

> the work of evaluation consists of collecting data, including relevant values and standards, resolving inconsistencies in the values, clarifying misunderstandings and misrepresentations, rectifying false facts and assumptions, distinguishing between wants and needs, identifying all relevant dimensions of merit, finding appropriate measures for these dimensions, weighting the dimensions, validating the standards, and arriving at an evaluative conclusion which requires a synthesis of all these considerations. (p. 86)

Program evaluation, although only one facet of evaluation, encompasses all these aspects of evaluation.

Programs and policies can be simultaneously good and bad, depending upon how the evaluation is conducted and the side effects incurred. The questions asked by the evaluator about the program and its policies would include: what are the uses, the foci, the audience, the training, what data must be collected, and so on. *Good* and *bad* are relative terms. The individuals involved in any single evaluation project will have different interests and will approach education with fairly clear but differing ideas about what are valid education and music education programs. Because these differences exist, clear statements of program purpose are required, as well as the ability on the part of the evaluator to understand the reasoning of those affected by the evaluation. Often the resources to fund program evaluation in education are inadequate for the length of time required for educational interventions to have any effect; thus the history of program evaluation in education appears to show that (most) interventions do not have a lasting effect on learning. Among the many types of program evaluation, two are distinctive. The first, associated with Scriven (1993, 1997), requires that the evaluator provide his or her interpretation of the data and make a judgment of the program's worth. Judgments and recommendations often require hard choices, and this type of evaluation brings evaluators close to or into the political arena of education. A second school of thought would have an external evaluator gather data, then put that data in the hands of the program manager for the stakeholders to interpret (Stake, 1991, 2000). Often this approach involves negotiating among all involved in the assessment to arrive at the meaning of the data and decisions to be made. This approach avoids, for the external evaluator, both the "summative" decision and the task of interpreting raw and derived scores, as well as establishing the significance of any differences.

Focus

Cronbach (1995) took issue with the general experimental model for gathering program evaluation data when he suggested that the primary purpose of an evaluator was to be a program *improver* (p. 27). He put the emphasis on formative rather than summative evaluation, suggesting that the primary purpose of evaluation might be to ascertain whether students can paraphrase, generate examples, use models, solve problems, identify the critical properties in a concept, give reasons why things are done, and as a final step synthesize complex arguments in favor of or against a relationship or concept. Cronbach's stance is that philosophical and conceptual beliefs are more powerful than lists of significant and nonsignificant differences; thus theories can be more successful in changing behaviors than lists of consequences for failure to change. Cronbach's thinking often does not satisfy the politician who wants to know why things are as they are—is there profiling, ineffective staffing, or incompetent teaching? To answer these questions the "hard" approach to assessment is needed. Often, however, the focus is not on whether success has been achieved but on providing documentation that there is equal participation and a proper allocation of resources. Equity concerns are addressed by gender, age, socioeconomic class, and race to ensure that no one group of individuals is disadvantaged due to, for example, physical handicaps, language, place of residence, or political affiliation.

Social Context

An important concept in program evaluation, especially that conducted through case studies and qualitative means, is putting all data into an appropriate context. Diversity issues prompt this concern, but other prompts stem from the recognition that there are major differences not only among individuals but also among classrooms, schools, and communities. In light of these differences, the question is raised as to whether all students and all teachers can or should be assessed through use of a single standard. Consideration of the social context allows educational outcomes to differ and still be equal. With the acceptance of different outcomes, the results of evaluation may need to be interpreted *relative* to floating standards. The support for relativity comes from constructivist philosophy. Humans can construct what is meant by *competent* and by *the good life;* as the goals of education are something society creates, society is free to construct various definitions of success.

Context influences outcomes. For the evaluator, established programs and their context increase the difficulty of conducting a meaningful assessment. If the school's band program has consistently won blue ribbons at marching band, jazz, and concert contests and festivals, ascertaining that the program does not meet the school's educational goals would require extremely compelling data. Even average programs are contextually influenced for evaluators of any persuasion. The constructivist would suggest that society values excellence arrived at through cooperative learning; thus the goals attained by the band are as valid as any goal the school's administration might propose. The connection between evaluation and the politics of education is most obvious in the assessment of long-established programs and those *perceived* by the public to be successful.

With knowledge of how the music program fits into the social, political, educational, and organizational context, a realistic look at its range of effects in each of the contexts is possible. The qualitative approach to program evaluation has advantages here: The evaluator can devote sufficient time on-site to become familiar with the local situation and its biases, traditions, and values, where liberal and conservative views are most likely to surface.

Another viable approach to program evaluation is to involve a limited number of external evaluators, perhaps only one, and to train the stakeholders to conduct a self-evaluation. Shadish and Cook (2000) suggest that communities differ in the way they construct reality, contributing to differences in how they perceive an evaluation, methods of observation, validations, reporting formats, and strategies for evaluation use (p. 45). Because of these differences, assessment training in self-evaluation situations is necessary; few teachers have had any systematic instruction in any form of evaluation. Robert Stake (1997) would like the stakeholders to discover for themselves what changes they wish to make—he believes if teachers have conducted or helped conduct the assessment, their personal investment will contribute to the possibility that the results will be used. Similar arguments are made by Fetterman (2001), who champions *empowerment evaluation,* where through the evaluation process the stakeholders are enabled (empowered) to make necessary changes and to defend the validity of current practices. How well a teacher or student should perform is a concept that is "constructed" by a school system or a teacher; thus multiple stakeholders must be involved in constructing or reconstructing the definition of acceptable performance if constructive use is to be made of the data collected.

Quantitative Versus Qualitative

During the 1990s and the first decade of the 21st century, program evaluation literature abounded with discussions about quantitative and qualitative assessment and the extent to which the two could be combined in a single assessment (House, 1994; Reichardt & Rallis, 1994; M. L. Smith, 1994). There are important differences between the two techniques, but these differences should not affect the actual evaluation. It appears that those empowered to make changes usually require *quantitative* data—there is a need to know the number of students who were successful as a result of an after-school program compared to the number of successful students who missed the offering. Success can have any number of important *qualitative* definitions, but they are usually not relevant to the need of school board members focused on costs, the number of students who do not graduate, the number of music students who fail, or even the number of students who have quit smoking as a result of a requirement in the after-school program. Quantitative data report the success or lack of success of a program in the simplest terms, a summative evaluation. Summative evaluations are used in comparing schools, states, and various remedial or gifted programs. A rich description, no matter how deep, of a student's experience in the school or in a classroom is seldom sufficiently generalizable or definitive to warrant school board action. Rich descriptions are more useful in formative evaluation, an evaluation that aids in changing classroom practices and classroom methods.

The methodology to be used in any assessment depends upon the subject matter and what it is that one wants to know. Until the content to be assessed is known, discussions about whether one should use quantitative or qualitative methodology in an assessment are not productive. The *problem* is the deciding factor. Teachers generally are not concerned with issues related to summative evaluation—it was not teachers who inspired the reform movement in education and its attendant content and performance standards. Teachers did not demand graduation examinations and, historically, have not requested information on how their class compares with other classes in the state or nation.

Currently evaluations in music that supposedly address program concerns through employment of qualitative data outnumber those that employ quantitative data, but those with quantitative data appear to be the more influential assessments in support of music programs. These data are not based on *musical outcomes;* data on higher academic tests scores, graduation rates, college acceptances, fewer delinquency incidents, better work habits, and such are the data that resonate with school administrators, school boards, and music activists. Qualitative data are more compelling on *instructional issues,* quantitative data on policy questions about the *value* of the program. A few qualitative assessments do not actually evaluate but are important instructional tools.

A major objection to the quantitative approach is that it reminds individuals of the pass-fail examination and all its related anxiety. The criticism of the quantitative evaluation involves the difficulty in teasing out the causes for any improvement or deficiencies from a summative score. The reference is usually to the "black box," meaning that administering a standardized test like the PRAXIS II examination provides a pass-fail based on the "cut-score" established by the state department of education, but the score provides little information to the candidate or his or her school on how to build upon successes or correct any weaknesses. The black box is the test that reveals nothing about what *caused* the score, whereas qualitative techniques are designed to observe frequently and in enough depth to identify probable causes of program weaknesses. It is not clear that observation, no matter how skillful, can assess many of the competencies required to be a successful teacher, but program evaluation is designed to look at programs, *not* individuals.

A Model

The current model for program evaluation in the arts is John Harland's *Arts Education in Secondary Schools: Effects and Effectiveness* (2000). A number of concerns in Great Britain prompted this study, among which were the following: There were fewer advisory services from local school districts, a decline in the arts content of initial training courses for primary teachers, a relaxation in the curriculum requirements to allow more time on literacy and numeracy, a worry that out-of-school programs were being boosted to replace in-school programs, and the promotion of the arts for their contribution toward combating social exclusion (p. 3). Harland's charge was to document the range of effects and outcomes attributable to school-based arts education, to examine the relationship between these effects and the key factors and processes associated with arts provision in schools, to illuminate good practice in schools' provision of high-quality education experiences in the arts, and to study the extent to which high levels of institutional involvement in the arts correlate with the qualities known to be associated with successful school improvement and school effectiveness. A survey of pupils in their junior year was conducted with interviews of employers and employees. The questions centered on objectives comparable to those in the United States; critical discrimination, aesthetic judgment, techniques, and skills at the key stage that was the end of required instruction, furthering of thinking skills, and the capacity to use the arts in their social, artistic, and cultural contexts and to prepare for a cultural life. Students in Great Britain ranked music as the least favorite subject with the highest proportion of responses that the curriculum had no impact on their abilities or attitudes.

The curriculum and the school were not as persuasive as the teacher, a conclusion that indicates the importance of selection and education of all teachers involved with music. A fine assessment of a teacher education program was completed by José Luis Aróstegui (2004).

Validity

Three Traditional Types

Validity has long been the sine qua non of research and evaluation. The term has been so misused that its meaning and even importance are subject to confusion. One can discuss validity only in relational terms; whereas a general statement that *results* were invalid might be quite appropriate. To establish validity, the gathering, interpreting, and reporting of data should be valid *in relation to* a concept or idea of importance. Traditionally, evaluators focused efforts to establish validity on one of three areas: content, criterion-related, or construct. *Content validity* indicates a match between the assessment techniques and the content of a course or program. High-stakes tests have been delayed in several states to ensure that the students have been taught the content that appears on the high-stakes examination. Students often recall an experience when there was little match between the content of classroom discussions and the final examination and when a legitimate complaint was lodged about the content validity of a test, especially tests that influenced the final grade in the course. *Criterion-related validity* matches the results of an assessment with an accepted measure of competence in the same domain. There should be a relationship between a medical student's passing "the boards" (a battery of tests) and his or her ability to diagnose standard illnesses. Criterion-referenced assessments are also expected to predict future performance. Some assessors separate predictive validity from validity established by a match between test results and current task competency. *Construct validity* has long been considered the most important validity check for many assessments in formal schooling. A construct is a trait or ability (like personality) that is difficult to assess directly. Observations should have construct validity. Musicality is a construct, a construct recognizable under special conditions but one whose fuzzy definition presents assessment problems. Musicality is currently assessed through an audition, through an improvisational or compositional task, by requiring one to distinguish a musical from a nonmusical event—seemingly different abilities.

More Recent Types

Other descriptors of validity better convey the value of an assessment, and additional types of validity are of concern. A common type is *consequential validity,* where one asks what are the consequences to students who succeed or fail on the assessment or the consequences to the school. The consequences of failing a high-stakes assessment can be greater than the consequences of passing it, although both scenarios have consequences.

Predictive validity has been teased out of criterion-related validity in many assessments due to the importance of admissions tests in many fields. For example, the question is regularly asked as to how well the SAT score predicts one's success in college.

Systemic validity is a concern in schools where it was decided to not just make minor revisions in a course but be bold and make systemic changes in how students are educated. Reducing the number of electives and increasing graduation requirements to 4 years of math, science, language arts, and social science is a systemic change in the philosophy of secondary education. The change from junior high to middle school was a systemic change. Multiple-intelligence schools see themselves as involved in systemic changes. Assessment of these changes requires systemic validity. The 1997 NAEP in music with its emphasis on creating and improvising along with a test of sight-reading ability could be judged on its systemic validity—to what extent did this new assessment capture a major change in the priority of objectives in the music curriculum?

The relationships between assessment and task in these types of validity are important because inferences on the meaning of the assessment results depend upon the strength of these validity relationships. If one were to find little relationship between the instruction in the high school band rehearsal and the tasks of the 1997 NAEP, a lack of instructional validity would be indicated. NAEP could have strong consequential validity should graduation from high school for these band members depend upon their NAEP scores. Strength and type of validity is a judgment call.

A Taxonomy of Objectives

Alignment of what is taught with what is tested is, perhaps, the most important step in assessment. Teachers do not teach from taxonomies, but a taxonomy is a critical tool in determining the extent to which there is alignment between the assessment and the instruction.

The Cognitive Domain

In the mid-1950s, Benjamin J. Bloom published his taxonomy in the cognitive domain (1956). It was a carefully worked out delineation of the many aspects of cognition, the ways in which the various aspects related to one another, and a hierarchical ordering of the development of cognition through its various aspects. Book 1 of *Taxonomy of Educational Objectives, Cognitive Domain,* opened up to educators a way of establishing clear objectives, sequencing these objectives, and assessing the extent to which the objectives were attained. Although the taxonomy was ordered from simple to complex, Bloom did not suggest that his sequence should necessarily be followed in instruction; teachers were expected to be simultaneously using several levels of the taxonomy. A striking feature of the taxonomy was that it consisted of multiple-choice and open-ended questions that looked, walked, and quacked like an assessment tool. Bloom's taxonomy demonstrated the importance of connecting the objectives of cognitive development with assessment and the necessity for the objectives to be clear and specific. Tremendous insights were gained by applying Bloom's taxonomy to a musical experience and constructing a task for each of the taxonomy categories. Such an exercise could serve as a check on the breadth and appropriateness of goal levels within one academic grade. The taxonomy was frustrating to music educators, as there was no accommodation for tasks that involved perceptual skills and knowledge. (Bloom's colleagues later constructed a taxonomy of the affective domain [Krathwohl, Bloom, & Masia, 1964, the second domain of learning], and independent researchers, especially Anita Harrow [1972] and Elizabeth Simpson [1966], constructed a taxonomy in the psychomotor domain, the third hypothesized dimension of learning. Krathwohl's major levels were receiving [attending], responding, valuing, organizing, and characterization by a value or value concept, while Simpson's levels were perception, set, guided response, mechanism, and complete overt response.)

Taxonomies are needed to provide clarity and coherence to all subjects. They are also necessary to organize different types of learning: content understanding, problem solving, metacognition, communication, teamwork, and collaboration (Herman, Baker, and Linn, 2004, p. 4). Review of the taxonomic levels provides a check on the balance and priorities of any assessment tool. Bloom's taxonomy has been found to be better than the NAEP framework in identifying important lifelong skills and in identifying consistency of test content (O'Neil, Sireci, and Huff, 2003–2004).

A Holistic Approach

Recently, influenced by the ideas of Howard Gardner and Bennett Reimer, education (including music education) has been moving toward a greater emphasis on cognition and broader definitions of learning. This new emphasis has given rise to the need for a new taxonomy, one that would reflect the new knowledge about learning. In 1998 A. Dean Hauenstein published *A Conceptual Framework for Educational Objectives: A Holistic Approach to Traditional Taxonomies*, which was an effort to update taxonomies in the three domains, Bloom's cognitive, D. Krathwohl's affective, and Simpson's psychomotor. In addition to making suggestions that allowed for constructivist thought, Hauenstein posits that the 63 categories contained in the three taxonomies were too many for teachers to use in curriculum planning.

He revised the three taxonomies and added a fourth "behavioral domain" taxonomy with five levels: acquisition, assimilation, adaptation, performance, and aspiration (containing 15 subcategories), for a total of 20 categories, rather than the 63 in the Bloom/Krathwohl/Simpson configuration. Hauenstein's revised categories are applicable to research, assessment, and thoughtful curriculum planning. The revised basic categories for the cognitive domain are conceptualization, comprehension, application, and synthesis; for psychomotor: perception, simulation, and conformation (short-term goals) and production and mastery (long-term goals). Psychomotor learning depends on the interrelationship of cognition and affect.

Hauenstein's retention of the affective domain (to the consternation of the pure cognitivists) is helpful to arts curriculum planning. He asserts that the affective domain is "equal to, if not more important than, the cognitive domain" (p. 59). The development of feelings, values, and beliefs and the development of lifelong interests, values, and appreciations such as for arts and music are crucial to the outcomes of education—knowledgeable, acculturated, and competent individuals (p. 60). The revised categories for the affective domain are: receiving, responding, valuing, believing, and behaving. These are organized similarly to the categories established by Krathwohl, as both have three subcategories for the first three categories and two each for believing and behaving. Believing and behaving replace Krathwohl's organization and characterization by value or value complex.

Other updates in the cognitive and psychomotor taxonomies better account for recent thinking about learning. The author was careful to ensure that the taxonomy was applicable and inclusive, that the categories were mutually exclusive, and that there were consistent "principles of order" for the categories (p. 31).

The purpose of this taxonomy is "for curriculum writers: no attempt is made to provide information on how to write objectives or measure achievement" (p. 123). The premise is that assessment takes its cue from the curriculum and that a profitable place to begin is with the taxonomies of the curriculum. The emphasis is on learning as a whole person. All three taxonomies are essential, with the fourth for curriculum research, and use of them makes education more organized. In the cognitive domain, conceptualization, comprehension, and application are short-term goals, evaluation and synthesis long-term. Taxonomies focus on objectives that enable students to explore, refine, or change prevailing dispositions, values, and beliefs as they form their own concepts. Education is dependent on the degree to which prescriptions and information/content are included in the curriculum for instruction. Space prohibits giving examples in music even for the 20 categories. Readers might wish to review the examples in my 1970 *Evaluation of Music Teaching and Learning* and write assessment exercises for the four Hauenstein taxonomies.

A Revision of Bloom's Taxonomy

A second new taxonomy appeared in 2001, written by a task force that included Krathwohl (*A Taxonomy for Learning, Teaching, and Assessing: A Revision of Bloom's Taxonomy of Educational Objectives*, edited by Lorin W. Anderson and David Krathwohl). It is an update of only the cognitive taxonomy and is two-dimensional: cognitive processes and knowledge. The revised cognitive processes are remembering, understanding, applying, analyzing, evaluating, and creating, premised on the assumption that these processes are linear in complexity. Knowledge consists of the factual, conceptual, procedural, and metacognitive, also arranged linearly, proceeding from concrete to abstract. The authors posit that use of the taxonomy provides a better understanding of objectives and of what is important in education (p. 6) and that a taxonomy helps one to plan, to select and design assessment instruments and procedures, and to thereby ensure that objectives, instruction, and assessment are consistent.

The alignment of objectives and assessment is basic to high-quality instruction. The different types of objectives that result not only from new knowledge but also from state and federal frameworks require different instructional approaches.

Another reason for revision is that Ralph Tyler's behaviors became confused with behaviorism, requiring that the word *behavior* be replaced with *cognitive processes* (Anderson & Krathwohl, 2001, p. 14).

The Marzano Taxonomy

A third new taxonomy of educational objectives, this one formulated by Robert J. Marzano (*Designing a New Taxonomy of Education Objectives* [2001]), reflects the philosophical shift to cognition and recognizes the role of new knowledge about how learning occurs. Marzano's taxonomy is a new guide to understanding cognitive development and a new way of appraising the appropriateness of objectives, curriculum, and assessment in education. It is a marked departure from the Bloom taxonomy and the two revisions, particularly in that it combines the cognitive and psychomotor domains. The foundation level of the taxonomy of educational objectives is knowledge, which is attained through three systems: a cognitive system, a metacognitive system, and a self-system. There is no allowance for an affective domain; emotion is subsumed under Level 6, Self-System. A further complication for music educators is the lack of clarity that concerns a possible perceptual domain. Reimer (1996) suggests that perception is a type of cognition, but this explanation only partially answers the question of how the attainment of perceptual skills fits into the music curriculum. Marzano concludes that *information* cannot be executed, an understandable argument if, and only if, perception is not considered. When musicians hear an unknown piece of music and mentally classify it to obtain deeper meaning, they are actually executing one type of information; their minds process the information and a response to the music so perceived occurs. Another concern of music educators will be the emphasis the cognitive approach places on verbalizing, for example, verbalizing about the music and the musical experience. A large part of the musical experience defies verbal description; one is reminded of Martha Graham's comment to the effect that "if I could describe it, I would not have to dance it."

For the researcher in music education this taxonomy offers a guide to exploring many aspects of the musical learning process that have not yet been considered. And although at first glance the taxonomy may seem beyond any practical application for the music teacher in the classroom, the taxonomy is in reality an excellent tool for *thinking* about the learning process, *planning* learning sequences, *recognizing* various kinds of learning not previously considered, and *helping* to ensure that assessment gets to the heart of the learnings the teacher deems of primary importance. The practicing music teacher may find the taxonomy initially formidable but with some small effort will be able to see the ways in which it opens up the nature and the facts of learning in a way that is applicable to the teacher's goals.

Levels   Knowledge consists of information, mental procedures, and psychomotor procedures; to obtain this knowledge it is necessary to consider the three systems: cognitive, metacognitive, and self. There are six levels to the taxonomy, four of them cognitive, plus the levels of *metacognition* and *self,* which are intact levels.

Level 1: Knowledge Retrieval

Level 2: Comprehension

Level 3: Analysis

Level 4: Knowledge Utilization

Level 5: Metacognition

Level 6: Self

The levels are not organized by complexity, as was the earlier Bloom and the two revised taxonomies; rather, they are based on how an individual processes the stimuli received. Although there are subcomponents to the systems of metacognition and self, there is no order to these subcomponents. There is, however, an implied order to the cognition system, beginning with Level 1 and advancing to Level 4. The numbering of the levels is confusing, as the first step in learning is to engage the *self*-system, followed by the *metacognition* system. The *cognitive* system is the last one to be engaged. This taxonomy, like the Anderson and Krathwohl, is a work-in-progress, with Marzano allowing that not every subcomponent of the six levels may be essential to all subjects.

Marzano's Taxonomy Applied to Music   In view of the uniqueness of music and the importance of perception in music, this taxonomy is not entirely satisfactory, because audiation, a subcompetence of perception, does not fit neatly into it. Music educators believe that a student should perceive chord changes, melodic motifs, and the extent to which performers are in tune with one another. If the student is a performer, the ability to sing chord tones or to play in tune can be observed, but performance is not essential to derive meaning from music. Music educators believe that there are degrees of perceptual ability; due to talent or learning, some individuals have a "James Levine ear," where the smallest deviation is perceived, while others are apparently satisfied with gross approximations of the tonality.

Subcomponents   Each of the six levels of the taxonomy has three subcomponents: information, mental procedures, and psychomotor procedures.

Information (sometimes called declarative knowledge) consists of (1) details and (2) organizing ideas. *Details* consist of vocabulary, facts, time sequences, cause/effect sequences, and episodes. Music vocabulary and facts are familiar to all of us. Less is done in music with the other components of information detail. A time sequence requires identifying important events that occur between two dates, such as 1792 and 1795, Haydn's period in London, when he wrote the *London* Symphonies. (We'll ignore 1792–1794, when he returned briefly to Vienna and took Beethoven as a pupil.) Cause/event sequences would require understanding the relationship between the valve for brass instruments and the change in brass music. An episode could be the riot created by the premier of Stravinsky's *Le Sacre du Printemps*. Details are not limited to information retrieval and Level 1 of the taxonomy. *Organizing ideas* consist of principles and generalizations. Principles can be either correlational, a change in one factor resulting in a change in another factor, or cause- and effect, where one factor *causes* a change in the other.

Mental Procedures (sometimes called procedural knowledge) consist of (1) processes and (2) skills. *Mental processes* could be organized into a simple hierarchy, as some are more complex than others. If all students were assigned to improvise on a theme or to compose a piece, the varying products could be assigned to a rough hierarchy, but an exact hierarchy is unlikely, as the improvisations would have different strengths. *Mental skills* consist of tactics, algorithms, and simple rules. Following a single rule would be the simplest mental process; the skills should be included in any rough hierarchy of mental processes.

Psychomotor Procedures consist of (1) processes, (2) skills, and (3) the same mental procedures. *Psychmotor processes* consist of complex combination procedures, such as performing one's part accurately and musically in a concert. *Psychomotor skills* are simple combination procedures and foundational procedures. A simple combination procedure would be double-tonguing, while a foundational procedure would be exhaling correctly.

For Bloom, knowledge was "little more than the remembering of the idea or phenomenon" (1956, pp. 28–29). Bloom's nine levels of knowledge were clear, but there was no provision for the mental operation that accompanied the behavior at each level. Marzano's argument is that there must be a process for retrieving and using the knowledge acquired. His stages indicate how the cognitive, metacognitive, and self-systems act upon the various knowledges. Declarative knowledge remains basic to learning, the taxonomy placing the emphasis on how vocabulary, facts, and criteria are used. To use knowledge requires attention to three kinds of memory: sensory memory, where we learn, briefly, from our senses; long-term memory which is the basis for knowing and understanding; and working memory, the memory used when focusing on a task.

Application to Assessment: Level 6, Self   Although much of the emphasis in the music classroom is on the cognitive requirements, the new taxonomy allows one to inspect the entire learning sequence. *Level 6: Self* is the first consideration. Bloom's taxonomy did not consider the self system.

Level 6: Self consists of examining importance, examining efficacy, examining emotional response, and examining motivation. Examining student motivation reveals a summary of the student's beliefs about importance, efficacy, and emotion. These differ in relative weight and combine to produce motivation.

The self-system of thinking addresses the question of whether to engage in the learning, how much energy to expend, what will be attended to, and to what extent this effort will satisfy a basic need. Personal goals are important in the self-system, as goals have to be at the personal level before one learns. Students may join music ensembles to have or be with friends, rather than to learn. The self-system begins to address the major questions of the purpose of life and to what extent the individual will need to change his or her environment to attain new goals. Bandura, Maslow, Buber, and other educational psychologists stress the importance of the student's investment in his or her own education.

In the self-system, the process is the same across the three domains of information, mental procedures, and psychomotor procedures. (Examples in this chapter are given only for the self and metacognition levels, as these are apt to be the most unfamiliar to the teacher.)

Self-system: Examining importance. The student decides what specific information is important:

Information

- *Details.* How important is it for me to know the events that surrounded the beginning of opera? Why do I believe this and how logical is my thinking?
- *Organizing ideas.* How important is it to me to know the principles of

bowing? Why would I need to know the principles; how valid is my thinking about this?

Mental procedures

- *Skills.* How important is it to audiate? Why is it important? How logical has my thinking been in establishing this importance?
- *Processes.* How important is the ability to compose? Why is composing important to me? How logical have I been in deriving this importance?

Psychomotor procedures

- *Skills.* How important is it to me to practice double-tonguing? Why would I want to double-tongue? How logical have I been in making this decision?
- *Process.* How important is it for me to be able to perform my part well in the chorus concert? Why do I want to be proficient? How valid is my thinking at ascertaining the importance of practicing with all the other things I have to do?

Self-system: Examining efficacy. The student must have the will (motivation) to change from not knowing to knowing. To what extent do I believe that I can improve my understanding or competence relative to this week's goals of the music class? (Determining efficacy likely does not generalize to all of the goals of the music experience.) Do I have the resources, the ability, the power to change my situation or the situation at school? What are the veridical or logical aspects that might demonstrate to me that I can accomplish the goals?

Information

- *Details.* How much can I increase my understanding of the conditions that surrounded the origin of the opera? What is my reasoning?
- *Organizing ideas.* How much can I improve my knowledge of the principles of bowing in different genres? Have I been logical and realistic in my reasoning?

Mental procedures

- *Skills.* To what extent will I be able to improve my ability to audiate? What is my reasoning and how logical is it that I can actually improve?
- *Processes.* To what extent will I be able to improve my skill at composing? How likely is it that this is possible?

Psychomotor procedures

- *Skills.* How much can I improve my double-tonguing and be able to perform the way I want to? How reasonable is this goal?
- *Processes.* How close can I come to getting everything right in next week's choral concert? How logical is my reasoning?

Self-system: Examining emotional response. Negative emotions dampen a student's motivation. Emotions, though we have limited control over them, can be powerful motivators. Many charismatic leaders appeal essentially to a person's emotions; patriotism and respect for the motherland are emotion-based reasons for action. Marzano suggests that the flow from emotion to cognition is stronger than the flow from cognition to emotion. The emotional response differs from other categories, as the objective is to understand the *pattern* of one's thinking. There is no basis for determining that one pattern is better than another or that change is in order.

Information

- *Details.* How do I feel about paying for music that I was able to get free from Napster? Why do I feel this way? How logical is this reaction? (What emotions do I have about the need to sell grapefruit in order for the school orchestra to have new music?)
- *Organizing ideas.* What feelings do I have about the time spent warming up in choral rehearsals? How did I arrive at this feeling about warming up?

Mental procedures

- *Skills.* Why do I get so upset when we are expected to audiate? Is this feeling logical? How and when did it begin?
- *Processes.* Why do I become so emotional about the music I compose? Why do I not want anything to be changed? How logical am I? What is my reasoning?

Psychomotor procedures

- *Skills.* Why do I believe that I can triple-tongue at MM = 142? Is this logical or just a feeling? What logic or reasoning did I use to believe I could improve that much?
- *Processes.* Why am I so emotional and sad after the final choral concert of the year? What reason do I have for making this so important yet so sad? Am I logical in behaving as I do?

Self-system: Examining motivation. Assessing the strength of motivation is identical to assessing the three components of the self-system of thinking. Students review their reaction to the importance of goals, to what extent they have the resources to meet the goals, and any emotional reaction that can interfere with accomplishment of these goals. The importance of the goal to the individual is usually the strongest motivator. It is useful, however, to have students reflect upon and write responses to the information, mental procedures, and psychomotor procedures involved in motivation even when the material draws solely from past reflections. (Space will not be taken here for examples, as motivation is a summary step.)

Application to Assessment: Level 5, Metacognition

Taxonomy level 5: Metacognition follows Level 6. It prepares the student to learn and assess the depth of interest and capacity for learning. Metacognition moves beyond cognition and consists of four categories: goal setting, process monitoring, monitoring clarity, and monitoring accuracy. Metacognition is a way of determining the functioning of the other types of thought. If there is a hierarchy, goal setting is the most important accompanied by three monitoring strategies.

Metacognition: Goal setting. For knowledge to occur, there must be a clear objective, a rough but thoughtful time line to accomplish that goal, and a knowledge of the resources required to meet that goal. There must be a clear picture of what the final product will look like and the relationship of any experiences to that product. Just practicing is not enough; one has to have an objective for any practice or drill. Where the student is involved in self-systems and in metacognition, the role of the teacher is changed.

Information

- *Details.* What is a goal that you might have relating to the Voluntary National Standards? What would you have to do to accomplish this goal?
- *Organizing ideas.* What goal would you suggest for yourself to improve your musical creativity? How might you accomplish that goal?

Mental procedures

- *Skills.* What goal might you set for your ability to audiate? What instruction and practice plan will enable you to reach that goal?
- *Processes.* Based upon your current competence, what goal do you have to learn to improvise in the genre of country and western music? What does your plan to accomplish this goal look like?

Psychomotor procedures

- *Skills.* State a terminal and intermediate goal that you have to improve your vocal high register. What resources will be required for you to meet these goals?
- *Processes.* What are your goals for this week to improve your musical understanding of the music we are singing in chorus? What are the procedures for improving understanding and how long would that process take?

Metacognition: Process monitoring. The function of this stage of monitoring is to assess the effectiveness of the algorithms, tactics, or rules used in a task. The taxonomy does not include monitoring the information stage, as the monitoring is to be authentic, that is, monitored in actual minutes required to accomplish a task. Thus the concern for the mental imagery of classifying a piece of music; little time elapses, and some classifying becomes almost automatic. Information such as vocabulary, facts, and causal sequences can be remembered and recalled but not acted upon. In ignoring perception to some extent, this definition indicates that much of the thrust of cognitive-based education could be *about* music, not *of* music. The mental and psychomotor skills that involve performance are unquestionably musical goals; there can be a question, however, about the importance in a music class of the extensive verbalization and reflection.

The student is to think about what he or she is doing *while* doing it. In some subjects, a verbal protocol is possible as it is in some music activities, but there are other situations where the opportunity to respond must be contrived, conducted after the experience.

Mental procedures

- *Skills.* To what extent were you able to hear every pitch mentally before you sang it?
- *Processes.* To what extent were you able to envision your composition before you performed it and how well were you able to interpret and perform your composition?

Psychomotor procedures

- *Skills.* Demonstrate a proper vocal warm-up. How effective were you at becoming more relaxed in your upper torso and getting the vocal cords to respond?
- *Processes.* As the student conductor of the orchestra, describe your musical thoughts into the tape recorder as you conduct. Comment on your effectiveness from your perception. I shall also stop you occasionally and ask you to orally evaluate your effectiveness at that point.

Metacognition: Monitoring clarity. The monitoring process is designed to assess any ambiguity in the goal or in how well the goal is to be attained. Often students do not understand all of the subgoals required in learning a piece of music and that more is required than getting the notes and rhythms correct. Clarity assists in establishing a disposition for learning the required tasks.

Information

- *Details.* Identify those sections of the test about which you were confused. What do you think caused your confusion on those sections? Are they related in some way?
- *Organizing ideas.* What concepts about appropriate breathing don't you understand? Be specific about the places in the music where you have inadequate breath support, where your breath support does not support the tone, and where your tone lacks a center due to your breathing.

Mental procedures

- *Skills.* Identify the places in the music where the score was confusing. What do you think caused this confusion?
- *Processes.* Identify the places in the score where the orchestra was unable to follow you. What is it about the music, the performers, or the situation that confused you?

Psychomotor procedures

- *Skills.* Identify those places in today's bowing exercises where you lost concentration. What do you think caused your inattention?
- *Processes.* Identify where in today's concert you missed the bowing pattern and became confused and played in the rests. What caused this confusion? Were you at letter B? With a downbow?

Metacognition: Monitoring accuracy. Accuracy is important in all subjects but none more so than music where the notes, rhythm, intonation, articulation, diction, and so forth must be precise. The student is to self-monitor to verify his or her own accuracy.

Information

- *Details.* How do you know that your explanation of Bach and Handel being the culmination of the Baroque period is an accurate explanation? What evidence do you have?
- *Organizing ideas.* What evidence do you have that you followed the compositional practices that were prevalent during the Classical period? What evidence do you have to verify that your composition authentically matches music of the Classical period?

Mental procedures

- *Skills.* Identify those parts of today's sight-reading exercise where you were able to audiate your part. How can you check your accuracy in audiating?
- *Processes.* Identify those computer programs that you used to help you arrange the music in the style of Ravel. What evidence do you have that your use of the programs provided a valid representation?

Cognitive System Processes   The four levels of the cognitive system detail the most familiar objectives, although some of the expected knowledge will require time-consuming assessments.

Level 1: Knowledge retrieval. Knowledge retrieval is defined as the ability to move knowledge from one's long-term memory to working memory. The level of knowledge is not sophisticated, consisting of facts and the simple structure of the topic. Questions about the style or genre of a piece of music satisfy Level 1.

Level 2: Comprehension. This level is comparable to comprehension in the Bloom taxonomy, except it does not include Bloom's extrapolation level. Synthesis in the new taxonomy matches Bloom's "interpretation." Comprehension is the process of preparing the major components of knowledge for inclusion in long-term memory. Knowledge specific to an experience may not be retained if it is not generalizable. The two stages of comprehension are synthesis and representation.

Level 3: Analysis. The basis for conducting an analysis is generation of new knowledge or new understanding. There are five types of analysis: matching, classifying, error analysis, generalization, and specification. For Marzano, analysis is comparable to Piaget's accommodation (1971), rather than assimilation or the idea of restructuring (which follows accretion and tuning), a system of Rumelhart and Norman (1981).

Level 4: Knowledge utilization. Level 4 is more advanced, if not more complex, than the other levels of cognition in the new taxonomy. The general categories are: decision making, problem solving, experimental inquiry, and investigation.

Assessment Strategies with the Marzano Taxonomy   As indicated by the length of the task descriptions, if music education programs were to be based upon this learning process, the assessments would need to parallel the objectives, follow the format suggested, and be embedded in the instruction.

Although retrieval of information is critical, as demonstrated in knowledge utilization, the most efficient way to assess a student's recall competence is through open-ended questions, multiple-choice, and on-demand type items.

Music notation could be used in matching, classifying, and demonstrating that the student understood the symbols of literacy. This assessment measure would satisfy a portion of Level 2: Comprehension and two of the methods of Level 3: Analysis, those of matching and classification.

Essays and oral reports are appropriate for all of the levels of the taxonomy except retrieval of information. Traditional sampling would constitute such a major source of variance that one could not determine the student's depth of knowledge of facts, definitions, time sequences, episodes, and cause/effect sequences; hence, new assessment formats are required.

Observation by teacher, peers, or outsiders is an inefficient and inaccurate assessment tool, because the observer brings too much baggage to the scene. Observing a student perform provides limited evidence of the range of the student's performing ability and even less of his or her comprehensive musical knowledge and skills. Observation provides partial information on a student's comprehension at one particular time and may provide partial information on the student's ability to retrieve information. In the best situations, the measurement error is great.

Performance tasks provide the opportunity to assess not only the student's cognitive competence but the metacognition and self levels when the performance task is substantive and on material worth knowing. A library assignment to conduct research and write a paper on an artist would not be very informative in assessing any of the nine Voluntary National Standards or one's basic musicianship. Administering one on-demand performance task will seldom produce adequate information. Even a complex task, if performed only once, is subject to substantial measurement error, less than that for the onetime high-stakes multiple-choice examination but of concern with any high-stakes assessment.

Assessment to improve (formative) must consist of frequent performance tasks, each scheduled to provide immediate feedback to the student and an opportunity to demonstrate that corrective action has been taken.

New Devices

The emphasis in this chapter is on assessment issues that will arise with new instructional modes and the appropriateness of both embedded and external assessments. The new knowledge about both thinking and learning, coupled with advances in technology, allows psychologists and educators to create truly diagnostic and adaptive systems in the areas of ability, learning, development, and achievement.

Some of these advances have resulted from new statistical techniques or new uses of old techniques that increase assessment efficiency or that better interpret the data. No effort is made here to explain the mathematical or statistical background of these techniques; the reader needs to seek statistical understanding elsewhere.

Processing and Strategy Skills

Snow and Lohman (1993) in editors Norman Frederiksen, Robert Mislevy, and Isaac Bejar's *Test Theory for a New Generation of Text* (1993) identify stimulus encoding, feature comparison, rule induction, rule application, and response justification as examples of processing skills that can now be identified in ability test performance. Most of these processes are assessed through the multicomponent latent trait approach that can arrange the factors being assessed to provide a powerful means of gathering data relevant to how and in what sequence certain concepts are understood. Most statistical techniques, however, contain assumptions that are less easily met in the real world than in the statistical laboratories where these programs are devised. Music educators need to know their students and their subject well in ascertaining whether the statistical assumptions apply to their teaching situation. With reasonable course requirements or electives in graduate programs for teachers, a new frontier in music education is possible. Should this new interest occur, it will represent a major change in the profession compared to past lack of serious interest in assessment. Student variations in self-regulation with respect to speed, accuracy, and sequence are three of the assumptions of computer testing about which little data are available on tasks in music. Widespread use of computer testing in music must await such data. The computer programs make assumptions about the problem-solving strategy being used, a strategy not dependent upon skill but on how one processes information, how one learns from responding to other test items, and whether one recognizes the characteristics of the test items. The research of Ippel and Beem (1987) and Kyllonen, Lohman, and Woltz (1984) is based on a computer-administered test that systematically manipulates strategy choices and strategy shifts based on student response. At issue in most of these computer-generated tests is an understanding of why an individual has difficulty with a particular item, as that understanding must be programmed into the machine. If this is a problem for language arts teachers, as it is, it will be a greater problem for music. The item analysis currently available from music achievement tests is spotty, and little analysis exists as to the effect of preceding and follow-up questions.

In aural perception, simple intervals, timbres, and patterns often have high difficulty indices, due perhaps to student expectation or experience, factors that have not been systematically investigated for even one style or genre of music. Cognitive psychologists believe that cognitive analyses can lead to computerized item generation that is more valid than items written by humans. If this process becomes a reality, the concerted effort of both humans and computers will be required to devise tests that can explain (measure) the "Aha!" in musical understanding that escapes verbalization. A major advantage of the computer is that it can alter the assumption about the test taker's basic ability and adjust accordingly, where humans have to assume that a single ability continuum underlies the various tasks to be solved. The computer can also accommodate additional distractors or sources of variation as they are identified during the test administration. Test theory depends upon the degree of focus or concentration required by a specific item and also must account for learning and responses that become automatic during the test taking. Some individuals use multiple strategies to solve problems, thus requiring computer programs based upon fluid reasoning to respond to students who grasp quickly the conceptual basis for the test. Cognitive psychology is gaining a better understanding of how various individuals learn; music educators may find this attention to learning unprecedented, but if they cooperate with educational psychologists, throughout the required trial-and-error process, music education assessment can arrive at a position to take advantage of "the possible."

Lohman (1988) suggests that our understanding of spatial ability tests has been superficial and that spatial abilities also involve multiple strategies, some of which are not at all "spatial." Research with spatial ability testing is pertinent to music education when arguments are made that experiences with music improve students' spatial and temporal-spatial abilities. In other areas also, questions are being raised as better descriptions are created about what occurs as students learn to perceive, memorize, reason, and solve problems. These descriptions are especially relevant to the use of portfolios where convergent and discrimination validity of contrasting portfolio scores can be established by computers through use of a set of structural equations and LISREL.

Reasoning and Understanding

Such advances have allowed educators such as Ann L. Brown and John C. Campione (1986) to conduct research on student reasoning and on transfer that has led to accepted principles in the field of education. Their ideas on the self-regulatory functions of planning, monitoring one's own progress, questioning, checking, and correcting errors are based upon research that used student responses. The promotion of teaching for understanding through semantic networks, schemata, scripts, prototypes, images, and mental models is also based upon recent advances in assessment that have provided a view of the acquisition and structure of knowledge different from that derived using data from multiple-choice tests only. The use of elaboration, chunking, connecting, restructuring, and similar basic ideas in connectionism arises from analyses of achievement, mainly in mathematics and science but increasingly applied to other basic subjects. Whether these instructional ideas apply to music education will depend upon the application of cognitive psychology and its assessment techniques to priority issues in the music curriculum. Accepting these methodologies without such assessment research is unwarranted. Some information on these techniques can be gained from interviews and teach-back procedures that should provide data on chunk size and some strategies on restructuring and elaboration. These mental processes are what humans use to reason, recall, reflect, and solve problems. Thus music educators must be cautious in suggesting that current curricular practices are efficient in aiding students in these various thinking and understanding strategies. Previous learning is critical in the research conducted in test development in other subjects, and music educators have little experience in collecting substantive data about previous learning. Mislevy (1993) argues that standard test theory failed to consider just how people know what they know and do what they do and the ways in which they increase these capacities. His ideas are supported by Snow and Lohman (1993), from whom I quote at some length:

> Cognitive psychology is now teaching us that to understand a particular individual's performance on a particular task, one must delve more deeply into its constituents—the configurations of knowledge, skill, understanding, belief, and attitude that underline particular responses. A richer, denser, more sensitive description is especially needed if tests are to be designed for diagnosis and classification in guiding instruction, rather than for summary selection and evaluation purposes only. This would seem to require test theories that use multivariate categorical as well as interval scale indicators and that apply to time series, not just to single-point assessments. The design of test items, the methods by which they are organized into tests, and the rules by which scores are assigned to responses must be guided by the purposes of testing. Modern theories of cognition and learning have described new, potentially useful constructs for measurement. One of the more important challenges for a new test theory and design, then, is to explore the measurement properties of these new scores. (p. 13)

Research on New Assessments

Computers Much of the research on new assessment procedures is based upon a general probability model and a Bayesian approach to estimating the parameters of the student and of the content to be assessed (Mislevy, Almond, Yan, & Steinberg, 2000). Shum's (1994) evidentiary reasoning derived from his Portal Project is a fundamental construct as investigators manage belief about a student's knowledge and skill (even that which is not observable) based upon what students say and can do. Content evidence is obtained in the context of a task that allows the computer to construct individualized tests, adding new tasks to each student's item pool and measuring different students with different items. The investigator builds the task model by describing the important features of a task (these must be known with certainty) along with the specifications for the work environment, the tools that the testee may use, the work products, stimulus materials, and any interactions between the testee and the task.

The model describes the mixture of tasks that go into an operational assessment, either a fixed or a dynamic task, and the model is built based upon probability consistent with knowledge about the underlying problem and the data collection process. The "unobservables" are obtained from responses to a given task from a large number of examinees. The test is continually updated, new items added, and the estimate of general proficiency changed by the Monte Carlo Markov Chain of estimation procedures. This technique has been applied to present tests that include the Graduate Record Examination and the ASVAB, in which the computer constructs an individual examination at the student's level. The ERGO computer program (Noetic Systems, 1991) provides probabilities for each student on as many as five skills. Multiple skill testing in one test is possible only when, in the initial test design, there is a coherent design for all of the skills.

At the heart of the development of computer-assisted assessment are the new psychometric models of learning where the purpose of assessment is not to establish the presence or absence of specific behaviors but to infer the nature of students' understandings of particular phenomena. There is little interest in the computer's ability to score isolated bits of knowledge; the goal is to develop programs that provide a model of understanding by individual students. The task is to design a set of questions that will expose different levels of understanding of a concept based on student response to several related questions, questions selected to reveal inconsistencies as well as consistencies in thinking. Computer-assisted assessments are not designed to replace current assessment measures that are appropriate to assess student learning of a body of factual material necessary in music and for which a well-designed multiple-choice format can reveal deep comprehension (Carroll, 1993).

Terminology and Concepts

Schemas   Cognitive psychologists who conduct research in learning suggest that schemas are one way to reflect the nature of the domain, the instruction, and the learner's knowledge about that domain. Schemas, however, are poorly defined in the literature; they are really just a collection of information organized like a story with a theme and characters. Individuals, based on their own experiences, use different schemas to solve the same problems. Individuals differ not only in the depth of each schema but also in their ability to search for the best schemas to solve new problems. With complex problems, individuals link several extant schemas, thus requiring a healthy long-term memory to solve substantive issues. The linking of schemas reveals the common elements that everyone uses in problem solving and is the value of schema theory (Marshall, 1993). (In computerized testing, each item contributes to the estimate of the contents of the schema and/or to its connecting links.) The data that can be provided to assessors is the extent to which students have acquired the schemas taught for problem solving, not whether students can produce the correct answer. Chomsky (1968) differentiated between competence and performance, competence being the knowledge of language and performance being the ability to use language. This distinction is followed by those who employ research in learning and assessment. Assessors are interested in the schema constructs (strategies, knowledge structure, and related components) as an indicator of competence and an indicator of the individual differences that are the student's span of abstract or general reasoning.

Latent Trait   Latent trait models are the psychometric standard for measuring ability, with the latent trait a mathematical model of the probability that an examinee passes a specific item, the Bayes probability mentioned earlier. The model is not based on the linear model of classical test theory but is sensitive to the nonlinear relationship of the probability of solving an item to the individual's actual ability. The relationship of item solving to actual ability (Rasch latent trait model) is an S-shaped curve in which the probability of .50 is reached when ability equals item difficulty. Verification of this model is often based on scores from the paper-folding spatial ability test that has become familiar to music educators as the dependent variable in the research of Shaw and Rauscher (1993). Test and item reliability are not based on the variance among student responses as is reliability in classical test theory but can be estimated through probability for each student.

Item Response Theory   This theory is loosely related to latent trait theory (although some would argue that it is philosophically at the other end of the continuum) in that it demonstrates the relationship of ability to performance in a nonlinear learning situation. The change in probability between any two abilities depends upon their relative location on the item response curve. An assumption is that there is more information when high-ability students do well on a difficult item and when low-ability students perform well on items appropriate for their ability. Pre- and posttests based on IRT must be designed to measure the same construct if gain scores are of interest; otherwise change score data are difficult to interpret. This change, however, is not measured on the same scale for individuals of different ability levels, thus providing a spurious negative relationship between change score and pretest score. Item response theory applies to dichotomously scored items although it probably can be used with more complicated responses; further research is needed. Despite accounting for individual differences, IRT assumes that there is a "characteristic" curve for each item that represents ability on that item. What IRT does best is assign a single, unidimensional continuum scale value to the examinee.

Behavioral Scaling   Behavioral scaling is a technique used to establish construct validity and is often not related to issues of generalizability or external validity. Scaling can be applied only to well-constructed tests, of adequate length and reliability. The assumption is that the task being measured is unidimensional and that a series of tasks of varying levels of difficulty can be constructed to measure this single construct. Reading skill, for example, is considered to be based on a single construct. Music educators Robert Miller (1979) and Lee Bartel (1992) separately investigated the potential of scaling, but their primary interest was in establishing the presence of constructs and not in developing classroom tests. There is inadequate research at present to indicate the extent to which this technique will be useful.

Another type of behavior scaling is used to establish anchor points on large-scale tests. The anchor points are verbal descriptions of a level of competence designed to be parametric descriptions that are both clear and objective. (Anchor points for the test developer need not be describable to the public, but the test developer must have a thorough acquaintance with the characteristics of the task, scale, or domain, in order to report any results or to use the results in further test development.) Anchor points were used to describe results of the music portion of the 1997 NAEP, but the data used to establish these were not provided.

Summary

The use of computers in assessment holds considerable potential should music educators devote some of their resources to gaining more information about what learning is important, the extent of current student competency, and the importance of the situation. Knowing how to interpret error remains one of the difficulties in several of the strategies used in computer-adapted testing. The assessment strategies being developed rely on a relationship between instruction, learning, and testing. The research results in fields such as mathematics indicate that deep understanding of complex subject matter is not easily attained and seldom present in today's students. To attain any such goal will require the systemic change in education emphasized in educational literature. That change could be a narrowing of the curriculum to allow for the needed time, a greatly extended school day or year, or the development of more effective teaching strategies than are known at present. A greater integration of subject matter is also an option, but one that has been fraught with outcomes of misunderstanding, wrong information, and a lack of constructs for further learning. Concepts that appear to be related in the classroom seldom have the same strong relationships in the real world. The solution to this problem, some argue, is to enable students to recognize that the goals of instruction and ordinary experience are the same; others argue that the schools need to change what today passes for ordinary experience. One cannot assess complex ideas without stimuli that build a framework equal in complexity to that of the ideas involved; in essay assessments, for example, a detailed question would be necessary to elicit the extent of a student's understanding. Subjects and connections that appear to be logical on the surface often are not learned in the same way, and students may use different schemas to solve problems in different subjects. Such issues require considerable more research before the premise that it is easy to integrate music into the teaming efforts of middle school teachers can be accepted.

Portfolios

The idea of a portfolio to better capture evidence of student learning appears in almost all contemporary educational literature. Assessment professionals recommend multiple measures to reduce the error that exists in any assessment, including scorer error in arriving at a composite score for a portfolio. The advantage of a portfolio in determining student competence is that it can contain evidence from multiple indicators; the portfolio is not the assessment tool, but it *contains* the results of valid and reliable assessments and enough information about the student and instructional goals to allow for interpretation of these materials. The rise of the portfolio challenged the testing establishment, with the result that Educational Testing Service, CRESST, and other large organizations have devoted major resources during the past decade to improving the portfolio and to investigating how it might be used in their programs (Gitomer & Dusch, 1994; Jones & Chittenden, 1995). The initial efforts to employ portfolios as assessment tools in state assessment plans such as those in Vermont, Kentucky, and California were too ambitious; the users did not understand the difficulties of scoring a group of items that were far from homogenous. Portfolios suffer from low reliability and questionable standards-based validity.

The California Learning Assessment System (CLAS) was modeled after the most current constructivist ideas in education, subjected to intense scrutiny by the public, and eventually vetoed by the governor, but not until extensive research had been conducted. CLAS was to be involved in making high-stakes decisions, those decisions requiring not only several types of validity but respectable (high) reliability for the indicators upon which these decisions are based. Percentiles are commonly used by the state or the school district to report assessment data to the public, as being in the upper half of a class is not only understandable but a reasonable generalization. American business leaders like to know that *all* high school graduates are competent but still need to know which students would make the "best" employees. Individuals opposed to assessment have effectively used the lack of stability in percentile scores on these state and national tests to attack their use. The argument, based upon test reliability, is impressive, usually computed at the 50th percentile, which allows portrayal of the most severe cases. (Large numbers of students are grouped in the middle, which means that a small change in a score can make a rather large difference in a student's rank or percentile standing among the total group of students being compared.) There is always error in teacher judgments, in observation, in classroom tests, in contest ratings, and in performances (an error that is greater in qualitative assessments). The user of assessment data of any kind needs to know the amount of this error, but reducing error is seldom the primary consideration in qualitative assessment. Could a student who has made noticeable progress over the course of a year actually obtain a lower percentile rank in the second year? According to Rogosa (1999), if a test had a reliability of .8, the probability of this occurring is .229 (20% of the time). A test needs to have a reliability of .9 to reduce this error to .133 and .95 to further reduce the error to .053. (These figures should be retained by the reader to assist in interpreting research results where the author reports a "satisfactory" reliability of .71!) Is it difficult to improve the reliability of assessments? Yes. To increase the reliability from .90 to .95 requires doubling the length of the test.

Portfolio scoring of the CLAS (Webb & Schlackman, 2000) enabled scorers to determine general competence, but the results were not adequate to justify inferences about individual student performance (p. 66). Portfolio data did, however, allow teachers and students to learn how the quality of student work related to California's dimensions of learning (dimensions of learning are similar to standards). Scoring of portfolios does not allow for comparisons or for obtaining a ranking or percentile, as portfolios contain both differing items and items produced under differing conditions for each student. The CLAS portfolios were in many respects models. They were not limited to exhibitions but contained multiple-choice test scores, performance tasks, and on-demand questions that were curricular embedded. Curriculum-embedded tasks in portfolios must provide evidence of the critical concepts of the discipline, as embedded tasks most often relate to the objectives mandated or expected by the community and state. On-demand tasks in a portfolio are more likely to reflect the priorities of the teacher and the school system.

Reliability of scoring of major portfolio items is improved when a larger number of competence levels is used. The American Council on the Training of Foreign Languages (1989) (Aschbaker, 1999) established 10 levels: novice-low, novice-mid, novice-high; intermediate-low, intermediate-mid, and intermediate-high; advanced, advanced-plus, superior, and distinguished. Ten levels in music are desirable. Though the often-recommended 3 levels are inadequate, some states are recommending only a 2-level (pass-fail), which invites serious assessment problems that extend beyond reliability, affecting student morale and beliefs. It is not unusual to find portfolio research that employs 3 or 4 levels and the investigator reporting reliability based on agreement and agreement within 1 level. With 3 levels, it should be obvious that chance will be a major factor in establishing "agreement" within 1 level!

The portfolio is not a simplistic and straightforward method of documenting student learning; a portfolio is to help students develop concepts, theories, strategies, practices, and beliefs that are consistent with the ways of knowing, arguing, and exploring. In music, material in a portfolio needs to conform to practices in learning, knowing, criticizing, discriminating, and exploring. Portfolios add additional ways of knowing but are not intended to replace extant methods. It is expected that students (as well as teachers) will be able to see changes in their understanding of music through the systematic and progressive change in conceptual structures displayed by the projects in the portfolio. Projects, therefore, cannot be randomly selected. Each student approaches his or her portfolio having a theory of how he or she comes to understand, a theory based upon the crucial concepts learned in and out of school. The teacher's task is to identify this theory and move that student toward theories that represent "best practices" in music. If this is done, the portfolio will eventually demonstrate to the student (he or she will discover) that the projects in the portfolio actually portray one or more ways of knowing and standards and practices in the field.

The projects in a portfolio might include demonstrations of competence in practiced performance ability, the ability to sight-read, to improvise, to compose, to write a reflective essay, to discuss the contributions of Stravinsky, and more, depending upon the extent of the instructional use of various frameworks and standards. An adjustment has to be made for each task to account for individual differences, as even the best student is not likely to be "best" in meeting each of the objectives currently espoused for music education. Thus instability—or lack of reliability—results not only from changes in the rater but also from the difficulty of establishing clear standards for the variety of tasks. It is not unusual for a rating to be based upon the student's improvement and/or the student's competence in relationship to his or her past competence and hypothesized ability. This basis is valuable but affects reliability. (Reliability can of course be improved when the most trivial tasks find their way into the portfolio as raters agree more easily on a level of competence in trivia.)

The New Standards Project

The New Standards Project, a partnership of 19 states and six urban school districts, has developed methods of assessment that are intended to function not as an "external" test but as integral elements within the system, thus increasing validity and reliability. The project recognizes that time requirements obviate the need to integrate assessment. The project's model for assessing understanding is derived from the military, where assessment practices effectively determine individual competence on problem solving, understanding, and ability to think. The success of the military is due to the clarity of their instructional goals and the acceptance that *every* soldier given a map and a compass and dropped into the middle of nowhere must be able to determine not only location but also the direction to the nearest mess hall. If public education is serious about all students reaching high standards, those standards and the projects that demonstrate knowledge and understanding of those standards must be equally clear. The New Standards Project found that teacher scoring of portfolios ranged from a reliability of .28 to .60, too low for most uses (Resnick, 1996). To raise the reliability, the project found it necessary to have multiple-choice or other on-demand items in the portfolio that provided evidence that the work in the portfolio was the student's own. Even with this stability, raising the reliability to a range of from .6 to .75 required constructing a clear course syllabus, setting the questions, describing the criteria for different grades, and establishing a grading sample. L. Resnick avers that a much more explicit theory of situated cognition is needed before performance assessment, the kind of assessment upon which portfolios are based, can progress (1996, p. 17).

Portfolio Validity

Student performance is sensitive to the assessment format (the context in which students are asked to perform, the type of task, and the conditions under which they assemble their portfolios). Portfolios, although authentic in one sense, differ from other authentic measures. For example, two-thirds of the students who were classified as capable on the basis of their portfolios were deemed not competent on the basis of a direct writing prompt, also an authentic measure. Observing students in the laboratory does not predict competent performance on a laboratory simulation. A number of researchers (Dunbar, Koretz, & Hoover [1991]; Linn, Burton, De Stefano, & Hansen [1995]; Shavelson, Baxter, & Gao [1993]; Shavelson, Baxter, & Pine [1991]; and Shavelson, Mayberry, Li, & Webb [1990]) have established that 15 to 19 tasks are needed in a portfolio for *each* objective if a portfolio is to serve as an assessment with a reliability of .80. The inclusion of one musical composition would reveal little about a student's musical understanding or about any of the reasons for asking the student to compose. In Vermont the average classroom teacher spent an additional 17 hours a month just managing the portfolios, leading 90% of the reporting principals to conclude that port-folios were helpful but probably too burdensome (p. 29).

Myford and Mislevy (1995) report that if AP Studio Art were viewed only as portfolio assessment, it would be nothing short of depressing (p. 13). What is learned from a portfolio in visual arts is an opportunity to assess not only skills and knowledge but also what students and judges value. The value component is more a social phenomenon than one in measurement (p. 13). The portfolio's greatest value is not in assessment but in improving learning, which, of course, is a major purpose of assessment when not used for accountability.

The Future

The lack of interest in assessment in music education may stem from music's low priority in the school, or, just as likely, it may be that the public is satisfied with the current status of music education. Another explanation is that the public is unconcerned about the music education *curriculum* and believes that any proposed outcomes will be positive but unimportant. The efforts of arts advocacy groups indicate that the public is uninformed about the music program and the student competencies it fosters. This lack of knowledge of outcomes is difficult to explain, as the music program is often highly visible in the community. The important outcomes may be the obvi-ous ones. Advocates of music education programs seldom, if ever, suggest improving or changing the program; the effort is totally on rallying the public to *support* music education in the schools. This support apparently does not include allocating additional instructional time, reducing the student-teacher ratio, increasing the music knowledge/skill base of the class-room teacher, or encouraging school boards and school administrators to place a higher priority on a quality music program. Rather, support means providing instruments for students or contributing to the fund-raising efforts required to maintain the current program. The objectives of the advocates do not easily fit into any of the taxonomies.

Without external pressure to demonstrate what students should know and be able to do on accepted objectives, little internal change will occur. This status quo situation is both positive and negative. The positive side is that music education comes to the reform table without any of the negative reports and baggage that accompany the basic subjects. Music education has no history of misusing multiple-choice and true-false tests; the primary as-sessment has been "evaluation" by friendly audiences. These evaluations have not been used diagnostically, needs assessment has not been conducted, and assessment data have not been used to justify the requests for resources. Teachers have not "taught to the test," and there are no national norms or competence standards. Parents do not expect grades in music, and if grades are given their meaning is obscure. Instrumental music may report student competence through chair placements that are then listed on the concert program, but few would accept this indicator as a measure of success of the music program, only that of the individual student. Music education has few leaders who champion any role for assessment. Charles Leonhard wrote a seminal article on evaluation in *Basic Concepts of Music Education* (1958), a book that initiated major changes in music education, but his chapter was ignored and Leonhard is remembered for other significant contributions but not for this effort.

Basic Music and Performance Programs

Music education can profit from the current interest in assessment only if the profession realizes that there are at least two distinct programs in the schools—a basic program and a performance program. These are so distinct that both the instructional and the assessment concepts differ, often substantially. Additional programs or variations on the programs may exist in various school systems, but both the performance and the basic program have a legitimate claim on curriculum resources. The basic or required program is a cognitive program (Phillips, 1995) and relates most closely to the educational reform movement. A third program, one focused on "instrumental" or nonmusical objectives, is not discussed in this chapter, despite its potential importance. Instrumental objectives include development of skills for lifelong learning and leisure activities, such skills as cooperation, responsibility, prioritizing, and numerous other worthwhile outcomes.

Although the two established music programs differ in significant ways, they are mutually supportive. Basic music that includes the required music program provides competencies that enhance the performance program; performance in turn can enhance understanding of some of the goals of the basic program. Mediocrity occurs when the priorities of the two programs are not observed and too much "overlap" is attempted. A school system may wish to support only a performance program *or* a basic program, and where this situation exists the difficulty of achieving challenging goals will be great. It is not realistic to accept goals when the resources to accomplish these goals do not exist. Music is a large and wonderful field, too broad for even the professional to feel competent in performance, musicology, composition, and music in general education.

Assessment and Educational Reform

The thrust of this chapter has been on assessment strategies for basic music, for music programs that match some of the programs in other basic subjects. Currently there are marked philosophical differences between the cognitivists and the situativists (Greeno, Collins, & Resnick, 1996), whether educational experiences are to be structured according to what we know about learning from the world of psychology and educational psychology or all learning is situated in a particular location, a particular time, and the sociocultural background of students and teachers. Eventually there will likely be some compromise; these substantive differences need not currently concern the music educator. Systemic reform in education is emphasizing learning strategies and issues of transfer rather than performance. Doing well on a standardized test is a performance, and although external assessment of performance is accepted by most educators, the current gathering and use of assessment data is for its potential in improving the learning process. Students who believe the purpose of education is to enable them to perform tend to select easy tasks they can do well; students who believe that education is for learning accept setbacks when they recognize that they are developing strategies, skills, and knowledges that move them toward worthwhile objectives. Education for these individuals is analogous to running a confidence course: If the course is too easy, it fails to build any lasting confidence. Confidence courses involve problem solving: The individual forms hypotheses of the best route and the best order of tasks and draws upon his or her extant knowledge and skills. With a cognitivist orientation, students will want to sing individually as well as offer individual reflections on a number of classroom experiences. The older behavioristic orientation adhered to outdated theories of motivation that emphasized the negative consequences of failure rather than what is now believed about motivation. There will never be adequate instructional time for the expected content and character of assessment unless the teacher changes his or her instructional procedures to include recording on a regular basis each student's competence in accordance with standards *and* that individual student's improvement. Even when embedded in instruction, such an assessment process will seem formidable to the teacher who is pressed for instructional time. The reform movement advocates that assessment be individualized to the extent possible, to record how well each student is learning in relationship to his or her sociocultural background as well as his or her competency on grade-level standards. Although the most extreme cognitivists or situativists (Anderson, Reder, & Simon, 1996) are fearful of the standards movement, all recognize the philosophical importance of educating all students to high standards. Standards require the assessing of students, individually and collectively, on developmentally appropriate grade-level goals. The assessment, however, is not for accountability but to assist the teacher and student in identifying what is yet to be accomplished. Teachers currently control grade-level objectives in the basic music program and can drastically reduce their goals to a manageable level. State and district curricula merely suggest. Textbooks for basic music, school district music curriculum guides, and state and national frameworks are not appropriate sources for establishing content validity of future assessments, as their suggestions for content do not take into account the resources available.

The instructional and assessment strategies recommended for the basic subjects are applicable to a basic music program that is focused on understanding music listened to in and out of class. Understanding music would enable a graduate of the program to listen to music with heightened aural abilities and knowledge of what is occurring in the music, to attend concerts, to be discriminating, and to use music in his or her daily life. The emphasis on cognition and problem solving means that students learn to identify musical problems, talk about musical issues, argue about the qualities of music, establish criteria for excellence in musical performance and in musical works, and be open to all quality music and musical experiences. The questions included in the Marzano taxonomy suggest the knowledge and skill that will be needed. The unsolved question is one of transfer. The expectation is that an understanding of the principles of music composition and performance will be an enabler for transfer. The ideas of Vygotsky imply that only if these principles are derived from the situation and the interaction with the music, individually and collectively, will transfer to different music in different situations be achieved (Brown & Farrar, 1985). New teachers in all subjects must think hard about these educational ideas and strategies and how they apply to their subject matter content, as educators are making these teaching suggestions based on face validity; they make sense in light of what we know today and in light of past failures. (Without past assessment, we do not know what aspects of the basic music program have failed; the only evidence is from the performance program.)

The basic music program will have to use all types of measurement devices. Low-level knowledge is required in sequential programs before high-level knowledge and its concomitant understandings can be attained at a level that makes transfer possible. Multiple-choice, single-answer, and matching tests will be part of instruction; equally necessary will be assessment of singing and perceptual skills—on a regular basis and recorded. Contemporary philosophy rejects the idea that instruction ceases for assessment and that all students take the same test at the same time. Individualized assessment requires more time, but if the skill or knowledge is worth teaching, it is worth each student's attaining that competence. Matching pitch and singing an arpeggio in tune is a low-level but necessary ability in most music programs. This low-level skill, however, must make sense to the student, or he or she will not be actively involved in the learning. Performance programs often involve passive learning; students seldom object to a class where little thinking is required. They are told what and how to perform, what to practice for the next lesson, and how well the lesson should be performed—a luxurious escape from the arduousness of active learning. Passive learning is less likely to transfer, thus making understandable the lack of transfer in many performance programs. A performance program will profit from tracking—not tracking by race, gender, or socioeconomic status but by competence. When all students have an equal chance to study, practice, and learn, tracking does not discriminate; it is not elitist. Excellent performance programs exist in all types of schools, from Phillips Exeter to Eisenhower High School.

The basic program can emphasize instruction where the historical and cultural factors of the community not only influence learning but also are indicators of the student's initial knowledge and the skills that are needed to participate in a community of practice. These classrooms emphasize the socially negotiated meaning to experiences (Eisenhart, Finkel, & Marion, 1996). The instruction is characterized by not only open demonstrations of perceptual abilities but also discussions about music that allow the teacher to identify misunderstanding, skipped sequences, and lack of competencies that will interfere with future learning. In traditional "general" music classes students do not develop the needed skills or knowledges and there is no provision for remedial work, resulting in an American population of musical illiterates.

Revising and correcting the traditional general music program will result in students' becoming engaged in learning in fundamentally new ways. The model would be the music critic; that is, the focus would be on hearing and understanding music. It is this discipline, not the discipline of the high school chorus, that provides the content and ways of "knowing" desired for all students. To assume that all students can learn music requires a new way of thinking on the part of both students and teachers. A large number of students (and adults) reject learning in music on the basis of lack of ability because the model presented to them has been an incorrect model. Self-assessment of knowledge in the constructive classroom is not only possible but also necessary. Self- and teacher assessments need not meet the same standards as published tests when they are frequent and used primarily to improve. Shepherd, in her hypothetical vision of the future, suggests that it is *possible* for teachers thinking systematically over time to develop highly accurate assessments of student learning (2001). The italics in the original indicate that this will not be easy even for the teacher with a small classroom.

The music critic is the suggested model as the emphasis is on understanding relationships—to other performance, to other musics, and to other times. This type of learning seldom occurs in a performance program, as it requires time for listening, researching, comparing, contrasting, and, most of all, discussing the *important* features of the music. The broader range of assessment tools required will likely also require attention to long-term musical and factual knowledge. It will necessitate students' recognizing and singing melodies, motives, unifying rhythmic patterns, and more. If this sounds ambitious, it is, but these competencies are only a few that involve higher order thinking and are prerequisite to problem solving. Identifying an incorrect note is a trivial event in problem solving and leads to more trivial problem solving (Leper, Drake, & O'Donnell-Johnson, 1997). With younger children more informal assessments will be needed, but these can be observation-based individual performances and responses and even the retelling of the stories in and of music.

Research by Camp (1992) indicates that students can articulate and apply critical criteria if given practice in doing so. This practice is necessary with portfolios, where the advantage is in analyzing past work. Portfolio scholars have found that it might be necessary to maintain two portfolios, instructional and performance, a near-impossibility in most music-teaching situations. Shepherd indicates that whether portfolios can be productively used for these two purposes is highly controversial even in basic subjects (2001). She indicates that the use of rubrics, which often accompany portfolios, is likely inappropriate in classrooms with young children. Rubrics are objectionable to others because of their resemblance to positivistic modes of assessment (Wile & Tierney, 1996). Other future assessment concerns center on the prescriptive nature of the scoring in using rubrics (Wolf & Reardon, 1996). A major need is research on rubric development. Their current use in teacher evaluation is unwarranted. Assessments should occur in the classroom as a normal part of instruction to take advantage of the social situation advocated by Vygotsky and to make assessment seem a part of learning. This description of assessment is not so different from current teacher efforts but demands new procedures and instruments. Assessments should not just judge competence as correct or incorrect, in-tune or out-of-tune, as might be expected in a performance program, but should also aid students in learning to distinguish quality of ideas, whether remarks are clear and accurate, whether previous knowledge is used in formulating a comment or reflection, and whether reference is made to standards. Assessment must also show the importance of *thinking* that occurs in reacting to musical experiences.

Assessment is ineffective whenever students do not have a clear understanding of the criteria by which their work will be assessed (Frederiksen & Collins, 1989). When required to become involved with self- and peer assessment, students become extremely interested in the criteria for excellence (Klenowski, 1995).

A Final Word

The suggestions for systemically changing education brought on by education's response to the reform movement are an idealization; research and experience are needed to determine their potential, including that for assessment. Teachers with successful music programs should not assume that these futuristic suggestions will automatically help their programs. Research has provided us with few cues, and those few are not based on current philosophies of education. Changing the culture of the music classroom to meet the new frameworks will change music education as it is currently practiced. Teachers cannot continue to randomly add and subtract experiences and objectives, as teaching for musical understanding requires focus on fewer objectives, fewer musical selections, and fewer types of music. The effort to develop assessment tools and dependent measures for research will occupy music educators for the next decade as not only the reliability and validity of even embedded measures need to be ascertained but also the requirements and substance of tools for program evaluation. Research in assessment needs to verify that NAEP has indeed established a working framework for the profession and to ascertain what are the alternatives. The teacher's rewards lie in positive feedback and the knowledge that one's efforts are worthwhile. More than a few of the ideas about the "mindful" school will require teachers to reflect on not only their own musical beliefs but also what they believe is possible for students to know and understand and what knowledge will be available to students on demand when performing, hearing, thinking about, and discussing music, in and out of school.

REFERENCES

Anderson, J. R., Reder, L. M., & Simon, H. A. (1996). Situated learning and education. *Educational Researcher, 25*, 5–11.

Anderson, L. W., & Krathwohl, D. (Eds.). (2001). *A taxonomy for learning, teaching, and assessing: A revision of Bloom's taxonomy of educational objectives.* New York: Longman.

Aróstegui, J. L. (2004). Much more than music: Music education instruction at the University of Illinois at Urbana-Champaign. In J. L. Aróstegui (Ed.), *The social context of music education.* Champaign: Center for Instructional Research and Curriculum Evaluation.

Aschbacher, P. (1999). Developing indicators of classroom practice to monitor and support school reform. (CSE Tech. Rep. No. 513). Los Angeles: UCLA CRESST.

Ashford, E. (2004). NCLB's unfunded arts programs seek refuge. *Education Digest, 70*(2), 22–26.

Baker, E., & Linn, R. (2004). Validity issues for accountability systems. In S. Fuhrman & R. Elmore (Eds.). *Redesigning accountability systems for education.* New York: Teachers College Press.

Bartel, L. (1992). The development of the cognitive-affective response test-music. *Psychomusicology, 11*(1), 15–26.

Beston, P. (2004). Senior student composition: An investigation of criteria used in assessments by New South Wales secondary school music teachers. *Research Studies in Music Education, 22*, 28–41.

Beyer, B. (1988). *Developing a thinking skills program.* Boston: Allyn and Bacon.

Biggs, J. B., & Collis, K. F. (1982). *Evaluating the quality of learning: The SOLO taxonomy.* New York: Academic Press.

Blakeslee, M. (2004). Assembling the arts education jigsaw. *Arts Education Policy Review, 105*(4), 31–36.

Blocker, L., Greenwood, R., & Shellahamer, B. (1997). Teaching behaviors of middle school and high school band directors in the rehearsal setting. *Journal of Research in Music Education, 45*(3), 457–469.

Blom, D., & Poole, K. (2004). Peer assessment of tertiary music performance: Opportunities for understanding performance assessment and performing through experience and self-reflection. *British Journal of Music Education 21*(1), 111–125.

Bloom, B. J. (Ed.). (1956). *Taxonomy of educational objectives: Book 1. Cognitive domain.* New York: Longman.

Brittin, R. V., & Sheldon, D. A. (1995). Comparing continuous versus static measurements in music listeners' preferences. *Journal of Research in Music Education, 43*, 36–45.

Brittin, R. (1996). Listeners' preference for music of other cultures: Comparing response modes. *Journal of Research in Music Education, 44*(4), 328–340.

Brittin, R., & Duke, R. (1997). Continuous versus summative evaluations of musical intensity: A comparison of two methods for measuring overall effect. *Journal of Research in Music Education, 45*(2), 245–258.

Broadfoot, P. (2000). Preface. In A. Filer (Ed.), *Assessment: Social practice and social product.* London: Routledge Falmer.

Brophy, T. (2000). *Assessing the developing child musician: A guide for general music or teachers.* Chicago: GIA.

Brown, A. L., & Campione, J. C. (1986). Psychological theory and the study of learning disabilities. *American Psychologist, 41,* 1059–1068.

Brown, A. L., & Farrar, R. A. (1985). Diagnosing zones of proximal development. In J. Weartsch (Ed.), *Culture, communication and cognition: Vygotskian perspectives* (pp. 273–305). Cambridge: Cambridge University Press.

Brown, C. (2000). A response to Anthony J. Palmer. *Philosophy of Music Education Review, 8*(2), 118–119.

Brynes, S. R. (1997). Different age and mentally handicapped listeners' response to Western art selections. *Journal of Research in Music Education, 44,* 569–579.

Buttsworth, L., Fogarty, G., & Rorke, P. (1993). Predicting aural performance in a tertiary music training programme. *Psychology of Music, 21*(2), 114–126.

Byrne, C., MacDonald, R., & Carlton, L. (2003). Assessing creativity in musical compositions: Flow as an assessment tool. *British Journal of Music Education, 20*(3), 277–290.

Camp, R. (1992). Portfolio reflections in middle and secondary school classrooms. In K. B. Yancey (Ed.), *Portfolios in the writing classroom* (pp. 61–79). Urbana, IL: National Council Teachers of English.

Cantu, N. (2000). *The use of tests when making high-stake decisions for students: A resource guide for educators and policy makers.* Washington, DC: U.S. Department of Education, Office of Civil Rights.

Cantwell, R., & Jeanneret, N. (2004). Developing a framework for the assessment of musical learning:Resolving the dilemma of the "parts" and the "whole." *Research Studies in Music Education, 22,* 2–13.

Carroll, J. B. (1993). *Human cognitive abilities.* New York: Cambridge University Press.

Chelimsky, E. (1992). Expanding evaluation capabilities in the General Accounting Office. In C. Wye & R. Sonnichsen (Eds.), *New directions for program evaluation: Vol. 5.* San Francisco: Jossey-Bass.

Chomsky, N. (1968). *Language and mind.* New York: Harcourt Brace Jovanovich.

Cibulka, James G. (2003). Educational bankruptcy, takeovers, and reconstitution of failing schools. In W. L. Boyd & D. Miretzky (Eds.), *American educational governance on trial: Change and challenges* (pp. 249–270). Chicago: University of Chicago Press.

Cizek, G. J., Bunch, M. B., & Koons, H. (2004). Setting performance standards: Contemporary methods. *Educational Measurement: Issues and Practices, 23*(4), 31–50.

Colwell, R. (1970). *The evaluation of music teaching and learning.* Englewood Cliffs, NJ: Prentice Hall.

Cook, E., Reimer, B., & Walker, D. (1974–1985). *Silver Burdett music, grades 1–6.* Morristown, NJ: Silver Burdett.

Cox, G. (2004). Charles Faulkner Bryan: His life and music. Review of Carolyn Livingston's 2003 publication. *British Journal of Music Education, 21*(2), 232–234.

Cronbach, L. (1995). Emerging roles of evaluation in science education reform. In R. O'Sullivan (Ed.), *New directions for program evaluation: Vol. 65* (pp. 19–29). San Francisco: Jossey-Bass.

Custodero, L. (1999). Constructing musical understandings: The cognition-flow interface. *Bulletin of the Council for Research in Music Education, 142*, 79–80.

Darling-Hammond, L. (2004). Standards, accountability and school reform. *Teachers College Record Special Issue: Testing; Teaching and Learning, 106*(6), 1047–1095.

Davis, A. P. (1998). Performance achievement and analysis of teaching during choral rehearsals, *Journal of Research in Music Education, 46*(1), 496–509.

Delandshere, G. (2003). Assessment as inquiry. *Teachers College Record, 104*(7), 1461–1484.

DeNardo, G., & Kantorski, V. (1995). A continuous response assessment of children's music cognition. *Bulletin of the Council for Research in Music Education, 126*, 42–52.

DeNardo, G. F., & Kantorski, V. J. (1998). A comparison of listeners' musical cognition using a continuous response assessment. *Journal of Research in Music Education, 46*(2), 320–331.

Developing an arts assessment: Some selected strategies, *The State Education Standard, 4*(4), 20–25.

Dunbar, S. B., Koretz, D. M., & Hoover, H. D. (1991). Quality control in the development and use of performance assessment. *Applied Measures in Education, 4*, 298–303.

Eisenhart, M., Finkel, E., & Marion, S. F. (1996). Creating the conditions for scientific literacy: A re-examination. *American Educational Research Journal, 33*, 261–295.

Ekholm, E. (2000) The effect of singing mode and seating arrangement on choral blend and overall choral sound. *Journal of Research in Music Education, 48*(2), 123–135.

Elmore, R. (2004). *School reform from the inside out: Policy, practice, and performance.* Cambridge: Harvard Education Press.

Evaluation Center. 2004. Checklists. http://www.wmich.edu/evalctr/checklists.

Fetterman, D. (2001). *Foundations of empowerment evaluation.* Thousand Oaks, CA: Sage.

Flinders, D. (2005). Multiple worlds, multiple ways of knowing: Elliot Eisner's contributions to educational research. In P. B. Uhrmacher & J. Matthews (Eds.), *Intricate palette: Working the ideas of Elliot Eisner.* Upper Saddle River, NJ: Pearson.

Flohr, J. (2000). *A contemporary rhythm skills assessment.* Champaign, IL: Electronic Courseware Systems.

Foshay, A. W. (2000). *The curriculum: Purpose, substance, practice.* New York: Teachers College Press.

Frankel, J. (2002). An evaluation of a web-based model of assessment for the New Jersey state core curriculum content standards in music. Unpublished doctoral dissertation, Teachers College, New York.

Frederiksen, J. R., & Collins, A. (1989). A systems approach to educational testing. *Educational Researcher, 18,* 27–32.

Frederiksen, N., Mislevy, R., & Bejar, I. (Eds.). (1993). *Test theory for a new generation of tests.* Hillsdale, NJ: Erlbaum.

Fredrickson, W. (1994). Band musicians' performance and eye contact as influenced by loss of a visual and/or aural stimulus. *Journal of Research in Music Education, 42*(4), 306–317.

Fredrickson, W. (1995). A comparison of perceived musical tension and aesthetic response. *Psychology of Music, 23*(1), 81–87.

Fredrickson, W. (1997). Elementary, middle, and high school student perceptions of tension in music. *Journal of Research in Music Education, 45*(4), 626–635.

Fredrickson, W. (1999). Effect of musical performance on perception of tension in Gustav Holt's First Suite in E-flat. *Journal of Research in Music Education, 47*(1), 44–52.

Fredrickson, W. E. (2001). The effect of performance medium on perception of musical tension. *Bulletin of the Council for Research in Music Education, 148,* 60–64.

Fremer, J. (2000, December). A message from your president. *Newsletter,* National Council on Measurement in Education.

Froehlich, H. (1995). Measurement dependability in the systematic observation of music instruction: A review, some questions, and possibilities for a (new?) approach. *Psychomusicology, 14,* 182–196.

Froseth, J., & Weaver, M. (1996). *Music teacher self-assessment.* Chicago: GIA.

Fullan, M. (2003). *The moral imperative of school leadership.* Thousand Oaks, CA: Corwin.

Gee, C. (1994). Artists in the classrooms: The impact and consequences of the National Endowment for the Arts' artist resident program on K–12 arts education, parts 1 and 2. *Arts Education Policy Review, 95*(3), 14–29, (4), 8–31.

Geringer, J. (1995). Continuous loudness judgments of dynamics in recorded music excerpts. *Journal of Research in Music Education, 43*(1), 22–35.

Gitomer, D., & Duschl, R. (1995). *Moving toward a portfolio culture in science education* (Document 94-07). Princeton, NJ: Center for Performance Assessment.

Goodlad, J., Mantle-Bromley, C., & Goodlad, S. (2004). *Education for everyone: Agenda for education in a democracy.* San Francisco: Jossey Bass.

Goodlad, J. I. (2004). *Romances with schools.* New York: McGraw Hill.

Goolsby, T. W. (1996). Time use in instrumental rehearsals: A comparison of experienced, novice, and student teachers. *Journal of Research in Music Education, 44*(4), 286–303.

Gordon, E. (1998). *Harmonic improvisation readiness record and rhythm improvisation readiness record.* Chicago: GIA.

Grant, S. G., Gradwell, J., & Cimbricz, S. (2004). A question of authenticity: The document-based question as an assessment of students' knowledge of history. *Journal of Curriculum and Supervision, 19*(4), 309–337.

Gray, K. (2004). Is high school career and technical education obsolete? *Phi Delta Kappan, 86*(2), 128–134.

Greene, J. P., Winters, M. A., & Forster, G. (2004). Testing high-stakes tests: Can we believe the results of accountability tests? *Teachers College Record Special Issue: Testing, Teaching, and Learning, 106*(6), 1124–1144.

Greeno, J. G., Collins, A. M., & Resnick, L. B. (1996). Cognition and learning.

In D. C. Berliner & R. C. Calfee (Eds.), *Handbook of educational psychology* (pp. 15–46). New York: Macmillan.

Gregory, D. (1994). Analysis of listening preferences of high school and college musicians. *Journal of Research in Music Education, 42,* 331–342.

Hair, H. (1997). Divergent research in children's musical development, *Psychomusicology, 16,* 26–39.

Hallam, S. (1998). *Instrumental teaching: A practical guide to better teaching and learning.* Oxford: Heinemann.

Hallam, S., & Prince, V. (2003). Conceptions of musical ability. *Research Studies in Music Education, 20,* 2–22.

Hallam, S., & Shaw, J. (2002). Constructions of musical ability. *Bulletin of the Council of Research in Music Education, 153/154,* 102–108.

Hardy, D. (1995). *The construction and validation of an original sight-playing test for elementary piano students.* Unpublished doctoral dissertation, University of Oklahoma, Norman.

Harland, J., Kinder, K., Lord, P., Stoff, A., Schagen, I., & Haynes, J. (with Cusworth, L., White, R., & Paola, R.). (2000). *Arts education in secondary schools: Effects and effectiveness.* Slough, UK: National Foundation for Education Research,

Harrow, A. (1972). *A taxonomy of the psychomotor domain.* New York: Longman.

Hauenstein, A. D. (1998). *A conceptual framework for educational objectives: A holistic approach to traditional taxonomies.* Lanham, MD: University Press of America.

Heck, R., & Crislip, M. (2001). Direct and indirect writing assessments: Examining issues of equity and utility. *Education Evaluation and Policy Analysis, 23*(3), 275–292.

Herman, J. L. Baker, E. L., & Linn, R. L. (2004, Spring). Accountability systems in support of student learning: Moving to the next generation. *CRESST LINE,* p. 4.

Hess, F. M., Rotherham, A. J., & Walsh, K. (2004). Conclusion. In F. M. Hess, A. J. Rotherham, & K. Walsh (Eds.), *A qualified teacher in every classroom? Appraising old answers and new ideas* (pp. 279–284). Cambridge: Harvard University Press.

Hickey, M. (1999, January). Assessment rubrics for music composition. *Music Educators Journal, 85*(4), 26–33.

Holcomb, A. (2003). An investigation of the concurrent validity of the discipline based professional teaching standards of music in Connecticut. Unpublished doctoral dissertation, University of Hartford, CT.

Hope, S. (2004). Art education in a world of cross-purposes. In E. W. Eisner & M. D. Day (Eds.), *Handbook of research and policy in art education.* Mahway, NJ: Lawrence Erlbaum.

House, E. R. (1994). Integrating the quantitative and qualitative. In C. Reichard & S. Rallis (Eds.), *New directions for program evaluation: Vol. 61. The qualitative–quantitative debate: New perspectives* (pp. 13–22). San Francisco: Jossey-Bass.

House, E. R. (1995a). Principled evaluation: A critique of the AEA guiding principles. In W. Shadish, D. Newman, M. A. Scheirer, & C. Wye (Eds.), *New directions for program evaluation: Vol. 66. Guiding principles for evaluators* (pp. 27–34). San Francisco: Jossey-Bass.

House, E. R. (1995b). Putting things together coherently: Logic and justice. In D. Fournier (Ed.), *New directions for program evaluation: Vol. 68. Reasoning in evaluation: Inferential links and leaps* (pp. 33–48). San Francisco: Jossey-Bass.

Ingram, D. Louis, K., & Schroeder, R. G. (2004). Accountability policies and teacher decision making: Barriers to the use of data to improve practice. *Teachers College Record Special Issue: Testing, Teaching, and Learning, 106*(6), 1258–1287.

Ippel, M. J., & Beem, L. A. (1987). A theory of antagonistic strategies. In E. DeCorte, H. Lodewijks, R. Parmentier, & P. Span (Eds.), *Learning and instruction: European research in an international context* (Vol. 1, pp. 111–121). Oxford: Pergamon Press.

Johnson, C. (1996). Musicians' and nonmusicians' assessment of perceived rubato in musical performance. *Journal of Research in Music Education, 44*(1), 84–96.

Jones, J., & Chittenden, E. (1995). *Teachers' perceptions of rating an early literacy portfolio* (Document 95-01). Princeton, NJ: Center for Performance Assessment.

Jorgensen, M. (2004). And there is much left to do. In M. Wilson (Ed.), *Toward coherence between classroom assessment and accountability* (pp. 2003–208). Chicago: University of Chicago Press.

Kivy, P. (1984). *Sound and semblance: Reflections on musical representation.* Princeton, NJ: Princeton University Press.

Klenowski, V. (1995). Student self-evaluation process in student-centered teaching and learning contexts of Australia and England. *Assessment in Education, 2,* 145–163.

Krathwohl, D., Bloom, B., & Masia, B. (1964). *Taxonomy of educational objectives: The classification of educational objectives handbook II: Affective domain.* New York: Longman.

Kupermintz, H. (2003). Teacher effects and teacher effectiveness: A validity investigation of the Tennessee value added assessment system. *Educational Evaluation and Policy Analysis, 25*(3), 287–298.

Kyllonen, P. C., Lohman, D. F., & Woltz, D. J. (1984). Componential modeling of alternative strategies for performing spatial tasks. *Journal of Educational Psychology, 76,* 1325–1345.

Lagemann, E. (2000). *An elusive science: The troubling history of education research.* Chicago: University of Chicago Press.

Lane, S., Parke, C. S., & Stone, G. A. (2002). The impact of a state performance-based assessment and accountability program on mathematics instruction and student learning: Evidence from survey data and school performance. *Educational Assessment, 8*(4), 279–315.

Lehman, Paul. (2004). Raising the bar: Paul Lehman assesses 10 years of national standards. *Teaching Music, 12*(2), 34–39.

Leonhard, C. (1958). Evaluation in music education. In N. Henry (Ed.), *Basic concepts of music education* [57th Yearbook of the National Society for the Study of Education], part 1. Chicago: University of Chicago Press.

Leper, M. R., Drake, M. F., & O'Donnell-Johnson, T. (1997). Scaffolding techniques of expert human tutors. In K. Hogan & M. Pressley (Eds.), *Scaffolding student learning: Instructional approaches and issues* (pp. 108–144). Cambridge: Brookline Books.

Lieberman, A., & Miller, L. (2004). *Teacher leadership*. San Francisco: Jossey Bass.

Linn, R. L. (2003a). Accountability: Responsibility and reasonable expectations. *Educational Researcher, 32*(7), 7–13.

Linn, R. L. (2003b). Requirements for measuring adequate yearly progress. *Policy Brief 6*. Los Angeles: UCLA, CRESST.

Linn, R. L., Burton, E., DeStefano, L., & Hanson, M. (1995). Generalizability of new standards project 1993 pilot study tasks in mathematics (CSE Tech. Rep. 392). Los Angeles: UCLA CRESST.

Lohman, D. F. (1988). Spatial abilities as traits, processes, and knowledge. In R. J. Sternberg (Ed.), *Advances in the psychology of human intelligence* (Vol. 4, pp. 181–248). Hillsdale, NJ: Erlbaum.

Lychner, J. (1998). An empirical study concerning terminology relating to aesthetic response to music. *Journal of Research in Music Education, 46*(2), 303–319.

Mabry, L. (1999, May). Writing to the rubric: Lingering effects of traditional standardized testing on direct writing assessment. *Phi Delta Kappan, 80*(9), 673–679.

Madsen, C. (1997a). Emotional response to music. *Psychomusicology, 16*, 59–67.

Madsen, C. (1997b). Focus of attention and aesthetic response. *Journal of Research in Music Education, 45*(1), 80–89.

Madsen, C. (1998). Emotion versus tension in Haydn's Symphony no. 104 as measured by the two-dimensional continuous response digital interface. *Journal of Research in Music Education, 46*(4), 546–554.

Madsen, C., Brittin, R., & Capprella-Sheldon, D. (1993). An empirical investigation of the aesthetic response to music. *Journal of Research in Music Education, 41*, 57–69.

Madsen, C., & Coggiola, J. (2001). The effect of manipulating a CRDI dial on the focus of attention of musicians/nonmusicians and perceived aesthetic response. *Bulletin of the Council for Research research in Music Education. 149*, 13–22.

Madsen, C., Geringer, J., & Fredrickson, W. (1997). Focus of attention to musical elements in Haydn's Symphony # 104. *Bulletin of the Council for Research in Music Education, 133*, 57–63.

Marshall, S. (1993). Assessing schema knowledge. In N. Frederiksen, R. Mislevy, & I. Bejar (Eds.), *Test theory for a new generation of tests* (pp. 155–180). Hillsdale, NJ: Erlbaum.

Marzano, R. J. (2001). *Designing a new taxonomy of educational objectives*. Thousand Oaks, CA: Corwin.

Masear, C. (1999). *The development and field test of a model for evaluating elementary string programs*. Unpublished doctoral dissertation, Teachers College, Columbia University, New York City.

McCurry, M. (1998). *Hand-chime performance as a means of meeting selected standards in the national standards of music education*. Unpublished doctoral dissertation, University of Georgia, Athens.

McGinn, D. (2005), January 9). Making the grade. *New York Times Magazine*, pp. 24–29.

McPherson, G. (1995). The assessment of musical performance: Development and validation of five new measures. *Psychology of Music, 23*(2), 142–161.

McPherson, G. E. (1996). Five aspects of musical performance and their correlates. *Bulletin of the Council for Research in Music Education, 127,* 115–121.

McPherson, G. E. (2005). From child to musician: Skill development during the beginning stages of learning an instrument. *Psychology of Music, 33*(1), 5–35.

McTighe, J. & Wiggins, G. (1999). *The Understanding by design handbook.* Alexandria, VA: ASCD.

Meier, D. (2000). *Will standards save public education?* Boston: Beacon.

Mikle, H. (1999). *The development of an individual sight reading inventory.* Unpublished doctoral dissertation, University of Minnesota, Minneapolis.

Miller, R. (1979). *An analysis of musical perception through multidimensional scaling.* Unpublished doctoral dissertation, University of Illinois at Urbana-Champaign.

Milner, M. (2000). *Program evaluation of a district's 5th grade music instruction in one component of the Texas essential knowledge and skills.* Unpublished doctoral dissertation, University of Houston, TX.

Mislevy, R. (1993). Introduction. In N. Fredrickson, R. Mislevy, & I. Bejar (Eds.), *Test theory for a new generation of tests* (pp. ix–xii). Hillsdale, NJ: Erlbaum.

Mislevy, R., Almond, R., Yan, D., & Steinberg, L. (2000) *Bayes Nets in educational assessment: Where do the numbers come from?* Los Angeles: Center for the Study of Evaluation.

Myford, C., & Mislevy, R. (1995). Monitoring and improving a portfolio assessment system (Document 94–05). Princeton, NJ: Center for Performance Assessment.

Newkirk, T. (2000). A manual for rubrics. *Education Week, 20*(2), 41.

Newman, F., Marks, H., & Gamoran, A. (1996). Authentic pedagogy and student performance. *American Journal of Education, 104,* 286, as cited in Grant, Gradwell, & Cimbricz (2004).

No Child Left Behind Act of 2001. (2002). Public Law Number 107–110, 115 Stat. 1425.

Noddings, N. (2003). *Happiness and education.* Cambridge: Cambridge University Press.

Norris, C. (1998). *The relationship of tonal memory tests of recognition and tonal memory tests of reproduction.* Unpublished doctoral dissertation, University of Illinois at Urbana-Champaign.

O'Neil, T., Sireci, S. G., & Huff, K. L. (2003–2004). *Educational Assessment 9*(3–4), 129–151.

Osgood, C., Suci, G., & Tannenbaum, P. (1957). *The measurement of meaning.* Urbana: University of Illinois Press.

Palmer, A. J. (2000). Consciousness studies and a philosophy of music education. *Philosophy of Music Education Review 8*(2), 99–110.

Persky, H., Sandene, B. & Askew, J. (1998). *The NAEP 1997 arts report card.* Washington, DC: U.S. Department of Education.

Phillips, D. C. (1995). The good, the bad, and the ugly: The many faces of constructivism. *Educational Researcher, 24,* 5–12.

Piaget, J. (1971). *Genetic epistemology* (E. Duckworth, Trans.). New York: Norton.

Popham, W. J (2004). Curriculum matters. *American School Board Journal, 191*(11), 30–33.

Pullin, D. (2004). Accountability, autonomy, and academic freedom in educator preparation programs. *Journal of Teacher Education: The Journal of Policy and Research in Teacher Education, 55* (4), 300–312.

Rauscher, F., Shaw, G., & Ky, K. (1993). Music and spatial task performance. *Nature, 365,* 611.

Reichardt, C., & Rallis, S. (1994). The relationship between qualitative and quantitative traditions. In C. Reichardt & S. Rallis (Eds.), *New directions for program evaluation: Vol. 61. The qualitative-quantitative debate: New perspectives* (5–12). San Francisco: Jossey-Bass.

Reimer, B. (1996). *Musical roles and musical minds: Beyond the theory of multiple intelligences.* Evanston, IL: Northwestern University Press.

Reimer, B. (2005). Eisner's thinking from a music educators' perspective. In P. B. Uhrmacher & J. Matthews (Eds.), *Intricate palette: Working the ideas of Elliot Eisner* (pp. 103–114). Upper Saddle River, NJ: Pearson.

Reimer, B., Hoffman, M., & McNeil, A. (1975–1982). *Silver Burdett music, grades 7, 8.* Morristown, NJ: Silver Burdett.

Rentz, E. (1992). Musicians' and nonmusicians' aural perception of orchestral instrument families. *Journal of Research in Music Education, 40*(3), 185–192.

Resnick, L. (1996). Performance puzzles: Issues in measuring capabilities and certifying accomplishments (CSE Tech. Rep. 415). Los Angeles: UCLA CRESST.

Reynolds, A., & Hyun, K. (2004). Understanding music aptitude: Teachers' interpretations. *Research Studies in Music Education, 23,* 18–31.

Richardson, E. (1992). The value of evaluation. In C. Wye & R. Sonnichsen (Eds.), *New directions for program evaluation: Vol. 55 Evaluation in the federal government: Changes, trends, and opportunities* (pp. 15–20). San Francisco: Jossey-Bass.

Rogosa, D. (1999). *Accuracy of Year 1, Year 2 comparisons using individual percentile rank scores: Classical test theory calculations.* Los Angeles: UCLA CRESST.

Rumelhart, D. E., & Norman, D. A. (1981). Accretion, tuning and restructuring: Three modes of learning. In J. W. Colton & R. Kaltzky (Eds.), *Semantic factors in cognition* (pp. 37–53). Hillsdale, NJ: Erlbaum.

Scott, S. (2000). An application of the SOLO taxonomy to classify the strategies used by grade 5 students to solve selected music-reading tasks. *Contributions to Music Education, 27*(2), 37–57.

Scriven, M. (1993). *New directions for program evaluation: Vol. 58. Hard won lessons in program evaluation.* San Francisco: Jossey-Bass.

Scriven, M. (1997). Truth and objectivity in evaluation. In E. Chelimsky & W. Shadish, *Evaluation for the 21st century: A handbook* (pp. 477–500). Thousand Oaks, CA: Sage.

Sedlacek, W. (2004). *Beyond the big test: Noncognitive assessment in higher education.* San Francisco: John Wiley.

Shadish, W., & Cook, T. (2000). As cited by M. Patton in Overview: Language matters, in R. Hopson (Ed.), *New directions in evaluation: Vol. 86. How and why language matters* (pp. 5–16). San Francisco: Jossey-Bass

Shadish, W., Cook, T., & Leviton, L. (1991). *Foundations of program evaluation: Theories of practice.* Newbury Park, CA: Sage.

Shavelson, R. J., Baxter, G. P., & Gao, X. (1993). Sampling variability of performance assessments. *Journal of Educational Measurement, 30,* 215–232.

Shavelson, R. J., Baxter, G. P., & Pine, J. (1991). Performance assessment in science. *Applied Measurement in Education, 4,* 347–362.

Shavelson, R. J., Mayberry, P. W., Li, W.-C., & Webb, N. M. (1990). Generalizability of job performance measurements: Marine Corps riflemen. *Military Psychology, 2,* 129–144.

Sheldon, D. (1994). Effects of tempo, musical experience, and listening modes on tempo modulation perception. *Journal of Research in Music Education, 42*(2), 190–202.

Sheldon, D., & Gregory, D. (1997). Perception of tempo modulation by listeners of different levels of educational experience. *Journal of Research in Music Education, 45*(3), 367–379.

Shepherd, L. (2001). The role of classroom assessment in teaching and learning. In V. Richardson (Ed.), *Handbook of research on teaching* (4th ed.). Washington, DC: American Educational Research Association.

Shulman, I. S. (2002). Making differences: A table of learning. *Change, 34*(6), 36–44.

Shum, D. A. (1994). *The evidential foundational of probabilistic reasoning.* New York: Wiley.

Siebenaler, D. J. (1997). Analysis of teacher–student interactions in the piano lessons of adults and children. *Journal of Research in Music Education, 45*(1), 6–20.

Simpson, E. (1966). *The classification of educational objectives, psychomotor domain.* (OE 5-85-104). Washington, DC: U.S. Department of Health, Education and Welfare.

Sizer, T. R. (2004). *The red pencil: Convictions from experience in education.* New Haven: Yale University Press.

Skadsem, J. A. (1997). Effect of conductor verbalization, dynamic markings, conductor gesture, and choir dynamic level on singers' dynamic responses. *Journal of Research in Music Education, 45*(4), 509–520.

Skinner, D. (2004). Primary and secondary barriers to the evaluation of change. *Evaluation, 10*(2), 135–154.

Smith, M. L. (1994). Qualitative plus/versus quantitative: The last word. In C. Reichardt & S. Rallis (Eds.), *New directions for program evaluation: Vol. 61. Approaches in evaluation studies* (pp. 37–44). San Francisco: Jossey-Bass.

Smith, N. (1992). Aspects of investigative inquiry. In N. Smith (Ed.), *New directions for program evaluation: Vol. 56. Varities of investigative evaluation* (pp. 3–14). San Francisco: Jossey-Bass.

Smith, N. (1995). The influence of societal games on the methodology of evaluative inquiry. In D. Fournier (Ed.), *New directions for program evaluation: Vol. 68. Reasoning in evaluation: Inferential links and leaps* (pp. 5–14). San Francisco: Jossey-Bass.

Smith, P. (2004). Curricular transformation: Why we need it; how to support it. *Change, 36*(1), 28–35.

Snow, R. E., & Lohman, D. F. (1993). Cognitive psychology, new test design, and new test theory: An introduction. In N. Frederiksen, R. Mislevy & I. Bejar (Eds.), *Test theory for a new generation of tests* (pp. 37–44). Hillsdale, NJ: Erlbaum.

Stake, R. E. (1991). Responsive evaluation and qualitative methods. In W. R. Shadish, T. D. Cook, & L. C. Leviton (Eds.), *Foundations of program evaluation: Theories of practice* (pp. 270–314). Newbury Park, CA: Sage.

Stake, R. E. (1997). Advocacy in evaluation: A necessary evil. In E. Chelimsky & W. R. Skadish (Eds.), *Evaluation for the 21st century* (pp. 470–478). London: Sage.

Stake, R. E. (2000). A modest commitment to the promotion of democracy. In K. E. Ryan & L. DeStefano, *New directions for program evaluation: Vol. 85. Evaluation as a democratic process: Promoting inclusion, dialogue, and deliberation* (pp. 97–106). San Francisco: Jossey-Bass.

Standerfer, S. (2003). *Perceptions and influences of the national board of professional teaching competency on secondary choral music teachers.* Unpublished doctoral dissertation. University of Virginia.

Steiner, D., & Rozen, S. (2004). Preparing tomorrow's teachers: An analysis of syllabi from a sample of America's schools of education. In R. Hess, A. Rotherham, & K. Walsh. (Eds.), *A qualified teacher in every classroom* (pp. 119–148). Cambridge: Harvard University Press.

Sternberg, R. J. (2003). What is an expert student? *Educational Researcher, 32*(8), 5–9.

Vispoel, W. (1992). Improving the measurement of tonal memory with computerized adaptive tests. *Psychomusicology, 11*(1), 27–43.

Webb, N., & Schlackman, J. (2000). *The dependability and interchangeability of assessment methods in science* (CSE Tech. Rep. 515). Los Angeles: UCLA CRESST.

Wei, H. (1995). *Development of a melodic achievement test for fourth grades taught by a specific music learning methodology.* Unpublished doctoral dissertation, University of Illinois, Urbana.

Weiss, C. H. (1998). *Evaluation* (2nd ed.). Upper Saddle River, NJ: Prentice Hall.

Wile, J. M., & Tierney, R. J. (1996). Tensions in assessment: The battle over portfolios, curriculum, and control. In R. Calfee & P. Perfumo (Eds.), *Writing portfolios in the classroom: Policy and practice, promise, and peril* (pp. 203–215). Mahwah, NJ: Erlbaum.

Winner, E., & Hetland, I. (2000). The arts in education: Evaluating the evidence for a causal link. *Journal of Aesthetic Education, 34*(3–4).

Wolf, D. P., & Reardon, S. F. (1996). Access to excellence through new forms of student assessment. In J. B. Baron & D. P. Wolf (Eds.), *Performance-based student assessment: Challenges and possibilities* (pp. 1–31). Chicago: University of Chicago Press.

Woodford, P. (2005). *Democracy and music education: Liberalism, ethics, and the politics of practice.* Bloomington: Indiana University Press.

Yarbrough, C., & Henley, P. (1999). The effect of observation focus on evaluations of choral rehearsal excerpts. *Journal of Research in Music Education, 47*(4), 308–318.

Qualitative Research Methodology in Music Education

LIORA BRESLER

ROBERT E. STAKE

A freckled third grader approaches the music teacher in the corridor and hands her a stack of 3 × 5 cards. "Thirty-six," he announces proudly. Back in her office Rebecca Grant puts the cards in an envelope on which she neatly writes, "Daniel Wang, 36," and posts it on the wall near three other envelopes. This latest is Daniel's entry in the Composer's Facts competition, this week featuring Aaron Copland. Were curious eyes to pry, they would find information about Copland's birthdate, milestones, compositions, and books. Winners will get musical handbags, musical rulers, musical paraphernalia which Rebecca orders (and pays for with her own money) from a mail-order firm specializing in music items.[1]

*   *   *

Public Act 84-126, effective August 1, 1985, amended The School Code of Illinois to include, for the first time in state history, a requirement that the goals for learning be identified and assessed. The fine arts were one of the six primary areas designated. Broad goals for Illinois school children include understanding the sensory, formal, technical, and expressive qualities for each of the arts; demonstrating the basic skills necessary to participate in the creation and performance of the arts; and identifying significant works in the arts from major historical periods and how they reflect societies, cultures, and civilizations, past and present.

Achievement of the goals would be assessed by paper and pencil tests. Music specialists, classroom teachers, and principals expressed anger and frustration about these new mandated tests. Among the main complaints were the loss and redirection of instructional time, the lack of empathy about teaching within existing constraints, the lack of responsiveness to teacher concerns, and the lack of financial support to help the teachers learn new skills. Mark Denman, principal in East Park, reacted as follows:

"It is not fair for the state to dictate this. Unless they teach us how to teach these areas it's not realistic. You can't just legislate improvement. You can't just say we are going to raise test scores. You've got to build the groundwork. You can't impose change from the top. You've got to ignite the interest of the staff. Oftentimes people in the State Department of Education will say: 'Do this, this, and this.' But we have no money to do it. We were not asked if we wanted to do it. We were not asked how we could do it. We work for years to improve something, then funding runs out and nothing further happens. So people are discouraged [shaking his head]. I know the intents of legislators are very good, but. . . .' "

*   *   *

It is a chilly Tuesday morning when Ms. Casieri and myself (in the role of observer, and not a very experienced one) are sitting in a half-full bus, with a group of third and fourth graders, on the way to the Civic Center to hear Humperdinck's *Hansel und Gretel*. When we are seated, a blue light is turned on, a series of Shhh's spreads in waves. The chaos subsides, an intense diminuendo, with some uncontrollable giggles as leftovers. The striking silence makes me uneasy, seems to invite a reaction. But no. The lights go down. The piano sounds.

Today's performance is a shortened version of the opera, 60 minutes rather than the 2 original hours. It is performed by a junior group of opera members, the orchestra parts transcribed to piano. An accomplished young woman plays flawlessly the difficult virtuoso part—rhythm and notes, articulations and phrasing, matching dynamics. There is much humor and jest as Hansel and Gretel tease and chase each other. Children laugh *with* the singers an honest laugh. A good channel to release the tension of the unfamiliar—singing culture, the new form.

In this chapter we review the basic theory and method of qualitative research in music education. Qualitative approaches come with various names and descriptions: case study, field study, ethnographic research, naturalistic, phenomenological, interpretive, symbolic interactionist, or just plain descriptive. We use "qualitative research" as a general term to refer to several research strategies that share certain characteristics: (1) *noninterventionist* observation in natural settings, (2) emphasis on *interpretation* of both emic issues (those of the participants) and etic issues (those of the writer), (3) highly *contextual description* of people and events, and (4) validation of information through triangulation. These constructs will be developed later in this chapter.

Educational researchers in America have increasingly come to value what researchers elsewhere have long emphasized: the personal and political nature of education. Part of the awareness is reflected in an increased interest in the unique circumstances of school programs and performances. The study of uniqueness can be handled in a disciplined and scholarly way with qualitative inquiry. The classroom community and societal contexts become more than abstract variables.

Our chapter begins with an overview of the intellectual and methodological roots of qualitative research, its basic assumptions and goals, plus identification of kinds of research questions of central interest. In the next section, we examine qualitative research in music. First, we examine models in pedagogy, ethnomusicology, and musical biography. Then we review key studies, focusing on their unique contributions to the field, their aims and objectives, and their primary issues and findings. Of special interest is the compatibility of research methods to the training of musicians regarding teaching as art form and classroom interaction as kinetic performance. We then focus on methods and criteria of qualitative studies. We conclude by pointing to some future directions and possibilities offered by qualitative research to the field of music education.

Roots of Qualitative Methodology

Just as music and education can be traced back across the centuries ultimately to the crude and custom-driven habits of primitive societies, qualitative inquiry has its roots in the intuitive and survivalist behavior of early peoples. For ages we have operated on hunches and emotions, increasingly using those that brought us safety and satisfaction. Gradually we saw the wisdom of what we already were doing by observing, questioning, keeping records and interpreting, respecting the experience and rumination of elders. Gradually we formed rules for study and names for our sciences. Music educators, too, increasingly drew from philosophers and social scientists to codify research procedures.

Intellectual Roots

The intellectual roots of qualitative methodology lie in the idealist movement—in particular, William Dilthey (1900) and Max Weber (1949), who found their philosophical origins in Kantian thinking. Immanuel Kant (1969) distinguished objects and events as they appear in experience from objects and events as they are in themselves, independent of the forms imposed on them by our cognitive faculties. The former he called "phenomena"; the latter, "noumena." All we can ever know, Kant argued, are phenomena. Rather than knowing the world directly, we sense, interpret, and explain it to ourselves. All experience is mediated by mind, and all human intellect is imbued with and limited to human interpretation and representation.

Phenomenologists follow Kant in the claim that immediate experiences and sensory observations are always interpreted or classified under general concepts. Their appeal to phenomena is therefore not an appeal to simple, uninterpreted data of sensory experience. Meaning is the target of phenomenology. Phenomenologists do not assume they know what things mean to others. Emphasizing the subjective aspects, they attempt to gain entry into the conceptual world of themselves and others. Giving accounts of their reality construction, phenomenologists believe that these inward construals derive from a developing understanding of self, others, and things. The relationships between these are not "givens" but dialectical, context bound, and processual.

Qualitative researchers tend to be phenomenological in their orientation. Most maintain that knowledge is a human construction. They reason as follows: Although knowledge starts with sensory experience of external stimuli, these sensations are immediately given meaning by the recipient. Though meaning originates in outside action, only the inside interpretation is known. As far as we can tell, nothing about the stimuli is registered in awareness and memory other than our interpretations of it. This registration is not necessarily conscious or rational.

In our minds, new perceptions of stimulation mix with old, and with complexes of perception, some of which we call generalizations. Some aspects of knowledge seem generated entirely from internal deliberation, without immediate external stimulation—but no aspects are purely of the external world, devoid of human construction.

Concepts of Reality   The aim of qualitative research is not to discover reality, for by phenomenological reasoning this is impossible. The aim is to construct a clearer experiential memory and to help people obtain a more sophisticated account of things. Sophistication is partly a matter of withstanding disciplined skepticism. Science strives to build universal understanding. The understanding reached by each individual will of course be to some degree unique to the beholder, but much will be held in common. Though the comprehension we seek is of our own making, it is a collective making. Each of us seeks a well-tuned comprehension, one bearing up under further human constructions: scrutiny and challenge.

The qualitative researcher chooses which realities to investigate. For researcher data or interpretation of findings, not every person's personal reality is of equal use. Society deems some interpretations better than others. People have ways of agreeing on which are the best explanations. Of course, they are not always right. There is no reason to think that among people fully committed to a constructed reality all constructions are of equal value. One can believe in relativity, contextuality, and constructivism, without believing all views are of equal merit. Personal civility or political ideology may call for respecting every view, but scientific study does not.[2]

Researchers interested in the uniqueness of particular teaching or learning find value in qualitative studies because the design allows or demands extra attention to physical, temporal, historical, social, political, economic, and aesthetic contexts. Contextual epistemology requires in-depth studies, leaving less time for the refinement of theme and construct. It is true that naturalistic and phenomenological case studies are likely to be undertaken by researchers with constructivist persuasions. Why this is is not clear, but it probably would be a mistake to conclude that more than a realist logic, a constructivist logic promotes contextualist epistemology or case-specific study. It is not uncommon to find case study researchers espousing a constructivist view of reality, but the two persuasions are not one and the same.

Cultural sciences need *descriptive* as well as explanatory and predictive powers. At the beginning, middle, and end of a program of research, the researcher at times needs to concentrate on interpretive understanding (*versteben*). The process of *versteben* involves the ability to empathize, to re-create the experience of others within oneself.

Dilthey and Weber perceived understanding as hermeneutic, resulting from a process of interpretation. The hermeneutic experience (encounter with a work of art) is historical, linguistic, dialectical. Understanding the meaning of any particular part of a text (a word or a sentence) requires an understanding of the meaning of the whole and vice versa. Thus, achieving a meaningful interpretation requires back and forth movement between parts and whole. Understanding cannot be pursued in the absence of context and interpretive framework. The hermeneutic perspective means that human experience is context bound and that there can be no context-free or neutral scientific language with which to express what happens in the social world. At best we could have laws applying to only a limited context for a limited time.

Ethnography and Biography

The roots of qualitative research methods can be traced to ethnography and sociological fieldwork as well as literary criticism, biography, and journalism. From the end of the nineteenth century, anthropologists advocated and practiced spending extensive periods of time in the natural setting, studying cultures with the intent of learning how the culture was perceived and understood by its members (cf. Boas and Malinowski). Bronislaw Malinowski, who found himself in New Guinea and unable to return to Poland because of the outbreak of World War I, was the first social anthropologist to spend long periods in a native village to observe what was going on. He was also the first professional anthropologist to dwell on how he obtained his data and what the fieldwork experience was like. Malinowski maintained that a theory of culture had to be grounded in particular human experiences, based on observation, and inductively sought.

Case study and ethnographic methods have been part of sociology's history since the 1920s and 1930s, when University of Chicago sociologists, under the influence of Robert Park, W. I. Thomas, and Herbert Blumer, were trained in the interpretive approach to human group life (Bogdan and Biklin, 1982; Denzin, 1989). Sociologists in succeeding generations turned away from the method, giving their attention to problems of measurement, validity, and reliability; survey methodologies; and laboratory experiments. Educational researchers recently have witnessed a surge of interest in interpretive approaches to the study of culture, biography, and human life. Central to this view has been the argument that societies, cultures, and the expressions of human experience can be read as social text, that is, the structures of representation that require symbolic statement (Denzin, 1989).

Literary models provide another important model for qualitative methodology. Eisner (1979, 1991) advocates the paradigmatic use of qualitative inquiry found in the arts and the world of art critics. Artists inquire in a qualitative mode both in the formulation of ends and in the use of means to achieve such ends. The art critic's task is to render the essentially ineffable qualities constituting works of art into a language that will help others perceive the world more deeply.

Thomas Barone (1987, 1990) follows Eisner in referring to works of art as relying on a continuum of scientific texts. All texts, claims Barone, are modes of fiction (borrowing the Geertz meaning of fiction—something fashioned). Each brings with it researcher/author subjectivity and personal bias, ideology, and visions, but with fictional works these are more visible, explicit. Barone reminds us that novelists do not spin their imaginary webs from within a world of pure illusion and fantasy, but that "since Henry Fielding, they also have relied upon observation of the minutae of human activity, observing social phenomena" (1987, p. 455). Often a novelist will construct a story out of the qualitative phenomena confronted in everyday experience: Sometimes they will intentionally transport themselves into the field to investigate facets of their emerging story's milieu, as did Dickens who, in preparation for *The Life Adventures of Nicholas Nickelby*, gained admittance to a notorious Yorkshire boarding school by assuming the false identity of someone seeking a school for the son of a widowed friend. The fictionalization process of the novelist, says Barone, is a rigorous and disciplined undertaking, a qualitative problem-solving process that even proceeds through several identifiable stages. A thesis, or central insight, is gradually constructed from patterned relationship between qualitative phenomena. A similar relationship between thesis and particulars exists in accomplished worlds of literary-style fiction such as autobiography, new journalism, and educational criticism. The crafting of an educational criticism closely resembles the dialectical problem-solving process of the novelist.

Rorty (1982) believes that all qualitative inquiry is continuous with literature. For Rorty, books serve the important role of advancing social and political goals of liberalism by promoting a genuine sense of human solidarity (Rorty, 1989).

Literature has been a methodological force. Biography and autobiography have become a topic of renewed interest in literary criticism (cf. Elbaz, 1987; Cockshut, 1984), as well as in sociology (cf. Denzin, 1989) and anthropology (cf. Geertz, 1988). Feminist views have had an important influence in this discussion (cf. Jelinek, 1980; Spacks, 1976; Grumet, 1988). Jean-Paul Sartre recognized the force of literature in the preface to *The Family Idiot, Gustave Flaubert*, Vol. 1, 1821–1857) (1981):

What, at this point in time, can we know about man? It seemed to me that this question could only be answered by studying a specific case. . . . For a man is never an individual; it would be more fitting to call him a *universal singular*. Summed up and for this reason universalized by his epoch, he in turn resumes it by reproducing himself in it as singularity. Universal by the singular universality of human history, singular by the universalizing singularity of his projects, he requires simultaneous examination from both ends. (pp. ix–x)

Biography has always been an important part of musicology and music history, with oral history gaining interest. While sociology focuses on *interpretive biography*—the creation of literary, narrative accounts, and representations of lived experience (Denzin, 1989)—the traditional use of biographies in music centers around life-events, especially family, patrons, and mentoring, a written account or history of an individual.

A second kind of biography (e.g., Von Gunden, 1983) is essentially a musical analysis, where biographical information of the composer and philosophy are brought in to interpret the music. Here, listening to musical works itself provides data, extending the examination of archives (e.g., documents, letters) and in-depth interviews of author and composer. Immersed in the music, the interviews, or observation data, the music education researcher attempts to find new patterns and meanings.

Qualitative Versus Quantitative Research

The quantitative research tradition, grounded in the positivist urge for a science of society, fostered adaptation of the methodology of the physical sciences to investigate social and human worlds. From the theological to the metaphysical, 20th-century positivism saw culmination of progress and human knowledge through scientific methods. Objects of study in the social sciences are to be treated in the same way that physical scientists treat physical things. The role of the social scientist is that of recorder and theory builder for a reality existing outside human experience.

Another assumption in positivist thinking was that in regard to values, social investigation can and should be a *neutral* activity. Hence, social scientists should eliminate all bias and value-laden preconception and not be emotionally involved with their subject matter. Knowledge derived from social investigation would eventually result in the same sort of technological mastery over the social world as physical science had for the physical world. The aims of practical application would be achieved by the discovery of social laws that point at relationships among social objects, aiming, like physical laws, at context-free social laws (Hempel, 1966; Popper, 1969).

Dilthey and Weber challenged the positivist point of view, arguing that social studies has a different ontological and epistemological status. They claimed that there we are both the subject and the object of inquiry: The subject matter concerns the product of human minds and as such is inseparably connected to our minds, bringing along all our subjectivities, cognitions, emotions, and values. Furthermore, the complexity of the social world and cultures makes it impossible to discover laws as in the physical sciences. Rather than a series of overarching casual laws, they said, emphasis must be on understanding the individual case or type.[3]

Philosophically, we are dealing here with two paradigms. The *quantitative paradigm* supports investigation of how reality exists independently of us. Ontological questions concerning what is can be kept separate from the epistemological questions about how we come to know "what is." According to that paradigm, knowledge and truth are questions of correspondence—what is true is what corresponds to reality. Done well, the activity of investigation does not affect what is being investigated.

In the *qualitative paradigm* there is a range of positions, from the idealist belief that social and human reality are created, to the milder conviction that this reality is shaped by our minds. But all the positions posit a degree of mind involvement with subject matter not acceptable to the quantitative, positivist, realist tradition. The idea that the process of investigation can be separated from what is being investigated is possible only within that realist perspective. In the realist view, an investigation is directed toward an external referent. In the idealist view, the process is external as well as internal, a part of the investigator's active participation in shaping the world (cf. Peshkin, 1988).

In actual life, no research study is purely qualitative or quantitative. In each qualitative study, enumeration and recognition of differences in amount have a place. And in each quantitative study, natural language description and interpretation are expected. The distinction as we see it is an epistemological distinction that can be identified as the distinction between inquiry for making explanations versus inquiry for promoting understanding. This distinction has best been developed by the Finnish philosopher of science Georg Hendrik von Wright (1971), who emphasized the epistemological distinction between formal explanations and experiential understanding.

Quantitative study was nourished by the scientific search for grand theory seeking generalizations that hold over diverse situations, trying to eliminate the merely situational, letting contextual effects "balance each other out." Quantitative researchers try to nullify context in order to find the most general and pervasive explanatory relationships. Research in education, including music education, has been dominated by this universalist approach, this grand search for explanation. Quantification occurs in order to permit simultaneous study of a large number of dissimilar cases, in order to put the researcher in a position to make formal generalizations about teaching and learning. Proposition-shaped knowledge obviously can be important.

It is apparent that much important knowledge about education (e.g., the calendar, the practice facilities) is situational. Qualitative researchers have a great interest in the uniqueness of the individual case, the variety of perceptions of that case, and the different intentionalities of the actors who populate that case. These interests force the researcher to find easy-access situations for repeated observations, to limit attention to small numbers of teachers and students, to rely little on objective measurement, and to probe in unexpected directions. Fixed designs are less necessary and can be less productive for providing understanding of particular cases. Still, in a discipline governed strongly by an existing composition or score, the musician may find the structures of quantitativism attractive and the open-field behavior of the qualitative researcher too improvisational.

Qualitative researchers are not devoid of interest in generalization, but it does not dominate their thinking. Often the qualitative researchers' commitments to multiple interpretations become manifest in a desire to assist practitioners to interpret the situations for themselves. The intent of research then may become the provision of vicarious experience for report readers, who will draw their own generalizations, combining previous experience with new. It often is research specially designed to assist practice. The choice of epistemological role for research and the immediacy of its assistance to practice should be part of our distinction between quantitative and qualitative inquiries.

Qualitative researchers, too, have interest in frequency, typicality, and generalizability (cf. Stake, Bresler, and Mabry, 1991). Still, their craft is distinguished by a too-holistic viewing of phenomena. They examine multiple situations but each at close quarters, not forcing them into comparisons, not fixated on common variables. It is not uncommon for a qualitative researcher to ask in midstudy: "Of all things, what is it that is most important to be learned from this case?" In music education, we have need for formal generalizations and need for experiential understandings of particular situations. We need high-quality research, both quantitative and qualitative.

Characteristics of Qualitative Research

1. It is holistic. Its contexts are well studied. It is case oriented (a case may be a student, a teacher, a classroom, a curriculum, any "bounded system"). It is relatively noncomparative, seeking more to understand its case than to understand how it differs from others.
2. It is empirical. It is field oriented, the field being the natural settings of the case. Its emphasis is on observables, including observations by informants. It strives to be naturalistic, noninterventionistic. There is a preference for natural language description. The researcher is the key instrument. For qualitative research, researchers typically spend considerable time in schools, homes, neighborhoods, and other locales learning about educational concerns. Data are collected on the premises. Qualitative researchers go to the particular settings because they are concerned with context. Action can be better understood when it is observed in the natural setting.
3. It is descriptive. Data take the form of words and graphics more than numbers. The written results of the research contain quotations to illustrate and substantiate the presentation.
4. It is interpretive. Its researchers rely on intuition, with many important

criteria not specified. Its on-site observers strive to keep attention free to recognize problem-relevant events. It is attuned to the fact that research is a researcher–subject interaction. Qualitative research is concerned with the different meanings that actions and events carry for different members.

5. It is empathic. It attends to the presumed intentions of those being observed. It seeks actor frames of reference, value commitments. Though planned, its design is emergent, responsive. Its issues are emic issues, progressively focused. Its reporting provides vicarious experience.

6. Some researchers emphasize working from bottom up (e.g., Glaser and Strauss's term *grounded theory*, 1967). Indeed, the direction of the issues and foci often emerge during data collection. The picture takes shape as the parts are examined.

7. When done well, its observations and immediate interpretations are validated. Triangulation, the checking of data against multiple sources and methods, is routine. There is a deliberate effort to disconfirm one's own interpretations. The reports assist readers to make their own interpretations, as well as to recognize subjectivity.[4]

Qualitative Research in Music Education

The first decades of research in music education, much as in general education, were characterized by adherence to quantitative models. Little research employed qualitative strategies to illuminate education problems. The late 1960s affected research mores, too. National foci on educational equity and back-to-basics curricula swung concern to values, feelings, and minority perspectives. Many recognized that we did not know enough about the educational experience of children "not making it." In general education, qualitative emphasis on understanding the perspective of all participants challenged the idea that the views of those in power are worth more than others. Student perspectives (Jackson, 1968) and the viewing of school as a system of discipline (Dreeben, 1968; Foucault, 1977; Henry, 1966) were widely considered. Concern about student achievement yielded some to concern for what students were actually doing in school. All this stimulated the need for different content, goals, and methods. It opened up educational researchers to qualitative approaches.

Music education, too, followed that route, perhaps delayed by a decade or so. The emphasis in formal music education research on quantitative methodology is reflected in books, reports, journal papers, and dissertations. But researchers and practitioners, teachers and conductors, have always used qualitative observations. To establish pedagogy requires illusive observation of students in order to pinpoint problems and suggest remedies. In an ancient example considered to be the first music pedagogy book, *L'Art de Toucher le Clavicin*, Francois Couperin expressed pedagogical assertions based on observations of student behavior: "It will be necessary to place some additional support under the feet of young people, varying in height as they grow, so that their feet not dangling in the air, may keep the body properly balanced." "With regard to making grimaces, it is possible to break oneself of this habit by placing a mirror on the reading-desk of the Spinet or harpsichord" (p. xx). "It is better and more seemly not to beat time with the head, the body, nor with the feet" (p. xx). The discipline of Couperin's observations and analysis is not known. Should we consider his writings research based?

As Couperin's book illustrates, pedagogical books on performance and conducting are designed to foster learning and remedy problems more than to arrive at causal explanations or understandings of the situation. Use of pictures to express good and bad technique is quite common (Kohut and Grant, 1990). Performance, like some aspects of pedagogy, involves a self-synchronous process of constant listening (either in one's own playing or in ensemble) and comparing it to the score. Through score preparation, the performer not only knows individual details—parts and sections of the score—but also develops a conception of the complete work. The style of performance best suited to any given work; a sound knowledge of music theory, harmonic analysis, and musical form; musicological knowledge to relate the piece to the composer's other works, as well as to other works of the period—all of these shape a performance.

Ethnomusicology is a field in music that draws its intellectual roots and methods from anthropology as well as from musicology. Merriam (1964) and Nettl (1983, 1987) discuss two major approaches in ethnomusicology. The first, a comparative study of musical systems and cultures, is standardized musicology, aiming to record and analyze music in order to produce an accurate structural analysis of the music investigated. Here, the study is primarily based on a fact-gathering descriptive approach, dealing with such questions as the modes of Persian or Indian music, names of instruments, how they are made, and who owns them.

The second approach, aiming to understand music in the context of human behavior, is an anthropological specialty. Here, the fieldworker tries to approximate the anthropologist, for the concern is with much broader questions of the use and function of music, the role and status of musicians, the concepts that lie behind music behavior, and other similar questions (Merriam, 1967; Nettl, 1987). The emphasis is on music but not on music divorced from its total context. The investigator attempts to emerge from the study with a broad and generally complete knowledge of both the culture and the music, as well as the way music fits into and is used within the wider context (Merriam, 1964, p. 42). This second approach is typically a field-oriented naturalistic study. The researcher stays at the site for a considerable amount of time, getting immersed in the culture. The issues, a combination of emic and etic, are progressively focused. The direction of the issues and foci often emerge during and after data collection.[5] With few exceptions (Keil, 1966; Oliver, 1960), ethnomusicological studies typically examine other cultures. Few ethnomusicological studies examine familiar music in familiar settings.

Even though these kinds of knowledge have not, until recently, entered the established domains of music education, research, the methods of observation, the interview, the use of archival material, and immersion in the case have long been important tools in music education, and in performance and musicology as well. A pioneering work that drew on these methods, done within the formal boundaries of music education research, was the Pillsbury Foundation Study (Moorhead and Pond, 1941, 1942, 1944, 1951). Initiated by people outside the field of music education (conductor Leopold Stokowski and composer Donald Pond), the Pillsbury Study was dedicated to the discovery of children's musical development through analysis of free, unhampered musical play. Amazed at the spontaneous outpouring of music in young children, Pond wanted to understand how and why children become musically expressive. Thinking along Deweian lines, he wanted to provide them with opportunities and materials so that they might function in their own ways as musicians. In the study, Pond made a conscious attempt to set aside adult notions about elements of music, processes of learning music, and ways of assessing musical development.

The Pillsbury Study was conducted with 3- to 6-year-old children attending a kindergarten designed specifically for research into musical creativity: an environment full of enticing instruments (e.g., sarong, Chinese and Burmese gongs, Indian drums, and tom-toms) and supportive, musically knowledgeable (but not intrusive) adults. The methods of study involved in-depth observation and analysis. Since the context of sound was of major importance, the observations included such activities as speech and physical movement. All sounds produced were considered musical or "embryonically of musical value." In his reports, Pond provided such examples as when a child calls from the sandbox, "I want a red spoon," in a rhythmic and tonal pattern or a child riding on a tricycle sings over and over to himself in unvarying rhythm, "I ran over a whole basket of cherries." The final report (Moorhead and Pond, 1951), was a set of three short case studies of individual children selected for individual differences and approaches. Data included biographical information such as age and personal, family, and school history.

Some naturalistic studies are taxonomic; others are not. Moorhead and Pond worked toward classification of the musical products. A classification of instrumental music, for example, included flexible and asymmetrical measures, exploring wide intervals, tone colors, and pitch contrast. Another category of sonic physical activity, "insistent and savage," was based on rigid and symmetrical rhythms, indifferent to melody and color variety. Pond distinguished between two types of spontaneous vocal utterances: "song," private rhythmically and melodically complex entities, and "chant," a more public utterance, often spontaneously improvised by groups of children. Social-personal context was seen to be highly relevant; most chants were developed first by one child and continued by that child or undertaken by others to form repartee series. Pond raised issues such as: Are these rhythmic patterns fundamental to the child's musical consciousness? What are the relationships between rhythmic patterns and physical rhythms?

The Moorhead and Pond study was holistic, case oriented, and noncomparative. The authors sought more to understand each child than to understand how children differ from each other. The natural setting was stressed, with an emphasis on observables. Moorhead and Pond did not try to intervene but rather to observe, describe, and understand.

The Pillsbury Study set a new direction for investigation of free musical activities and improvisation. For music education research, it provided methodological direction and legitimation of the use of naturalistic methods. In the late 1970s and 1980s, music education saw a spurt of qualitative works, independently done in different locations and universities across the country. Jeanne Bamberger of Massachusetts Institute of Technology (1977) examined two subjects' perceptions of a melody, noting the strategies used by each to compose a melody and the relationship between perceptions, models, strategies, and the completed melody. A protocol analysis employing an innovative computer-based recording system to study compositional process was included.

Most reported qualitative studies have been dissertations, works of solitary, inexperienced researchers, backed by little financial resource (cf. Gerber, 1975; Freundlich, 1978; Cohen, 1980; Lewers, 1980; L'Roy, 1983; Thiel, 1984; Garrison, 1985; Krueger, 1985; Upitis, 1985; Bresler, 1987; DeLorenzo, 1987; Harwood, 1987). Observing spontaneous musical behavior of children, Douglas Freundlich (1978) of Harvard explored two fifth-grade children's musical thinking, especially focusing on spontaneous solutions to musical problems. Students were to improvise on a simple diatonic xylophone within a traditional musical frame of standard 12-bar blues. The data were collected in the context of a structured "jam session." The research was qualitative not because the situation was loosely structured but because the researcher was refining his interpretation with every observation. Freundlich found that development proceeded down from the chorus-as-a-whole and up from a self-generated two-bar motif. Addressing improvisation's pedagogical value, Freundlich pointed out that the child can generate authentic musical ideas without reference to notation, and that musical concepts furnished by the improvisation procedure are logically organized.

Veronica Cohen (1980) of the University of Illinois also examined the generation of musical ideas in a loosely structured situation. Discussing her methods, Cohen noted the following:

> This is not a conventional study in which the researcher set up a plan and then followed it, reporting in what ways it was successful or not. Instead, borrowing on the naturalistic, exploratory and yet scientific tradition exemplified in some of the most important of Piaget's studies, it searched through observations over many years . . . focusing finally on a few of two children's musical productions that held the most promise for revealing the underlying structure and dynamics of children's spontaneous music. (p. 1)

Data collection included a 3-year period of general background observation and immersion in children's free musical play in the kindergarten, followed by a rigorous and detailed study of videotaped data involving two kindergarten children. Cohen discussed the role of intuition and accumulated knowledge of the whole field of music in making the thousands of decisions in data collection in the field. "The researcher becomes the chief instrument who selects, interprets and synthesizes evidence in order to break through to the mind of the child" (p. 2). Engagement in musical dialogues with children was a focus. Descriptors included the role of kindergarten music, teacher special interest, and the *participant-observer* role of the researcher. Cohen reported that she was constantly involved in planning the music curriculum, taught demonstration classes for university students, demonstrated ways of interacting with children at the music center, and discussed and analyzed children's work for classroom teachers, parents, and university students.

Cohen investigated musical gestures, noting how the children organize sounds into "musical ideas." Using videotapes for data collection, Cohen found that such behavior could be nicely placed into three broad categories: exploration, mastery, and generation of musical gestures. She speculated that even at this early age children tended to specialize: some almost always engaged in "mastery" activities (reproduction of known melodies) whereas others "improvised" their own gestures.

Influences of culture and society on the musical behavior of children is a relatively sociology-based area studied by qualitative researchers. In Israel, Devorah Kalekin-Fishman (1981, 1986) investigated the nature of music in kindergartens, examining it from teacher as well as from child perspectives. A kindergarten was chosen as the case because it is here the child encounters society as officially organized by educators and is exposed to conceptual frameworks deliberately arranged to fit at least a dozen years of life in educational organizations. Kalekin-Fishman made intensive observations and conducted semistructured interviews. An analysis of sonal patterns in kindergartens in Germany and Israel showed that with minimal framing (intended pitch and intended rhythm), children produced varieties of typified music making. The framing, however, was not that most commonly employed by kindergarten teachers, who usually have a relatively narrow field of musical knowledge.

Ethnomusicology provides an important model for music education research. At the University of Wisconsin, Madison, Virginia Garrison (1985) examined the transmission process of folk music, a process that is as vital to that tradition as is its product, the music. If folk music is to be included in formal music educational settings, then it is important that those social and musical aspects of the folk music tradition that are essential to that tradition are identified. In order to investigate the transmission process and the effect of changed instructional context on that process, Garrison used ethnomusicological methods of extensive and intensive naturalistic observations of 72 practicing fiddlers and 49 beginning fiddling students in a variety of contexts for a period of 6 years, as well as open-ended interviews and photography.

In a similar vein, Eve Harwood (1987) of the University of Illinois opened her dissertation discussing the difficulty researchers have studying music of a culture different from their own. Whereas at one time it was considered sufficient to analyze musical artifacts in the form of tape recordings and transcriptions, using terms appropriate to traditional Western musicology, modern ethnomusicology holds that understanding and describing the cultural context in which music making occurs is a necessary part of understanding the music of a given group. An outsider's analytical tools and observations are not necessarily invalid, but an insider's view of what is significant about the music are thought to illuminate our understanding in a unique way.

In the case of North American children, folklorists and musicians were collecting children's repertoires before 1900, but little scholarship had been directed toward the singers themselves. Harwood's study was based on the assumption that children's music and musical world are distinct from adult counterparts, that what is considered beautiful, attractive, or good to sing and is cherished by children may be different. Not a naturalistic study, Harwood's procedures included semistructured interviews in which the 15 children sang all the songs they could remember, discussed how they had learned each song, and described their singing habits and preferences. A parent of each child answered questions regarding the child's singing habits and preferences and the musical life of the family. Interviews and singing were taped and transcribed, and a fieldwork journal of impressions and visual observations was kept. In conclusion, Harwood once again asserted the need to study children's music as one would that of any outside culture, attempting to appreciate both the insider's and the outsider's view of the material.

In the studies just reviewed, researchers examined relatively uncharted territories in order to understand musical activities in context. The study of innovation is another such uncharted territory. Qualitative methodology not only allows but features the study of contexts. One innovation has been the introduction of instructional computer programming that many music educators claim dramatically affects the music education scene. Case studies are one of many ways to examine accommodation of computers into music classes.

At Stanford, Liora Bresler (1987) studied the integration of computers into a college-level introductory music theory class. The learning environment into which the computer is integrated is far too complex to be condensed to one or even several variables. Complications ranged from implicit and explicit curricula of the music theory class to multiple goals and values of instructors, program designers, and students, all interacting with beliefs, musical aspirations, and perceptions of the innovation. Intensive observations of student work at the computer and unstructured and semistructured interviews with the participants provided the main data, supplemented with questionnaires, computer logs, and collection of materials (e.g., syllabi, tests, and students' composition answer sheets).

Even though initially the class seemed an ideal setting for the use of computers for education (e.g., perfect match between contents of software and curriculum-individualized instruction for a musically heterogeneous population, stable teaching over a number of years), the results fell well short of expectations. Many important issues such as the relevance of music practice to the computer program and the aesthetics of music in the computer program emerged at the site.

Focusing on social and cultural contexts, Saville Kushner (1985) of the University of East Anglia studied an innovative, 3-year course for third- and fourth-year students at the Guildhall School of Music and Drama in London. The course, a response to fundamental misgivings about the education of musicians in conservatories, arranged student performances and workshops in a range of unconventional community sites. Rather than judging the merits of the training, Kushner was commissioned to collect information that participants would find useful in making such judgments. His report was rich in description of program development over time, noting student and teacher perception and audience response. Through vignettes and vivid pictures, it conveyed conservatory life, its inside rivalries, competitions, participant experiences, implicit and explicit goals, and values. The personal debates about destination, the dreams, the dilemmas—so personal, yet so common to performance-oriented people—captured a reality pertinent to musical lives, innovations, and experiences. The portrayal of student perspectives, including those at the lower social strata, captured personal and cultural meanings of music, confusion over what the role of the professional musician should be, as well as the social context of repertoire.

Case studies are typically confined to one setting. A series of eight case studies portraying ordinary arts instruction in the United States was conducted by the Center for Instructional Research and Curriculum Evaluation (CIRCE) at the University of Illinois under the auspices of the National Arts Education Research Center, funded by the National Endowment for the Arts (see Stake, Bresler, and Mabry, 1991). Described in detail were the fundamental differences in program offering for music education specialists and general classroom teachers, not only in curricula and pedagogy but also in impact on scheduling, resources, and use of curricular organizers as well. One etic (original design) issue was the role of community resources and performances. Classroom observations brought out the "hidden curriculum"—art as relief from schoolwork and the regularity with which music was presented without background or interpretation, whether for class participation or as background activity to eating, doing worksheets, or reading. As usual, the emphasis was not on what ought to be, but the study did provide researcher interpretation as to what is needed.

In another federally funded project, the Elementary Subjects Study (funded by the U.S. Department of Education) at Michigan State University, music and the visual arts were studied along with mathematics, science, social studies, and literature. The program focused on conceptual understanding, higher order thinking and problem solving in elementary school teaching through a series of case studies of music and visual arts instruction

(May, 1990). Research questions included the following: What content is taught when teaching for conceptual understanding and higher level learning? How do teachers negotiate curricular decisions? How do teachers concentrate their teaching to use their limited resources best? In what ways is good teaching subject matter specific?

In the mid-1990s, qualitative views and methods became prominent in music education inquiry. This new presence is a result of several forces. Almost all areas of educational research have been affected by the spread of qualitative research. The spread is reflected in the multiple editions of the *Handbook of Qualitative Research* (Denzin and Lincoln, 1994, 2000, 2006) and in journals specifically centered on qualitative research, such as *Qualitative Inquiry* and the *International Journal of Qualitative Research*. Qualitative research has been widely present in other arts education disciplines— visual arts, dance, and drama. Music education research burgeoned as well.

Seminal in this process were the two qualitative conferences at the University of Illinois (1994 and 1996) and the publication of their keynote addresses, as well as selected papers in the *Bulletin of the Council for Research in Music Education* (CRME). Although this was the first concentrated presence of qualitative research in a music education research journal, qualitative methods have been increasingly present in international conferences (e.g., International Society of Music Education, Research in Music Education) and in established, as well as new, research journals (*British Journal of Music Education*, *Research Studies in Music Education*, *Music Education Research*, *The Quarterly Journal of Music Teaching and Learning*, and the *Asia-Pacific Journal of Arts Education*).

How is the growth of qualitative research influencing the field of music education? Examination of the literature of the past 15 years shows that cultural, institutional, and personal contexts came to the forefront. On the cultural level, globalization seems to blur distinctions between national, regional, and local musical communities. At the same time, globalization discloses musical diversity and heterogeneity through increased hybridization, highlighting historical, social, and cultural contexts. The intensification of these processes in the past 20 years promoted research on folk and indigenous music. The prevalence of popular music, combined with the postmodernist erosion of the traditional distinction between high art and low art, accelerated the research on various types of folk, popular, and rock music.

In this process, the interests of ethnomusicologists, sociologists, and music educators have moved closer. The Society for Ethnomusicology features a special interest group of music education, and ethnomusicologists and sociologists of music are invited to keynote music keynote music education conferences. Leading figures in these area—Bruno Nettl (2002), Kofi Agawu and Meki Nzewi (Nzewi, 2002; Herbst, Nzewi, and Agawu, 2003), Tom Turino (2000), Simon Frith (1996), and Tia DeNora (2000)—have added to the understanding of educational issues.

Researchers in music education with a strong background in ethnomusicology have made special contributions. Patricia Campbell (1991, 1998,

2002), for example, has explored the roles music plays in children's lives and the manner by which various folkways, technologies, and institutional settings help them perpetuate and preserve particular musical expressions and experiences. In her various studies, Campbell explored children's membership in social and cultural units and the inevitable influences those units have on musical ideas, values, and behaviors.

In an African framework, dance and music are usually holistically integrated and often inclusive of costume, ritual, and stories framed within a particular cosmology. In Namibia, Minette Mans (cf. 2000, 2002, 2004) examined how young Namibian children engage with music, what and when do they play, and how they are educated in the performing arts. Mans focuses on an informal, community-based arts education. She pointed out that indigenous music, prevalent in the community, is typically not part of the formal schooling system, where educators are often trained in Western traditions.

Indeed, playgrounds and homes are fertile grounds for tapping and honing children's artistic potentials. Teachers' expertise and training are in Western music, and their lack of knowledge about indigenous music is common. At the same time, the massive migrations from rural areas to cities threaten indigenous music, stirring an urgency in capturing it and, when possible, restoring it to the school. Ghana, like some other African countries, has embarked on school reforms and policies to make school music reflect the culture of the local communities. The role of indigenous music in formal educational settings has become critical (cf. Flolu, 2000; Leung,[6] 2002, 2004; Mans, 2000; Oppondo, 2000), spurring debate and research. Akosua Addo (1996) conducted a visual ethnography of the Ghanaian school child's music world, through the performance of songs for singing games. She examined the cultural norms evident in the performance and practice of Ghanaian children's play song. Addo explored the interests of the children, their collective and individual backgrounds, and how these reflect on their concepts of culture. Focusing on the sound and structural features of children's play songs, she looked at similarities and differences between these and those of adult music cultures. She explored the contribution that the performance and practice of play songs make to the acquisition and development of concepts of culture among children on school playgrounds in the Ghana.

Mary Dzansi (2003) examined Ghanaian cultural values and expressions embedded in children's playground repertoire, describing and interpreting children's informal performances of these songs (sung in schools' playgrounds during recess time, as well as in community festivals). Indigenous music is part of many countries in various parts of the world. In Ireland, Kari Veblen (1996) has conducted an ethnographic study of Irish teaching and learning practices by examining cultural assumptions and constructs of time, space, and relationships of daily incidents.

Methodologically, these studies mirror the qualitative scene outside music education. Different qualitative-genres-reflect-various traditions of ethnographic work, initially of outsiders studying others' cultures and, increasingly, the voices of insiders studying their own culture but reporting to "foreign" audiences (Mans, 2000). As part of the dramatic increase of world universities, many from other cultures learn in Western countries, mostly in the United States, United Kingdom, and Australia (cf. Addo, 1996; Dzansi, 2003; Leung, 2002).

A related area of study concerns teaching musics of other cultures and the impact on the curriculum. In the United States, Rita Klinger (1996) examined the practical problems surrounding the application of "multicultural music" to the elementary school curriculum as reflected in one music teacher's attempt to enlarge the scope of her teaching to include the music of Africa. Klinger examined musical materials selected for the performance, instructional strategies, the use of instruments and the development of instrumental accompaniment, and the extent to which the teacher contextualized the music during class time. In particular, she was interested in the fit to the goals of multicultural education, the extent to which authenticity was a concern from the music teacher's perspective, and the contextualization of music with nonmusical materials in the elementary music class. In Australia, Kathy Marsh (1995) conducted a case study of preservice music education focused on preservice student-teachers' attitudinal change to indigenous music. In addition to the studies of ethnicity, research examined teaching music for minority populations, for example, problems regarding teaching music to Muslims in England, based on observations and interviews with pupils and adults (Harris, 2002).

In a globalized world, the opportunities for musical learning about distant cultures become widespread. In her participant-observation work, Kimberly Powell 2003, 2004, 2005) has examined musical practices that transmit deep cultural values through the contemporary art of Japanese drumming, *taiko*, a growing artistic and political movement in North America with more than 150 *taiko* ensembles. Powell described the teaching and learning processes in the apprenticeship of *taiko* drummers, highlighting the ways in which cultural knowledge is embodied through participation in socially and culturally prescribed systems of meaning and how such participation serves to organize sensory experience into knowledge of art, self, and self in relation to learning.

These studies illuminate ways of operating with qualitative methods. Whereas Powell's work involved an immersion experience in the learning, gradually making her an insider, Campbell, Addo, and Dzansi (for Addo and Dzansi, working within their own culture) maintained themselves as outsiders—adults looking at children's repertoire.

Like ethnomusicology, sociology has had a tradition of using qualitative methods to understand phenomena in context. In her fine "Social and Cultural Contexts of Music Teaching and Learning: An Introduction" for *The New Handbook on Music Teaching and Learning*, Marie McCarthy (2002) pointed out the lack of sociological research tradition. Recently, some music education scholars have been increasingly coming to view music as social action and to examine even more closely music teaching and learning as embedded in social and cultural values. Theoretical perspectives in sociology that originated in social constructivism, critical theory, and situated cognition provide important perspectives to life in various social educational settings, in and out of the classroom.

Research in music education flows from changes in communication technology that have afforded unprecedented diversity in the range of music produced and consumed, particularly in popular, commercial music. Although the use of communication technology evolved over a long period, it reached a point of rapid acceleration in the last 20 years. In the process, it has fundamentally changed our interactions with music. Recording technologies, combined with speed of communication, eliminated barriers of time and geographical distance. The traditional listening spaces, such as churches and concert halls, gave way to homes, hotel rooms, and cars. Children, like adults, are constantly exposed to recorded music—in particular, to its popular forms.

Although the interest in popular music in music education has long been present, research on popular music has thrived in the past decade (Byrne and Sheridan, 2000; Dunbar-Hill and Wemyss, 1999, 2000; Herbert and Campbell, 2000; Green, 2001; Soderman and Folkestad, 2004). Research topics include perspectives on teaching popular music in schools, the role of popular music in children's and adults' lives and society (Crafts, Cavicchi, and Keil 1993), and the close examination of communities of music (Green, 2001). The interest in urban and popular music is reflected in special issues of research journals, for example, the *International Journal of Music Education*, with its focus on popular music as an educational phenomenon and the effects of the music on teenage culture and on society as a whole (Folkestad, 2000).

In this endeavor, the important work of the MayDay group provided valuable contributions featuring the ideas of Tom Regelski, Marie McCarthy, Terry Gates, and Wayne Bowman (see, for example, the special issue in the *Council of Research in Music Education*, June 1998, and http://education .nyu.edu/music/mayday/maydaygroup/events/amherst.htm.

One focus of sociological research is the organization of society in groups. Among the well-researched characteristics are ethnicity, gender, social class, religion, and nationality. In England, Lucy Green studied the gendered nature of the musical experience in schools (1993, 1997). Green's work inspired other empirical studies on gendered musical practices and experiences and how they may affect students' expectations and products of composition (cf. Charles, 2004). In their chapter on gender in the *New Handbook of Music Teaching and Learning*, Lamb, Dolloff, and Howe (2002) point out that music education lagged behind other disciplines in addressing feminist theories but provide groundwork for branching out. Many of the first studies centered on historical research (Koza 1990, 1993), including black women music educators, but others examined current issues (Lamb, 1990, 1996).

The use of qualitative research has brought increasing attention to the institutional contexts that shape the curriculum (Bresler, 1998). Personal contexts highlight the perspectives of students' voices in diverse educational levels. Researchers have focused on students' experiences, learning processes, and the forms of acquisition of knowledge in which they participate. (cf. Aróstegui, 2004; Finney, 2003; Kokotsaki, Davidson, and Coimbra, 2001; Silva, 2004; Silvey, 2004a, 2004b; Stalhammar, 2000).

The focus on teachers' perspectives and beliefs opened up the diversity of views on good teaching. Through participant-observations and interviews, Schmidt (1998) explored the definitions of "good" teaching held by four student teachers of instrumental music. Their understandings were constructed from a variety of experiences with parents, peers, teachers, cooperating teachers, and students—experiences that they explicitly and tacitly transformed into principles of good teaching. Each student teacher engaged in ongoing refinement of a personal definition of good music teaching, consistently filtering potential elements of that model through an interpretive lens—the desire, as the student teachers said, to be "themselves" in the classroom. Observations of their instructional practices revealed that their definitions of "good" teaching were influenced by the university music education courses but that, because of the strengths of personal beliefs, each one learned a different version of what was taught.

Action research of teachers emphasizes the study of one's own practice, leading to possible improvement. Some action research has oriented toward one's own classrooms (Treacher, 1989; Miller, 1994–1995, 1997; 2004); others are part of bigger projects (Strathclyde Consortium for Action Research in Learning Approaches and Teaching Techniques in Inventing Project, Byrne and Sheridan, 2001).

In the area of musical cognition, qualitative methods became highly influential in the traditionally quantitative domains of perception, creativity, and composition (including that facilitated by computers). Argyris and Schon (1974) described two types of theories: (1) espoused theories reflecting knowledge *about* action and (2) theories *in* action—the knowledge actually used in action. Research on children's mental processes, composition, and creativity often draw on both types of theories. Pioneered by Donald Pond in the 1940s, Bertil Sundin in Sweden in the early 1960s (Sundin, McPherson, and Folkestad, 1998), Jeanne Bamberger (1977, 1991), and Rena Upitis (1992), prominent voices in the field include Margaret Barrett (2000, 2001, 2003), Pamela Burnard (1995, 1999; Burnard and Younker, 2004), Rivka Elkoshy (2004), Magne Espeland (2003), Joyce Gromko (1996), Maude Hickey (2003), Sandra Stauffer (1999, 2001, 2002), Jackie Wiggins (1994, 1999/2000, 2002), and Betty Ann Younker (2003; Younker and Smith, 1996). The role of computers in facilitating composition is growing (Folkestad, 1996; Folkestad, Lindstrom, and Hargreaves, 1997; Hickey, 2003; Stauffer, 2001). Eva Brand (1998) drew on theories in action, identifying and describing children's in-action mental model of their learning. The model was inferred from observation of children's behavior as they learned a song.

Important differences across (and sometime within) genres have to do with the type of research questions, the unit of analysis, the length of study, the level of contexts sought (micro, meso, or macro), and the extent to which the research is open-ended, reflecting the intellectual traditions from which they evolve.

Some research in music is done by nonmusicians, where music is but one subject among several others, chosen to highlight larger patterns. Such was a study by Benjamin Bloom (1985), who was interested in the development of talent in a variety of domains—music, math, sculpture, athletics—and the roles of families, teachers, and schools in discovering, developing, and encouraging unusually high levels of competence. The commonalities of music with other domains, as well as its unique properties, were presented by Sosniak (1985).

Music Concepts to Aid Qualitative Study

Extensive use of observation in natural settings with little intervention encourages us to discern the complexity of music education. Taped interviews can capture participant voices, views, and struggles. Qualitative methodology promotes the pursuit of questions like, What music do teachers cherish and participate in outside of school? How are school reform and the accountability movement affecting how teachers perceive the teaching of music? What are children's assumptions about music, about what is beautiful, attractive, or well formed? What musical events are to be found in prekindergarten settings? In school settings? In jam sessions? Are there ways that teachers are using MTV for legitimate music instruction? Qualitative researchers can examine events that reflect latent as well as manifest learning. They can study interrelationships of school, home, media, and culture as they shape musical skills and attitudes. They do this by studying individual cases, problems, and settings.

Capturing reality in its complexity opens up research studies to additional modes of representation: vignettes, photographs, audio- and videotapes, films, and various artifacts of performing and teaching music.

Using tapes to capture musical nuances and qualities in performances as well as intonations of "everyday speech" is useful for musicians, for whom intonation, rhythm, and pitch are specially meaningful.

Having discussed the content and representations that qualitative methodology offers music education research, we now want to draw attention to the symbiotic relation between musicianship and intellectual inquiry—noting that much can be developed along qualitative lines. Musical approach can be an asset in qualitative research in general education. Music educators who turn to research in education can use their musical background to contribute to structural conceptualizations and analysis of school life and teaching.

Teaching and classroom life should sometimes be regarded through aesthetic lenses (cf. Eisner, 1979; Goodman, 1968; Brophy and Good, 1986;

Kagan, 1989). Here, it is important to make the distinction between an artwork and a phenomenon analyzed through aesthetic parameters (Dewey, 1958). As Eisner has stated, we can pay attention to the aesthetic qualities of a teaching performance in order to perceive what is later described as its qualitative aspects or its feelingful character. The performance itself may not be artistic; that is, it may not have coherence and unity and might not be particularly inventive. Nevertheless, it still can have aesthetic properties. The opposite of aesthetic is anaesthetic, the thwarting of feeling. Objects, situations, or events that are aesthetic evoke or elicit feeling. Whether the situation of performance is artistic, it can be argued, is another matter (Eisner, private communication, 1990).

Art affords us the unique experience of apprehending the result of one individual's (the artist's) inquiry into the structure of reality and the structure of a medium (Olson, 1978; Arnheim, 1986; Eisner, 1988). Teachers, like artists, create articulated, planned experiences[7] and the portrayal of experience can be disciplined by qualitative methods. Analysis of a lesson, like a work of art in general and a musical work in particular, can benefit by allusion to arts' structural properties: rhythm, line, orchestration, texture, form. Lessons can create drama—introduction, building of tension, and resolution. Formal qualities play a major role in the educational communication, interacting with specific messages and contents to create the impact. These properties help provide standards for teaching, drawing attention to coherence, sequentiality, and comprehension.

Let us examine some musical parameters that we have found helpful for conceptualizing qualitative research, particularly in examining curricula and pedagogies: (1) *Form* relates to the organization of parts and whole, arrangement of repetition and variation, unity and variety. Teaching uses and builds on these. A number of educational models point to the importance of form in teaching: setting up introductory anticipation, development and closure, or the creation of suspense, a dramatic climax and resolution as the summing up of the lesson or of a topic. Every lesson has a form, created by the interplay of new and old material, repetition and variation. A lesson may be conceptualized as a Baroque suite—a series of little, related movements (except for parameters like tonality and orchestration)—or as a classical sonata form, tightly organized, fully developed, and well balanced. (2) *Style.* Just as categorization of musical style[8] is useful for perception and analysis, so is the categorization of teaching style. Parameters of style are qualitative lenses for classroom life, pedagogies, and curricular materials.

Form and style are broad categories, referring to complexes or syndromes. The qualities of melody (or line), tempo and rhythm, orchestration and texture, are more specific. (3) *Tempo* is the pace, quick and slow and all the gradations in between. *Rhythm* refers to relationships of tempi over time as well as to temporal patterns. What are the paces of the lesson? How fast do the ideas flow? How rapidly does the teacher change topic, focus, and assignment? How does this pace raise anticipation or a sense of development and evaluation? (4) *Orchestration* refers to the character of the interplay among players or participants. What is the character of interplay between teacher and students? How does the teacher get the students to take more initiative? Presentations can be didactic, the teacher assuming the soloist's role, dominating the presentation. Alternatively, the teacher assumes the conductor's role, facilitating student dialogue, yet maintaining control over content and form. Classroom life can take the form of chamber ensembles, a measure of student leadership and autonomy. Orchestration reveals the "colors" of voices in the classroom, for example some extroverted (brass versus string instruments) in higher registers, intense, and interacting. (5) *Melody* refers to the "plot line," its direction ascending, descending, or flat. Is the unit of thought a long one, or are there many shorter units? What are the interrelations of the shorter idea units to the whole lesson? Are they complementary, autonomous, or unified? What is the inner form (in terms of anticipation and drama) within each of these plot lines? (6) *Texture* refers to the interrelations of simultaneous lines and their development over time during the lesson. Under the category of texture, the presentation of topics, such as at a board meeting, can be homophonic or contrapuntal, several voices echoing, confronting, or ignoring each other.

These music concepts, as well as special concepts of education, are expected content and representation in qualitative music education research. Most important are their contributions to expressivity. Though unobtrusive, the researcher interacts with teaching and learning phenomena, bringing unique experience and scholarship into interpretation. Along with relatively uncontestable descriptions, traces of the researcher's deepest personal understandings are presented. The character and the art form of the researcher are not hidden.

Some qualitative works have examined methodological issues, for example, in ethnographic work, the nature of cultural assumptions and discrepancies (e.g., Veblen, 1996; Bresler, 2002). Other issues relate to a wider array of qualitative genres, for example, discussion of methods (Powell, 2005) or ethics (Bresler, 1997).

Arts-based inquiry is a growing area of experimentation. Exploring voice and narrative style, Peter DeVries studied himself as a music teacher, using a compelling autobiographical narrative (de Vries, 1999), and combined with theater educator Barbara Poston-Anderson in collaborative voices (Poston-Anderson and de Vries, 2000). Their work outlines an unfolding arts-based collaboration in a tertiary institution in the context of creating a musical play for preschool children. Written from both educators' perspectives, this work discusses their collaborative process from the scripting and composition through to the rehearsal and performance stages, identifying the main characteristics that they believe contributed to their perceptions of a successful collaboration. Other researchers that experiment with voice are Peter Gouzouasis and Karen Lee (Gouzouasis and Lee, 2002), exploring through musical forms of fugues multiple voices related to the research inquiry.

In a quest for finer attention to the temporal dimensions of personal and cultural experience, as well as relationships with participants, coresearchers, and the audiences of research, Bresler (2005, forthcoming) has explored the ways in which the various musical processes of listening, performing, and composing can inform the processes of educational research. Central themes across these domains include improvisation empathy, and embodiment.

Methods and Criteria

The primary task of the researcher is interpretation (with interpretations presented eventually not just as findings but as assertions; Erickson, 1986). The most obvious work of the qualitative researcher is data gathering in the field. The ethic of qualitative research calls for abundant description, sufficient for readers to participate in verification of the researcher's interpretations and to make some of their own (Stake, 1978). Thus, most of the methodological advice in the literature has to do with data gathering. If we were limited to a single recommendation, we would name Schatzman and Strauss (1973), *Field Research: Strategies for a Natural Sociology*.

Data Collection

The examples of music education research described earlier identify the main methods for qualitative research: intensive observation in natural settings, examination of documents and other artifacts, and interview. Even when audio- or videotaped, the principal "instrument" is the researcher, a constant arbiter of what is important, of the need for further data, for probing, and for small or large redesign of the study. The design of the study is said to be emergent or progressively focused (Strauss, 1987). The design is based not only on a strong sense of the research questions or issues at hand (Smith, 1978) but also on the growing body of interpreted observations in the classroom or wherever.

When assuming the more common nonparticipant role, the researcher observes ordinary activities and habitat, the people, the exercise of authority and responsibility, the expression of intent, the productivity, and especially the milieu. Believing that important understandings are situationally rooted, the researcher carefully describes the contacts, noting not just space and time characteristics, but social, economic, political, historical, and aesthetic contexts. The nonparticipating observer is as invisible and nonintrusive as possible, often even refraining from appearing to record what is going on.

In a participant-observer role, the researcher engages in the ordinary activities of the group or program being studied but tries not to redirect those activities. Participation may be marginal, perhaps the role of helpmate with some sharing of interests and problems (Spindler, 1982), or more extensive, such as the teacher as researcher in her own classroom or the researcher as consultant providing in-service training to teachers (Cohen, 1980; Stake and

Easley, 1978; Stanley, 1990; Wagner, 1990). The growing interest in action research (teacher as researcher; Carr and Kemmis, 1986) is apparent in recent meetings of the American Education Research Association. Here especially, but even in the more passive roles, as interpreter, the researcher is seen as an interactive force in events.

Document review is an essential component of data collection (Andre, 1983). Needed data on inspiration, obligation, and constraint on personal or group action are often disclosed in formal and informal documents. Many useful documents are fugitive records, stored in places no one can remember, making it necessary for the researcher to look through countless papers to find a useful one. Often the information needed is a marginal notation or not even a document at all, such as an inscription on a trophy or notes on a calendar. Browsing is a common activity for the researcher, with half a mind for the research question but another half just trying to comprehend what sort of place it is.

Interviews are conducted not as surveys of how people feel but primarily to obtain observations that the researcher is unable to make directly, secondarily to capture multiple realities or perceptions of any given situation, and, finally, to assist in interpreting what is happening. When standardized information is needed from large numbers of people, the written survey is more efficient, but most qualitative researchers want to probe more deeply than is possible with questionnaires. With a structured interview, the researcher assumes questions are comprehensible and consistent in meaning across respondents. Semistructured interviews, with topics or questions predetermined, allow latitude for probing and following the interviewee's sense of what is important. Unfortunately, they are costly to administer and time-consuming in analysis. The degree of structure for individual questions, for the interview as a whole, or for the project as a whole are key decisions to be made and remade (Mishler, 1986).

The qualitative researcher seeks to be unobtrusive, knowing that the more attention is drawn to the study, the more posturing there will be and less ordinary activity available for observation. Even interviewing and testing are interventions, drawing attention to the presence and purpose of the research. The researcher takes advantage of indications of accretion and use, such as graffiti on walls or repair records for tape recorders. Gene Webb and his Northwestern colleagues provided many examples of unobtrusive measures (Webb, Campbell, Schwartz, and Sechrest, 1966), but one of the authors, Don Campbell, later expressed the concern that heavy use of such methods persuade readers that social scientists are covert and deceptive, undermining the credibility of all research. Researchers, often in effect guests at the work space and in the private spaces of others, should be considerate. With its probing orientation, qualitative research easily intrudes into the personal affairs of others. Making the report anonymous is often insufficient to avoid the risk of harming people. Handling data is an ethical as much as a technical matter (Rainwater and Pittman, 1969).

Data Analysis

Techniques vary widely. Both qualitative and quantitative analyses of data are used by the qualitative researcher. Quantitative analysis is used more to work toward generalization across specifics observed in the field. It proceeds largely by coding, classifying, and aggregating observations (Miles and Huberman, 1984). Thus, for example, teaching episodes are increasingly seen to be of perhaps three kinds, and the length of student deliberation in choosing a musical instrument is treated statistically. Uniqueness of each particular situation is given little attention: the typical, aggregate, and generalizable are given more attention. Such an approach is often followed in policy analysis (Yin, 1984).

Qualitative analysis is organized more around the notes and stories the researcher keeps, increasingly focused on a small number of issues or themes. The researcher selects the most revealing instances, identifies vignettes, and composes narratives from day to day, then uses an even smaller selection of them in the final presentation (Goetz and LeCompte, 1984). The choice of what to report is subjective, evolving, emphasizing more what contributes to the understanding of the particulars observed than relating to cases and situations elsewhere, usually giving no more than minor attention to comparisons, not worrying much about typically or representativeness. Thus, the integrity, complexity, and contextuality of individual cases are probed. Readers fit them in among cases they have known. If theory building is the ultimate intent of the researcher here, qualitative analysis paces it not by years but by decades.

Multiple case studies require a kind of analysis that remains largely unformalized. One tries to preserve the uniqueness of the individual case, yet produce cross-site conclusions. The usual reporting procedure is to present a long or short summary of each case, then chapters on understanding the aggregate (Huberman and Miles, 1984). Panels of interpreters, some of whom may not have observed at any sites, are often useful for enriching and challenging the interpretations—but require more comprehensive site summaries than site-visiting researchers usually provide for themselves. For self-use, panel, or instructional purposes, such summaries provide a synthesis of what the researcher knows about the site, tentative findings, and quality of data supporting them, even indicating what is still left to find out, and perhaps indicating an agenda for the next wave of data collection (Bogdan and Taylor, 1984).

For most qualitative projects, data analysis is an informal and often overwhelming task. There are too many data to keep records of and too few that support prevailing impressions. The researcher works with those seeming most likely to advance understanding, describing them in detail, and frequently restating the issue being pursued. Data analysis is an art form.

Criteria of Quality

The characteristics of quality in quantitative studies are widely agreed upon: representativeness of the sample, reliability and validity of measurement, objectivity in interpretation, and the probabilities of Type I and Type II errors, to name several (Campbell and Stanley, 1966). No such summary of characteristics of quality has been developed for qualitative research. Many of the same concepts are worthy of consideration, but when purposes are different (e.g., a low interest in broad generalization), then the criteria will be different. Whether the alternative purposes are legitimate is a question that researchers continue to debate (Smith and Heshusius, 1986).

The most important criterion for any research is that it is about something important, important to readers as well as to researchers. Researchers are given great respect for recognizing what needs to be studied, and they should not abuse that privilege. Perhaps an overly large share of music education research is the psychological study of musical skills and knowledge; perhaps too little is the study of curriculum change and that of music teaching. Still, the health of any research enterprise depends more on intellectual curiosity, studying what needs to be better understood, rather than on what can be funded or will be pleasing to patrons and readers.

In a response to critics of naturalistic inquiry, Lincoln and Guba (1985, 1988) asked methodologists and philosophers of science for evidence that well-crafted research grounded in qualitative and phenomenological traditions *could* be judged and found (1) systematically congruent with the context, that is, valid; (2) not subject to aberrations in research process or instrumentation, that is, reliable; and (3) not open to charges of bias, prejudice, or political advocacy of the investigators. Lincoln and Guba rejected these more quantitative or positivist criteria on grounds that they were incompatible with the axioms of naturalistic research. They saw the naturalist's criteria to be (1) credibility (rather than internal validity), (2) transferability (rather than external validity or generalizability), (3) dependability (rather than reliability), and (4) confirmability (rather than objectivity). These alternative terms were advocated primarily to make clear the inappropriateness of conventional criteria for qualitative research (House, 1980).

To illustrate these criteria, consider a naturalistic case study of a program for training teachers of introductory band. As does a quantitative researcher, the qualitative researcher unconsciously or deliberately takes into account the experience, sophistication, curiosity, and concerns of the eventual audience and seeks to say mostly what will be credible to them. But unlike the quantitative researcher, the qualitative researcher intends to build upon the uniqueness of personal understanding, offering for each reader a credible account and a vicarious experience for substantiation or modification of existing generalizations.

Transferability refers to the extent to which the research facilitates inferences by readers regarding their own situations and responsibilities. Such are petite generalizations rather than the grand generalizations of the theory builder, relatively context-free, and a basis for general policy. Good transfer is based on similarity of situations, intuitively weighted as to what is important and unimportant in the match.

Our campus researcher seeks to describe band director trainees meaningfully to readers, with observations transferable to their situations. Rather than measuring with instrument or frequency count, he observes and portrays the band teacher training experience, clearly describing people, dialogue, settings, expressions of intent and frustration, and so on, so as to enable the reader to associate this new vicarious experience with previous experience, recognizing ordinary use of both reasoning and intuition in clarifying views and improving understanding.

Confirmability is a sophisticated way of suggesting accuracy. With qualitative data we seldom have an accurate impression the first time we look; we have to confirm or triangulate[9] (Denzin, 1970), and when we can we have others, including our readers, confirm the finding. The researcher is not content to note available confirmatory evidence but deliberately seeks new facts that might refute the present facts (Popper, 1969). What are facts? It always happens that several important facts are in some degree interpretations (e.g., a professor's apparent lack of interest in band appearance, particularly synchronous movement—whether or not she confirms it), the meanings differing from observer to observer. The researcher triangulates the observations, working toward some common perception, but expects and reports on certain differences in perception (for example, between male and female faculty members) and goes out of his way to relate certain ways he, with background and value commitment showing, interacted with the scene and arrived at assertions. With different backgrounds, the readers, too, interpret the account differently. Confirmability is an aim, not an ideal, to be tempered by the indefiniteness of reality and by sticking with questions that matter.

Drawn by his persuasion toward constructed reality, our quantitative researcher finds it of little use to hypothesize some "true account" of the band director training program, an account independent of human observers, an ideal to which actual accounts might be compared. Even those parts of the account most agreed upon are not good grounds for considering "validity"—for many of those easily confirmed facts are of little interest, and one way to get confirmation is to omit things, even important things, that people see differently. The account should be dependable among relatively neutral readers, portraying much of what they would have seen, had they been there, and omitting most of what they would have found irrelevant and distracting. The researcher is greatly privileged in what to attend to, but the audience can invalidate, at least for their purposes, the account as off-the-mark and incomplete.

Complete objectivity is unattainable and unsought in this research paradigm (Dilthey, 1900; Barone, 1990). The researcher seeks to diminish subjectivity that interferes with comprehension and to exploit subjectivity for deeper interpretation (Peshkin, 1988). He exposes himself, preferably with grace. Although most readers have little interest in reading the researcher's track record, autobiographical and opinion statements are useful footnotes for deliberately revealing lack of experience, alliances, and value positions. And to carry the handling of subjectivity further, the competent qualitative researcher finds ways of including contrary views and alternative explanations.

The criteria for high-quality inquiry and for high-quality reports are not one and the same. The inquiry process belongs largely to the researcher. Each of the data-gathering and analysis methods has its own criteria, sources for which we have footnoted. The criteria for reports (reports being communications requiring both a sender and a receiver) lie in the hands of both the researcher and the user of the research. With quantitative measurement, it is not the test or instrument that has validity, it is each use of the measurements that is valid or invalid (Cronbach, 1971). Similarly with qualitative research, the meanings arrived at by individual readers and the applications to new practice are the ultimate indexes of validity of the reports (Howe and Eisenhart, 1990). A final assection might be that in the program studied here, band directors are reconsidering their roles in protection and perpetuation of local culture. If readers misinterpret this as indicating the graduates thus are hostile to change, the finding should be considered invalid. The researcher can do much to increase the quality of his work, but it serves no more than to facilitate cautious and insightful use of his accounts.

Strengths and Weaknesses

As summarized by Miles and Huberman (1984), the weakest aspect of qualitative research is its contribution to basic research generalizations and policy study—but such is not its intent. Its purpose is to facilitate understanding of the particular. Still, by charging the researcher with spontaneous responsibility in the field, it lacks good protection against

1. excessive subjectivity in observations
2. imprecise language in descriptions
3. vague descriptions of the research design
4. unwieldy and voluminous reports
5. implication of generalizability when little is warranted
6. cost and time overrun
7. unethical intrusion into personal lives

But the strengths of qualitative study are impressive as well. We would summarize those strengths as

1. a holistic, systemic purview, emphasizing inner workings and contexts
2. a strong, empirical commitment to triangulated description of teaching
3. an obligation and opportunity to get the most from fieldwork interpretations

4. a sense of empathy enhancing the utility of use for applied practice in education

These features have not characterized the majority of the music education research in our journals. Certainly it would be a mistake, were all the issues and developments of music education to be studied naturalistically—but that imbalance is far away.

To close this chapter we would like to quote from Kushner's (1985) case study, his final words:

> As can be read throughout this report, the participating students are formidable critics and evaluators—and no one has been spared their scrutiny. MPCS offers a rare occasion in music training for trainees to support each other in a discussion forum and they use it with effect. Guildhall tutors, guest speakers, professional collaborators, prospective employers, those who seek to advise and the principal himself, have all found themselves having to defend statements they have made to MPCS groups in the face of often considerable pressure. There is no evidence on this course, at least, for the often-heard assertion that music students are inarticulate or reticent. This may be both heartening and worrying for the conservatoire facing the prospect of trying to integrate an educational curriculum with a training curriculum. The implications of curriculum integration go beyond finding appropriate slots on a timetable for optional sessions. If there is a vision of new practice enshrined in the Project then it might prove increasingly hard to protect other teaching areas in the School from the consequences of that vision. . . . To date the Project has undoubtedly enjoyed many successes—but it is still a curriculum 'fledgling' enjoying the attention and tolerance needed to nurture it. Its musical products are of a quality which still worry Peter, in educational terms its aims and outcome are still hit-and-miss. There is no certainty that the course will interest conservatoire students other than those (still small) numbers who opt to join and remain on the course. And, of course, MPCS has not had to withstand confrontation with critics one of the few experiences so far denied it.

NOTES

1. Vignettes quoted herein are from Stake, Bresler, and Mabry, *Custom and Cherishing*, 1991.

2. Guba and Lincoln (1981) have identified gradations of belief in an independent versus a constructed reality. One's belief is linked to belief in how we come to know what we know—but ontology and epistemology are not interdeterminate. Belief in independent reality does not fix one's belief in a simple world, the worlds of Stravinsky's *Firebird* or seasonal fund drives. Nor does belief in constructionism fix belief in a heterogenous, particularist world. Realists too believe that generalizations are regularly limited by local condition. "Do teachers always prefer authoritarian milieus or only under certain conditions?" Though idealists, relativists, situationalists, contextualists, and other champions

of local knowledge often resist broad generalizations and are found to support constructivist ontology, their support for a contextualist epistemology is a correlate, not a derivative, of that ontology.

3. Rorty's perspective on both idealism and positivism moves us toward the role of literature in qualitative methodology. Kant and Hegel, claims Rorty (1989), went only halfway in their repudiation of the idea that truth is "out there." They were willing to view the world of empirical science as a made world, to see matter as constructed by mind. But they persisted in seeing mind, spirit, the depths of the human self, as having an intrinsic nature, one that could be known by a kind of nonempirical superscience called philosophy. Thus, only half of truth, the bottom, scientific half, was made. The truth about mind, the providence of philosophy, was still a matter of discovery rather than creation. The idealists confused the idea that nothing has intrinsic nature with the idea that space and time are unreal, that human beings cause the spatiotemporal world to exist. Claiming that truth is not out there, Rorty says that where there are no sentences, there is no truth, that sentences are elements of human languages, and that human languages, as whole vocabularies, are human creations.

4. See naturalistic generalizations, Stake and Trumbull (1982).

5. According to the emic approach, the issues, concepts, and meanings are of the people under study. In the etic approach, researchers apply their own concepts to understand the social behavior of the people being studied (Taylor and Bogdan, 1984). The emic categories of meaning are called first-order concepts. The etic categories are called second-order concepts, since they are "constructs of the constructs made by actors on the social scene" (Schutz, 1962).

6. Here, qualitative interviews supplemented quantitative surveys.

7. The fact that some teachers teach artistically does not necessitate that they articulate it. We find teachers who provide meaningful aesthetic experience in their lessons yet seem unable to articulate it, just as some musicians create excellent music but find it difficult (and unnecessary) to talk about it. Time and again, we are confronted with the difference between "know how" and "know about."

8. Pathos/Dyonsian/Romantic versus Ethos/Apolonian/Classic is a distinction of musical idiom prominent since Plato. Ethos, associated with restraint and serenity, canon and norm, implies belief in absolute, unalterable values. Pathos, associated with strong feeling, motion, and action implies the personal quest (cf. Sachs, 1946).

9. The term *triangulation* was coined by Webb et al. (1965), an internal index to provide convergent evidence, "the onslaught of a series of imperfect measures." Triangulation is supposed to support a finding by showing that independent measures (checking with different sources, applying different methods, corroborated by different researchers, and examined through different theories) of it agree with it, or at least, don't contradict it.

REFERENCES

Addo, A. (1996). A multimedia analysis of selected Ghanaian children's play songs. *Bulletin of the Council for Research in Music Education 129*, 1–28.

Andre, M. (1983). Use of content analysis in educational evaluation. *Discourse, 4*(1).

Argyris, C., & Schon, D. 1974. Theory in practice: Increasing professional development. San Francisco: Jossey Bass.

Arnheim, R. (1986). *New essays on the psychology of art.* Los Angeles: University of California Press.

Aróstegui, J. L. (2004). Much more than music: Music education instruction at the University of Illinois at Urbana-Champaign. In J. L. Aróstegui (Ed.), *The social context of music education* (pp. 127–210). Urbana, IL: CIRCE, University of Illinois.

Bamberger, J. (1977). In search of a tune. In D. Perkins & B. Leondar (Eds.), *The arts and cognition.* Baltimore: Johns Hopkins University Press.

Bamberger, J. (1977). Intuitive and formal musical knowing. In Stanley S. Madeja (Ed.), *The arts, cognition, and basic skills.* St. Louis: CEMREL.

Bamberger, J. (1978). In search of a tune. In D. Perkins & B. Leondar (Eds.), *The arts and cognition.* Baltimore: Johns Hopkins University Press.

Bamberger, J. (1991). *The mind behind the musical ear: How children develop musical intelligence.* Cambridge, MA: Harvard University Press.

Barone, T. (1987). Research out of the shadows: A reply to Rist. *Curriculum Inquiry, 17*(4), 453–463.

Barone, T. (1990). *Rethinking the meaning of vigor: Toward a literary tradition of educational inquiry.* Paper presented at the annual meeting of the American Education Research Association, Boston.

Barrett, M. S. (2000). Windows, mirrors and reflections: A case study of adult constructions of children's musical thinking. *Bulletin of the Council for Research in Music Education, 145* 43–61.

Barrett, M. S. (2001). Constructing a view of children's meaning-making as notators: A case-study of a five-year-old's descriptions and explanations of invented notations. *Research Studies in Music Education, 16*, 33–45.

Barrett, M. S. (2003). Invented notations and mediated memory: A case-study of two children's use of invented notations. *Bulletin of the Council for Research in Music Education, 153/154*, 55–62.

Berg, B. L. (1989). *Qualitative research methods for the social sciences.* Boston: Allyn and Bacon.

Bloom, B. (Ed.). (1985). *Developing talent in young people.* New York: Ballantine.

Bogdan, R., & Biklen, S. K. (1982). *Qualitative research for education: An introduction to theory and methods.* Boston: Allyn and Bacon.

Bogdan, R., & Taylor, S. (1984). *Introduction to qualitative research methodology.* New York: John Wiley.

Brand, M. (1987). A review of participant observation: Study of a fourth grade music classroom—Cynthia Rhodes Thiel. *Bulletin of the Council for Research in Music Education, 92.*

Brand, E. (1998). The process of identifying children's mental model of their own learning as inferred from learning a song. *Bulletin of the Council for Research in Music Education, 145*, 47–61.

Bresler, L. (1987). The role of the computer in a music theory class: Integration, barriers and learning. Unpublished doctoral dissertation, Stanford University, Stanford, CA.

Bresler, L. (1997). Towards the creation of a new code of ethics in qualitative research. *Bulletin of the Council of Research in Music Education, 130*, 17–29.

Bresler, L. (1998). The genre of school music and its shaping by meso, micro and macro contexts. *Research Studies in Music Education, 11*, 2–18.

Bresler, L. (2002). The interpretive zone in international qualitative research. In L. Bresler & A. Ardichvili (Eds.), *International research in education: Experience, theory and practice* (pp. 39–81). New York: Peter Lang.

Bresler, L. (2005). What musicianship can offer to research. A keynote address presented in Research in Music Education, Exeter, England (to be published in *Music Education Research*, 2005).

Bresler, L. (forthcoming). The music lesson. In L. Bresler (Ed.), *Handbook of research for arts-based inquiry*. Thousand Oaks, CA: Sage.

Brophy, J., & Good, T. L. (1986). Teacher behavior and student achievement. In M. C. Wittrock (Ed.), *Handbook of research on teaching* (3rd ed.). New York: Macmillan.

Burnard, P. (1995). Task design and experience in composition. *Research Studies in Music Education, 5*, 32–46.

Burnard, P. (1999). Bodily intention in children's improvisation and composition. *Psychology of Music, 27*(2), 159–174.

Burnard, P., & Younker, B. A. (2004). Problem solving and creativity: Insights from students' individual composing pathways. *International Journal for Music Education, 22*(1), 59–76.

Byrne, C., & Sheridan, M. (2000). The long and winding road: The story of rock music in Scottish schools. *International Journal of Music Education, 36*, 46–57.

Byrne, C. & Sheridan, M. (2001). The Scarlatti papers: Development of an action research project in music. *British Journal of Music Education, 18*(2).

Campbell, D. T., & Stanley, J. C. (1966). Closing down the conversation: The end of the quantitative/qualitative debate among educational inquirers. *Educational Researcher, 1*(4), 20–24.

Campbell, P. S. (1991). The child-song [*sic*] genre: A comparison of songs by and for children. *International Journal of Music Education, 17*, 14–23.

Campbell, P. S. (1998). *Songs in their heads: Music and its meaning in children's lives*. New York: Oxford University Press.

Campbell, P. S. (2002). The musical culture of children. In L. Bresler & C. Thompson (Eds.), *The arts in children's lives: Context, culture, and curriculum* (pp. 57–70). Dordrecht: Kluwer.

Carr, W., & Kemmis, S. (1986). *Becoming critical: Education, knowledge and action research*. London: Falmer.

Charles, B. (2004). Boys' and girls' constructions of gender through musical composition in the primary school. *British Journal of Music Education, 21*(3), 265–277.

Cockshut, A. O. J. (1984). *The art of autobiography*. New Haven: Yale University Press.

Cohen, V. (1980). The emergence of musical gestures in kindergarten children. Unpublished doctoral dissertation, University of Illinois at Urbana-Champaign.

Couperin, F. (1933). *L'Art de toucher le clavecin*. Wiesbaden, Germany: Breitkopf & Hartel. (Originally published in 1717)

Crafts, S., Cavicchi, D., & Keil, C. (1993). *My music*. Hanover, NH: Wesleyan University Press.

Cronbach, L. J. (1971). Test validation. In R. L. Thorndike (Ed.). *Educational measurement,* 2nd ed. (pp. 443–507). Washington, DC: American Council on Education.

DeLorenzo, L. (1987). An exploratory field of sixth grade students' creative music problem solving processes in the general music class. Unpublished doctoral dissertation, Teachers College, Columbia University, New York.

DeNora, T. (2000). *Music in everyday life.* Cambridge: Cambridge University Press.

Denzin, N. K. (1970). *The research act.* New York: Aldine.

Denzin, N. K. (1989). *Interpretative biography.* Beverly Hills: Sage.

Denzin, N., & Lincoln, Y. (Eds.). (1994). *Handbook of qualitative research.* Thousand Oaks, CA: Sage.

Denzin, N., & Lincoln, Y. (Eds.). (2000). *Handbook of qualitative research,* 2nd ed. Thousand Oaks, CA: Sage.

Denzin, N., & Lincoln, Y. (Eds.). (2006). *Handbook of qualitative research,* 3rd ed. Thousand Oaks, CA: Sage.

De Vries, P. (1999). *The researcher as subject: Using autobiography to examine the nature of being a classroom primary music teacher.* Unpublished doctoral dissertation, Griffith University, Queensland, Australia.

Dewey, J. (1958). *Art as experience.* New York: Putnam's.

Dilthey, W. (1900/1976). *Selected writings.* (H. P. Rickman, Ed. & Trans.). Cambridge: Cambridge University Press.

Dilthey, W. (1910). *The construction of the historical world of the human studies. (Der Aufbauder Welt in den Geisteswissen-schaften).* Gesammelte Schriften I–VII. Leipzig: B. G. Teubner, 1914–1927.

Dreeben, R. (1968). *On what is learned in school.* Reading, MA: Addison-Wesley.

Dunbar-Hall, P., & Wemyss, K. (1999). Analysis and popular music: A challenge for music education. *Research Studies in Music Education, 13,* 40–55.

Dunbar-Hall, P., & Wemyss, K. (2000). The effects of the study of popular music on music education. *International Journal of Music Education, 36,* 23–34.

Dzansi, M. P. (2002). Some manifestations of Ghanaian indigenous culture in children's singing games. Retrieved from *http://ijea.asu.edu/v3n7/.*

Eisner, E. (1979). *The educational imagination: On the design and evaluation of school programs.* New York: Macmillan.

Eisner, E. (1988). The primacy of experience and the politics of method. *Educational Researcher, 17*(5), 15–20.

Eisner, E. (1991). *The enlightened eye: Qualitative inquiry and the enactment of educational practice.* New York: Macmillan.

Elbaz, R. (1987). *The changing nature of the self: A critical study of the autobiographical discourse.* Iowa City: University of Iowa Press.

Elkoshy, R. (2002). An investigation into children's responses through drawing, to short musical fragments and complete compositions. *Music Education Research, (4)*2, 199–211.

Elkoshy, R. (2004). Is music "colorful"? A study of the effects of age and musical literacy on children's notational color expressions. *International Journal of Education and the Arts, 5*(2). Retrieved from http://ijea.asu.edu/v5n2/.

Erickson, F. (1986). Qualitative methods in research on teaching. In Merlin C. Wittrock (Ed.), *Handbook on teaching,* 3rd ed. New York: Macmillan.

Espeland, M. (2003). The African drum: The compositional process as discourse and interaction in a school context. In M. Hickey (Ed.), *Why and how to teach music composition: A new horizon for music education* (pp. 167–192). Reston, VA: MENC.

Finney, J. (2003). From resentment to enchantment: What a class of thirteen year olds and their music teacher tell us about a musical education. *International Journal of Education and the Arts, 4*(6). Retrieved from http://ijea .asu.edu/v4n6/.

Flolu, J. (2000). Re-thinking arts education in Ghana. *Arts Education Policy Review, 101*(5), 25–29.

Folkestad, G. (1996). *Computer-based creative music making: Young people's music in the digital age*. Published doctoral dissertation, ACTA University, Gothenburg, Sweden.

Folkestad, G. (2000). Editorial. *International Journal of Music Education, 36*, 1–3.

Folkestad, G., Lindstrom, B., & Hargreaves, D. (1997). Young people's music in the digital age: A study of computer based creative music making. *Research Studies in Music Education, 9*, 1–12.

Foucault, M. (1977) *Discipline and punish: The birth of the prison* (Trans. A. Sheridan). New York: Pantheon.

Freundlich, D. (1978). The development of musical thinking case-studies in improvisation. Unpublished doctoral dissertation, Harvard University, Cambridge.

Frith, S. (1996). *Performing rites: On the value of popular music*. Cambridge: Harvard University Press.

Garrison, V. (1985). *Traditional and non-traditional teaching and learning practices in folk music*. Unpublished doctoral dissertation, University of Wisconsin, Madison.

Gerber, L. (1975). An examination of three early childhood programs in relation to early childhood music education. Unpublished doctoral dissertation, University of Illinois at Urbana-Champaign.

Geertz, C. (1973). *The interpretation of cultures*. New York: Basic Books.

Geertz, C. (1988). *Works and lives: The anthropologist as author*. Stanford, CA: Stanford University Press.

Glaser, G. A., & Strauss, A. L. (1967). *The discovery of grounded theory: Strategies for qualitative research*. Chicago: Aldine.

Goetz, J. P., & LeCompte, M. D. (1984). *Ethnography and qualitative design in educational research*. San Francisco: Academic Press.

Goodman, N. (1968). *The languages of art*. Indianapolis: Hackett.

Gouzouasis, P., & Lee, K. V. (2002). Do you hear what I hear? Musicians composing the truth. *Teacher Education Quarterly, 29*(4), 125–141.

Green, L. (1993). Music, gender and education: A report of some exploratory research. *British Journal of Music Education, 10*, 219–253.

Green, L. (1997). *Music, gender, education*. Cambridge: Cambridge University Press.

Green, L. (1999). Research in the sociology of music education: Some introductory concepts. *Music Education Research, 1*(2), 159–169.

Green, L. (2001). *How popular musicians learn: A way ahead for music education*. Aldershot, England: Ashgate.

Gromko, J. (1996). In a child's voice: An interpretive interaction with young composers. *Bulletin of the Council for Research in Music Education, 128*, 47–58.

Grumet, M. (1988). *Bitter milk: Women and teaching.* Amherst: University of Massachusetts Press.

Guba, E., & Lincoln, Y. (1981). *Effective evaluation.* San Francisco: Jossey-Bass.

Habermas, J. (1971). *Knowledge and human interests.* (J. J. Shapiro, Trans.). Boston: Beacon.

Hamilton, D. (1977). Making sense of curriculum evaluation: Continuities and discontinuities in an educational idea. *Review of Research in Education, 5,* 318–347.

Harris, D. (2002). A report on the situation regarding teaching music to Muslims in an inner-city school. *British Journal of Music Education, 19*(1), 49–60.

Harwood, E. (1987). The memorized song repertoire of children in grades four and five. Unpublished doctoral dissertation, University of Illinois at Urbana-Champaign.

Hempel, C. (1966). *Philosophy of natural sciences.* London: Prentice Hall.

Henry, J. (1966). *On education.* New York: Random House.

Herbert, D., & Campbell, P. (2000). Rock music in American schools: Positions and practices since the 1960s. *International Journal of Music Education, 36,* 14–22.

Herbst, A., Nzewi, M., & Agawu, K. (Eds.). (2003). *Musical arts in Africa: Theory, practice and education.* Pretoria, South Africa: University of South Africa Press.

Hickey, M. (Ed.). (2003). *Why and how to teach music composition.* Reston, VA: National Association for Music Education (MENC).

House, E. (1980). *Evaluating with validity.* Beverly Hills, CA: Sage.

Howe, K., & Eisenhart, M. (1990). Standards for qualitative (and quantitative) research: A prolegomenon. *Educational Researcher, 19*(4), 2–9.

Huberman, A. M., & Miles, M. B. (1984). *Innovation up close: How school improvement works.* New York: Plenum.

Jackson, P. (1968). *Life in classrooms.* New York: Holt, Rinehart and Winston.

Jelinek, E. C. (Ed.). (1980). *Women's autobiography: Essays in criticism.* Bloomington: Indiana University Press.

Kagan, D. M. (1989). The heuristic value of regarding classroom instruction as an aesthetic medium. *Educational Researcher, 18*(6), 11–18.

Kalekin-Fishman, D. (1981). Ts'lilim ufikuach: R'chisshath mussag hamusika b'ganei Y'lakim [Sounds and control: The acquisition of the concept of music in the kindergarten.] *Mah'beroth L'mebkar ul'vikoreth [Notebooks of Research and Criticism],* 6 5–16.

Kalekin-Fishman, D. (1986). Music and not-music in kindergartens. *Journal of Research in Music Education, 34*(1), 54–68.

Kant, I. (1969). *Kritik der Urteilskraft* (S. H. Bergman, Trans.). Copyright by The Bialik Institute, Jerusalem.

Keil, C. (1966). *Urban blues.* Chicago: University of Chicago.

Klinger, R. (1996). From glockenspiel to mbira: An ethnography of multicultural practice in music education. *Bulletin of the Council for Research in Music Education, 128,* 29–36.

Klofas, J. J., & Cutshall, C. R. (1985). The social archeology of a juvenile facility: Unobtrusive methods in the study of institutional culture. *Qualitative Sociology, 8*(4), 368–387.

Kohut, D., & Grant, J. (1990). *Learning to conduct and rehearse.* Englewood Cliffs, NJ: Prentice Hall.

Kokotsaki, D., Davidson, J., & Coimbra, D. (2001). Investigating the assessment of singers in a music college setting: The students' perspective. *Research Studies in Music Education, 16,* 15–32.

Koza, J. (1990). Music instruction in the nineteenth century: Views from Frody's *Lady's Book,* 1830–77. *Journal of Research in Music Education, 38*(4), 245–257.

Koza, J. (1993). The "missing males" and other gender issues in music education: Evidence from the *Music Supervisors' Journal,* 1914–1924. *Journal of Research in Music Education, 41*(3), 212–232.

Krueger, P. J. (1985). Influences of the hidden curriculum upon the perspectives of music student teachers. Unpublished doctoral dissertation, University of Wisconsin, Madison.

Krueger, P. J. (1987). Ethnographic research methodology in music education. *Journal of Research in Music Education, 35*(2), 69–77.

Kushner, S. (1985). Working dreams: Innovation in a conservatoire. Unpublished report, University of East Anglia, United Kingdom.

Kushner, S. (1989). St. Joseph's Hospice: A music performance and communication skills evaluation case study. Unpublished report, University of East Anglia, United Kingdom.

L'Roy, D. (1983). The development of occupational identity in undergraduate music education majors. Unpublished doctoral dissertation, North Texas State University, Denton.

Lamb, R. (1990). Are there gender issues in school music? *Canadian Music Educator, 31*(6), 9–13.

Lamb, R. (1996). Discords: Feminist pedagogy in music education. *Theory into Practice, 35*(2), 124–131.

Lamb, R., Dolloff, L., & Howe, S. (2002). Feminism, feminist research, and gender research in music education. In R. Colwell & C. Richardson (Eds.), *The new handbook on music teaching and learning* (pp. 648–674.) New York: Oxford University Press.

Leung, C. C. (2002). The role of Chinese music in secondary school education in Hong Kong. Unpublished doctoral dissertation, RMIT University.

Leung, C. C. (2004). Curriculum and culture: A model for content selections and teaching approaches in music. *British Journal of Music Education, 21*(1), 25–39.

Lewers, J. M. (1980). Rehearsal as the search for expressiveness: Implications for music reading in the high school mixed chorus. Unpublished doctoral dissertation, Teachers College, Columbia University, New York.

Lincoln, Y. S., & Guba, E. G. (1985). *Naturalistic inquiry.* New York: Sage.

Lincoln, Y. S., & Guba, E. G. (1986). But is it rigorous? Trustworthiness and authenticity in naturalistic evaluation. In D. D. William (Ed.), *Naturalistic evaluation: New directions for program evaluation,* No. 30. San Francisco: Jossey-Bass.

Lincoln, Y. S., & Guba, E. G. (1988). *Criteria for assessing naturalistic inquiries as reports.* Paper presented at the annual meeting of the American Education Research Association, New Orleans.

Mans, M. (1995). Music education in Namibia: An overview. In L. Lepherd (Ed.), *Music education in international perspective: National systems* (pp. 52–65). Toowoomba, Australia: University of Southern Queensland Press.

Mans, M. E. (2000). Using Namibian music/dance traditions as a basis for reforming arts education in Namibia. *International Journal of Education & the Arts, 1*(3).

Mans, M. E. (2002). Playing the music: Comparing children's song and dance in Namibian education. In L. Bresler & C. Thompson (Eds.), *The arts in children's lives: Context, culture, and curriculum* (pp. 71–86). Dordrecht, Netherlands: Kluwer.

Mans, M. E. (2004). The changing body in Southern Africa: A perspective from ethnomusicology. In L. Bresler (Ed.), *Knowing bodies, moving minds: Embodied knowledge in arts education and schooling* (pp. 77–96). Dordrecht, Netherlands: Kluwer.

Marsh, K. (1995). Children's singing games: Composition in the playground? *Research Studies in Music Education, 4*, 2–11.

Marsh, K. (1999). Mediated orality: The role of popular music in the changing tradition of children's musical play. *Research Studies in Music Education, 13*, 2–11.

May, W. (1990). Teaching for understanding in the arts. *Quarterly, 1*(1 & 2), 5–16.

McCarthy, M. (1999). Gendered discourse and the construction of identity: Toward a liberated pedagogy in music education. *Journal of Aesthetic Education, 33*(4), 109–125.

McCarthy, M. (2002). Social and cultural contexts of music teaching and learning: An introduction. In R. Colwell & C. Richardson (Eds.), *The new handbook on music teaching and learning* (pp. 563–565). New York: Oxford University Press.

Merriam, A. (1964). *The anthropology of music.* Chicago: Northwestern University Press.

Merriam, A. (1967). *Ethnomusicology of the Flathead Indians.* Chicago: Aldine.

Miles, M. B., & Huberman, A. M. (1984). *Qualitative data analysis: A sourcebook of new methods.* Beverly Hills, CA: Sage.

Miller, B. (1994–1995). Integrating elementary music instruction with a whole language first-grade classroom. *Bulletin of the Council for Research in Music Education, 123*, 36–38.

Miller, B. A. (1997). Collaboration: The bonus prize in the research package. *Teacher Research: The Journal of Classroom Inquiry, 5*(1), 57–74.

Miller, B. A. (2004). Designing compositional tasks for elementary music classrooms. *Research Studies in Music Education, 22*, 59–71.

Mishler, E. G. (1986). *Research interviewing.* Cambridge: Harvard University Press.

Moorhead, G., & Pond, D. (1941, 1942, 1944, 1951). *Music of young children* (Vols. 1–4). Vancouver: Pillsbury Foundation.

Nash, R. J. (1987). The convergence of anthropology and education. In G. Spindler (Ed.), *Education and cultural process.* Prospect Heights, IL: Waveland.

Nettl, B. (1983). *Twenty-nine issues and concepts.* Urbana: University of Illinois Press.

Nettl, B. (1987). *The radif of Persian music: Studies of structure and cultural context.* Champaign, IL: Elephant & Cat.

Nettl, B. (2002). What's to be learned? Comments on teaching on teaching music in the world and teaching world music at home. In L. Bresler & C. Thompson (Eds.), *The arts in children's lives: Context, culture, and curriculum* (pp. 29–42). Dordrecht, Netherlands: Kluwer.

Nzewi, Meki (2002). Backcloth to music and healing in traditional African society. [online] *Voices: A World Forum for Music Therapy*. Retrieved October 5, 2005, from http://www.voices.no/mainissues/Voices2(2)nzewi.html

Olson, D. (1978). The arts as basic skills: Three cognitive functions of symbols. In S. S. Madeja (Ed.), *The arts, cognition, and basic skills* (pp. 59–81). St. Louis: CEMREL.

Oppondo, P. (2000). Cultural policies in Kenya. *Arts Education Policy Review, 101*(5), 18–24.

Peshkin, A. (1988). In search of subjectivity—One's own. *Educational Researcher, 17*(7), 17–21.

Popper, K. (1959). *The logic of scientific discovery*. New York: Basic Books.

Popper, K. (1969). *Conjectures and refutations*. London: Routledge & Kegan Paul.

Poston-Anderson, B., & de Vries, P. (2000) The Peter Piper pickled pepper mystery: Arts educators collaborate to create a musical play for pre-schoolers. *International Journal of Education and the Arts, 1*(5).

Powell, K. (2003). *Learning together: Practice, pleasure and identity in a Taiko drumming world*. Unpublished doctoral dissertation, Stanford University.

Powell, K. (2004). Apprenticing the mind in Japanese American *Taiko* drumming. In L. Bresler (Ed.), *Knowing bodies, moving minds: Towards embodied teaching and learning* (pp. 183–196). Dordrecht, Netherlands: Kluwer.

Powell, K. (2005). Inside-out and outside-in: Participant observation in taiko drumming. In G. Spindler & L. Hammond (Eds.), *Innovations in educational ethnography: Theory, methods and results*. Mahwah, NJ: Lawrence Erlbaum.

Rainwater, L., & Pittman, D. (1969). Ethical problems in studying a politically sensitive and deviant community. In G. J. McCall & J. L. Simmons (Eds.), *Issues in participant observation*. Reading, MA: Addison-Wesley.

Rorty, R. (1982). *Consequences of pragmatism*. Minneapolis: University of Minnesota Press.

Rorty, R. (1989). *Contingency, irony and solidarity*. Cambridge: Cambridge University Press.

Sartre, J.-P. (1981). *The family idiot: Gustave Flaubert* (Vol. 1 1821–1857). Chicago: University of Chicago Press. (Originally published 1971)

Schatzman, L., & Strauss, A. (1973). *Field research: Strategies for a natural sociology*. Englewood Cliffs, NJ: Prentice Hall.

Schmidt, M. (1998). Defining "good" music teaching: Four student teachers' beliefs and practices. *Bulletin of the Council for Research in Music Education, 138*, 19–46.

Schutz, A. (1962). *Collected Papers, Vol. I: The problem of social reality* (M. Natanson, Ed.). The Hague: Martinus Nijhoff.

Silva, W. (2004). Keeping on the sunny side: A case study of teaching and learning music in an American old-time string band ensemble. In J. L. Aróstegui (Ed.), *The social context of music education* (pp. 81–126). Urbana: CIRCE, University of Illinois.

Silvey, P. E. (2004a). Ingrid and her music: An adolescent choral singer comes to know musical works. In J. L. Aróstegui (Ed.), *The social context of music education* (pp. 11–45). Urbana: CIRCE, University of Illinois.

Silvey, P. E. (2004b). Acquaintance knowledge of musical works in the secondary choral classroom. *Arts and Learning Research Journal, 20*(1), 111–133.

Smith, J. K., & Heshusius, L. (1986). Closing down the conversation: The end of the quantitative-qualitative debate among educational inquirers. *Educational Researcher*, 4–12.

Smith, L. M. (1978). An evolving logic of participant observation, educational ethnography and other case studies. In L. Shulman (Ed.), *Review of research in education* (Vol. 6). Chicago: Peacock.

Soderman, J., & Folkestad, G. (2004) How hip-hop musicians learn: Strategies in informal creative music making. *Music Education Research*, 6(3), 313–326.

Sosniak, L. A. (1985). Learning to be a concert pianist. In B. Bloom (Ed.), *Developing talent in young people* (pp. 19–67). New York: Ballantine.

Spacks, P. (1976). *Imagining a self: Autobiography and novel in eighteenth-century England*. Cambridge: Harvard University Press.

Spindler, G. (Ed.). (1963). *Education and culture*. New York: Holt, Rinehart, & Winston.

Spindler, G. (1982). *Doing the ethnography of schooling*. New York: Holt, Rinehart, & Winston.

Stake, R. E. (1978). The case study method in social inquiry. *Educational Researcher*, 7(2), 5–8.

Stake, R. E., Bresler, L., & Mabry, L. (1991). *Custom and cherishing*. Urbana: Council for Research in Music Education.

Stake, R. E., Easley, J., Denny, T., Smith, M. L., Peskin, A., Welch, W. W., et al. (1978). *Case studies in science education*. Washington, DC: U.S. Government Printing Office.

Stake, R. E., & Trumbull, D. (1982). Naturalistic generalizations. *Review Journal of Philosophy & Social Science*, 7(1–2).

Stalhammar, B. (2000). The spaces of music and its foundation of values: Music teaching and young people's own music experience. *International Journal of Music Education*, 36. 35–45.

Stanley, J. (1990). Doing democracy: Cato Park School and the study of education in school settings. Paper presented at the annual meeting of the American Education Research Association, Boston.

Stauffer, S. L. (1999). Sociological and cultural cues in the compositions of children and adolescents. In M. S. Moore, G. E. McPherson, & R. Smith (Eds.), *Children and music: Developmental perspectives*. (Proceedings of the second Asia-Pacific Symposium on Music Education Research). Launceston, Australia: University of Tasmania.

Stauffer, S. L. (2001). Composing with computers: Meg makes music. *Bulletin of the Council for Research in Music Education*, 150, 1–20.

Stauffer, S. L. (2002). Connections between music and life experiences of young composers and their compositions. *Journal of Research in Music Education*, 50, 301–322.

Strauss, A. (1987). *Qualitative analysis for social scientists*. Cambridge: Cambridge University Press.

Sundin, B., McPherson, G., & Folkestad, G. (1998). *Children composition*. Malmo and Lund, Sweden: Malmo Academy of Music and Lund University.

Thiel, C. R. (1984). Participant observation: Study of a fourth grade music classroom. Unpublished doctoral dissertation, University of Illinois at Urbana-Champaign.

Treacher, V. 1989. Classroom issues in assessment and evaluation in the arts. Reading, England: Berkshire Local Education Authority.

Turino, T. (2000). *Nationalists, cosmpolitans, and popular music in Zimbabwe.* Chicago: University of Chicago Press.

Upitis, R. (1985). Children's understanding of rhythm: The relationship between development and musical training. Unpublished doctoral dissertation, Harvard University, Cambridge.

Upitis, R. (1992). *Can I play you my song? The compositions and invented notations of children.* Portsmouth, NH: Heinemann.

Veblen, K. (1996). Truth, perception, and cultural constructs in ethnographic research: Music teaching and learning in Ireland. *Bulletin of the Council for Research in Music Education, 129,* 37–52

Von Gunden, H. (1983). *The music of Pauline Oliveros.* London: Scarecrow.

Von Wright, G. (1971). *Explanation and understanding.* London: Routledge & Kegan Paul.

Wagner, J. (1990). Field research as a full participant in schools and other settings. Paper presented at the annual meeting of the American Education Research Association, Boston.

Webb, E., Campbell, D. T., Schwartz, R. D., & Sechrest, L. (1966). *Unobtrusive measures: Nonreactive research in the social sciences.* Chicago: Rand McNally.

Webb, E., Campbell, D. T., Schwartz, R. D., & Sechrest, L. (1981). *Nonreactive measures in the social sciences.* Boston: Houghton Mifflin.

Weber, M. (1949). *Methodology of the social sciences.* (E. Shils & H. Finch, Trans.). Glencoe, IL: Free Press.

Wiggins, J. H. (1994). Children's strategies for solving compositional problems with peers. *Journal of Research in Music Education, 42*(3), 232–252.

Wiggins, J. (1999–2000). The nature of shared musical understanding and its role in empowering independent musical thinking. *Bulletin of the Council for Research in Music Education, 143,* 65–90.

Wiggins, J. (2002). Creative process as meaningful music thinking. In T. Sullivan & L. Wilignham (Eds.), *Creativity and music education* (pp. 78–88). Terrance Bay, ON: Canadian Music Educators' Association National Office.

Yin, R. K. (1984). *Case studies in research design: Design and methods.* Beverly Hills, CA: Sage.

Younker, B. A. (2003). Fifth grade students' involvement in composition: A teacher's internationality. *Music Education International, 2,* 22–35.

Younker, B. A., & Smith, W. H. (1996). Comparing and modeling musical thought processes of expert and novice composers. *Bulletin of the Council for Research in Music Education, 128,* 25–36.

Zeller, N. (1987). A rhetoric for naturalistic inquiry. Unpublished doctoral dissertation, Indiana University, Bloomington.

Contemporary Issues in Qualitative Research and Music Education

8

DAVID J. FLINDERS

CAROL P. RICHARDSON

In the first edition of the *Handbook of Research on Music Teaching and Learning,* Donald Casey (1992) used the broad term "descriptive research" to include common forms of qualitative inquiry. In the introduction to his chapter, Casey said: "Despite some speculation to the contrary, descriptive research should by no means be conceived as any less vigorous, worthwhile, or useful than other research modes" (p. 115). Although critics remain (e.g. Shavelson & Towne, 2002), qualitative researchers today face less "speculation to the contrary." Leading universities, journals, and book publishers now give qualitative studies an increasingly high profile. Professional organizations, such as the American Educational Research Association, have institutionalized qualitative approaches as a viable alternative to large-sample, statistical studies, and doctoral programs now provide expanded training in qualitative methods. Together with these opportunities, the number of qualitative researchers has multiplied. Their ranks have grown so quickly over the past decade that it is difficult to find a more prominent trend in the field of educational research. Who and what have contributed to this trend are among the questions raised in this chapter.

We will argue that the growth of qualitative research is more than simply a matter of numbers. Instead, recent developments revolve around large issues, as researchers rethink the questions of what counts as a rigorous, worthwhile, and useful study. To take one example, research methodologists have increasingly questioned the value of applying quantitative criteria to qualitative work. We no longer ask qualitative researchers for hypotheses stated specifically to test causal relationships. We no longer ask for independent and dependent variables, let alone that these variables be operationalized in a way that allows for objective measurement. Qualitative researchers do begin their work with what Malinowski (1922/1984) called "foreshadowed problems" (p. 9). They are also interested in the perceived antecedents of what they observe. Today, however, the distinctions between hypotheses and orienting questions, or between causes and perceived antecedents, are recognized more widely and regarded as more important than they once were.

This growing differentiation among genres of empirical research has been motivated partly by a proliferation of traditions and approaches within qualitative inquiry itself. Earlier qualitative work drew primarily on its parent disciplines in the social sciences. Thus, a qualitative study was often viewed as falling within the same family as its more quantitative siblings. Today qualitative researchers draw on a broader gene pool, so to speak. In addition to the social sciences, they look to the arts, the humanities, and a range of professional studies. As a result, many of the recent approaches represent more distant kin, relatives who live by different customs and different cultures. Having more voices around the table has presented both challenges and opportunities. In this chapter we also consider these challenges and opportunities.

One challenge worth mentioning is that researchers who now turn to qualitative inquiry face what may seem like a bewildering array of possibilities for how to conceptualize, carry out, and write up a qualitative study. These possibilities open the door to new research questions, thereby serving a critical function, but they also heighten the need for researchers to explicitly situate their work within the traditions of which it is a part. With more options, less can be taken for granted. One cannot assume, for example, that a qualitative study participates in ethnographic traditions simply because it employs qualitative methods (Eisner, 1998; Wolcott, 1982). It would be a categorical mistake to fault educational criticism, school portraiture, biographic case studies, narrative inquiry, and other nonethnographic approaches because they do not adhere to the canons set down by the likes of Malinowski, Mead, or even Geertz.

For this reason, in this chapter we seek to acknowledge the variety of qualitative approaches now used in education. Overall, the chapter is divided into two sections. The first section surveys qualitative trends, approaches, and continuing dilemmas within the field of educational research at large. As such, the focus of our survey is necessarily broad. On all counts, however, it should not be viewed as comprehensive because the relevant literature is now so large that we have left out far more than we have included. In deciding what to include, our aim has been to highlight some of the major landmarks of qualitative inquiry as a field of methodological study. Where details are provided, we have done so largely to illustrate broader categories or characteristics of qualitative work. We have also limited our review to the period of the 1960s to the present. Although the disciplinary roots and contributions to qualitative research go back much further, qualitative work has made its most significant gains in the field of education only over the past 4 decades.

The second section of the chapter examines trends and issues in qualitative research that are specific to music education. Here the literature is less extensive, but qualitative research on music teaching and learning is often similar to as well as distinctive from the broader contours of educational research. In this context, both similarities and differences deserve close attention.

The Rise of Qualitative Research and Its Aftermath

The rise of qualitative research in education defies simple explanation. Its exact causes and extent are especially difficult to pin down for at least two reasons. First, we are referring not to a single trend but to multiple changes in how researchers think about and carry out their work. Patterns in the overall development of qualitative research run parallel and intersect at various points, forming a confluence of permutations around similar but not identical themes. Like the field itself, its development has been anything but linear or monolithic.

Second, qualitative research has a range of different meanings. Even the name *qualitative* has been debated (Eisner, 1998, p. 5; Lincoln & Guba, 1985, p. 7). A few of its potential synonyms, for example, include *naturalistic, descriptive, interpretive, case study,* and *field-based research.* We will use the term *qualitative* because it is currently the most common and inclusive way in which researchers describe this broad style, category, and means of inquiry. Deciding on a label, however, only begs the larger question: What is qualitative research? For our purposes, we define qualitative research as work that illustrates at least some of the following characteristics. First, qualitative studies are a systematic form of empirical inquiry that usually includes some type of fieldwork. Artifacts such as textbooks and curriculum materials may be the focus of study, but qualitative work is typically field based, so that researchers may attend to the context in which events unfold. Second, once in the field, qualitative researchers are expected to do more than mechanically record their observations. To put this another way, their ability to see and hear is regarded as an achievement rather than a task, and knowledge is viewed as something constructed rather than as something given, found, or existing independently of the researchers. Third, qualitative studies usually assume an interpretive focus. Researchers may seek to understand the meanings of educational experiences from the participants' perspective (the so-called emic view), with respect to theory (the etic view), or both. The point, however, is that qualitative research is designed to examine *meaning* as a social, psychological, or political phenomenon. Fourth, data analysis strategies in qualitative research are typically thematic and sometimes emergent throughout the course of a study. Fifth, qualitative researchers usually work with small samples of voluntary participants (see also Bogdan & Biklen, 1998, pp. 4–7; Eisner, 1998, pp. 27–41).

These five characteristics are typical but not strict criteria for doing qualitative research. Some qualitative researchers work with large-sample data sets, some collect data solely at their office computers via the internet (which is fieldwork of a different sort), and some researchers, those who do observational studies, do not work directly with participants at all. Our point is not to limit the definition of qualitative research by laying claim to a specific set of theories, techniques, or beliefs. Rather, as Wolcott (1992) writes,

> to claim competence in qualitative research is, at most, to claim general familiarity with what is currently being done, coupled perhaps, with experience in one or two particular facets (e.g., to "be good at" collecting and interpreting life histories, or to "be" a symbolic interactionist). (p. 4)

This lack of precise definitions and clear criteria is sometimes viewed as problematic, but it does not seem to have prevented qualitative research from gaining increased acceptance over the past four decades.

The 1960s: Germination

Our review begins with the 1960s, a decade that represents not so much growth per se as rather the germination of renewed interest in qualitative work. At that time, educational research remained largely in the embrace of what Cronbach and Suppes (1969, p. 45) called "the heyday of empiricism" and especially its legacy of quantification. The broader foundations of this legacy stretch back directly through Edward L. Thorndike and his aspirations for a "complete science of psychology." Such a science, Thorndike (1910) wrote, "would tell the cause of every change in human nature, would tell the result which every educational force . . . would have" (p. 6). Thorndike's analogies were with physics and chemistry, suggesting that psychological and educational research should strive toward similar aims. As already implied, the aims he specified were those of prediction and control.

Today his view is often regarded as naive, if not utopian in an ignoble sense. Forty years ago, however, most educational researchers still looked to experimental science and its underlying epistemology of logical positivism as the model for their work. Qualitative and interpretive studies were carried out, but these studies generally went unnoticed even when researchers dressed them up to appear more "scientific" than they actually were. Denzin and Lincoln (1994, p. 8) refer to this period as "the golden age of rigorous qualitative analysis," citing Becker, Geer, Hughes and Strauss's (1961) study of medical education, *Boys in White,* as a "canonical" text of the period. In part, such studies reflect an effort to align qualitative research with the type of conventional criteria outlined in Campbell and Stanley's popular 1963 monograph on experimental and quasi-experimental research designs. Qualitative studies also looked to minor but well-established traditions in the sociology of education (e.g., Waller's classic 1932 study *Sociology of Teaching*) and to the case study work of the Chicago School sociologists (Bogdan & Biklin, 1998, pp. 8–11).

Anthropological studies of education represent what was perhaps the only other home for qualitative work in the 1960s. In particular, George Spindler edited two volumes, *Education and Anthropology* (1955) and *Education and Culture* (1963), that helped provide the foundations for the ethnography of schooling, which would soon become a productive category of qualitative research. Looking back on the 1963 volume in a later work, Spindler and Spindler (1992) commented: "The fact that the commitment to direct observation is more apparent in the papers that deal with educational process in non-Western societies than those at home is an indication that anthropologists had only begun their work in our own society" (p. 57). Here the Spindlers were noting the beginnings of domestic anthropology, another trend that would further opportunities for qualitative researchers in education. Nevertheless, ties with traditional anthropology in the 1960s remained important for establishing the legitimacy of qualitative research as a form of discipline-based inquiry.

Other sources (e.g., Vidich & Lyman, 1994) have reviewed the history of qualitative research in fields such as sociology and anthropology. In education, most of the early qualitative studies were conducted by researchers whose primary identifications were with their parent disciplines rather than with the field of education itself. Philip Jackson's classic study *Life in Classrooms* (1968) is in some ways an exception that proves the rule. Its significance was the rarity of an educational researcher spending a year observing classes in an actual school. Jackson's work also overlapped quantitative and qualitative traditions, but if nothing else his style suggested broader possibilities for educational research. As Eisner (1998) writes: "What resulted from Jackson's observations was an insightful, artistically crafted book remembered more for its metaphors and insight than for the nods Jackson gave to the quantitative data he presented in its second half" (p. 13).

The decade of the 1960s was not known for producing a wealth of exemplar qualitative studies in education, although as we have already noted, sociological and anthropological field-based research continued to build on earlier traditions. Probably more influential in educational circles were books outside the field suggesting alternative perspectives on the structure and processes of research at large. Two such books foreshadowed future debates. The first was Thomas Kuhn's book *The Structure of Scientific Revolutions* (1962). Kuhn's historical perspective on science popularized the notion that researchers conceptualize topics of study and carry out their work within broad theoretical frameworks represented by the paradigm of a field. Kuhn's work brought two assumptions into question: the logical progression of science and, because a priori paradigms help determine what count as data, the objectivity of science in deciding questions of fact (see also Donmoyer, 1990, pp. 179–181; Phillips, 1990, pp. 31–34). A second book was Barney Glaser and Anselm Strauss's *Discovery of Grounded Theory*. Glaser and Strauss's perspective emphasized the mutual interaction between theory and data. Although largely a technical approach, grounded theory served to broaden the conventional assumptions that the primary aims of research are restricted to theory testing or theory verification (see also Creswell, 1998). Instead, qualitative researchers could view their work as a means of generating theory through repeated observations and emergent themes.

The 1970s: Growth

Qualitative developments in education signaled both continuity and change during the 1970s. Continuation of discipline-based studies not only held steady but also embraced a wider range of research. In educational anthropology, the term *ethnography* found its way into the field, and the ethnography of schooling increasingly focused on individual cases (Spindler & Spindler, 1992, pp. 57–58). Moreover, these cases were closer to home than previous studies had been. Domestic ethnographies of this decade are illustrated by Harry Wolcott's book *The Man in the Principal's Office* (1973) and Alan Peshkin's *Growing Up American* (1978). Although Peshkin's title looks back to the work of Mead, his reference predates (as does his book eschew) the 1960s tendency to drape qualitative studies in the names and games of experimental science.

A more general break from this tendency is also found in Clifford Geertz's book *The Interpretation of Cultures* (1973). This widely read book is remembered for popularizing Gilbert Ryle's term "thick description." For Geertz, the point of thick description was not to produce an objective record of culture but to make sense of events in local settings through the process of writing. When confronted with a puzzling experience, ethnographers write, and writing was seen as a matter of interpretation rather than the discovery of scientific laws. Geertz's emphasis on thick description as a means to understand "local knowledge" (Geertz, 1983) served to further distinguish the aims of qualitative inquiry. Interpretation, in this respect, provided a point on which qualitative researchers could begin defining their own rules rather than trying to play by the rules of someone else's game.

Seeking alternatives to the language of experimental science, qualitative researchers found support and guidance on other fronts as well. Hermeneutic philosophers, for example, were in the midst of epistemological debates that questioned whether knowledge is somehow waiting to be discovered, independent of the discovery and its discoverers, or contingent on the history and context in which it is produced. In particular, qualitative researchers were drawn to the work of Jürgen Habermas (1971, 1975) and Hans-Georg Gadamer (1975), who to different degrees argued for the contingency of knowledge (Smith, 1993). Their arguments again gave increasing support to the interpretive dimensions of inquiry. "Hermeneutics has a practical bent," Noddings (1995) later wrote. "It tries to make sense out of history and contemporary contexts without tying either to a rigid theoretical foundation" (p. 71).

Qualitative research in education also received help from a closer and often unrecognized source; that is, quantitative researchers who were beginning to abandon Thorndike's aspirations for a "complete science" of education. Some of these researchers, once hard-nosed positivists, came to align themselves with constructivist views of knowledge. Lee Cronbach is the most prominent example in this category. In his 1974 address to the American Psychological Association, Cronbach (1975, p. 123) acknowledged that the complexity and changeability of culture prevented the social sciences from accumulating the type of generalizations found in the natural sciences. Cronbach's stature as a psychometrician—who he was—no doubt put tremendous weight behind his concerns. He was not, however, the only leading figure to rethink his earlier beliefs with respect to quantitative and qualitative forms of research. In 1963, Donald Campbell and Julian Stanley described case studies as the least defensible design for social research. By the end of the 1970s, however, Campbell (1979, p. 52) had nearly reversed his position, arguing that when qualitative studies contradict quantitative results, "the quantitative results should be regarded as suspect until the reasons for the discrepancy are well understood" (quoted in Scholfield, 1990, p. 206).

These developments gave qualitative researchers the opportunity to promote their work as a distinctive genre of educational inquiry, and subsequent lines of scholarship have pursued this goal. At the close of the 1970s, however, some researchers had begun another trend by proposing approaches that departed not only from large-sample, quantitative research but also from the leading forms of discipline-based qualitative inquiry. Elliot Eisner, in *The Educational Imagination* (1979), proposed one of the first alternatives to conventional ethnographic and case study research. Two chapters in this book outline "educational criticism and connoisseurship," which Eisner describes as a qualitative form of educational inquiry and evaluation that "takes its lead from the work that critics have done in literature, theater, film, music and the visual arts" (p. 190). Drawing on Dewey's (1934) aesthetic philosophy, as well as the work of Susanne Langer (1957) and Rudolf Arnheim (1969), Eisner argued that the arts could powerfully inform the work of educators and researchers alike.

The 1980s: New Ventures

With the beginning of the 1980s, other writers looked to the arts and humanities as a basis for conceptualizing educational research. Sarah Lawrence Lightfoot's work exemplifies this trend. Like many other qualitative researchers of her generation, Lightfoot was originally trained in the conventions of disciplined social science. Her contributions, however, departed from these traditions as she sought to develop a form of case study research known as "school portraiture." Her book *The Good High School* (1983) includes both a methodological discussion of this approach and portraits of two urban, two suburban, and two elite high schools. Others in secondary education turned to both formal and informal qualitative fieldwork to inform books such as Theodore Sizer's *Horace's Compromise* (1984) and Arthur Powell, Eleanor Farrar, and David Cohen's *The Shopping Mall High School* (1985). Unlike Lightfoot, these authors did not set out specific approaches. However, they did use qualitative methods in novel ways. Sizer used composite descriptions, for example, and Powell, Farrar, and Cohen enlisted metaphors to extend the theoretical significance of their work. An even more decided departure from social science is found in the work of Madeleine Grumet (1980). Grumet combined phenomenological and autobiographical methods from literary traditions to use as models for studying curriculum, teaching, and teacher education.

While qualitative researchers were emphasizing the continuities between systematic inquiry and other fields, broader critiques of quantitative research were emphasizing the discontinuities between the rigors of science and its relevance for practice. In 1983, Donald Schön's book *The Reflective Practitioner* directly challenged the assumed relationship between scientific knowledge and "applied" fields ranging from medicine to music. Widely recognized in education, Schön's argument was that the products of science, such as generalizations based on statistical probabilities, neither readily transfer to professional practice nor find fertile ground in the conditions under which professionals work. Such generalizations address central tendencies and broad principles of how aspects of the social or physical word operate under controlled or ideal conditions. Practitioners, however, are concerned with individual cases under conditions, to use Schön's words, of "complexity, uncertainty, instability, uniqueness, and value-conflict" (1983, p. 39).

Similar concerns were also being raised by an increasing number of feminist scholars in the 1980s. Like Schön, these writers were concerned with the neglect of anomalies and the "detachment" of science as an epistemological ideal that lifts knowledge above the interests, desires, and histories of those who seek it. Evelyn Fox Keller's biography of Barbara McClintock, *A Feeling for the Organism* (1983), served as an example of how a researcher's attachment to the subject of her research could enhance rather than detract from science. In education, Belenky, Clinchy, Goldberger, and Tarule's *Women's Ways of Knowing* (1986) reported the results of interviews with women college students and former college students. These researchers focused on their participants' conceptions of teaching, curriculum, and knowledge. The themes developed from their data again challenged traditional notions of objectivity and universal truth by suggesting that such notions often hid or disparaged the experience of women.

Feminist scholars who sought to redefine subjectivity were joined by others, including some anthropologists and educational ethnographers. Alan Peshkin (1982, 1988, 2000), for example, began a series of articles on the roles of subjectivity in qualitative research. Although he initially regarded his own subjectivity as an "affliction," Peshkin came to argue that researchers cannot and should not exorcise it from the processes of research. Instead, subjectivity should be pursued as a way for researchers to better understand their own accounts of research (see also Rosaldo, 1989).

What we are describing is a confluence of trends that served a dual purpose: to distinguish qualitative work as a separate genre of inquiry and to challenge the leading assumptions of conventional, quantitative research. Neither of these trends went unchallenged. On the contrary, debates in the 1980s were rife between the proponents of quantitative and qualitative research, and the more researchers began to view qualitative inquiry as a legitimate alternative, the more intense the debates became. The conflict was often played out in leading journals. In 1983, for example, a classic exchange between Denis Phillips and Elliot Eisner appeared in the *Educational Researcher*. Phillips's article, entitled "After the Wake: Postpositivistic Educational Thought," cautioned researchers against prematurely assuming the demise of what Phillips correctly predicted would be the continuing dominance of a more modest but by no means vanquished positivist tradition. Eisner (1983) responded in the same issue, arguing for pluralism in both our conceptions of knowledge and the means by which it is obtained.

The qualitative versus quantitative debates were increasingly fueled by researchers on both sides who viewed the two traditions as resting on incommensurable epistemologies. On the qualitative side, Yvonna Lincoln and Egon Guba (1985, 1989) exemplify leading researchers who defined the assumptions of qualitative research as a rejection of, or at least in direct opposition to, the foundations of quantitative work. Their widely cited book *Naturalistic Inquiry* (1985) drew loosely on Kuhn's perspective in framing the debate as a case of conflicting paradigms. The assumptions of what Lincoln and Guba labeled the *positivist paradigm* included the following: (1) Reality viewed as independent; (2) research aims defined as developing "nomothetic," cause-and-effect generalizations; and (3) the use of procedural objectivity as the criterion for validity. They characterized the *naturalistic paradigm* as focusing on multiple realities constructed by the researcher, the development of "ideographic" knowledge, and the value-laden nature of inquiry (pp. 37–38). In later work, Guba and Lincoln (1989) renamed the naturalistic perspective the *constructivist paradigm*. They also became increasingly insistent that qualitative researchers give up the search for concepts and criteria that would mirror quantitative research.

Not all researchers, however, accepted the incommensurability of the two perspectives. Some argued that quantitative traditions offered valuable standards or, at least, applicable criteria to inform qualitative studies. In their sourcebook *Qualitative Data Analysis* (1984), for example, Matthew Miles and Michael Huberman sought methodological sophistication over epistemological dualism. Their work represented the strategy of making qualitative research more rigorous in the conventional sense by adapting some of the logic and design techniques of quantitative research. Other researchers found it readily possible to blend qualitative and quantitative approaches within the same study (e.g., Shuy, 1986). Miles and Huberman's work focused largely on issues of design and method, as did other books published during this period, including Bogdan and Biklen's *Qualitative Research in Education* (1982), Jaeger's *Complementary Methods for Research in Education* (1988), and Van Maane's *Tales of the Field* (1988).

Methods per se, however, were not at the center of this decade's debate. Rather, the arguments focused on epistemological questions regarding the validity of qualitative research and thus its legitimacy as a whole. The persistence of such basic concerns were reflected in a small conference on qualitative research hosted by the Graduate School of Education at Stanford University in 1988. The conference brought together such diverse scholars as Denis Phillips, Matthew Miles, Michael Apple, Yvonna Lincoln, Egon Guba, Henry Wolcott, Howard Becker, Madeleine Grumet, and Philip Jackson. Their conference papers were later published in *Qualitative Inquiry in Education: The Continuing Debate* (1990), a book edited by the conference organizers, Elliot Eisner and Alan Peshkin. Both the conference and book organized the study of qualitative inquiry around five topics: subjectivity and objectivity, validity, generalizability, ethics, and the uses of qualitative research. Although these topics encompassed a broad range of issues, epistemological questions remained the center of gravity and the main points of contention. For many qualitative researchers, the field was characterized by what Eisner and Peshkin's book title had suggested, a series of continuing debates.

Yet, regardless of unresolved tensions, developments in the 1980s anticipated future growth in qualitative research on two counts. First, researchers continued to emphasize issues and methods specific to qualitative research. Reflecting this trend, the first issue of the *International Journal of Qualitative Studies in Education* was published in 1986. Second, qualitative research had gained a modest but strong foothold in mainstream educational research. This trend represented integration, so to speak, rather than separately building the field from within an already established circle of researchers. The third edition of the *Handbook of Research on Teaching,* for example, included new chapters on both qualitative methods (Erickson, 1986) and the "cultures of teaching" (Feiman-Nemser & Floden, 1986). Earlier editions of the handbook had defined research on teaching almost exclusively in terms of a quantitative framework (Gage, 1963). Qualitative approaches also made their way into the field of program evaluation research, which, like research on teaching, had initially been established as the sole province of quantitative measurement. That orientation changed with writers such as Michael Patton (1980) and Robert Stake (1986), both of whom saw qualitative methods as a means of increasing the relevance and impact of evaluation results. In short, qualitative research was being advanced on two scenes: both in publications devoted specifically to qualitative inquiry and side-by-side with quantitative studies across areas of specialization.

The 1990s: New Challenges

Developments continued on both of these venues throughout the 1990s. The number of publications devoted specifically to qualitative approaches and methods grew so quickly that efforts to survey the field became major undertakings. *The Handbook of Qualitative Research* (Denzin & Lincoln, 1994), for example, revealed a scope and body of scholarship that most would have considered presumptuous a mere 10 years earlier.

The integration of qualitative approaches into mainstream research progressed as well. By the 1990s, classic, multiple-edition textbooks on educational research were including one or more chapters on qualitative methods alongside their standard chapters on quasi-experimental and survey research design. Illustrating this trend, the sixth edition of Meredith Gall, Walter Borg, and Joyce Gall's introductory text *Educational Research* (1996) included two new chapters, one addressing case study methods and the other focusing on qualitative orientations. The latter chapter, entitled "Qualitative Research Traditions," represents an ambitious attempt to map what had by then become a broad terrain. The chapter identifies 17 separate traditions classified into three groups based on the type of phenomena each tradition investigates. In the first group, "Investigation of Lived Experience," the authors included traditions such as cognitive psychology, life history, and phenomenology. In the second group, "Investigation of Society and Culture," they included traditions such as cultural studies, ethnography, and symbolic interactionism. In the third group, "Investigation of Language and Communication," they included traditions such as hermeneutics and semiotics.

The Gall, Borg, and Gall survey was one of the most inclusive attempts to organize the qualitative work being done in the 1990s (see Creswell, 1998; Wolcott, 1992). Space was found for traditions that overlap with quantitative research, as in the case of cognitive psychology. However, such inclusions are useful in now recognizing the past contributions that leading psychologists made to qualitative studies. Jerome Bruner's work, for example, strongly supported interpretive inquiry. In *Acts of Meaning* (1990), Bruner argued that "to insist upon explanation in terms of *causes* simply bars us from trying to understand how human beings interpret their worlds and how *we* interpret *their* acts of interpretation" (p. xiii, emphasis in original). Overall, figures such as Bruner, the new inclusiveness of textbooks, and a growing list of publications all signaled the ongoing expansion of qualitative research.

Methodological work in the 1990s continued to draw on philosophical traditions as well, especially hermeneutics and phenomenology. Yet scholars in this group expressed their alliance to these traditions in ways that were significantly different from those followed by their predecessors. The more contemporary scholars were increasingly explicit in aligning methods with epistemological assumptions and less apologetic about emphasizing the postmodern elements of their work. Max Van Manen's *Researching Lived Experience* (1990), for example, proposed a "hermeneutic phenomenological approach to human science research." The approach not only drew on interpretive traditions but attempted to integrate research and writing as a means to illuminate the researcher's stance within the context of his or her own study. Steinar Kvale (1996), to cite another example, integrated similar philosophical assumptions with interview methods to reconceptualize data as meanings coconstructed between researcher and participant.

The postmodern in research both extended and broke with Continental philosophy by reasserting the partiality of all knowledge and the view that objectivity is in itself a form of bias. This view also came to emphasize multiple identities based on gender, race, class, and ethnicity. These identities implied multiple epistemologies as well (Donmoyer, 1996), raising challenges that we will return to in the next section. The postmodern also called attention to the constitutive functions of language (i.e., as we speak language, it speaks us), and this view more broadly came to be known as the "interpretive turn" in social research. Perhaps most significant, the partiality of knowledge meant that its production in both research and education was also an expression of power (Bowers & Flinders, 1990, pp. 157–191; Clough, 1992, p. 8).

Although these perspectives were not new, postmodernism gave critiques of all research a hard political edge. As Howard Becker (1993) wrote, "Attacks on qualitative research used to come exclusively from the methodological right, from the proponents of positivism and statistical and experimental rigor. But now the attack comes from the cultural studies left as well" (p. 218). To the extent that qualitative work had been accepted into educational research, its advocates found themselves in a new role, that of centrist. The irony of this position came from qualitative researchers soon finding themselves criticized for reasons similar to the ones they had recently been using against quantitative research (for a recent example, see English, 2000).

Qualitative researchers responded to their postmodern critics in a variety of ways. First, many researchers welcomed more focus on the sociology of knowledge and the politics of research, even if it meant shifting attention away from other issues. Those who had participated earlier in the "paradigm wars" were already accustomed to seeing definitions of knowledge as expressions of power. Elliot Eisner, best known as an advocate for epistemological pluralism, had long argued that established methods of inquiry represented the interest and investment of those who used them. In the introduction to *The Enlightened Eye* (1991), Eisner wrote: "Which particular forms of representation become acceptable in the educational research community is as much a political matter as an epistemological one" (p. 8). At least on this count, qualitative researchers and their postmodern critics were not entirely at odds.

Second, qualitative researchers responded by renewing their efforts to reflexively place themselves within their work. Petra Munro (1993, p. 164) describes research self-reflexivity as a means of "establishing collaborative and nonexploitive research relationships" that avoid an objectification of research participants. Munro and others (e.g., Glesne, 1999, pp. 102–105) turned to feminist scholarship to inform the complexities of what "nonexploitive research relations" should mean in the context of qualitative fieldwork and reporting. This scholarship, especially the work of Nel Noddings (1999), cast researcher-participant relations in ethical as well as political terms. On the ethical side, qualitative researchers struggled with notions of friendship, intimacy, and rapport. Interest in such issues represented a shift away from using the two great ethical systems of philosophy—utilitarianism and Kantian ethics—as the only source from which to draw moral guidance (Flinders, 1992). The shift to relational ethics, or what Noddings (1992) referred to as an "ethic of care," complemented conventional approaches in a powerful way. Rather than locate moral reasoning largely within an individual agent or actor, as had utilitarian and Kantian principles, an ethic of care emphasizes relationships and intersubjective perspectives. Among other implications, this view meant that researchers needed to negotiate much of their work with their participants.

An emphasis on relational approach is also reflected in action research, a third trend that was and continues to be influenced by postmodern ideas. Action research is a broad label for several forms of inquiry, most but not all of which employ qualitative methods. While action research developed earlier, renewed interest in the 1990s was characterized by a responsiveness to the local problems of research participants and a commitment to collaboration. Some forms (such as political action and emancipatory action research) focused specifically on problems related to the oppression of socially, economically, or educationally marginalized groups. Ernest Stringer (1993, 1996), for example, developed a form of action research from his work with Aboriginal groups in West Australia. Stringer called his approach "socially responsive educational research," grounding it in the work of scholars such as Paulo Freire (1970). The approach was characteristic of action research in several ways. First, it took a problem-solving orientation by focusing the outcomes of inquiry on plans, policies, or program services. Second, the methods of the approach were described in a nontechnical language, widely accessible to lay participants. Third, the approach placed particular emphasis on the words and stories of participants themselves throughout the planning, methods, analysis, and reporting of research.

As postmodernism challenged researchers to think broadly, more established trends in qualitative research continued as well. We noted earlier, for example, the ongoing popularity in traditional forms of ethnography. The 1990s were also a decade in which increasing numbers of qualitative researchers used personal computers to help them with tasks such as recording and sorting data (see Gahan & Hannibal, 1998; Weitzman & Miles, 1995). Across this range of developments, however, our overview has emphasized the recent proliferation of qualitative approaches and the rise of postmodern perspectives. These two developments are of special interest because they have set the stage for many of the field's contemporary and continuing dilemmas. We identify three such dilemmas here and suggest some of the challenges they currently pose for the theory and practice of research.

Continuing Dilemmas

The first dilemma stems from epistemological pluralism in general and specifically as it relates to categories such as race, class, gender, and ethnicity. If cultural experience and identities within these broad categories imply different epistemologies, what Noddings (1995, pp. 192–194) calls "standpoint" epistemologies, then researchers (and readers of research) within each group are in a privileged position to conduct and evaluate that research. This argument can lead to a number of tensions, one of which is in deciding who is appropriate to judge the usefulness and rigor of different types of research. To draw an analogy from schools of thought in psychology, for example, one could question whether a Skinnerian behaviorist is the appropriate person to evaluate a study based on psychoanalytic theories. From the perspective of standpoint epistemologies, a similar question could be raised about cultural groups. In either case, however, within-group variations are often large. As a result, standpoint epistemologies could be defined with ever-increasing specificity, leading to an infinite regress (Donmoyer, in press).

Another tension posed by standpoint epistemologies is that such a view of knowledge, as already noted, implies a privileged position for researchers within a given group. Pressing the point further, one could argue that only women researchers should study gender oppression, that only black researchers should study the lived experience of black participants, and so forth. Such balkanization, however, would contradict the postmodern call for research to include multiple voices and perspectives, a prospect that defeats the purpose of having different standpoints in the first place (Noddings, 1995, p. 184). To avoid these tensions, researchers can view different standpoints as in some ways compatible. Yet this view only raises another question: Compatible on what basis? Because postmodernism itself offers little guidance on exactly this point, the potential fragmentation of epistemological perspectives remains a contemporary challenge.

A second dilemma stems from a contemporary skepticism of all epistemological claims. In some ways, postmodernism can be viewed as an anti-epistemology in its rejection of Descartes' aloof knower, free choice, and the notion of an autonomous subject. This rejection has brought into focus the historical and situated inevitability of all research. As Noddings (1995, p. 75) points out, however, some feminists are concerned that philosophers are declaring the "death of the subject" at the very time that women and other marginalized groups are finally gaining recognition in areas that value autonomous achievement. Beyond the frustration of feeling like the rules have been changed in the middle of the game, the challenge for qualitative researchers is in reconciling the partiality of all knowledge with the trend toward conceptualizing research specifically as a means of empowerment.

A third dilemma stems from the increasing number of qualitative researchers who look to the arts and humanities rather than the social sciences as models for their work. Eisner (1997, 1999), for example, has recently argued that because science can be viewed as a subcategory of inquiry, we should not demand that all qualitative research in education be scientific. Responding to Eisner, Mayer (2000) objected to this view on the grounds that to admit nonscientific methods would "diminish the reputation of our field" (p. 38). One response to concerns over the field's reputation would be to demonstrate that nonscientific forms of inquiry can be just as rigorous and useful on the basis of other criteria. The challenge of identifying such criteria is in its wide disparity, compared with what researchers usually have come to expect, from forms of systematic inquiry. Ambiguity in the arts, for example, functions in critical ways to convey meanings that cannot be stated literally. Ambiguity keeps a work of art open to interpretation, which allows for and promotes meaningful engagement. If we admit ambiguity into research, however, by what criteria would it be assessed? Does it make sense to speak of "rigorous" ambiguity or of a rigorously ambiguous study?

Another area in which criteria may be difficult to pin down involves the persuasive functions of language. As qualitative researchers turn to more literary uses of metaphor, narrative forms, and poetic transcriptions of data, skillful writing might readily subvert as well as enhance the aims of research. In discussing the "rhetoric of inquiry," Henry St. Maurice (1993, pp. 202–204) argues that all types of educational research, both quantitative and qualitative, employ rhetorical forms and thus privilege those who know how to use the rules of the discourse to their advantage. The politics of this issue have a long history with respect to artistic traditions. It was Plato, after all, who banished poets (even Homer) from his utopian republic because of their ability to incite emotions and thereby persuade the unsuspecting. For contemporary qualitative researchers, however, appropriate use of representational forms may be most pressing as an ethical rather than political concern. As such, researchers find scant guidance in conventional research ethics such as informed consent, avoidance of harm, and confidentiality. Qualitative researchers who have addressed stylistic issues (see, for example, Wolcott, 1990a, 1990b), imply the role of a different ethic, one that emphasizes craft, balance, fairness, and attention to detail. Working out criteria in these areas, nevertheless, remains a largely unfinished task.

Qualitative Research and Music Education

The remaining sections of this chapter focus on qualitative research in music education by highlighting the ways that the major issues surrounding qualitative research in education have played out in music education research. We first address the context in which qualitative methodology came to be considered a viable research tool for studying music teaching and learning and offer an analysis of the critical issues that have impacted the quality of the qualitative research genre in music education and its current position within the discipline. Second, we present a range of exemplary music education research studies that used a wide variety of qualitative methodologies. In conclusion we propose promising points of departure for future research in music education using qualitative methodology.

Issues in Context

The description of the development of qualitative research in education during the decades from 1960 through 1990 presented earlier in this chapter has, not surprisingly, parallels with the important features of the development of qualitative research as a viable methodology for inquiry in music education. Greatly influenced by research trends of the time and dominated by the need to achieve mainstream stature, music education researchers of the late 1950s and 1960s engaged in studies that produced quantifiable outcomes exemplified in the work of experimental psychologists. In addition to these were curriculum studies (projects in which a year's worth of teaching content was organized into a dissertation-length document) and status studies (typically, an uncritical look at the music program of a particular school district and academic unit, focused not on learning outcomes or teacher satisfaction but on aspects such as number of participants and budget). (See Colwell [1967] for a more detailed description of this era.) During this period, while education researchers such as Philip Jackson went into classrooms as ethnographers, music education researchers such as Ed Gordon and Richard Colwell developed psychometric tests to help practitioners quantify students' musical aptitude and achievement. With the invention of these measures, music education research entered the heyday of quasi-experimental, experimental, and descriptive studies designed to use the new psychometric measures of musical aptitude and achievement to quantify effects on dependent variables. Emboldened by Gordon and Colwell, many novice researchers were encouraged by their doctoral advisors to develop their own purpose-built "measures" of whatever construct they wished to study, often without any specialized coursework or expertise in measurement and evaluation. Such tests and checklists were often the sole source of data in the dissertation study, yet the measures themselves typically were unproven as valid or reliable measures of the construct under investigation. The tendency to look to psychometrics as the answer to many of the discipline's questions and to encourage novices to dabble in test construction during this era brought music education research under what Shirley Brice Heath has called "the punishing influence of psychology" (Heath, 1999, p. 204). She continues: "During the 1970s, the discipline of psychology, with its attendant concepts of controls, variables, and quantifiable indicators, increasingly dominated estimations of sound research."

The problem with this limited focus was that the typical doctoral dissertation project sampled too few students and offered treatments that were either not well designed and controlled or not administered over a period of time long enough to reflect measurable changes in students' skills or achievement. Alan Schoenfeld (1999) characterized the results of this approach this way: "I do not think it overly harsh to say that the wholesale and inappropriate adoption of statistical methods into small-scale studies was, in large measure, a triumph of scientism over common sense" (p. 181). He continued: "There are few findings of any lasting significance emerging from such statistics-dominated small-scale work in education over more than the quarter-century from the 1950s and 1960s through the 1970s" (p. 182).

Music education research has always been a hybrid field, its practitioners relying on such widely flung disciplines as education, psychology, sociology, anthropology, and even ethnomusicology for both methods of inquiry and organizing constructs, attempting to adapt and apply these methods to the study of music teaching and learning. The appropriation by music education researchers of the emerging qualitative methodology during the 1980s and 1990s followed the pattern of the earlier appropriation of the quantitative/ experimental canon: Add the new topic (qualitative methodology) to the extant research course syllabus and then rely on crosscampus departments or schools (education, sociology, "ed psych") to give doctoral students further expertise in "the real thing." The underlying assumptions behind this approach, which continue to guide doctoral programs in the current century, are that the music education doctoral student can successfully adapt the "new" research method to the discipline of music education and that the same student, when transformed into a novice music education researcher upon achieving candidacy, can derive deep and meaningful insights from data gleaned through any of the multitude of qualitative methodologies mastered in a single three-hour survey course. The insertion of "music education" where "education" appears in the following quotation summarizes succinctly the result of predicating practice on this pair of faulty assumptions.

> Researchers in education who call their ad hoc attempts to make sense of dialogue "discourse analysis," are not only bad scholars: they are giving education a bad name. The same could be said for those who make cavalier use of "clinical interviews," "protocol analysis," and so on. (Schoenfeld, 1999, p. 180)

The current generation of senior faculty who train music education researchers were themselves trained during the heyday of positivism and may have never expanded their own research expertise beyond its confines nor have any reason or interest in doing so. It is no surprise, then, that the language used in major refereed research publications in music education still bears the trappings of the positivist paradigm exclusively: hypothesis, variables, and objective measurement have not been replaced by the "orienting questions" and "perceived antecedents for what's observed" described earlier in this chapter. Eisner's assertion (1997) that "which particular forms of representation become acceptable in the education research community is as much a political matter as an epistemological one" (p. 8) certainly applies to the way the leadership of the music education research community has regarded qualitative studies in our discipline. One might be tempted to think that the paradigm wars are over, at least in the greater education research community, for qualitative studies and their frameworks have assumed a position of equal prominence alongside the more positivist research methods (as evidenced by a cursory read through the program of the annual meeting of the American Educational Research Association). However, the fallout from this particular war appears to be not unlike the aftermath of the Civil War in this country, with hostilities still being played out, however politely, more than 100 years later. Lagemann describes the current political climate thus: "Quantitative types challenge qualitative types, and the reverse; discipline-based scholars question the rigor of studies undertaken by education-based scholars, and education-based scholars query the relevance of studies done by their discipline-based colleagues" (Lagemann, 1999, p. 8). Such partisan wranglings are not absent from the music education research community, either. Qualitative research and its trappings have yet to be fully embraced. For example, the directives to editorial boards of the major refereed journals look much the same today as they did in 1967, using the language and criteria of the positivist paradigm to evaluate manuscripts for publication. When the manuscript is "qualitative," the reviewer might not find the requisite problem statement and research questions on first glance, or ever. There may be no apparent conclusions or implications but plenty of prose. The way qualitative researchers use language to create their research reports can be problematic, both for themselves and the editorial board members who are unschooled in the genre.

For many of those trained in the positivist era, the terminology of qualitative research can be a forbidding foreign country, requiring a new lexicon. Evidence of exactly how different and extensive this new research language is from the old can be found in Thomas Schwandt's 1997 book *Qualitative Inquiry: A Dictionary of Terms*. This important volume was conceived as "an inviting overview of critical terms in the discourses of qualitative inquiry" (p. ix). The 215 terms, ranging from "action research" to "Weltanschuung," are presented in short annotations that offer both the philosophical orientation and methodological explanation. Though not exhaustive, this text demystifies the qualitative research language in an intellectually inviting way that the current generation of doctoral advisors and their students might find enlightening.

The use of the term "qualitative research" as it has come to be used in the music education context is one of the critical issues that needs to be addressed here. In their very fine chapter on qualitative research methodology in the first *Handbook of Research on Music Teaching and Learning*, Bresler and Stake (1992) defined qualitative research as a

> general term to refer to several research strategies that share certain characteristics: (1) noninterventionist observation in natural settings; (2) emphasis on interpretation of both emic issues (those of the participants) and etic issues

(those of the writer); (3) highly contextual description of people and events; and (4) validation of information through triangulation. (p. 76)

They elaborate further, listing seven additional characteristics of qualitative research that refine their definition considerably: holistic, empirical, descriptive, interpretive, empathetic, formulated from the bottom up (grounded theory), and validated (p. 79). The composite definition is illustrative of the specific meanings the term carries in education research. However, the term's meaning within the music education research discipline is much broader. For many reasons, including lack of familiarity on the part of music education researchers, less distinction has been made when applying the term, and the operant definition has come to be "research that relies on some form of verbal data rather than numerical data," often but not always coupled with "research based on observation of a music classroom setting (field work)." This imprecision resulted from the confusion proliferated, in part, by thesis advisors challenged to keep abreast of methodological developments in qualitative inquiry. Hence, when applying Bresler and Stake's definition to qualitative music education studies that were undertaken in the last 10 years, many would be more appropriately labeled "descriptive." This is not a criticism of the discipline but rather a sign of the era in which we work: one where a proliferation of new knowledge, new research methods, and new forms of representation make the task of preparing new generations of researchers daunting. Schoenfeld (1999) describes our era this way: "There is no canon, there are no core methods, this is not a time of normal science, and there are myriad models of mentoring [young researchers], even among those especially talented in it" (p. 167).

Schoenfeld goes on to argue that the single most important research skill we can instill in the new generation of researchers is the ability to find and frame important problems to solve: problems that are more than just "interesting" because they go after the deeper meanings behind phenomena. A concomitant skill we would argue for is the ability to write in a voice that frees the reader to find the meaning of the qualitative research report. Laurel Richardson (1994) asks: "How do we put ourselves in our own texts, and with what consequences? How do we nurture our own individuality and at the same time lay claim to 'knowing' something? These are both philosophically and practically difficult problems" (p. 517). The best qualitative work brings the reader in close contact with the setting, the participants, and interactions among these. The very best writing is required in the qualitative genre, for the whole enterprise rests on the ability of the researcher to portray, illustrate, and explain. However, the typical graduate-level research methods survey class continues to initiate novices in the use of the positivist paradigm's omniscient third person, rather than "I." It is no wonder that our research students' first efforts at reading and writing qualitative studies often leave them wondering, "Is this research?"

Music educator/researchers operate under the additional pressure to answer the pragmatic question: "What difference does this study make?" Because the qualitative genre asks the reader to make her or his own meaning from the study, as well as subsequently create her or his own application in the form of new music classroom or rehearsal practice, the answer to the pragmatic question is not immediate but rather comes to the reader upon further reflection. The reader's interpretation depends entirely on the researcher's ability to provide a rich, in-depth, accurate description of the phenomenon as experienced by the researcher, along with an indication of how the researcher made her or his interpretive choices. Alan Peshkin (2000) offers one way of portraying the interpretive process through a series of "metanarrative reflections" that describe what he terms "problematics": offset paragraphs, in the body of the prose narrative, that explain not only the interpretive choices that were made but also the options that were discarded. The result offers the reader a glimpse of the influence of the researcher's subjectivity at each decision-making step of the interpretive process. Peshkin emphasizes that "to be forthcoming and honest about how we work as researchers is to develop a reflective awareness that . . . contributes to enhancing the quality of our interpretive acts" (p. 9). Music education researchers may take another 10 years to become accustomed to the fact that qualitative studies often yield insights that have parallels with the insights gained from musical experiences, for both can be powerful, emotion-laden, and difficult to put into words.

Exemplars of Qualitative Research in Music Education

The qualitative studies in music education included in this section exemplify the broader operant definition of "qualitative" rather than the Bresler/Stake definition. They are included here to illustrate how various species of qualitative methodology have been used to study some aspects of music teaching and learning. Included in this summary are case studies, participant observation, action research, ethnography, and verbal protocol analyses.

Case Studies

The purpose of a case study, according to Stake (1994), is "not to represent the world, but to represent the case" (p. 246). Stake emphasizes the need to "optimize understanding of the case rather than generalization beyond" (p. 246). Stake describes three general categories for types of case studies: intrinsic, instrumental, and collective. The intrinsic case study is undertaken because the researcher has an intrinsic interest in a particular setting or teacher. In an instrumental case study, the particular case is less important than the insight it can provide into a specific issue of theory. A collective case study is an "instrumental case study expended to several cases" (p. 237). Collective cases are selected because of the researcher's belief that "understanding them will lead to better understanding, perhaps better theorizing, about a still larger collection of cases" (p. 237).

Two examples of case studies are included here: one is the work of a research team made up of experienced researchers, the other a doctoral dissertation. Both exemplify, to differing degrees, the qualitative genre's ability to enable the researcher to get closer to the subject under consideration.

Stake, Bresler, and Mabry's (1991) look at what actually happened in the arts in several school districts around the United States focused on one middle school and seven primary schools to get an "understanding of particular situations" in a variety of locations and quality of arts programs (p. 6). In what is described as a "constructivist case study," the findings are experiences that the researchers constructed in an attempt "not to minimize but to preserve interactions between researcher and phenomena" (p. 11). The following six research issues guided the observations (p. 9):

1. Is there attention to aesthetics, to beauty, to intellectual understanding of the arts?
2. Are teachers encouraged to meet arts education needs by integrating arts activities into the teaching of other subject matter?
3. When studying significant artists and their works, are popular and multicultural arts included?
4. Does the responsibility to achieve measurable goals diminish the attention given to arts events and experiences happening outside the classroom?
5. Are there advocates for more discipline-based arts education or other high-quality curricula to replace present custom?
6. What forms of arts education leadership are present and how do they match the needs for leadership?

Each of the research team members developed their own list of specific questions from this broad list and spent 9 to 12 days at individual sites. The resulting report presents lively portraits of practice; each site is portrayed in an individual chapter authored by a single research team member.

The findings were not particularly flattering. The arts existed on the margins of the school day, dominated by popular arts and crafts rather than fine art and a discipline-based approach. "The message from the community to the school was 'Keep art and music part of the curriculum; keep it modest and conventional; continue the traditional performances and exhibits' " (p. 342). No connections to facilitate arts education improvement were found between the observed teachers and the public advocates of music and art education, such as academics, authors of disciplinary journals, or professional organizations such as the Music Educators National Conference (MENC) (p. 345).

The second example of the case study genre is L'Hommedieu's (1992) observational case study of a master studio performance teacher. The purpose of this study was to develop a pedagogical profile of the factors that define extraordinary master teaching in the one-to-one instructional environment of the performance studio. L'Hommedieu looked specifically at four factors of studio teaching, cues, participation, reinforcement, and feedback/correctives, and then considered how these teacher moves were interpreted by the students and how well the students' interpretation matched the teacher's intent.

The study is an important example of a young researcher's shift from one paradigm to another as the result of using an observation schedule in the pilot study. L'Hommedieu found that his musical expertise and experience made the observation schedule checklist data categories seem trivial and found Eisner's "connoisseur" model a better lens through which to consider the master teachers. He then used field notes to record his impressions during the 17 hours of lessons he observed in the study. Other data sources included videotapes of the observed lessons and interviews with the master teachers and their students. The resulting portraits of the individual teachers, though focused on the four pedagogical constructs described earlier, show the rich variety of differences between them, as well as pointing out individual instances of excellent teaching.

Participant Observation

Participant observation studies involve the researcher in some sort of role in the setting that is the focus of the study. There are gradations of amount and type of participation within this definition, as well as of how transparent the researcher's role is to the participants (Atkinson & Hammersley, 1994, p. 249). Each of these variations influences the outcomes of the study and needs to be addressed at the outset when using participant observation.

Berg's (1997) study examined how students in two small high school chamber ensembles reached conclusions about musical interpretation through social interaction. Two questions guided this study: Do identifiable patterns of music thought and action exist within the ensembles? How do these patterns reveal ways that student interactions, tools, and social structures assist or constrain movement through Vygotsky's zone of proximal development toward increased music awareness? During a 5-month period Berg was a participant observer of the two string ensembles during 13 rehearsals, 16 coaching sessions, and 6 performances. Her data sources included video- and audiotapes, transcribed dialogue, 11 interviews with ensemble members and coaches, field notes, and other miscellaneous documents. Berg found that there were similarities (in both groups members challenged each other to clarify, elaborate, and justify the problem solution) and differences (members of the two groups exchanged roles differently and used unique rehearsal strategies) between the social interaction pattern of the two groups. Berg's well-written dissertation portrays collaborative learning in music as a multifaceted process that can both help and hinder the individual performer's musical growth.

Action Research

Action research in music teacher education includes studies in which teachers use their own classroom or rehearsal as a place to implement untried teaching strategies, solve specific teaching-related problems, or document their own reflections on what they do in the course of a school day. There is often an evaluative component to this type of work, with teachers documenting the changes resulting from the innovation. Action research has achieved a resurgence in recent years with the advent of school-university collaborative research partnerships. (See Burnaford, Fischer, & Hobson [1996] for a detailed look at one institution's implementation of action research projects within school communities.)

O'Toole's (1994) action research study of power dynamics in the choral rehearsal class addressed the question of why anyone would be willing to participate in the typical performance ensemble, in which the individual's opinions, thoughts, and feelings are subordinated in favor of the director's opinions, thoughts, and feelings. The research questions focused on replacing the traditional power relations of the choral music classroom with a series of three 8-week projects that implemented feminist pedagogy in three choral ensemble settings. Working in collaboration with two high school choral directors and her own choir, O'Toole used their classroom concerns to design projects that would give more voice to individual students' responses, musical decision-making, and input. O'Toole attempted to involve the students' feelings, needs, and reactions in the rehearsal setting through activities ranging from large group discussion of the poetic text, journal entries about the rehearsals, and student interviews about their experiences. The data included field notes, teacher interviews, student interviews, student-conducted interviews, and researcher journals.

O'Toole's dissertation is noteworthy for both its attempt to apply feminist pedagogical principles in the choral rehearsal and its experimentation with a "postmodern format." The narrative, in first person, is juxtaposed with tales (classroom events) and with critical commentary, nonlinear drama (five unrelated scenes documenting individual and group interview analysis), verbal "snapshots" of interesting moments from the classroom projects, "montages" (a series of images that play with the point of view established in the snapshots), and "slippage" (the author's admission of personal or philosophical contradiction). The result is a rich, thought-provoking example of a more artistic way to represent qualitative research findings.

Ethnography

A form of participant observation that typically explores a particular case in detail by gathering extensive field note and interview data, the ethnographic analysis focuses on the interpretation of "meaning and functions of human actions" and is usually in the form of verbal description and explanation (Atkinson & Hammersley, 1994, p. 248). The main requirement for the ethnographer is to ask the right questions, and skill at interviewing is the prerequisite for data gathering in an ethnographic study.

The process of transmission of traditional music in Ireland and the "nature of both stability and change as seen through the role of the traditional music teacher" was the subject of Veblen's 1991 ethnographic study (p. xii). Her research questions focused on the role of the teacher and the musical network and formal structures for transmission of Irish folk music and the perceptions of teachers and participants' judgments of Irish music traditions as active or passive.

Veblen's 9 months in Ireland allowed her to observe the teaching of two well-known instrumental teachers and interview them. She then corroborated or refuted their points of view via interviews with 13 other teachers of traditional Irish folk music from around the country and interviewed another 26 people representing Irish music organizations. Data included audiotaped interviews, lesson observation notes, field notes, publications of organizations, and videotaped materials and photos.

The format chosen for this work enhances Veblen's excellent writing. The extensive quotations, typical of ethnography, feature the participants' voices, woven together with contextual, interpretive prose that skillfully preserves the flavor and local color experienced by the researcher. Veblen offers the reader an unusually high level of interpretation through tables that tally the findings from each section, followed by a detailed prose summary. Veblen's major finding, that the traditional means of transmission has shifted from being an informal, home-based, individual pursuit to a more organized, classroom endeavor, is offered with some reservation, given the powerful indictment of institutionalized music instruction offered early in the work by one informant: " 'I was rejected by the music teachers as being the only person who didn't have a musical ear and I'm the only one who ever did anything with music out of the entire class' " (p. 61).

Verbal Protocol Analysis: "Think Alouds"

Verbal protocol analysis is a method of data gathering in music education research that relies on the informant's ability to tell the researcher everything he or she is thinking while engaged in some musical task. The authoritative text on "think alouds" is Ericsson and Simon's *Protocol Analysis: Verbal Reports as Data* (1993). The methodology is drawn from the tradition of experimental psychology, where the researcher gives scripted prompts at regular intervals and does not deviate from the procedure. The resulting verbal data or "protocols" are analyzed for patterns of cognitive processes.

Though verbal protocol analysis is clearly a positivist methodology, it has come to be known as a qualitative research method in music education because of its reliance on verbal data. There has been some confusion about the difference between interview data and think aloud data, with "think aloud" used in a cavalier fashion by researchers whose questions to informants were clearly interviews rather than invitations to "tell me what you're thinking" while engaged in a musical activity. The methodology is included here because of its potential to reveal not only the cognitive processes of informants but the meanings they create when engaged with music.

Richardson's work with Cambodian refugee children was part of a research program focused on the cognitive processes involved in the music listening experience (Richardson, 1988, 1994, 1995, 1996, 1998, 1999). Sixty children in grades 1 through 8, designated "new arrivals," as they had just arrived in Sydney from Thai refugee camps, were asked to "think aloud" while listening to four short recorded examples of music drawn from western European classical music and four examples of traditional Cambodian music. The transcripts of their verbalizations were analyzed for evidence of cognitive processes found to be present in an adult musical connoisseur and musically trained elementary-aged children in a Chicago suburb. The results showed that the refugee children exhibited the same cognitive processes as their musically sophisticated age-mates, leading the researcher to conclude that human beings appear to be "hard wired" with universal cognitive processes that operate regardless of culture or education.

More recently, Richardson (2002) took a "postpositivist" look at the same data as a source of insight into the way these children create meaning while listening to both familiar and unfamiliar music. Their individual stories were brought to words in the clinical setting of the "think aloud" procedure by listening to the music of their homeland. Their tales of growing up in a state of constant danger and of leaving the green countryside of Cambodia for urban Sydney are a powerful contrast to the "data" reported in the earlier study, revealing the potential of think alouds to offer a window on children's affective lives as well as their cognitive processes.

Points of Departure for Future Studies

What kinds of music teaching and learning issues could best be studied using qualitative methodologies? We conclude by proposing a few possibilities.

Case Studies

- Studies of exemplar teachers and conductors, particularly ensemble directors and private teachers: What are the "teaching moves" that these individual practitioners do that result in highly skilled and musically expressive performances?
- What patterns of development occur in music teacher education students? How do their skills and understandings develop during the junior year 2-semester methods sequence?
- Further investigation of classroom practice to learn what is involved in teaching music for enhanced understanding, "interweaving the empirical with the conceptual" (Ball, 1999, p. 374)

Observational/Ethnographic Studies

What musical learnings result from enrichment and entertainment programs, such as artists-in-the-schools programs?

Ethnographic Case Studies

How has "school music" integrated with "real life" music in various settings? What meanings do kids have about each?

Verbal Protocol Analysis

What kinds of music learning can best be enhanced with technology? How do learners make meaning from their encounters with technology? What musical learnings happen? How is this integrated with what they learn in the classroom or ensemble?

REFERENCES

Arnheim, R. (1969). *Visual thinking*. Berkeley: University of California Press.

Atkinson, P., & Hammersley, M. (1994). Ethnography and participant observation. In N. K. Denzin & Y. S. Lincoln (Eds.), *Handbook of qualitative research* (pp. 248–261). Thousand Oaks, CA: Sage.

Ball, D. L., & Lampert, M. (1999). Multiples of evidence, time, and perspective: Revising the study of teaching and learning. In E. C. Lagemann & L. S. Shulman (Eds.), *Issues in education research: Problems and possibilities* (pp. 371–398). San Francisco: Jossey-Bass.

Becker, H. S., Geer, B., Hughes, E. C., & Strauss, A. L. (1961). *Boys in white: Student culture in medical school*. Chicago: University of Chicago Press.

Becker, H. (1993). Theory: The necessary evil. In D. J. Flinders & G. E. Mills (Eds.), *Theory and concepts in qualitative research* (pp. 218–229). New York: Teachers College Press.

Belenky, M. F., Clinchy, B. M., Goldberger, N. R., & Tarule, J. M. (1986). *Women's ways of knowing*. New York: Basic Books.

Berg, M. H. (1997). *Social construction of musical experience in two high school chamber music ensembles*. Unpublished doctoral dissertation, Northwestern University, Evanston.

Bogdan, R. C., & Biklin, S. K. (1998). *Qualitative research for education* (3rd ed.). Boston: Allyn and Bacon.

Bogdan, R. C., & Biklin, S. K. (1982). *Qualitative research in education*. Boston: Allyn and Bacon.

Bowers, C. A., & Flinders, D. J. (1990). *Responsive teaching*. New York: Teachers College Press.

Bresler, L., & Stake, R. E. (1992). Qualitative research methodology in music education. In R. Colwell (Ed.), *Handbook of research on music teaching and learning* (pp. 75–90). New York: Schirmer Books.

Bruner, J. (1990). *Acts of meaning.* Cambridge, MA: Harvard University Press.

Burnaford, G., Fischer, J., & Hobson, D. (1996) *Teachers doing research: Practical possibilities.* Mahwah, NJ: Erlbaum.

Campbell, D. T. (1979). Degrees of freedom and the case study. In T. D. Cook & C. S. Reichardt (Eds.), *Qualitative and quantitative methods in evaluation research* (pp. 49–67). Beverly Hills, CA: Sage.

Campbell, D. T., & Stanley, J. C. (1963). *Experimental and quasi-experimental designs for research.* Chicago: Rand McNally.

Casey, D. E. (1992). Descriptive research: Techniques and procedures. In R. Colwell (Ed.), *Handbook of research on music teaching and learning* (pp. 115–123). New York: Schirmer Books.

Clough, P. T. (1992). *The end(s) of ethnography: From realism to social criticism.* Newbury Park, CA: Sage.

Colwell, R. J. (1967). Music education and experimental research. *Journal of Research in Music Education, 25*(1), 73–84.

Creswell, J. W. (1988). *Qualitative inquiry and research design.* Thousand Oaks, CA: Sage.

Cronbach, L. (1975). Beyond the two disciplines of scientific psychology. *American Psychologist, 30,* 116–127.

Cronbach, L., & Suppes, P. (Eds.). (1969). *Research for tomorrow's schools.* New York: Macmillan.

Denzin, N. K., & Lincoln, Y. S. (Eds.). (1994). *The handbook of qualitative research.* Thousand Oaks, CA: Sage.

Dewey, J. (1934). *Art as experience.* New York: Perigee Books.

Donmoyer, R. (1990). Generalizability and the single-case study. In E. W. Eisner & A. Peshlein (Eds.), *Qualitative inquiry in education* (pp. 175–200). New York: Teachers College Press.

Donmoyer, R. (1996). Educational research in an era of paradigm proliferation: What is a journal editor to do? *Educational Researcher, 25*(2), 19–35.

Donmoyer, R. (in press). Paradigm talk reconsidered. In V. Richardson (Ed.), *Handbook of research on teaching* (4th ed.). Commerce, GA: Baker & Taylor Books.

Eisner, E. W. (1979). *The educational imagination.* New York: Macmillan.

Eisner, E. W. (1983). Anastasia might still be alive, but the monarchy is dead. *Educational Researcher, 12*(5), 13–14, 23–24.

Eisner, E. W. (1991). *The enlightened eye.* New York: Macmillan.

Eisner, E. W. (1997). The promise and perils of alternative forms of data representation. *Educational Researcher, 26*(6), 4–10.

Eisner, E. W. (1999). Rejoinder: A response to Tom Knapp. *Educational Researcher, 28*(1), 19–20.

Eisner, E. W., & Peshkin, A. (Eds.). (1990). *Qualitative inquiry in education: The continuing debate.* New York: Teachers College Press.

English, F. W. (2000). A critical appraisal of Sara Lawrence Lightfoot's *portraiture* as a method of educational research. *Educational Researcher, 29*(7), 21–26.

Erickson, F. (1986). Qualitative methods in research on teaching. In M. C. Wittrock (Ed.), *Handbook of research on teaching* (3rd ed., pp. 119–161). New York: Macmillan.

Ericsson, K. A., & Simon, H. A. (1993). *Protocol analysis: Verbal reports as data* (rev. ed.). Cambridge, MA: MIT.

Feiman-Nemser, S., & Floden, R. E. (1986). The cultures of teaching. In M. C. Wittrock (Ed.), *Handbook of research on teaching* (3rd ed., pp. 505–526). New York: Macmillan.

Flinders, D. J. (1992). In search of ethical guidance. *International Journal of Qualitative Studies in Education, 5*(2), 101–115.

Freire, P. (1973). *Pedagogy of the oppressed*. New York: Seabury Press.

Gadamer, H. (1975). *Truth and method* (G. Bardon & J. Cumming, Trans. and Eds). New York: Seabury Press.

Gage, N. L. (1963). *Handbook of research on teaching*. Chicago: Rand McNally.

Gahan, C., & Hannibal, M. (1998). *Doing qualitative research using QSR NVB IST*. Thousand Oaks, CA: Sage.

Gall, M., Borg, W. R., & Gall, J. P. (1996). *Educational research: An introduction* (6th ed.). White Plains, NY: Longman.

Geertz, C. (1973). *The interpretation of cultures*. New York: Basic Books.

Geertz, C. (1983). *Local knowledge: Further essays in interpretive anthropology*. New York: Basic Books.

Glaser, B. G., & Strauss, A. L. (1967). *The discovery of grounded theory: Strategies for qualitative research*. Chicago: Aldine.

Glesne, C. (1999). *Becoming qualitative researchers* (2nd ed.). New York: Longman.

Grumet, M. (1980). Autobiography and reconceptualization. *Journal of Curriculum Theorizing, 2,* 155–158.

Guba, E., & Lincoln, Y. (1989). *Fourth generation evaluation*. Newbury Park, CA: Sage.

Habermas, J. (1971). *Knowledge and human interests* (J. Shapiro, Trans.). Boston: Beacon Press.

Habermas, J. (1975). *Legitimation crisis* (T. McCarthy, Trans.). Boston: Beacon Press.

Heath, S. B. (1999). Discipline and disciplines in education research: Elusive goals? In E. C. Lagemann & L. S. Shulman (Eds.), *Issues in education research: Problems and possibilities* (pp. 203–223). San Francisco: Jossey-Bass.

Jackson, P. W. (1968). *Life in classrooms*. New York: Holt, Rinehart and Winston.

Jaeger, R. M. (Ed). (1988). *Complementary methods for research in education*. Washington, DC: American Educational Research Association.

Keller, E. F. (1983). *A feeling for the organism: The life and work of Barbara McClintock*. New York: Freeman.

Kuhn, T. (1962). *The structure of scientific revolutions*. Chicago: University of Chicago Press.

Kvale, S. (1996). *Interviews: An introduction to qualitative research interviewing*. Thousand Oaks, CA: Sage.

Lagemann, E. C. (1999). An auspicious moment for education research? In E. C. Lagemann & L. S. Shulman (Eds.), *Issues in education research: Problems and possibilities* (pp. 3–16). San Francisco: Jossey-Bass.

Langer, S. (1957). *Problems of art*. New York: Scribner's.

LeCompte, M. D., Millroy, W. L., & Preissle, J. (1992). *The handbook of qualitative research in education*. New York: Academic Press.

L'Hommedieu, R. L. (1992). *The management of selected educational process variables by master studio teachers in music performance*. Unpublished doctoral dissertation, Northwestern University, Evanston.

Lightfoot, S. L. (1983). *The good high school*. New York: Basic Books.

Lincoln, Y. S., & Guba, E. G. (1985). *Naturalistic inquiry*. Thousand Oaks, CA: Sage.

Malinowski, B. (1988). *Argonauts of the Western Pacific: An account of native enterprise and adventure in the archipelagoes of Melanesian New Guinea*. London: Routledge. (Original work published 1922)

Mayer, R. E. (2000). What is the place of science in educational research? *Educational Researcher, 29*(6), 38–39.

Miles, M. B., & Huberman, A. M. (1984). *Qualitative data analysis*. Beverly Hills, CA: Sage.

Munro, P. (1993). Continuing dilemmas in life history research. In D. J. Flinders & G. E. Mills (Eds.), *Theory and concepts in qualitative research* (pp. 163–177). New York: Teachers College Press.

Noddings, N. (1992). *The challenge to care in schools*. New York: Teachers College Press.

Noddings, N. (1995). *Philosophy of education*. Boulder, CO: Westview Press.

Noddings, N. (1999). Care, justice, and equity. In M. S. Katz, N. Noddings, & K. A. Strike (Eds.), *Justice and caring* (pp. 7–20). New York: Teachers College Press.

O'Toole, P. A. (1994). *Redirecting the choral classroom: A feminist poststructural analysis of power relations within three choral settings*. Unpublished doctoral dissertation, University of Wisconsin, Madison.

Patton, M. (1980). *Qualitative evaluation and research methods*. Newbury Park, CA: Sage.

Peshkin, A. (1978). *Growing up American*. Chicago: University of Chicago Press.

Peshkin, A. (1982). The researcher and subjectivity: Reflections on ethnography of school and community. In G. Spindler (Ed.), *Doing the ethnography of schooling* (pp. 20–47). New York: Holt, Rinehart and Winston.

Peshkin, A. (1988). In search of subjectivity of one's own. *Educational Researcher, 17*(7), 17–22.

Peshkin, A. (2000). The nature of interpretation in qualitative research. *Educational Researcher, 29*(9), 5–9.

Phillips, D. C. (1983). After the wake: Postpositivistic educational thought. *Educational Researcher, 12*(5), 4–12.

Phillips, D. C. (1990). Subjectivity and objectivity: An objective inquiry. In E. W. Eisner & A. Peshkin (Eds.), *Qualitative inquiry in education* (pp. 19–37). New York: Teachers College Press.

Powell, A. G., Farrar, E., & Cohen, D. K. (1985). *The shopping mall high school*. Boston: Houghton Mifflin.

Richardson, C. P. (1988). *Musical thinking as exemplified in music criticism*. Unpublished doctoral dissertation, University of Illinois, Urbana-Champaign.

Richardson, C. P. (1994). The music listening processes of the child connoisseur: A developmental model. *Proceedings of the Third International Conference for Music Perception and Cognition of the European Society for the Cognitive Sciences of Music, Liège, Belgium* (pp. 153–154). Liège: European Society for the Cognitive Sciences of Music.

Richardson, C. P. (1995, April). *Toward a global model of children's music listening processes*. Paper presented at the annual meeting of the American Educational Research Association, San Francisco.

Richardson, C. P. (1996, April). *Finding the voice within the data: Think alouds in music.* Paper presented at the annual meeting of the American Educational Research Association, New York City.

Richardson, C. P. (1998). The roles of the critical thinker in the music classroom. *Studies in Music, 17,* 107–120.

Richardson, C. P. (1999). The music listening processes of Cambodian refugee children. *Bulletin of the Council for Research in Music Education, 142,* 91.

Richardson, C. P. (2002). Eastern ears in Western classrooms: Cambodian refugee children in the general music class. In B. Hanley & T. Goo'sby (Eds.), *Musical Understanding: Perspectives in theory and practice.* Victoria: Canadian Music Educators Association.

Richardson, L. (1994). Writing: A method of inquiry. In N. K. Denzin & Y. S. Lincoln (Eds.), *Handbook of qualitative research* (pp. 516–529). Thousand Oaks, CA: Sage.

Rosaldo, R. (1989). *Culture and truth.* Boston: Beacon Press.

Schoenfeld, A. H. (1999). The core, the canon, and the development of research skills: Issues in the preparation of education researchers. In E. C. Lagemann & L. S. Shulman (Eds.), *Issues in education research: Problems and possibilities* (pp. 166–203). San Francisco: Jossey-Bass.

Schofield, J. W. (1990). Increasing the generalizability of qualitative research. In E. W. Eisner & Alan Peshkin (Eds.), *Qualitative inquiry in education* (pp. 201–232). New York: Teachers College Press.

Schön, D. (1983). *The reflective practitioner.* New York: Basic.

Schwandt, T. A. (1997). *Qualitative inquiry: A dictionary of terms.* Thousand Oaks, CA: Sage.

Shavelson, R. J., & Towne, L. (2002). *Scientific research in education.* Washington D.C.: National Academy Press.

Sherman, R. R., & Webb, R. B. (1988). *Qualitative research in education: focus and methods.* New York: Falmer Press.

Shuy, R. (1986). Secretary Bennett's teaching. *Teaching and Teacher Education, 2*(4), 315–323.

Sizer, T. R. (1984). *Horace's compromise: The dilemma of the American high school.* Boston: Houghton Mifflin.

Smith, J. K. (1993). Hermeneutics and qualitative inquiry. In D. J. Flinders & G. E. Mills (Eds.), *Theory and concepts in qualitative research* (pp. 183–200). New York: Teachers College Press.

Spindler, G. (Ed.). (1955). *Education and anthropology.* Stanford, CA: Stanford University Press.

Spindler, G. (Ed.). (1963). *Education and culture: Anthropological approaches.* New York: Holt, Rinehart, and Winston.

Spindler, G., & Spindler, L. (1992). Cultural process and ethnography: An anthropological perspective. In M. D. LeCompte, W. L. Millroy, & J. Preissle (Eds.), *The handbook of qualitative research in education* (pp. 53–92). New York: Academic Press.

Stake, R. E. (1986, April). *Situational context as influence on evaluation and use.* Paper presented at the annual meeting of the American Educational Research Association, San Francisco.

Stake, R. (1994). Case studies. In N. K. Denzin & Y. S. Lincoln (Eds.), *Handbook of qualitative research* (pp. 516–529). Thousand Oaks, CA: Sage.

Stake, R., Bresler, L., & Mabry, L. (1991). *Custom and cherishing: The arts in elementary schools.* Urbana, IL: Bulletin Council for Research in Music Education.

St. Maurice, H. (1993). The rhetorical return: The rhetoric of qualitative inquiry. In D. J. Flinders & G. E. Mills (Eds.), *Theory and concepts in qualitative research* (pp. 201–217). New York: Teachers College Press.

Stringer, E. T. (1993). Socially responsive educational research. In D. J. Flinders & G. E. Mills (Eds.), *Theory and concepts in qualitative research* (pp. 141–162). New York: Teachers College Press.

Stringer, E. T. (1996). *Action research: A handbook for practitioners.* Thousand Oaks, CA: Sage.

Thorndike, E. L. (1910). The contribution of psychology to education. *Journal of Educational Psychology, 1,* 5–12.

Van Maanen, J. (1988). *Tales of the field.* Chicago: University of Chicago Press.

Van Manen, M. (1990). *Researching lived experience.* Albany: State University of New York Press.

Veblen, K. K. (1991). *Perceptions of change and stability in the transmission of Irish traditional music: An examination of the music teacher's role.* Unpublished doctoral dissertation, University of Wisconsin, Madison.

Vidich, A. J., & Layman, S. M. (1994). Qualitative methods: Their history in sociology and anthropology. In N. K. Denzin & Y. S. Lincoln (Eds.), *Handbook of qualitative research* (pp. 23–59). Thousand Oaks, CA: Sage.

Waller, W. (1932). *Sociology of teaching.* New York: Wiley.

Weitzman, E., & Miles, M. (1995). *Computer programs for qualitative data analysis.* Thousand Oaks, CA: Sage.

Wolcott, H. F. (1973). *The man in the principal's office: An ethnography.* New York: Holt, Rinehart and Winston.

Wolcott, H. F. (1982). Differing styles of on-site research or, if it isn't ethnography, what is it? *Review Journal of Philosophy and Social Science, 7*(1,2), 154–169.

Wolcott, H. F. (1990a). On seeking—and rejecting—validity in qualitative research. In E. W. Eisner & A. Peshkin (Eds.), *Qualitative inquiry in education* (pp. 121–152). New York: Teachers College Press.

Wolcott, H. F. (1990b). *Writing up qualitative research.* Newbury Park, CA: Sage.

Wolcott, H. F. (1992). Posturing in qualitative research. In M. D. LeCompte, W. L. Milroy, & J. Preissle (Eds.), *The handbook of qualitative research in education* (pp. 3–52). New York: Academic Press.

Trends in Data Acquisition and Knowledge Development

9

LEE R. BARTEL

Research is "a systematic process by which investigators gather information, organize it in a meaningful way, and analyze and interpret it" (Asmus & Radocy, 1992, p. 141). While this definition does not indicate why investigators gather and work with information, a clue is in "a meaningful way"—the research process should be meaningful. Organizing, analyzing, and interpreting is a process of developing knowledge. Another way to express this is to say that research is a systematic process of data acquisition and knowledge development. The terms "data acquisition" and "knowledge development" resonate clearly with the current computer lexicon (Knowledge Discovery in Databases or KDD). This is intentional because technology is one of the most influential forces affecting research in the past 30 years. I have selected these terms to serve as "lenses" with which to examine trends in research.

A trend is direction of movement, a course, an inclination. To identify a trend means to note change over time and then to project the "direction" and "movement" of the change into the future. I am not a futurist. Nevertheless, I identify seven trends in research:

1. *Construct complexity*—researchers are taking into account more dimensions, facets, or connections as they construct research problems and build conceptual frameworks for studies;
2. *Ethical complexity*—recognizing and honoring the complexity of constructs such as teaching and learning takes the researcher into dimensions of students' lives that have strong ethical implications. This trend intersects with a growing attention to individual and human rights and requires compromise with traditional design principles;
3. *Methodological complexity*—the pursuit of satisfying answers to questions

343

consisting of complex constructs requires greater diversity and multiplicity of method;

4. *Data complexity*—multivariate and multimethod studies result in complexity in data as a whole and within specific types of data such as video recordings;

5. *Analytical complexity*—data and construct complexity dictates analytical complexity in the process of fitting most appropriate analyses with specific questions and data, and developing knowledge through patterns, relationships, similarities and differences, and so on;

6. *Representation complexity*—technological developments are providing new and easier ways of presenting data, data reductions, and knowledge claims, while epistemological argument is redefining what counts as "knowledge," with the result that knowledge representation is becoming increasingly complex; and

7. *Dissemination complexity*—website postings, e-journals, teleconferences, video journals, CD-ROMs are current indicators of dissemination opportunity, choice, and complexity.

Perhaps there are two mega trends: the use of technology and the increasing complexity in all facets of the process. Due to constraints on length, my focus is principally on three of the areas in which complexity is increasing.

I draw attention to complexity because the natural function of research is to simplify. Complexity, a property of an object, idea, phenomenon, organism, or system, stems from "compoundness"—multiple parts, layers, or dimensions. In addition, complexity lies not only in an entity as multiple components but also in the interconnectedness or interwovenness of the parts, each of which may depend on or influence the other, neither of which is in a fixed relationship or quantity, nor is related to a fixed behavior. For example, learning is complex. Learning depends on the many attributes of the learner, the home, the teacher, the curriculum, the school, and the environment. Each of these in turn is complex, with related and dependent dimensions. Considering learning without considering these interconnected dimensions would be to deny the essential nature of learning. Complexity, as a quality of being differentiated yet integrated, is commonly regarded as "the direction in which evolution proceeds" (Csikszentmihalyi, 1993, p. 157). Since I am looking at trends or changes in research, my perspective is a view over time.

Explanation of changes in complexity over time, or simply explanation of complexity itself is the focus of Complexity Theory. Although I am not making a direct application of Complexity Theory (or Chaos Theory), the implication of my observations and explanations may have some commonalities with it. An important assumption of Complexity Theory is its inherent dialectic of simplicity and complexity: "What looks incredibly complicated may have a simple origin, while surface simplicity may conceal something stunningly complex" (Briggs & Peat, 1999, p. 79). In its application in research, the most important premise of Complexity Theory is that complexity and simplicity are not so much "inherent in objects themselves, but in the way things interact with each other, and we, in turn, interact with them" (Briggs & Peat, 1999, p. 89).

To understand the seven trends more fully, we need to reconceptualize research in terms of "knowledge development" and "data acquisition." This may transcend the qualitative-quantitative division by focusing on essential processes of research.

Knowledge Development

Constructs as Knowledge

Graduate student Pierre plays with questions of creativity for a research study. He wonders whether it is an inherent potential or learned ability and then realizes he needs to clarify what he means by "creativity." Pierre reflects on instances when he was told he was especially creative. He remembers the feelings of anguish when he had to improvise in music class and the sense of euphoria when he crafted an exceptional poem. He describes the characteristics of some people he considers creative. He realizes the meaning "creativity" has in his mind is an accumulation of at least (1) personal experiences that were designated "creative," (2) demonstrations of others engaging in "creativity," (3) stories involving "creativity," and (4) the meanings of other words associated with creativity like spontaneous, artistic, novel, unique, and special. Pierre has constructed this set of meaning connections with creativity over many years. A complex construct relates to and depends on a multitude of other constructs; it constantly and continuously develops.

In research, the term *construct* generally means a defined concept, a formalized description of an informal notion, a distillation of an idea so that it can be operationalized with a "test" or checklist or categorical assignments. Researchers use the term *construct* to reflect individuals' active mental involvement in building a definition, the engagement in a constructive process to give clear meaning to an idea. The mind selects some things, rejects some things, connects some things. For example, *creativity* as a commonly used term clearly has a shared meaning that communicates something to many people in our culture. But, to study it in a formal research context, a researcher might define creativity in a way related to manipulation of materials, to certain procedures, or to observable products with defined characteristics; in other words, as an operational definition.

An infant's first recognitions of a violin and its associated sound, Pierre's association with "creativity," or the researcher's theoretical construct all share the feature of being a locus of meaning *constructed* by a mental process of selection and association from a host of "perceptual data." "Cronbach has concluded that all human action is constructed, not caused, and that to expect Newton-like generalizations describing human action, as Thorndike did, is to engage in a process akin to 'waiting for Godot' " (Donmoyer, 1990, p. 178, referring to Cronbach, 1982).

Many constructs begin as object recognition in nonlinguistic modes. Others begin almost as dictionary linguistic descriptions but as such are essentially "empty" constructs (like web pages that have only one thing on them and with no further links). Connotations can be added to these basic constructs through verbal and visual connections, but active experience is what essentially develops the richness of the construct. Clearly, a parent or teacher cannot simply "transfer" a fully-formed construct to the child. The person must engage perceptual data and build (construct) or organize it into a mental structure.

Basic constructs exist in a descriptive, denotative "noun" form, to which connotations are added through active experience. Qualitative descriptive constructs—adjectives and adverbs—emerge from attributions or characterizations of basic constructs and tend to take on values on a dichotomous continuum (e.g., hot versus cold, excellent versus mediocre, loud versus soft). Explanatory, or "theory-making," constructs develop as mental structures that encompass the links and relationships among constructs. Kelly (1955) refers to these in his *Psychology of Personal Constructs*; they are also the constructs described by schema theory. The relational, explanatory construct can be seen as a hypothesis or, with development, a theory. It acts as a means of making predictions about the world. As the person experiences a stream of sensory data from any or all the bodily senses, these hypothesis constructs offer "explanations" of the data by allocating them to existing constructs and relationships among constructs previously experienced or by introducing "modifications" to existing constructs.

In most cases in this chapter, I refer to descriptive and explanatory level constructs simultaneously. Where necessary, I differentiate by referring to schema-type constructs as "explanatory constructs." For example, knowledge is the sum of consciously and intentionally accessible constructs (in this case, both descriptive and explanatory types). In addition, I assume that constructs exist not only linguistically as word meanings but also in relation to all perceptual modes (phenomenal, linguistic, kinesthetic, affective, and performance; see Perlmutter and Perkins, 1982) and to all forms of intelligence (Gardner, 1999).

Knowledge development and understanding is concerned with (1) increasing the complexity of constructs (adding pages with more on them to the Website), (2) increasing the associations among constructs (creating more links between sites), (3) increasing the complexity of explanatory constructs, (4) increasing the extent of construct consciousness or clarity, (5) making associations more readily accessible, and (6) increasing facility at accessing and using the links, thereby (7) increasing the accuracy of explanatory constructs to anticipate and predict the future. The purpose of research is knowledge development.

Constructs in Research Design   Fine (1998) asserts, "What science makes is knowledge, which includes concepts and theories, along with things and even facts" (p. 4). Research is about constructing knowledge. Especially in the social sciences, where most music education research is methodologically situated, research works with constructs. We rarely work with objects or matter, as physicists do, where only the most radical constructivists might argue properties do not exist apart from representations of them. The things that concern music educators are more likely theoretical constructs such as musicianship, creativity, aptitude, preferences, attitudes, abilities, effectiveness, competence, artistry, achievement, excellence, learning, response, or understanding, for which we normally use "indicators" or representations from which we infer what we can know. What our research efforts are aimed at, then, is to refine, elaborate, or clarify our constructs.

Research design is generally a data acquisition and analysis plan for the purpose of developing knowledge. It is possible to make a plan to acquire data without a clear view of what knowledge exactly will be developed, but in most cases, even in research trying to develop "grounded theory," the researcher has a prediction of the type of knowledge, the category of constructs, that will emerge. The way to acknowledge this prediction is in the form of a question. A real question, one without an already formulated answer, is the means to examining the nature and adequacy of constructs. A question demands a method of answering. The plan to secure an answer is the research design. The constructs a researcher will think to question, the kinds of questions, and the kinds of methods admissible as legitimate for answering those questions are culturally influenced—whether that is a religious, societal, or research culture.

A researcher may decide to further knowledge in a defined area, on one facet of a problem, or a simple construct, but must recognize that resulting "incompleteness" and, thus, the possible irrelevance of the knowledge to the holistic and complex essence of education and life. Simplifying a construct in research may clarify method and design but risks distortion. Imposing a favorite method or design on possible questions thereby eliminates potentially useful and important questions. In addition, exploring phenomena one or two unidimensional constructs at a time is a slow process within a changing context. Cronbach (1975) stresses this problem of social science research: "The trouble, as I see it, is that we cannot store up generalizations and constructs for ultimate assembly into a network. It is as if we needed a gross of dry cells to power an engine and could only make one a month. The energy would leak out of the first cells before we had half the battery completed. So it is with the potency of our generalizations" (p. 123).

Construct contemplation and analysis is of greatest importance as a step toward research design. The next step, deciding what data will provide the sources of information from which knowledge can be advanced is just as crucial. What cannot be overemphasized is that all that can be obtained is a "representation" of the construct under study. The number on an ability test is a representation (or estimate in statistical terms) of ability-related tasks as defined by a theory-driven testmaker. If a student is observed demonstrating behaviors that are physical, verbal, or musical representations one may infer something about that student's ability. An interview with a person will obtain a linguistic representation, as well as some gestural representation, of an internal state.

Researchers are concerned about construct validity, that is, the extent to which the data being obtained adequately represent the construct theorized. If we are studying creativity, data might be observations of the manipulation of materials, of certain procedures, or of observable products with defined characteristics. Such data, selected to relate to a theoretical construct, may well ignore many aspects of the "creative experience" like the creator's feelings, some of the thought process occurring during the process of creation, the kinesthetic abilities limiting realization of an idea, or the ideas rejected during the process. A serious concern for researchers of creativity is one of construct validity, that is, do the dimensions included in the "observables" or the "test" really match the richness of meaning we give the word *creativity*. The problem may be that a complex construct is simplified into a "theoretical construct" that is too one-dimensional, too reliant on the immediately evident, or too poorly understood by the researcher.

Theoretical construct validity depends both on how well one knows the "common" construct and on how faithful the selected representations are to the "reality" they are taken to represent. If the constructs are thoroughly known, questions can be anticipated and the research design improved. If the complexity entailed in a situation is not understood, or if the researcher believes there may be unanticipated questions from incomplete construct-awareness, the research may begin exploring the environment and attend to the constructs being "tweaked" by the incoming data. The researcher then is becoming aware of the constructs employed in classifying and filing incoming data. Whether through formal "instruments" or mentally analyzed informal observations, this is a process of data acquisition and knowledge development.

Constructs and Analysis   Given that the data in a large database are of various types, a program to make sense of them must be flexible enough to accommodate the diversity. One way is to apply to software the concepts of Kelly's (1955) *Psychology of Personal Constructs*. The fundamental principle holds that a person's psychological processes are directed by explanatory constructs. Kelly sees the main function of explanatory constructs (or schemas) as creating personal predictions about the world. The person then tests the predictions, and the construct is reinforced or changed depending on how well the experiential reality matches the prediction. Data mining software begins with constructs of postulated relationships among data. These anticipatory constructs are then confirmed, altered, or mutated in an iterative process. Knowledge constructs are "discovered" in the database by the computer.

In a similar manner, the researcher conducting a case study of a classroom acquires a constant stream of "data." These data are processed with existing explanatory constructs—the result of all previous "learning" (knowledge development). As the researcher's explanatory constructs encounter data that cannot be accommodated by existing structures, new ones are created or existing ones modified. This process of the mind is essentially the same as that of normal living that results in our "informal" knowledge or common sense. However, when the researcher makes the process conscious by making the construct structure conscious, it is clearly recognizable as an analysis process. Researchers gathering verbal, gestural, artistic, or emotive representations must be especially aware of the "data mining" nature of their analysis.

The quantitatively descriptive researcher engages in virtually the same process but in a slower and more linear manner. Data are representations, believed to have validity related to the constructs under study. The representations are analyzed with an existing construct and the degree to which they coincide with the construct is made conscious. The researcher then decides whether the basic construct or the anticipatory/explanatory construct is confirmed or requires modification.

Implication of Constructs for Method

If Cronbach (1982) is correct that all human action is constructed, not caused, and the explanations we have presented are plausible, then research method begins with and accounts for the nature of the constructs to be studied. Furthermore, method and analysis must acknowledge that in social science, the phenomena of interest are usually enmeshed with the construct structure of each individual in the study. That emphasizes the urgent need for attention to construct validity in any study and that validity probably rests to a great extent on the complexity of the representations as well as what Keeves (1997a) calls "band width" (range of manifestations) and "fidelity" (observational unidimensionality). To honor the complexity inherent in most constructs, researchers must plan for a program of research, multiple data types, multimethods, or close identification with a "family" of studies contributing to a shared knowledge.

Data Acquisition

A Basic Research Process

Without data, there is no research. The data employed in knowledge development may not be recent but nonetheless are data and should be recognized as such. The philosopher engaged in criticism of a praxial approach to music education may employ constructs acquired from Kant or Sparshott 10 years ago. The historian may have strong personal memories of participation in an organization she is now studying. The experimenter gathers his computer file of data. The anthropologist writes copious field notes, creates audio and video recordings, and gathers representative objects. Data acquisition is crucial in every case.

Types of Data

All data are representations. An achievement test score is a representation of the student's achievement (itself a theoretical construct). Numbers are not quantities, they are mental surrogates for quantities. The numeral "7" in and of itself is an indication of "sevenness" in whatever property to which it is applied. The words in the interview transcription are not the meanings and thoughts of the interviewee, they are surrogates for those meanings. Therefore, to understand the types of data, we must explore types of representations. (Just to clarify the obvious, we are assuming there is a reality apart from representations of it.)

Representations of knowledge are both internal (the way we represent images and concepts internally) and external (the way we represent our knowledge to communicate it to others). For example, through internal representation, we create a construct we label "up" by about kindergarten. It develops with every lift off the floor or climbing of the stair (kinesthetically), with tossing a toy or pointing to the sky (spatial), with making a vocal glissando (musical), with counting while building the block tower (mathematical), and with adding words to all these experiences (linguistic). We can communicate something about "up" to others through external representations—moving our hand upward (gestural), pointing upward (symbolic), drawing an arrow pointing to the "top" of the page (iconic), saying the word "up" (linguistic), saying a series of numbers representing increasing quantities (numeric), or making a sound increasing rapidly in pitch (musical). Representations fall at least into the areas of Gardner's (1999) basic intelligences: linguistic, logical-mathematical, musical, bodily-kinesthetic, spatial, and, probably, intra- and interpersonal, and possibly even naturalist and spiritual. Within each there are different expressions and forms. For example, linguistic representations may be a single word, a logical proposition, a poem, or a story. Bodily-kinesthetic representations may include symbolic gestures such as sign language, kinesthetic analogues, dance, or pantomine. The important conclusion here is that all forms of external representation can be regarded as "data" and therefore recorded and analyzed.

Roles of Data

Data, as knowledge representation, have distinct roles. Davis, Shrobe, and Szolovits (1993) identify five roles of a knowledge representation that are pertinent to artificial intelligence applications on computers. Three are particularly relevant here. The first and most obvious is the basic role of a knowledge representation as a surrogate—something that substitutes for the thing itself. The second role of data is as a "set of ontological commitments." External reality can be represented in various ways, and no representation is perfect. Each attempted representation captures some things but necessarily omits others. Therefore, every time researchers decide what they will focus on in the world and how they will represent it, they are "making a set of ontological commitments. The commitments are in effect a strong pair of glasses that determine what we can see, bringing some part of the world into sharp focus, at the expense of blurring other parts" (Davis, Shrobe, & Szolovits, 1993, p. 20).

A third role a knowledge representation fulfills is as a "medium of human expression." This is most important in research in terms of communicating knowledge developed in the research process. An important point here is that knowledge as a construct is generally complex, and the selection of a means of representing it again focuses on some facets and ignores others. Expression and communication are different. A person may choose a way to express knowledge and it may satisfy that person, but it may not communicate what was intended or meant. It is one thing to record video data of a conductor's gesture, analyze the gestures as knowledge representations, and reshape existing knowledge about musical problem solving, and quite another to appear in front of a research conference and demonstrate that knowledge only with gestures. Gesture may be needed to communicate aspects of knowledge that are not easily represented in words, but words are pragmatically useful. Anyone traveling in a country where his or her language is not understood knows how difficult gestural communication alone is. At the same time, in many contexts, seeing another's gestures enhances communication accuracy.

Data Acquisition Concerns

The primary requirement of data, of a representation as a surrogate, is that it is something out of which we can make meaning that is warranted and that the meaning it contributes is supported or at least not contradicted through multiple perspectives (i.e., it is valid). Although validity often appears to hinge on methodology (e.g., randomization and control in experiments, population and sampling in descriptive, triangulation in interpretivist), validity is primarily about credible, defensible meaning-making from the selected representation. Cronbach (1971) asserts, "One validates, not a test, but an interpretation of data arising from a specified procedure" (p. 447). Zeller (1997) explains, "it is not the indicant itself that is being validated, but rather, it is the purpose for which the indicant is being used that is submitted to validation procedures" (p. 824). If a professor uses a highly "valid" music history examination as a measure of achievement in a musical acoustics class, there certainly would be indefensible meaning-making.

Because the constructs we deal with in social science are complex, selecting any one representation from which we can credibly infer meaning is nearly impossible. Consequently, researchers concerned about validity may need to draw on several types of representations (complex data) and multiple methods. Zeller (1997) argues, "A valid inference occurs when there is no conflict between messages received as a result of the use of a variety of different methodological procedures" (p. 829).

Seven Trends

Trend 1: Construct Complexity

The most fundamental trend affecting the social and behavioral science dimensions of music education research is the growing recognition by researchers of complexity as a central characteristic of all constructs and phenomena and the increasing complexity of the constructs themselves. Constructs do not exist in external reality—only the sources for our constructs do. Constructs are mental creations and develop toward complexity. Complexity is characterized by "compoundness"—multiple parts, layers, or dimensions—and interconnectedness of the parts, each of which may depend on or influence the other, none of which are in a fixed relationship or quantity, nor are related to a fixed behavior. For example, the researcher today may acknowledge that "self-concept" as a research construct is more complex than researchers thought 15 years ago, but the self-concept construct in the typical research subject's mind may be more complex today than it was 25 years ago, because of an increase in comparative images from the media, peer comparisons through Internet chat lines, or societal standards resulting from cultural diversity.

The complexity problem was first described in relation to the problem of generalizability of specific research findings. The hope enunciated by E. L. Thorndike (1910) was to "tell every fact about everyone's intellect and character and behavior, . . . the cause of every change in human nature . . . the result which every educational force . . . would have" (p. 6). In 1957, Cronbach reiterated this hope, but argued that to accomplish this researchers would have to focus on the effects of interactions rather than the effects of treatments. Frustration from inconsistent findings from similar studies led Cronbach (1975) to conclude as we said earlier:

> Once we attend to interactions, we enter a hall of mirrors that extends to infinity. However far we carry our analysis—to third-order or fifth-order or any other—untested interactions of still higher order can be envisioned. (p. 119)

A major part of the problem seemed related to changing cultural context and the speed with which studies can be done. Cronbach concluded:

The trouble, as I see it, is that we cannot store up generalizations and constructs for ultimate assembly into a network. It is as if we needed a gross [12 dozen] of dry cells to power an engine and could only make one a month. The energy would leak out of the first cells before we had half the battery completed. So it is with the potency of our generalizations. (p. 123)

A problem for research is that we are dealing with complex constructs within a complex context that is evolving rapidly toward greater complexity. One social science reaction to this problem may be the rise of qualitative research. "Qualitative" researchers frequently point to the simplifying, linear approach of quantitative researchers as focusing on phenomena or constructs that have no relevance in the complicated real world. Quantitative researchers have been slow to respond with analytic techniques that can accommodate the complexity inherent in education or even to acknowledge the complexity. The arguments between the two groups have been so drenched in philosophic fundamentals of Cartesian reductionism, hermeneutics, epistemology, realism, relativism, constructivism, and so on, that the more practical issues of construct complexity have been lost behind the smokescreen of the paradigm wars in educational research. Cziko (1989) observes that "the debate, centered on issues related to quantitative versus qualitative approaches to research, has at the very least raised serious questions. . . . There appears, however, to have been little discussion among educational researchers of what may be an even more basic issue, that is, the possibility that the phenomena studied in the social and behavioral sciences are essentially unpredictable and indeterminate [complex]" (p. 17). Evolution toward increasing complexity has not only affected the social sciences. Perhaps not yet openly perceived as a paradigm war in "hard science," limitations of the Newtonian Paradigm are showing and "a major fault line has developed in the episteme" (Hayles, 1991, p. 16). The wedge now driving open this fault is Complexity Theory.

Qualitative researchers reacted to the simplicity and linearity problem of traditional scientific research by abandoning formal measurement and calculation. Naturalistic contexts are inherently complex and make credible analysis and understanding difficult. Complexity-informed researchers in social science are responding now in several ways. One is to imitate the physical scientists in searching for "chaotic order in dynamic data sets measured across very large numbers of time points" (Byrne, 2000, p. 2) with statistically rigorous analysis of the dynamics of chaos in social science data. Another approach is the development through computer-based simulations "of very elegant graphical representations of the behavior of uninterpreted deterministic chaotic expressions" (Byrne, 2000, p. 3). This allows for the examination, for example, "of whole system properties corresponding exactly to Durkheim's conception of social facts, and allows for examination of their emergence and transformation over time" (Byrne, 2000, p. 3).

A third way complexity-informed social science researchers are changing is to look in a new way at both quantitative and qualitative approaches. In quantitative research, we either have or can envision large and complex data sets—of the sort acquired through national assessments, polls, census, market surveys, government revenue data, school evaluations, and so on. These data sets are complex because they contain varied data about individuals and groups in a time-series manner. Perhaps logistic regression and loglinear procedures are appropriate analysis techniques because of the possibility for handling interaction. However, Bryne (2000) says—and Cronbach (1975) might agree—"It has been unfortunate that the emergent complexity generated by interaction has so often been reduced to terms in linear equations. A way of thinking informed by complexity leads us to treat procedures which enable the identification of significant interaction as qualitative exploratory devices rather than as ways of establishing law-like models . . . Instead of generating models which seek to describe determinants of outcomes, and writing interactions as terms in those models, we can see interactions as signs of the presence of complexity in general" (Byrne, 2000, p. 4). In qualitative research, we are seeing a trend toward computer-assisted analysis. The influence of Complexity researchers will probably result in an emphasis on time-ordered data and analysis that looks for development and change.

Trend 2: Ethical Complexity

At least three factors have contributed to a trend of increasing ethical complexity in conducting music education research. The first is the increasing complexity of the constructs under study. No longer are rigorous researchers satisfied to administer a short paper-pencil test and claim, for example, it is a valid measure of self-concept. The acknowledgement of construct complexity means researchers are probing deeper into sensitive areas—psychological issues, home and private matters, relationships, roles and perceptions—all of which potentially can destabilize the participant's mental state or raise questions that provoke transformative reflection. Also, some constructs studied in music education are diversified and include topics that may touch on sensitive or confidential data, for example, mentoring (Lamb, 1997b, 1998, 1999), peak experience (Gabrielsson, 1991; Sundin, 1989), negative feedback (Cameron & Bartel, 2000; Jacques, 2000), or brainwave manipulating sounds (Bartel, 2000).

A second factor is the increasing complexity of the social environment within which music education takes place. In cosmopolitan cities, cultural diversity continues to increase. Not long ago, a researcher in Canada or the United States could send a letter requesting permission written in English to parents with considerable confidence that it could be read and understood. Today in Toronto, for example, most schools have upwards of 30 language groups represented among the students and many of the families are recent immigrants. Although students are learning English, parental permission for research necessitates extensive translation of letters and further raises fears among many people of privacy invasion through student observation or questioning. Subject diversity of language, culture, or religion becomes a prominent issue in the interpretation of data representing most constructs. This is less of a problem with simple constructs but a serious problem in complex constructs. An ethical issue resides in the integrity of our interpretations—do we really understand and correctly represent what people know, believe, experience, perceive, or achieve?

A third factor increasing ethical complexity is "the rights revolution" (Ignatieff, 2000). Beginning with the 1948 Universal Declaration of Human Rights, the past 50+ years have seen a constant struggle for freedom, civil rights, equal rights, self-government, or human rights. Often the battle has been between individual rights versus special group rights. The development of an increasingly litigious culture has exacerbated the situation. One consequence of these struggles has been a climate where both subjects and researchers are much more aware, and ethical watch-dog agencies are much more cautious. As a result researchers must anticipate and clarify procedures and effects, communicate clearly and accurately to all touched by the research, and obtain legally defensible permissions for all research.

Trend 3: Methodological Complexity

Research methodology is the plan employed to acquire data and make meaning (develop knowledge) out of those data. It is an intentional process to reshape or confirm existing constructs (knowledge). In education, this process has always been relatively complex, because educational research is inherently multidisciplinary—the concerns of education draw on many disciplines. Historical and philosophical research have methodological traditions pursued in music education research. Psychology as a discipline developed in the past 120 years, and has two, at times competing, orientations—experimental and correlational (Cronbach, 1957; Shulman, 1988). Both psychological research orientations have been prominent in music education research. Musicology, in addition to its historical dimension, is an analytic approach, one that is applied in music education research. Sociological research in the past relied heavily on surveys—questionnaires and interviews. This is one of the most common approaches in music education research. Anthropology has had less application in music education research until recently, but ethnomethodology has been rising in popularity. Some disciplines, such as linguistics, economics, and demography, have had little effect on music education research.

Educational research is inherently multilevel—concerned about both individuals and groups. Educational research deals with problems that are inherently complex: "It is rare that a problem in educational research can be reduced in such a way that it can be viewed in terms of only two constructs or variables" (Keeves, 1997b, p. 278). Educational research often examines learning over time making multiple or repeated measures necessary.

As a result of being multidisciplinary, multilevel, and inherently complex, educational research is multimethod. However, the existence of many methods, if these were clearly differentiated but not integrated, would demonstrate diversity but only limited complexity. The growing acceptance of multiple epistomologies, however, adds another layer of real complexity.

The often heated paradigm wars in educational research that attempted to demonstrate the "rightness" of one paradigm over another, assumed that distinct paradigms existed and that, if so, only one could be "true." There are serious flaws in the concept of distinct paradigms (Walker & Evers, 1997), but as foundational theories for a specific set of research methodologies they do have utility. Walker and Evers (1997) explain:

> In offering a broader, three-way taxonomy of research to account for diversity in inquiry, Popkewitz (1984, p. 35) says: "the concept of paradigm provides a way to consider this divergence in vision, custom and tradition. It enables us to consider science as procedures and theories of social affairs." He assumes that "in educational sciences, three paradigms have emerged to give definition and structure to the practice of research." After the fashion of "critical theory" (Habermas, 1972), he identifies the paradigms as "empirical-analytic" (roughly equivalent to quantitative science), "symbolic" (qualitative and interpretive or hermeneutical inquiry), and "critical" (where political criteria relating to human betterment are applied in research). (p. 23)

The coexistence of these epistomological perspectives is important. They do not supersede each other as paradigms in the way natural sciences are assumed to do (although that is now in question as well), or as Lincoln and Guba (1984) seem to assume with their "paradigm eras."

Another facet of research methodology has greatly affected the overall complexity of knowledge development processes in the past 15 years—theoretical orientation. These orientations are differentiated in specific ways from each other, with common features between some, and selective discipline and paradigm acceptance among them. Babbie (1995) argues that these orientations coexist and cocontribute to a complete view of social and behavioral phenomena because each "offers insights that others lack—but ignores aspects of social life that other[s] . . . reveal" (p. 41).

Babbie (1995) and Rothe (1993) identify the following as distinct theoretical orientations affecting methodological decisions: (1) social Darwinism—research finding factors predicting or facilitating survival of the fittest (e.g., finding characteristics of band students most likely to succeed); (2) conflict theory—questions related to class or group (e.g., how "ethnic minorities" are excluded from mainstream musical culture through the maintenance of "racial" stereotyping); (3) symbolic interactionism—concerns about how the individual constructs an image of self through interactions with groups and individuals, is able to take on the perspective of the other, and then tailors communication in anticipation of the reaction of the "generalized other." For example, orchestra members may have a view that conductors are volatile, passionate, dictators. Consequently, they act cautiously, await instructions, and tolerate abusive behavior. The conductor sees them as musicians to be instructed, controlled, and manipulated, possibly by dramatized anger in order that they will play with adrenalin and passionate vigor. The interaction between the group and the individual is symbolic; (4) role theory—examinations of how taking on a role restricts or permits certain behaviors, for example, the role of passionate conductor. Dolloff (1999) focuses on how music teachers have an image of "teacher" that sets behavioral expectations for themselves when they assume the role of teacher; (5) ethnomethodology—examines a culture in context to make sense of how people live and what meaning they give to their reality, assuming that people's realities are constructed in cultural context. For example, a community choir can be a distinct culture and the researcher could "live" awhile in this culture to discover the realities experienced there; (6) structural functionalism—organizations or societies are systematically structured like organisms—consisting of components that each contribute to the function of the whole (e.g., what distinguishes tenured professors from untenured professors from graduate students from undergraduate students by examining values, norms, community types, or individual roles); (7) feminist theory—an orientation that has common features usually including a rejection of positivism, a ubiquitous concern with gender, stress on the value-ladeness of all research, the adoption of liberatory methodology, and the pursuit of nonhierarchical research relationships (Haig, 1997, pp. 180–181); (8) exchange theory—examination of the rationality applied in weighing costs and benefits of all choices (Homans, 1974). A researcher might examine what constitutes music students' cost and benefit ledger related to time-intensive practice and the benefits of musical achievement; (9) phenomenology—a focus on how people internalize the objective world into consciousness and negotiate its reality in order to make it livable and shareable, for example, what is it like being a musical child prodigy? (10) conversational analysis—assumes conversation is central in interpersonal behavior. Particular interest is in status and power revealed in conversational structure, for example, through interruptions and overlaps. The "talk" between trumpet teacher and trumpet student might be the means of studying student/teacher relationship; (11) social Ecology—assumes "physical properties of territory act as reference points for people's interactions with one another" (Rothe, 1993, p. 56). A field experiment manipulating music room environment would address its social ecology; (12) action research—not so much a theory as an attitude with focus on improvement. A teacher might enlist the cooperation of a choir to record, in a reflective journal, responses to some innovative strategies to build a sense of community. Analysis of the students' and teacher's journals would serve as data to determine whether the innovations result in improvement.

Other discipline-related orientations are surely possible, but these serve to illustrate the complexity that develops as paradigm, discipline, and orientation interact in the creation of research method. Music education research does not reveal all of these orientations, but a basic trend is toward a greater emphasis on sociology of music, constructivism, and the social aspects of music making and learning, and with that will come specific social research orientations (McCarthy, 1997, 2000; Paul, 2000).

The relevance of discipline, paradigm, and orientations to research method is evident if one sees research method not simply as the data acquisition method but, rather, as an interaction among the question posed, the analysis required to answer the question, and the data appropriate for the analysis. An important role of the orientations is in influencing what questions will be asked, but they also influence who will be asked, how answers will be obtained, what will count as valued representations and as knowledge, and what analyses will be conducted.

I must make an important observation: The primary form of data (representation) in empirical-analytic research is the numeral, hence the common designation "quantitative." The primary form of data (representation) in symbolic and critical research is the word. Words allow for use of adjectives and adverbs, the description of qualities, and hence the designation "qualitative." I differentiate, however, among quantitative methods on the basis of: (1) How the data are acquired (by asking questions requiring ratings it could be survey, by asking questions on a "test" it could be an experiment or a correlational study, and by counting checkmarks on a list representing behaviors it could be an observational study); (2) from whom the data are acquired (random sample assigned to comparative groups could be an experiment, or a single group volunteer sample might be a survey); (3) what happens between data acquisition efforts (if a planned treatment is administered it may be an experiment); and (4) what analysis is planned for the acquired data (if two sets of scores from a group of individuals are compared for relationship it is correlational, if the averages are compared it could be an experiment). The question(s) that motivate the research are directly answered by the analysis and so have an important defining role for methodology.

These four aspects of research: how the data are *acquired,* from *whom* the data are acquired, what *happens* between data acquisition efforts, and what *analysis* is planned for the acquired data, along with the defining role of the research questions and their explanatory intention, determine method. They do so in "quantitative" research and they do so in "qualitative" research. Consequently, the general category of qualitative research contains many specific methods. However, the definition of these methods may not be settled, because the field is still evolving.

The most direct way to methodological relatedness is in multimethod studies. Exploring complex constructs raises multiple questions that frequently demand multiple methods. In the past, these were most likely methods within a single epistomological paradigm, but researchers are beginning to combine "quantitative" and "qualitative" methods in a single study. Zeller (1997) asserts that "one method used in isolation does not provide compelling answers to many research problems. The reason for this is clear. Different techniques differ dramatically in their purposes, goals, objectives, tactics, strategies, strengths, and weaknesses. The original questions that prompt the research and the new questions that emerge from its results require a blending of methods" (p. 828). In the discussion of validity in research, Zeller argues further that "inferences about validity do not lend themselves to solely quantitative or statistical solutions. On the contrary, an interactive research strategy combining quantitative and qualitative is advocated. A valid inference occurs when there is no conflict between messages received as a result of the use of a variety of different methodological procedures" (Zeller, 1997, p. 829).

Trend 4: Data Complexity

All data are representations, intentionally acquired or captured for study. An achievement test score sets a fixed point, a freeze-frame of sorts, for the individual's ever developing achievement. A video recording of a piano lesson can later be viewed and reviewed. The image on the video screen is not the actual lesson—it is a representation of the lesson. It is selected for study and is fixed (selected, made stable, not repaired) to the extent that it can be repeatedly viewed.

The researcher's selection of the phenomenon or representation for study is one of the most important and urgent decisions in any research effort. In traditional empirical-analytic research, this is done early in the process, and study design is created accordingly. In interpretivist approaches, the researcher may decide that some aspect of teaching may be studied, commence video recording many episodes of teaching, and delay the decision on what specific phenomena or representations to describe or interpret. But, regardless of delay, or multiple viewings of a tape, eventually the researcher selects the words, actions, or gestures to include in the analytic and interpretive process.

Ways to fix representations for study include: (1) audio recorded language (often transcribed into written form); (2) written language of various types; (3) audio recorded sound; (4) video recordings of the phenomena; (5) test scores; (6) verbal or numeric categorical assigments; (7) numeric rating or rank values; (8) graphic displays; (9) photographic or pictorial prints; (10) artifacts; and (11) symbols and symbolic notations. Obviously, categories and subcategories are possible. For example, audio recorded sound could have subcategories such as music, ambient room noise, subject's nonverbal sounds, and so on.

There is a simple to complex specificity range in fixed data. Consider the following: a checkmark in a category, the number on a rating scale, or the test score; an audio recording of an interview or a written narrative account; a video recording of an interpretive dance; or an artist's self-portrait. All hold meaning and can be interpreted; however, the layers, strands, connections, and interrelationships of meaning in the latter are considerably greater.

An important characteristic to note about different types of data is data depth. Certain types of data, such as categorical assignments or test scores, have a simple relationship with the construct they represent. Other data types, however, are more complex. The data fixed by a video recording of a band rehearsal can be subjected to various theoretical orientation "lenses" or to various research questions. Such data has "depth" that can be mined and refined repeatedly before its store is depleted. The more complex the data type is, the more depth it offers for data mining.

Trend 5: Analytical Complexity

Despite the increasing complexity of constructs, methodology, and data, analysis is essentially a process of simplification, a process of creating order within the represented reality that allows for meaning making (interpretation). Analysis is a process of clarification, a process of reducing unknowns. In a computer systems context, complexity is defined as "the existence of unknowns" (Kafre Systems International, 1998). The goal of research is to eliminate unknowns through the development of knowing, and it may do so by imposing a simplification system. It is in analysis that the tension between complexity and simplification exists most obviously. In statistical analysis, the researcher lets a number represent a phenomenon, manipulates the collected numbers to reduce them to a number representing something new, and postulates an implication of the number for the original observed phenomenon. In qualitative analysis, the researcher frequently transcribes or notates the representations, categorizes and classifies these for further comparative examination, and postulates an explanation or interpretation about the observed phenomena. However, the phenomena and constructs of interest to music educators are complex and analyses leading to unidimensionality, simple linearity, or "stories that dissolve all complexity" (Shenk, 1997, p. 157), are no longer useful if progress in research is to be made.

General Responses to Complexity

In educational research, attendance to complexity can be seen as giving greater place to individual uniqueness and context, to multiple perspectives, and different representations. Several developments in research design, analysis, and measurement illustrate how these requirements can be accommodated.

Rasch Analysis Rasch analysis recognizes the inevitable interaction of a measurement technique with the person being measured (Keeves, 1997a). The technique links qualitative analysis to quantitative methods by converting dichotomous and rating scale observations into linear measures. It is often misclassified under item response theory or logit-linear models. These describe data. "Rasch specifies how persons, probes, prompts, raters, test items, tasks, etc. *must* interact statistically for linear measures to be constructed from ordinal observations. Rasch implements stochastic Guttman ordering, conjoint additivity, Campbell concatenation, sufficiency and infinite divisibility" (Linacre, 1995).

Single-Case Design and Change Measurement   Recognizing complexity raises serious doubt about the generalizability of results from large samples. When researchers average results from groups of subjects, they omit considerable richness in the data (Sharpley, 1997, p. 451). Practitioners' concerns with individuals rather than aggregates mean that the scientific theory generalized from research actually has limited application in practice. "Even statistically significant findings from studies with huge, randomly selected samples cannot be applied directly to individuals in particular situations; skilled clinicians will always be required to determine whether a research generalization applies to a particular individual, whether the generalization needs to be adjusted to accommodate individual idiosyncrasy, or whether it needs to be abandoned entirely with certain individuals in certain situations" (Donmoyer, 1990, p. 181). As a result, research aimed at establishing the utility of specific interventions rather than at establishing scientific principles is finding single-case design particularly useful (Jutai, Knox, Rumney, Gates, Wit, & Bartel, 1997).

Single-case studies can have a macrofocus (Stake, Bresler, & Mabry, 1991) or a microfocus (Jutai et al., 1997) and can be designed to yield various types of data. For those generating numeric data, the measurement of change in the interrupted time series is the primary analytic task. In the past, there was debate between advocates of simple visual analysis of a graphic representation of research participants' change and advocates of statistical analysis. The problem was that graphic representation was easily distorted and that traditional statistical procedures were not properly applicable because simple pre and postcomparisons were not adequate. One of the concerns influencing analysis is both the within person change and the between person change. Least-squares regression analysis has been used for within person change and weighted least-squares regression analysis for between person change. However, recent developments have made change measurement more powerful, assuming the collection of considerable longitudinal data. High-quality analysis of within- and between-person models can be conducted with hierarchical linear modeling (Bryk & Raudenbush, 1992) or with covariance structure analysis (Willett & Sayer, 1994, 1995).

Meta-Analysis   Glass (1976) coined the term *meta-analysis* for an approach that allows the quantitative, analytic integration of the results from many studies on a particular phenomenon. Although the statistical procedure treats the studies selected for integration as being alike, in actual fact the meta-analysis merges multiple perspectives and varying definitions of constructs. It is then a form of analysis that simplifies the complexity inherent in research in a particular field. If "reality" is complex and any one study cannot adequately encompass that complexity to form an explanation of it, then integrating all attempts at such explanation in a meta-analysis may more adequately honor the complexity.

Integration of analyses from multiple independent studies had been done in some form before Glass (1976). Cotes (1722) describes how astronomers' observations were combined by using weighted averages. Pearson (1904) integrated five separate samples by averaging estimates of correlation. Birge (1932) attempted to integrate results in physics by weighting combinations of estimates; Cochran (1937) and Yates and Cochran (1938) did so with agricultural experiments. Tippett (1931) and Fisher (1932) proposed a method of combining probability values.

The use of meta-analysis has been increasing, especially in the past 15 years. Barrowman (1998), surveying the use of meta-analysis in medical research, found two or three studies per year in the early 1980s, increasing to about 10 per year by the mid-1980s, and to 80 by the end of the 1980s. Egger and Smith (1997, p. 1) found this trend continued, with close to 800 meta-analysis studies reported in Medline by 1996. In music education, few meta-analysis studies have been done. A search of the major journals revealed two, Standley (1996) and the more sophisticated Hetland (2000). However, "meta-analysis seems well suited . . . to make a larger and larger contribution to the social and behavioral sciences, and to a broad range of policy-relevant research" (Wachter & Straf, 1990, p. 28).

The most common approach to meta-analysis is to calculate the effect size on each study selected for inclusion. Effect size is basically the mean of the treatment group minus the mean of the control group divided by the standard deviation of the control group (Light & Pillemer, 1984). The pattern of effect sizes can then be examined visually by plotting them on frequency distributions or funnel displays that plot effect size, for example, against sample size. Statistical procedures are used to calculate cumulative effects, for example, overall mean effect size (Glass, McGraw, & Smith, 1981; Hunter, Schmidt, & Jackson, 1982; Rosenthal, 1991).

Criticisms of meta-analysis focus primarily on three issues: independence, the "apples" and "oranges" problem, and the "file drawer" problem. When a single study consists of multiple "experiments," several effect-size estimates result. These cannot be used separately in a meta-analysis, because they may be drawn from the same sample and, consequently, are not independent. Glass et al. (1981) acknowledge the problem and suggest calculating an average effect for the study as a whole. As these individual study effects are mostly related to distinct variables, critics argue that averaging them is not an adequate solution (Chou, 1992). This is a criticism that focuses on the tension between the complexity of reality and the analytic drive to simplify for understanding. The "apples" and "oranges" problem is somewhat related. Critics point out that meta-analysis integrates effects from variables based on different theoretical constructs. Glass et al. (1981) argue that researchers constantly aggregate data from different individuals who are like "apples" and "oranges." The important consideration is that the meta-analysis concern must be about "fruit," and then "apples" and "oranges" can be included. The "file drawer" problem is based on the premise that researchers selecting studies for inclusion in a meta-analysis will favor published studies because of availability and that there is a publication bias: The selection process for publication tends to favor studies that show significance (the studies that do not reject the null hypothesis remain in the file drawer) (McGaw, 1997). Rosenthal (1991) argues this problem does not exist, but Glass et al. (1981) show that effects from meta-analyses of theses and dissertations are weaker than effects from published studies.

Recent developments with Bayesian statistics have been applied to meta-analysis with considerable promise. DuMouchel (1990), Efron (1996), and Smith, Spiegelhalter, and Thomas (1995) demonstrate that Bayesian methods provide a framework for handling meta-analytic issues such as fixed-effects versus random-effects models, appropriate treatment of small studies, possible shapes of the population distribution, and how to include covariates (Barrowman, 1998).

Concept Mapping   The concept map is familiar to most teachers as an efficient teaching strategy; it has more recently been used as a technique in interpretivist research. Specifically, it can be used to probe and visualize the complexity of constructs residing in a research participant's mind. Novak (1990) employed the concept map in research with elementary students as a means of facilitating analysis of interview data by applying this structural device for representing a student's understanding of a complex phenomenon. The visual, often hierarchical, display of ideas does clarify participants' understanding, but the common two-dimensionality of visualization may distort or at best inadequately represent the participants' knowledge. "The limitation [of concept mapping in a research context] is inherent in a hierarchical representation of knowledge in which complex concepts, or complexes of concepts, are established in a superordinate/subordinate relationship. The concept complexes situated in the subordinate positions are, however, multilevel entities whose constituent parts often relate in a complex manner to the focus concept" (Lawson, 1997, p. 294).

An alternative to the "hand-drawn," hierarchical, qualitative concept maps has been emerging. Particularly when a group of participants is involved, a method described by Trochim (1989a, 1989b) that draws on multivariate analysis can be used. The concept or domain to be mapped is focused for the group, statements are generated through brainstorming, the statements are placed on cards, each participant sorts the cards into piles that make sense to the person (not a forced distribution like Q-sort), statements are rated (e.g., on priority or preference), the cards in sorted piles are then analyzed through cluster analysis and nonmetric multidimensional scaling, and finally displayed in various maps for interpretation. Although this approach is described by Trochim (1989b) as "soft science or hard art," it is an indication of a trend in analysis of complex constructs—the use of statistical analysis with "qualitative" data and attention to complexity by statistical analysts.

Dual Scaling   One of the most common analysis techniques of interpretivist research is the identification of "themes" in data—essentially a process dependent on the categorization of observations (verbal statements or descriptions of behavior). Computer programs now assist in categorization, or at least in tracking and retrieving, of text data for purposes of thematic analysis. Using the categorization for further analysis by doing numeric, statistical analysis on the categorical data, however, is not so common. A recent method designed to extract quantitative information from nonnumerical (qualitative) data is dual scaling (Nishisato, 1980, 1994; Nishisato & Nishisato, 1994). It addresses simultaneously in analysis a number of the characteristics of complex data—it is descriptive, optimal, multidimensional, and multivariate. For example, it will derive the most reliable scores for respondents from multiple-choice data, as well as provide all the necessary coordinates for multidimensional representation of data. It handles both incidence data and dominance data. Its potential for music education research is still to be explored.

Analysis Preceding Theory

Scientific research typically begins with theory. Growing out of philosophical inquiry, scientific method requires the researcher to begin by engaging in the essence of philosophical thinking, conceptual analysis. This process of examining and defining constructs culminates in the postulation of relationships and the design of a means of acquiring empirical data to test the theory. Analysis is driven by the theory under investigation. Now data-gathering techniques are such that researchers can be faced with databases so large and complex that analysis must begin without a coherent theory in place. The process of investigating data acquired and stored by a computer is now essentially the same as that of investigating the data acquired and stored by the mind—the sifting, sorting, categorizing, and classifying, with constructs that modify and mutate as the analysis proceeds.

Data Mining   Data mining is, in a sense, a computer-based "grounded theory" analysis approach. Rather than the scientific, verification-based approach (establish theory and use analysis to verify it), it is a discovery approach to analysis (hence "knowledge discovery in databases"). "Data mining is a set of techniques used in an automated approach to exhaustively explore and bring to the surface complex relationships in very large datasets" (Moxon, 1996, p. 1). Although most frequently applied to largely tabular databases, "these techniques can be, have been, and will be applied to other data representations, including spatial data domains, text-based domains, and multimedia (image) domains" (Moxon, 1996, p. 1). The computer programs that do the data mining use algorithms that can examine many multidimensional data relationships concurrently and highlight dominant or exceptional ones. In nontechnical terms, the data mining computer programs employ a form of Kelly's (1955) *Psychology of Personal Constructs*. The computer begins with a set of rather simple predictor constructs. As it attempts to handle the flow of data with these constructs, anomalies reshape the constructs in the process. These newly mutated constructs are then tested against the data. In this way the computer "learns" and refines constructs very much as people do.

Data mining analysis focuses on a variety of possible productive courses to make sense of the data including: association, sequence, clustering, classification, estimation, case-based reasoning, fuzzy logic, genetic algorithms, and fractal-based transforms. Problems in data mining (Moxon, 1996, p. 4) stem from (1) Its susceptibility to "dirty" data—database errors due to magnitude and multiple source input; (2) inability to "explain" results in human terms—do not fit simple if-then terms; and (3) the data representation gap—problems in combining data forms from different computers and database types.

Database sources of potential research value for music education are increasing. "Big Brother" governments, financial institutions, and Internet companies are collecting vast amounts of data potentially relevant to aspects of music in society. These include government census, national survey and assessment data (Burke, 1997), public and private institutional data banks and data archives (Anderson & Rosier, 1997), and commercial data. For example, music Websites may offer their "free" service in exchange for user profile data and then track all music and music-video use. They invite users to create preference lists, to rate individual songs, and so on. This information is stored in a database (now called a data warehouse). Access to government census databases is relatively easy. Access to commercial data may be more difficult. However, the data acquisition is constant; knowledge development is the responsibility of researchers.

Exploratory Data Analysis   EDA, first defined by Tukey (1977), is, in a sense, a manual form of data mining. In the strict scientific method, all analyses are for verification, based on hypotheses articulated before data gathering. Scientific analysis takes its inferential validity from this approach. Consequently, " 'playing around' with data is not 'good' science, not replicable, and perhaps fraudulent. Many experienced researchers pay lip service to this view, while surreptitiously employing ad hoc exploratory procedures they have learned are essential to research" (Leinhardt & Leinhardt, 1997, p. 519). EDA is gaining greater importance, because desktop computer analysis makes "snooping" easier, and there is more recognition that finding pattern in nature, the purpose of EDA, is inherently a subjective enterprise. "Exploratory analyses incorporate the wisdom, skill, and intuition of the investigator into the experiment" (Palmer, 2000, p. 2). As an analysis method, EDA blatantly recognizes the "constructive" dimension of scientific research—searching does go on in research. EDA is particularly necessary in educational research because often data is gathered on a hunch, intuition, or just because it can be gathered and might be useful.

The analyses deemed "exploratory" now often include various dimensional analyses (correspondence, canonical, principal components, smallest space, multidimensional scaling, configuration comparison, factor scoring, metric dimensional scaling) as well as nonhierarchical and hierarchical cluster analyses. All have a pretheory or theory formulation function. For statistically rigorous analysis, EDA cannot be combined with confirmatory analysis on the same data set. One way to accommodate this is to acquire a large enough data set to allow its division into an exploratory subset and a confirmatory subset.

Theory-Confirming Analysis

The current mind-set in research is increasingly accepting exploratory analysis as not only permissible but necessary. Confirmatory analysis, however, is the natural follow-up. Exploration leads to theory which then must be subjected to confirmatory procedures. Most traditional parametric and nonparametric statistical analyses serve this purpose (Asmus & Radocy, 1992). Statistical-based modeling is particularly powerful in theory confirmation and Asmus and Radocy (1992) identify path analysis and linear structural relations analysis (latent trait modeling) as important approaches. They observe that, "Many in the field of music have claimed that a variety of important musical concepts are simply unmeasurable. Latent trait modeling provides a means of accounting for these "unmeasurable" concepts in complex systems" (Asmus & Radocy, 1992, p. 165).

"A prominent theme in methodological criticism of educational research during the 1980s was the failure of many quantitative studies to attend to the hierarchical, multilevel character of much educational field research data. ... Perhaps more profound than such technical difficulties, however, is the impoverishment of conceptualization which single-level models encourage" (Raudenbush & Bryk, 1997, p. 549). An important analytic response to this problem is hierarchical linear modeling also referred to as multilevel linear models, random coefficient models, and complex covariance components models. Effective explanations of hierarchical linear modeling are given by Goldstein (1987), Bock (1989), Raudenbush and Willms (1991) and Bryk and Raudenbush (1992).

Exploration-Confirmation Dynamic

Although technically and ideally the analyses described under the previous two headings precede theory or confirm theory, most analysis realistically is a constructive, dynamic process in which there is some interplay between exploration and explanation, prediction and confirmation. An example of such an approach is Q-methodology (McKeon & Thomas, 1988). Although not strictly a form of analysis, it is a technique that has real potential for exploring intrapersonal relations and as such it is a "qualitative" technique.

Q-methodology also lends itself easily to theory confirmation. As an analytic technique it drew serious criticism from strict statisticians, but its blending of qualitative and statistical aspects is causing a resurgence of use in preference-oriented research in political science and psychology.

Repertory Grid Technique is another approach that interacts with analysis to explore and explain. It is designed to carry out effectively the process of trying to find out how people view the world from their own perspective (analysis of the person's own internal representation of the world) (Bryce, 2003). A variety of mathematical analyses can be conducted (Fansella & Bannister, 1977), but recent developments in concept mapping and dual scaling have potential with repertory grids as well.

Event history analysis, also known as survival analysis or hazard modeling, is an approach to exploring whether and when events occur. For example, a researcher might explore when a music student learns a particular skill or when people stop playing their band instruments. An analytic challenge is the problem that some people may not have developed the musical skill at the time the researcher is studying it or this skill may never develop. Event history analysis provides a sound mathematical basis for dealing with such anomalies through predictive modeling (Singer & Willett, 1991; Willett & Singer, 1991).

A battery of new techniques has developed for qualitative data analysis. Since qualitative research often focuses on a "grounded theory" approach, these analytic methods tend to contribute both to exploration and confirmation. Contingency Table Analysis, Correspondence Analysis, and Configural Frequency Analysis can be subsumed under Dual Scaling, described previously. Galois Lattice or G-lattice is a graphic method of examining and representing knowledge structures within small groups (Ander, Joó, and Merö, 1997). Social Network Analysis is an approach that allows for the examination of complex (multiplex, meaning multistranded) social relationship networks through mathematical models instead of simple sociograms (Scott, 1991).

Trend 6: Knowledge Representation Complexity

The earlier sections on types of data and roles of data explained many aspects of representation. Here the focus is primarily on the way knowledge is represented to others in a process of communicating the results of a research study. As a basic premise, research is the systematic development of knowledge. Knowledge, like intelligence, exists in multiple forms or types. Knowledge, therefore, can be represented in multiple forms. In the past, a particular type of knowledge has been favored by the "research culture"; propositional written representation of the researcher's understanding has been the "privileged representation." Even at conferences where oral presentations were made, the basic mode of presentation has been to "read the paper." Numeric forms have been a staple of research. Other forms of linguistic and nonlinguistic representation are now emerging as research presentations.

The forms of knowledge representation emerging as research communication can be typified as fitting on related continua: hermeneutically closed to hermeneutically open, propositional to nonpropositional, discursive to nondiscursive. One of the common aspects of these continua is the perception of interpretive control. Propositional, discursive, hermeneutically closed communication, mainly in written form, is generally perceived as most interpretively controlled by the researcher. Consisting of a linear series of assertions and logical argumentative support, such communication attempts to limit interpretive range and the possibilities of inference. Nonpropositional or nondiscursive forms are more hermeneutically open, assuming an interpretive, knowledge-constructing role for the receiver of the knowledge communication. Commitment to either extreme of a positivist or constructivist ontology leads to a commitment as well on the representation continua. Recently, there has been a growing shift toward constructivist ontology. The result is a trend toward greater use of nonpropositional and nondiscursive forms of representation of research knowledge.

Written Linguistic Forms

The way language is used to construct thoughts and ideas varies in different forms of literature. Within written language, there is a range of hermeneutic control, from propositional argument to artistic, nonpropositional forms. A poem carries meaning or represents knowledge in a way quite different from a laboratory experiment report or philosophical argument. But language has a central role in constructing or mediating the construction of our internal representations of reality. Postman (1999) says that "language is a major factor in producing our perceptions, judgments, knowledge, and institutions" (p. 70). Postman in this context quotes Einstein saying, "The only justification for our concepts and systems of concepts is that they serve to represent the complex of our experiences; beyond this they have no legitimacy" (p. 70). A problem with language, however, is how to represent "the complex of our experience." Since the 18th century, "scientific" writers have argued or assumed that our experience of reality is best and fully communicated in expository, propositional prose. In the 20th century "almost every field of scholarship—including psychology, linguistics, sociology, and medicine—was infused with an understanding of the problematic relationship of language to reality" (Postman, 1999, p. 71). Despite extreme postmodernists' criticisms of language to represent reality accurately, "We cannot experience reality bare. We encounter it through a system of codes (language, mathematics, art). . . . They [the postmodernists] mean to disabuse us of linguistic naivete, to urge us to take account *how* our codes do their work and enforce their authority" (Postman, 1999, p. 71). We must, however, distinguish among "our codes" as to how they carry meaning. To read poetry as propositional argument is to miss its real meaning. To read every sentence of a story as literal "truth" is probably to miss the real meaning of the story. Each form of literature carries meaning in a particular way. If we restrict ourselves to expository prose, we restrict the kinds of meanings we can take from "research," limit our knowledge, limit our communication power, and distort understanding.

Expository Prose The expository, propositional essay remains one of the most effective ways of communicating a researcher's knowledge to others. One of the changes in the past 10 years, however, has been in the "voice" of such writing. There is now increasing recognition that all knowledge is someone's knowledge rather than objective truth. With this recognition comes a need for ownership. Consequently, use of first person is replacing the air of depersonalized, scientific objectivity associated with third-person expressions. The austerity of expository prose is now being recognized as a form of rhetoric and is often moderated with the inclusion of informal speech transcription from interview or observational data, personal journal notes, or other forms of language. Philosophy and criticism are a special form of argumentative propositional literature.

History According to Barzun & Graff (1992) in their classic book, *The Modern Researcher*, all research reporting is writing history. However, there is a form of literature we recognize as history. It is in essence telling a story in propositional form, consciously interpretive particularly when it is analytic, thematic history. Biography frequently attempts to be thematic and analytic but also to capture aspects of personality and character through enlivened stories. In the form of autobiography or personal diary, which is gaining a place within research methods like personal narrative, the text can be less propositional and more reflectively poetic (Karsemeyer, 2000, Kernohan, 2005).

Story Since ancient times, stories, myths, tales, and epics have been used to communicate ideas, truths, and knowledge essential to the cultures that gave rise to them. For example, the parables in the New Testament clearly have meaning. The perceived meaning may vary from person to person, yet the general point is powerfully understood. That same point could not be made as powerfully with a propositional essay. Barone (1983), Adler (2002), and others have demonstrated that constructing knowledge gained from research as a story communicates aspects of knowledge beyond the propositional.

Poetry The "poetic" nature of language resides in the way meaning constructs are accessed. In propositional statements, the specific form of a construct, the precise meaning to be made out of a particular word, is controlled by the syntax and context. In poetic expressions, the constructs, with all their potential multiple meanings, are activated. New links between constructs are explored by putting words next to each other that might not ordinarily be thought of together, thereby requiring a reexamination of each construct's contents. The nondiscursive nature of poetic language results potentially in both richer connotative, affective meaning and less denotative meaning. The lack of contextual meaning specification and the juxtaposition of constructs can thereby make conscious links, such as emotional memories, not accessed in the more controlled form of propositional discourse. Although relatively rare at this point, there are signs that researchers are exploring these hermeneutically open forms of poetry (Adler, 2002; Leggo, 2001; Kernohan, 2005), prosetry (Andrews, 2000), or metaphorically rich reflections (Denton, 1996). The "hermeneutically open" research report still allows the research reporter some meaning-making power by the very selection of words, metaphors, images, anecdotes, narratives, or interview quotes. However, what meaning is made from the words and images selected is entrusted to the reader.

Drama (as Script)   The dialogic interaction of questionnaire and respondent, of interviewer and interviewee, or of observed and observer naturally evokes the essence of drama. Dramatic interaction is not, however, simply text followed by text; it is "dramatic" in the sense that the text is enlivened with additional meaning conveyed by inflection, vocal tone, pacing, gesture, facial expression, and so on. The transcription of an interview does not capture these layers of meaning communicated by the person interviewed. "Stage directions" written into the "script" may convey some of these meaning dimensions as the drama stimulates imagination and is re-created in the mind of the reader. Consequently, researchers are beginning to write at least parts of research reports in this form. Reynolds (1996) included the script for a radio play as preface to the dissertation. Lamb (1991, 1994), Baskwill (2001), O'Toole (1994), and Adler (2002) reported significant dimensions of their research as a drama script. At times, participants in research presentations are enlisted to enact these scripts as reader theater. Vitale (2002) expressed the core of his findings in a movie script. The challenge for the researcher attempting to communicate additional meaning through written dramatic dialogue is first the selection of a potent transcript. More important, as writing style, the challenge is described by Van Manen (1990). For a good dramatic script, we want "language that lets itself be spoken and used as thought" (p. 32). However, what is to be represented, as fully and richly as possible, is still only the knowledge discovered, supported, or clarified in the intentional research process. To go beyond that risks the imposition of personal interpretive agendas.

Spoken Language

An oral research report carries a dimension of meaning not present in a written report. Nondiscursive, suprasegmental sounds (Farahani, Panayiotis,

Georgiou, & Narayanan, 2004) that we hear as vocal inflection, emphasis, and tone indicate importance, certainty, excitement, and the like in specific parts of the report. In addition, gesture and facial expression carry meaning that clarifies and enhances understanding. These dimensions are important because communication of meaning is enhanced if multiple representations (linguistic, gestural, tonal, visual) are employed. However, the presenter's persuasiveness and appeal may affect the acceptance of the research. There is a research culture, and norms within that culture may favor a specific style of presentation. For example, in *The Little Prince* (Saint-Exupery, 1943), the Turkish astronomer makes a discovery and "On making his discovery, the astronomer had presented it to the International Astronomical Congress, in a great demonstration. But he was in Turkish costume, and so nobody would believe what he said. Grown-ups are like that" (p. 17). John Kenneth Galbraith (quoted in Smithrim, Upitis, Meban, & Patteson, 2000) observed, "There are a significant number of learned men and women who hold that any successful effort to make ideas lively, intelligible, and interesting is a manifestation of deficient scholarship. This is the fortress behind which the minimally coherent regularly find refuge." There is a trend toward livelier, more multirepresentational communications of research knowledge.

Numeric Representations

Numbers are an important form of representation in research reports but a form that communicates more than information about the phenomenon the numbers are representing. For many people in our society, statistical numbers mean "scientific" research, and the credibility of any attendant assertions rises. At the same time, for many the numbers are baffling and intimidating, with the result that few of those who might benefit from the knowledge intended to be communicated actually understand and receive the communication. Unfortunately, the group that sees numbers as "scientific" includes not only readers of research but also some researchers, who have minimal understanding of the numbers they employ. Numbers can be misleading, especially when they are separated from what they represent. A recent trend in research reporting, especially in the popular press, is describing the effect of, for example, a new treatment as percent improvement or likelihood, rather than in terms of significance or actual probabilities. For example, Altman (1999) reports in the *New York Times* that a new drug produces a 76 percent reduction in breast cancer. In actual fact, 1 percent of the study's participants who took a placebo over three years got breast cancer, while a quarter of 1 percent taking the drug got the disease. The "76 percent improvement" sounds impressive but does not communicate the importance or significance of the finding and becomes highly misleading (Smallwood, 2000, p. 17).

Graphic Representations

Graphic representations of research knowledge are designed to communicate information through the complex visual processing system. In the process of communicating, we can entertain, persuade, inform, or mislead. Wilkenson (1988) argues, "Many designers of quantitative graphics confuse these functions or subordinate informing to other goals. Sometimes this is intentional, as in graphic propaganda, but often it is inadvertent, as in popular newspaper graphs which distort their message with bright colors and 'perspective' views" (p. 61). Because computer statistics and graphics programs make it easy, and almost the only choice, researchers increasingly use three-dimensional bar graphs and pie charts (e.g., Asmus, 1994, pp. 18–21). In every case, the three-dimensional perspective makes the graphic more "entertaining" but less clear and, therefore, less informative. For example, in the bar graphs Asmus (1994) presents, it is very difficult to determine to what point on the vertical axis the bar corresponds. There is no doubt about the potential for graphic representation to enhance the communication of knowledge in both written and oral presentations. However, we must resist trendy "entertainment" and choose clear information.

"To envision information—and what bright splendid visions can result— is to work at the intersection of image, word, number, art" (Tufte, 1990, p. 9). But the challenge in this process of "envisioning information" stems from the fact that "the world is complex, dynamic, multidimensional; the paper is static, flat. How are we to represent the rich visual world of experience and measurement on mere flatland?" (Tufte, 1990, p. 9). The use of three-dimensional perspective in graphs is not the answer. The multidimensionality lies in meaning, not in perspective. The flatland is not simply the paper or video screen surface but the simplicity of representation. The escape from the "flatland" is through "progress of methods for enhancing density, complexity, dimensionality, and even sometimes beauty" (Tufte, 1990, p. 33).

Artistic Representation

Musical   Although music is an artistic, nonpropositional phenomenon, music education researchers have been slow to embrace the trend in educational research toward arts-based, or arts-informed inquiry. The problem for music is essentially our inability to see how making music could be an expression of knowledge gained through research. The key is in the research question asked. If the data required to answer the question are musical, then presenting samples of data can inform the communication of knowledge gained. In fact, the musical data, as representations of the phenomenon being studied, are the only way to communicate a dimension of meaning involved. For example, if the researcher is asking what musical decisions expert conductors make to balance musical perfection and the limited abilities of musicians, the best data would be actual rehearsal events. Once the researcher "knows" the answer, the communication of that knowledge would be through the researcher demonstrating the same ability with an ensemble. That might be a research report at a research conference. Music as an additional layer of meaning in a research presentation has been used and is discussed in this chapter under combination forms.

Theater   Drama scripts were earlier described as a form of representation. Staging an actual theatrical production is the next step. Just as an oral report enhances a written paper, an acted drama is more powerful than a written one. Just as actually performing music requires a different level of understanding than merely talking about or analyzing music, so "acting" the new knowledge about a teacher role, a student's struggle, or a parent's dilemma requires and presents a different level of insight. The act of communicating in a dramatic way also embodies in a holistic manner a representation of knowledge. An example of such a dramatic production was *Hong Kong, Canada*, written by the researcher, Tara Goldstein (2000). The script was "based on four years of ethnographic research in a multilingual, multiracial school" (program notes) and was refined as a result of the feedback from two workshop readings of the play by graduate students in the researcher's classes. The staged, one-act play was a representation of the knowledge gained in the research.

Visual Images   A 4-page photo essay in a magazine may be more powerful in communicating elements of a phenomenon than a 40-page written essay might be. At least, the photo essay would communicate something unique and different from the written essay. For this reason, researchers now may include visual images as a data source and an integral part of a research report (Neilsen, 2001). Methodology like visual anthropology (Banks, 1998) and visual sociology (Harper, 1998) is developing. Karsemeyer (2000) used one photograph to represent the central meaning of her dissertation on dance. Woolley (2000) included a photo essay as representation of children's engagement. Huberman (2004) used both photographs and children's drawings as data and as a means of reporting her findings. Illustration instead of photograph could function in the same way.

Combination Forms

Many of the previously mentioned modes of representation are used within the context of another, such as numbers in a propositional essay or graphs in an oral report. There are possibilities that combine more modes, particularly the artistic.

Documentary   The video documentary is a form being explored in video journals like Gale's *The Video Journal of Education*. The potential of this medium is to combine researcher comment (in the propositional argument form) with other oral presentation, graphs, actual research participant comment, dramatic episodes, photographic images, and illustrations, with background or interlude music. The modes of representation could encompass all types of intelligence and knowledge. The visual is a substantial part of the documentary. "Photographs get meaning, like all cultural objects, from their context" (Becker, 1998, p. 88). The documentary form offers a rich, multifaceted context, controlled to a great extent by the researcher-documentary maker. As such, it has powerful potential for the communication of complex knowledge. An oral history of a significant leader or a case study of a school program might be the core of such a documentary, but the potential is for great creative flexibility. An example from sociology is the documentary *"You're blind": Black athletes and ads* (Harrison, 2001).

Paper Performance   Performance texts, described by Denzin (1997) as "poems, scripts, short stories, dramas that are read, and performed before audiences" (p. 179), may border on performance art or a monologue drama but involve parallel representational "performances." An example is the paper performance delivered in several academic contexts entitled "Dorothy troubles Musicland" (Lamb, 1997). In this presentation, Lamb read a formal, expository essay in parallel with a series of recordings from Tchaikovsky to current alternative rock groups, while transforming her appearance step by step by the removal and addition of clothing and ornamentation, from wool-suited professor to "leather dyke." The two nonlinguistic modes of representation were illustrative of the propositions of the essay, serving interactively in the meaning construction of the audience. They were parallel communications, each adding its own set of meanings but also creating a reflexive whole greater than its parts.

The trend in representation of research knowledge is clearly toward diversity and integration into multiple mode presentations. The later artistic and combination forms are particularly more complex because they are multirepresentational, have representational depth (multiple attempts to understand the representation may lead to different meanings), and are richer in meaning (inherently more construct links), with less specific, researcher-controlled interpretation. This means the research communication act can no longer effectively be a one-way communication, a short 15-minute session, or definitive in meaning. The researcher now engages in a communication process that encounters the knowledge "recipient" and reflexively constructs meaning from research efforts.

Researcher Bias

Researcher bias is an important consideration in all forms of representation. The term *bias* itself is a problem. Traditional scientific researchers may take "bias" to mean an expression of the researcher's voice in the report, evidence of the researcher's personal construct-oriented interpretation, or research that involves data gathering through intentional experience. However, obscuring the researcher's voice may create bias: All research has someone's interpretation, and all research data gathering is done through a construct structure, regardless of the form of representation or the "fixing" method. Bias is more a matter of researcher integrity. Bias in representation is a form of error resulting from the researcher's misperception of phenomenal features due to existing construct rigidity, lack of fidelity to a consensus of perception, or a deliberate mis-"representation" of knowledge due to conscious or unconscious allegiance to a preexisting construct. Traditional scientific researchers believed that adherence to methodological formulae and descriptive propositional reporting of results would prevent bias. What was not recognized was that the "objective," "scientific," "truth" aura that clung to such reports could communicate a "bias" (an erroneous representation of knowledge) despite the researcher's best intentions. Furthermore, the limited range of questions that could be explored with these "scientific" methods indicated a bias through ontological commitment in the very choice of methodology. Since the possibility of misperception, misrepresentation, or failure to develop a broad enough consensus among instruments or perceivers is inherent in all research, describing the intentionality of data acquisition, personalizing the knowledge claims, and acknowledging the interpretive act are essential criteria for researcher integrity.

The most researcher-controlled forms of representation of knowledge are the written expository essay and its oral presentation. Within the restricted range of knowledge communicated by propositional language and to the extent that language can encode meaning in the least ambiguous way, such research reports minimize potential misinterpretation and unrecognized bias. When the researcher chooses a form of representation that is less propositional, there is more complex meaning—more levels or layers of meaning drawing on more types of intelligence (more hot buttons on the website being accessed). The potential for misinterpretation (or the construction of a personal interpretation) rises as well, leaving those with an ontological commitment to objective "truth," which can be discovered through empirical evidence and logical reasoning, quite worried. If one recognizes that knowledge is constructed and personal, and that research is ultimately about knowledge development, then research-derived, knowledge representations that serve as stimuli to personal knowledge construction should be clear but potent. Multiple forms of representation have the best chance of altering the receiver's knowledge structure, because each form contributes a dimension the others lack.

Although multiple forms of representation contribute dimensions of meaning, the forms are not equal in communicative power. Marshall McLuhan gave us the concept of a hot medium (television) versus a cool medium (print). We recognize now that it is more than media. The anecdote (story) is a particularly powerful form. Shenk (1997) writes that "anecdotage is a particular problem in the context of today's media age. 'With the sophisticated mental apparatus we have used to build world eminence as a species,' Robert Cialdini says of this catch-22, 'we have created an environment so complex, fast-paced, and information-laden that we must increasingly deal with it in the fashion of the animals we long ago transcended' " (p. 159). According to Shenk, we deal with life's complexity by clinging to simple stories. Social psychologists show how meeting a particular case (e.g., a brutal prison guard) can overshadow considerable statistical data about the general category (e.g., all prison guards) (Shenk, 1997, pp. 156–157). Researchers selecting story and other artistic forms of representation must be fully aware of the power of their selected communication medium, exercise caution, and demonstrate integrity in how they shape the meaning of the communication. Shenk (1997) expresses the caution: "Beware stories that dissolve all complexity" (p. 157).

Trend 7: Dissemination Complexity

Research dissemination is about facilitating knowledge development in others. Frequently researchers believe, or at least act as if, dissemination is about "putting the information out there" and others may read and try to understand if motivated. However, communication can be more active and more reflexive—researchers have a responsibility for developing knowledge in others.

There are two important issues related to dissemination of research-derived knowledge: In whom knowledge should be developed, and how. Until recently, new research-derived knowledge was primarily communicated to other academic researchers. Researchers have lamented the lack of application of research by practitioners, yet have lived in and perpetuated a system that does not value practical dissemination. Now practitioners and the general public are coming to expect that research findings may inform aspects of their daily lives from diet choices to what music they play for their babies.

In Whom Is Knowledge to Be Developed?   The groups to whom research knowledge should be communicated are now more numerous than they were even a decade ago. These now include (1) researchers in music education; (2) researchers in other disciplines; (3) users of research—researchers and their university establishments must learn to value direct communication with teachers through in-service workshops, demonstrations, and the development of pedagogical resources, as highly as they value refereed publication; (4) advocacy groups; (5) the music industry—music education researchers may be uncomfortable with the industrial R&D approach, but often there is "product" development potential in research. Conflict may, of course, arise between research "objectivity" and desired outcomes in research intentionally conducted for advocacy groups or proprietary purposes; and (6) the public.

To communicate effectively with teachers, advocacy groups, the music industry, and the general public the researcher needs to take a "public relations" view. One important requirement is the elimination of jargon. Although we may be dealing with complex phenomena and ideas, understanding starts with simplification rather than complexification. This may be through a potent visual image, story, or specific case example. The temptation is to sensationalize and thereby distort as well as to allow bias to enter the communication. Although the researcher targets communication to specific groups, what is communicated must be the result of real research.

How Is Knowledge to Be Developed? "How" to communicate research knowledge depends to some extent on "to whom" it is to be communicated, but today there are several ways to reach almost every target population. Three variables influence the choice of dissemination medium: time, cost, and form of representation required. The effect of electronic media on time is obvious. The need for face-to-face meeting and discussion versus electronic forms has the largest bearing on cost. The form the knowledge representation takes greatly affects the choice of medium for dissemination. When knowledge was represented only in static visual graphics or text, print publication was efficient. The recognition that knowledge exists in gesture, image, or sound requires alternative forms of knowledge communication. Knowledge performances require "in person" presentation or must be captured on video. Combining text, talk, music, and photographed or computer animated video images can be done by the new media forms such as DVD, CD-ROM, or Internet-based Web productions. As there is a trend in music education research toward multiple forms of representation of research knowledge, more complex media will be employed in dissemination.

An example of the "public relations" approach to research dissemination is described in detail by Smithrim, Upitis, Meban, and Patteson (2000). The premise of the article is that researchers must go "public or perish." Efforts to communicate to their "publics" have included reports at nine academic conferences, papers for refereed journals, interviews on morning radio, photographs in the university newspaper, a story for the local paper, an exhibit of children's art work from the project, articles in the participant research school newspapers, creation of a website, a video describing the project, and a glossy brochure to accompany press releases or for conference distribution. The researchers became advocates for their own research project.

Conclusion

This chapter has essentially been about ontology and epistemology, reality and knowledge, external and internal representation. I have argued that reality is complex but exists apart from representations of it, and that knowledge about reality is constructed through a process of prediction, verification, or accommodation. The mind is engaged in a process of acquiring data related to reality and, from these data, constructing knowledge in a systematic way. Research is the same process, only formalized. Because all the senses provide data for the knowledge constructing process, knowledge exists in multiple forms. If knowledge exists internally in multiple forms, it is most accurately represented externally in multiple ways.

The general trend I have explored has a twofold manifestation: Phenomena in which researchers are interested are increasing in complexity, and there is increasing recognition that all human behaviors and characteristics are inherently complex. I have argued this means that mental constructs associated with all human behavior and expression must be regarded as interrelated and multifaceted, and that theoretical research constructs must reflect this complexity. What follows from this is that data have multiple meanings and connections, yet do not represent fully the associated phenomena. To address complex constructs, given the limitation of data, a variety of research methods must be employed. Multiple data and varied method lead to complex analyses to accommodate multiple levels, hierarchical structures, nonlinear relations, and nonpropositional, nondiscursive data.

Although not directly applying complexity theory (chaos theory), I have purposefully aligned some of my rhetoric with it. One of the most important implications of complexity theory is that researchers will never be able to make a complete description and will never be able to completely predict phenomena. This is implied by Cronbach's (1975) "hall of mirrors" (p. 119) or empty "first cells before we had half the battery completed" (p. 123).

Can research exist without a drive to predict and control? Is research not about theory, theory not about predicting, and predicting not about controlling? The hope of researchers has been to find that "other elusive variable," another interaction, a more detailed path analysis. We know that students do not simply drop out of band because their aptitude is low and they are assigned to an instrument for which they do not like the timbre. But, we believe if we also account for intelligence, teacher behavior, home support, socioeconomic status, and early music experiences, we will be closer. And we assume one day we could account for 100% of the variance and predict who will stay and who will drop out.

The prospect of not being able to discover answers or even partial answers to many of our problems and challenges is probably frightening to music education researchers. As mentioned earlier, each researcher functions in a research culture. Ours is one influenced by the fact that we are musicians, educators, and researchers. Musicians in the Western European tradition are masters of replicative music making in which minute control of every muscle, pitch, rhythm, timbre, and nuance is practiced through hours and hours of repetitive, disciplined effort. Most challenges must be solved before a successful performance is realized. As educators, we function in a milieu where the normal need for class control is amplified by the noisiness of our art and our love of large group performance. The public performance pressure makes efficiency and learning management paramount. As researchers, we live in an era of rational science in which the central purpose is prediction and control.

So how can we respond to the challenge of complexity? We can draw on our unique strengths as music education researchers—persistence, discipline, and creative thinking. But, in addition, we need to be more rigorous in conceptual analysis to understand the constructs we encounter. We must be ingenious in identifying the form of data that most validly represent the phenomena we value. We must be flexible and open-minded in selecting methods to provide reliable observations. We must be disciplined in analysis to transcend the easy answer, the known analytic technique, or the simple solution. We must be daring, confident, and willing to engage the people who matter to music education in the development of knowledge.

In the face of complexity, we also must realize that we are not going to solve the whole puzzle and find every answer. As a result, we may ask different questions. Although we cannot manage the whole system, we are a part of the system and need to realize how we are connected to others. We may ask questions that help us understand another's perspective, another's plight, another's joy. Second, we can change from a perspective of only finding problems to which we can match solutions to one where we see beauty in life's chaos, and describe that beauty. Third, we must engage in "lateral thinking"—encountering the complexity to find imaginative new solutions. Fourth, we must believe in small, local efforts that can have global results. A common metaphor in chaos theory is the assertion that a butterfly flapping its wings in China can affect the weather in New York. Although our power is limited, we are in a dynamic system, and we do have influence. Finally, we must learn to discover, attend to, and appreciate life's rich subtleties.

REFERENCES

Adler, A. (2002). A case study of boys' experiences of singing in school. Unpublished doctoral dissertation, University of Toronto.

Altman, L. K. (1999). Drug slashes breast cancer risk, study shows. *New York Times*, June 16, p. A21.

Ander, C., Joó, A., & Merö, L. (1997). Galois Lattices. In J. P. Keeves (Ed.), *Educational research methodology, and measurement: An international handbook* (2nd ed., pp. 543–549). Tarrytown, NY: Pergamon Elsevier Science.

Anderson, J., & Rosier, M. J. (1997). Data banks and data archives. In J. P. Keeves (Ed.), *Educational research methodology, and measurement: An international handbook* (2nd ed., pp. 344–349). Tarrytown, NY: Pergamon Elsevier Science.

Andrews, B. (2000). Land of Shadows. *Language and literacy: A Canadian educational e-journal*, 2(1). Retrieved from http://educ.queensu.ca/~landl/

Asmus, E. (1994). Motivation in music teaching and learning. *Quarterly Journal of Music Teaching and Learning* 5(4), 5–32.

Asmus, E. P., & Radocy, R. E. (1992). Quantitative analysis. In R. Colwell (Ed.), *Handbook of research in music teaching and learning* (pp. 141–183). New York: Schirmer.

Babbie, E. R. (1995). *The practice of social research* (7th ed.). Belmont, CA: Wadsworth.

Banks, M. (1998). Visual anthropology: Image, object and interpretation. In J. Prosser (Ed.), *Image-based research: A sourcebook for qualitative researchers* (pp. 9–23). London: RoutledgeFalmer.

Barone, T. (1983). Things of use and things of beauty: The story of the Swain County High School Arts Program. *Daedalus, 112*(3), 1–28.

Barrowman, N. (1998). *A survey of meta-analysis: Dalhousie University.* Retrieved from www.mscs.dal.ca/~barrowma/ma.html

Bartel, L. (2000). A foundation for research in the effects of sound on brain and body functions. In H. Jørgensen (Ed.), *Challenges in music education research and practice for a new millennium* (pp. 58–64). Oslo, Norway: Norges musikkhogskole.

Barzun, J., & Graff, H. F. (1992). *The modern researcher* (5th ed.). Belmont, CA: Wadsworth.

Baskwill, J. (2001). Performing our research and our work: Women principals on stage. In L. Nielsen, A. L. Cole, & J. G. Knowles (Eds.), *The Art of writing inquiry* (pp. 132–158). Halifax, NS, Canada: Backalong.

Becker, H. S. (1998). Visual sociology, documentary photography, and photojournalism: It's (almost) all a matter of context. In J. Prosser (Ed.), *Image-based research* (pp. 84–96). New York: RutledgeFalmer, Taylor & Francis.

Birge, R. T. (1932). The calculation of errors by the method of least squares. *Physical Review, 40,* 207–227.

Bock, R. D. (Ed.). (1989). *Multilevel analysis of educational research.* New York: Academic Press.

Briggs, J., & Peat, D. (1999). *Seven life lessons of chaos.* New York: HarperCollins.

Bryce, P. (2003). Meaning-making in music: The personal constructs of musicians. Unpublished doctoral dissertation, University of Toronto.

Bryk, A. S., & Raudenbush, S. W. (1992). *Hierarchical linear models: Applications and data-analysis methods.* Beverly Hills, CA: Sage.

Burke, G. (1997). Census and national survey data. In J. P. Keeves (Ed.), *Educational research methodology, and measurement: An international handbook* (2nd ed., pp. 323–327). Tarrytown, NY: Pergamon Elsevier Science.

Byrne, D. (2000). Complexity theory and social research. *Social Research Update, 18,* 1–7. Retrieved from www.soc.surrey.ac.uk/sru/SRU18.html

Cameron, L., & Bartel, L. (2000). Engage or disengage: An inquiry into lasting response to music teaching. *Orbit, 31*(1), 22–25.

Chou, S. L. (1992). *Research methods in psychology: A primer.* Calgary, AB: Detselig.

Cochran, W. G. (1937). Problems arising in analysis of a series of similar experiments. *Journal of the Royal Statistical Society (Supplement), 4,* 102–118.

Cotes, R. (1722). Aestimatio Errorum in Mixta Mathesi, per Variatones Partium Trianguli Plani et Sphaerici. Part of Cote's *Opera Miscellanea,* published with *Harmonia Mensurarum,* ed. R. Smith. Cambridge, MA: Harvard University Press.

Cronbach, L. (1957). The two disciplines of scientific psychology. *American Psychologist, 12,* 671–684.

Cronbach, L. (1971). Test validation. In R. L. Thorndike (Ed.), *Educational measurement* (2nd ed.). Washington, DC: American Council on Education.

Cronbach, L. (1975). Beyond the two disciplines of scientific psychology. *American Psychologist, 30,* 116–127.

Cronbach, L. (1982). Prudent aspirations for social inquiry. In W. Kruskal (Ed.), *The social sciences: Their nature and lines* (pp. 61–82). Chicago: University of Chicago Press.

Cziko, G. A. (1989). Unpredictability and indeterminism in human behavior: Arguments and implications for educational research. *Educational Researcher, 18*(3), 17–25.

Csikszentmihalyi, M. (1993). *The evolving self: A psychology for the third millennium.* New York: HarperCollins.

Davis, R., Shrobe, H., & Szolovits, P. (1993). What is a knowledge representation. *AI Magazine, 14*(1), 17–33.

Denton, D. (1996). In the tenderness of stone: A poetics of the heart. (Doctoral dissertation, Ontario Institute for Studies in Education, University of Toronto, 1996). *Dissertation Abstracts International, 58*(06), 2085.

Denzin, N. (1997). Performance texts. In W. G. Tierney & Y. S. Lincoln (Eds.), *Representation and the text: Reframing the narrative voice* (pp. 179–217). New York: State University of New York Press.

Dolloff, L. (1999). Imagining ourselves as teachers: The development of teacher identity in music teacher education. *Music Education Research, 1*(2), 191–207.

Donmoyer, R. (1990). Generalizability and the single-case study. In E. W. Eisner & A. Peshkin (Eds.), *Qualitative inquiry in education: The continuing debate* (pp. 175–200). New York: Teachers College Press.

DuMouchel, W. (1990). Bayesian meta-analysis. In D. A. Berry (Ed.), *Statistical methodology in the pharmaceutical sciences.* New York: Dekker.

Efron, B. (1996). Empirical Bayes methods for combining likelihoods. *Journal of the American Statistical Association, 91,* 538–565.

Egger, M., & Smith G. D. (1997). Meta-analysis: Potentials and promise. *British Medical Journal, 315,* 1371–1374.

Fansella, F., & Bannister, D. (1977). *A manual for repertory grid techniques.* London: Academic Press.

Farahani, F., Panayiotis G., Georgiou, P. G., & Narayanan, S. S. (2004). Speaker identification using supra-segmental pitch pattern dynamics. Proceedings of ICASSP, 2004, Montreal. Retrieved from http://sail.usc.edu/publications/icassp_2004_farhad.pdf

Fine, A. (1998). Scientific realism and antirealism. In E. Craig (Ed.), *Routledge encyclopedia of philosophy online.* Retrieved from http://www.rep.routledge.com

Fisher, R. A. (1932). *Statistical methods for research workers* (4th ed.). London: Oliver and Boyd.

Gabrielsson, A. (1991). Experiencing music. *Canadian Journal of Research in Music Education, 33* (ISME Research Edition), 21–26.

Gardner, H. (1999). *Intelligence reframed.* New York: Basic Books.

Glass, G. V. (1976). Primary, secondary, and meta-analysis. *Educational Researcher, 5,* 3–8.

Glass, G. V., McGraw, B., & Smith, M. L. (1981). *Meta-analysis in social research.* Beverly Hills, CA: Sage.

Goldstein, H. (1987). *Multilevel models in educational and social research.* Oxford: Oxford University Press.

Goldstein, T. (2000). Program notes for *Hong Kong, Canada*. University of Toronto.

Grace, A. P. (2001). Poetry as narrative inquiry. In L. Nielsen, A. L. Cole, & J. G. Knowles (Eds.) *The art of writing inquiry* (pp. 26–31). Halifax, NS, Canada: Backalong.

Haig, B. D. (1997). Feminist research methodology. In J. P. Keeves (Ed.), *Educational research methodology, and measurement: An international handbook* (2nd ed., pp. 180–185). Tarrytown, NY: Pergamon Elsevier Science.

Harper, D. (1998). An argument for visual sociology. In J. Prosser (Ed.), *Image-based research: A sourcebook for qualitative researchers* (pp. 24–41). London: RoutledgeFalmer.

Harrison, C. K. (2001). *"You're blind": Black athletes and ads*. Produced by P. E. Hamilton. The Paul Robeson Centre for Academic and Athletic Prowess. Ann Arbor: University of Michigan.

Hayles, N. K. (1991). *Chaos and order*. Chicago: University of Chicago Press.

Hetland, L. (2000). Listening to music enhances spatial-temporal reasoning: Evidence for the Mozart effect. *The Journal of Aesthetic Education, 34*, 3–4.

Homans, G. C. (1974). *Social behavior: Its elementary forms*. New York: Harcourt Brace Jovanovich.

Huberman, A. (2004). The experience of growing up in tandem with another and its implications for parenting and educating: An inquiry into the stories of twins and other multiples. Unpublished doctoral dissertation, University of Toronto.

Hunter, J. E., Schmidt, F. L., & Jackson, G. B. (1982). *Meta-analysis: Cumulating research findings across studies*. Beverly Hills, CA: Sage.

Ignatieff, M. (2000). *The rights revolution*. Toronto: House of Anansi.

Jacques, B. (2000). Abuse and persistence: Why do they do it? *Canadian Music Educator, 42*(2), 8–13.

Jutai, J., Knox, R., Rumney, P., Gates, R., Wit, V., & Bartel, L. (1997, May). *Musical training methods to improve recovery of attention and memory following head injury*. Paper presented at the Executive Function and Developmental Psychopathology: Theory and Application Conference, University of Toronto.

Kafre Systems International. (1998). On eliminating risk by managing complexity. *Technical Reports KSI-TN-100102*. Retrieved from http://www.ksiinc.com/onrisk

Karsemeyer, J. (2000). *Moved by the spirit: A narrative inquiry*. Unpublished doctoral dissertation, University of Toronto.

Keeves, J. P. (1997a). Introduction: Advances in measurement in education. In J. P. Keeves (Ed.), *Educational research methodology, and measurement: An international handbook* (2nd ed., pp. 705–712). Tarrytown, NY: Pergamon Elsevier Science.

Keeves, J. P. (1997b). Introduction: Methods and processes in educational research. In J. P. Keeves (Ed.), *Educational research methodology, and measurement: An international handbook* (2nd ed., pp. 277–285). Tarrytown, NY: Pergamon Elsevier Science.

Kelly, G. (1955). *The psychology of personal constructs*. 2 vols. New York: Norton.

Kernohan, L. (2005). Finding my way: Experiencing audition as a sightless musician. Unpublished doctoral dissertation, University of Toronto.

Lamb, R. (1991). Medusa's aria: Feminist theory and music education. In J. Gaskell & A. McLaren (Eds.), *Women and education* (pp. 299–320) Calgary, AB: Detselig.

Lamb, R. (1994). Aria senza accompagnamento, *Quarterly Journal of Music Teaching and Learning, 4*(4), *5*(1), 5–20.

Lamb, R. (1997a, February). *Dorothy troubles Musicland.* Paper presented at the Faculty of Music, University of Toronto.

Lamb, R. (1997b). Music trouble: Desire, discourse, and the pedagogy project. *Canadian University Music Review, 18*(1), 84–98.

Lamb, R. (1998, May). *Mentoring: Master teacher/student apprentice as pedagogy in music.* Paper presented at the Canadian University Music Society, University of Ottawa.

Lamb, R. (1999). "I never really thought about it": Master/apprentice as pedagogy in music. In K. Armatage (Ed.), *Equity and how to get it: Rescuing graduate studies* (pp. 213–238). Toronto: Inanna Publications and Education.

Lawson, M. J. (1997). Concept mapping. In J. P. Keeves (Ed.), *Educational research methodology, and measurement: An international handbook* (2nd ed., pp. 290–296). Tarrytown, NY: Pergamon Elsevier Science.

Leggo, C. (2001) Research as poetic rumination: Twenty-six ways of listening to light. In L. Nielsen, A. L. Cole, & J. G. Knowles (Eds.), *The art of writing inquiry* (pp. 173–195). Halifax, NS, Canada: Backalong.

Leinhardt, G., & Leinhardt S. (1997). Exploratory data analysis. In J. P. Keeves (Ed.), *Educational research methodology, and measurement: An international handbook* (2nd ed., pp. 519–528). Tarrytown, NY: Pergamon Elsevier Science.

Light, R. J., & Pillemer, D. B. (1984). *Summing up: The science of reviewing research.* Cambridge, MA: Harvard University Press.

Linacre, J. M. (1995). *Rasch measurement: Construct clear concepts and useful numbers!* University of Chicago. Retrieved from http://www.winsteps.com/

Lincoln, Y. S., & Guba, E. G. (1984). *Naturalistic inquiry.* Beverly Hills, CA: Sage.

McCarthy, M. (1997). The foundations of sociology in American music education, 1900–1935. In R. Rideout (Ed.), *On the sociology of music education* (pp. 71–80). Norman: School of Music, University of Oklahoma.

McCarthy, M. (2000). Music Matters: A philosophical foundation for a sociology of music education. *Bulletin of the Council for Research in Music Education, 144,* 3–9.

McGaw, B. (1997). Meta-analysis. In J. P. Keeves (Ed.), *Educational research methodology, and measurement: An international handbook* (2nd ed., pp. 371–380). Tarrytown, NY: Pergamon Elsevier Science.

McKeon, B., & Thomas, D. (1988). *Q-methodology.* Newbury Park, CA: Sage.

Moxon, B. (1996, August). The hows and whys of data mining, and how it differs from other analytical techniques. *DBMS Data Warehouse Supplement,* 1–3.

Neilsen, A. (2001). Are paintings texts?: Making the strange familiar again. In L. Nielsen, A. L. Cole, & J. G. Knowles (Eds.), *The art of writing inquiry* (pp. 283–291). Halifax, NS, Canada: Backalong.

Nishisato, S. (1980). *Analysis of categorical data: Dual scaling and its applications.* Toronto: University of Toronto Press.

Nishisato, S. (1994). *Elements of dual scaling: An introduction to practical data analysis.* Hillsdale, NJ: Lawrence Erlbaum.

Nishisato, S., & Nishisato, I. (1994). *Dual scaling in a nutshell.* Toronto: MicroStats.

Novak, J. (1990). Concept mapping: A useful device for science education. *Journal of Research in Science Teaching, 27*(10), 937–949.

O'Toole, P. A. (1994). Redirecting the choral classroom: A feminist poststructural analysis of power relations within three choral classrooms. *Dissertation Abstracts International, 55*(07), 1864. (UMF No. AAT 9426965)

Palmer, M. (2000). *Hypothesis-driven and exploratory data analysis.* Retrieved from http://www.okstate.edu/artsci/botany/ordinate/motivate.htm

Paul, S. J. (2000). The sociological foundations of David Elliott's "Music Matters" philosophy. *Bulletin of the Council for Research in Music Education, 144,* 11–20.

Pearson, K. (1904). Report on certain enteric fever inoculations. *British Medical Journal, 2,* 1243–1246.

Perlmutter, M. L., & Perkins, D. N. (1982). A model of aesthetic response. In S. S. Madeja & D. N. Perkins (Eds.), *A model for aesthetic response in the arts* (pp. 1–29). St. Louis, MO: CEMREL, Inc.

Postman, N. (1999). *Building a bridge to the eighteenth century.* New York: Alfred A. Knopf.

Raudenbush, S. W., & Bryk, A. S. (1997). Hierarchical linear modeling. In J. P. Keeves (Ed.), *Educational research methodology, and measurement: An international handbook* (2nd ed., pp. 549–556). Tarrytown, NY: Pergamon Elsevier Science.

Raudenbush, S. W., & Willms, J. D. (1991). *Schools, classrooms, and pupils: International studies of schooling from a multilevel perspective.* New York: Academic Press.

Rosenthal, R. (1991). *Meta-analytic procedures for social research* (rev. ed). Newbury Park, CA: Sage.

Reynolds, J. L. (1996). Wind and song: Sound and freedom in musical creativity. (Doctoral dissertation, University of Toronto, 1996). *Dissertation Abstracts International, 58*(06), 2127.

Rothe, J. P. (1993). *Qualitative research: A practical guide.* Toronto: PDE.

Saint-Exupery, A. (1943). *The little prince* (trans. Katherine Woods). Orlando, FL: Harcourt Brace.

Scott, J. (1991). *Social network analysis: A handbook.* Newbury Park, CA: Sage.

Sharpley, C. F. (1997). Single case research: Measuring change. In J. P. Keeves (Ed.), *Educational research methodology, and measurement: An international handbook* (2nd ed., pp. 451–455). Tarrytown, NY: Pergamon Elsevier Science.

Shenk, D. (1997). *Data fog: Surviving the information glut.* New York: Harper Edge.

Shulman, L. (1988). Disciplines of inquiry in education: An overview. In R. M. Jaeger (Ed.), *Complementary methods for research in education* (pp. 3–17). Washington, DC: American Educational Research Association.

Singer, J. D., & Willett, J. B. (1991). Modeling the days of our lives: Using survival analysis when designing and analyzing longitudinal studies of duration and the timing of events. *Psychological Bulletin, 110*(2), 268–298.

Smallwood, B. (2000). News that's hard to swallow. *Adbusters 29*, 17.

Smith, T. C., Spiegelhalter, D. J., & Thomas, A. (1995). Bayesian approaches to random-effects meta-analysis: A comparative study. *Statistics in Medicine, 14*, 2685–2699.

Smithrim, K., Upitis, R., Meban, M., & Patteson, A. (2000). Get public or perish. *Language and Literacy: A Canadian Educational E-Journal, 2*(1). Retrieved from http://educ.queensu.ca/~landl/

Stake, R., Bresler, L., & Mabry, L. (1991). *Custom and cherishing: The arts in elementary schools*. Urbana-Champaign, IL: Council for Research in Music Education.

Standley, J. M. (1996). A meta-analysis on the effects of music as reinforcement for education/therapy objectives. *Journal of Research in Music Education 44*(2), 105–133.

Sundin, B. (1989). Early music memories and socialization. *Canadian Journal of Research in Music Education, 30*(2), 154–161.

Thorndike, E. L. (1910). The contribution of psychology to education. *Journal of Educational Psychology, 1, 5*–12.

Tippett, L. H. C. (1931). *The methods of statistics*. London: Williams & Norgate.

Trochim, W. (1989a). An introduction to concept mapping for planning and evaluation. *Evaluation and Program Planning, 12, 1*–16.

Trochim, W. (1989b). Concept mapping: Soft science or hard art? *Evaluation and Program Planning, 12, 87*–110.

Tufte, E.R. (1990). *Envisioning information*. Cheshire, CT: Graphics Press.

Tukey, J. W. (1977). *Exploratory data analysis*. Reading, MA: Addison-Wesley.

Van Manen, M. (1990). *Researching lived experience: Human science for an action sensitive pedagogy*. Albany, N.Y.: State University of New York Press.

Vitale, J. L. (2002). The effect of music on the meanings students gain from film. Doctor of Education Thesis, Ontario Institute for Studies in Education, University of Toronto.

Wachter, K. W., & Straf, M. L. (Eds.). (1990). *The future of meta-analysis*. New York: Russell Sage Foundation.

Walker, J. C., & Evers, C. W. (1997). Research in education: Epistomological issues. In J. P. Keeves (Ed.), *Educational research methodology, and measurement: An international handbook* (2nd ed., pp. 22–31). Tarrytown, NY: Pergamon Elsevier Science.

Wilkenson, L. (1988). *SYSGRAPH*. Evanston, IL: SYSTAT.

Willett, J. B., & Sayer, A. G. (1994). Using covariance structure analysis to detect correlates and predictors of change. *Psychological Bulletin, 116, 363*–381.

Willett, J. B., & Sayer, A. G. (1995). Cross-domain analyses of change over time: Combing growth modeling and covariance structure analysis. In G. A. Marcoulides & R. E. Schumaker (Eds.), *Advanced structural equation modeling: Issues and techniques*. Hillsdale, NJ: Lawrence Erlbaum.

Willett, J. B., & Singer, J. D. (1991). From whether to when: New methods for studying student dropout and teacher attrition. *Review of Educational Research, 61*(4), 407–450.

Woolley, J. C. (2000). *Making connections: Pre-reading reader response and mother-research from one family's perspective*. Unpublished doctoral dissertation, University of Toronto.

Yates, F., & Cochran, W. G. (1938). The analysis of groups of experiments. *Journal of Agricultural Science, 28,* 556–580.

Zeller, R. A. (1997). Validity. In J. P. Keeves (Ed.), *Educational research methodology, and measurement: An international handbook* (2nd ed., pp. 822–829). Tarrytown, NY: Pergamon Elsevier Science.

Index

a priori comparisons, in analysis of variance, 117–119
ability, musical, 206–207
accountability, assessment framework for, 204–205
achievement, 206
acquisition, assessment of, 232
action research, 357
    in qualitative research, 290, 295, 324, 329, 334
adaptation, assessment of, 232
advisor, major, for dissertation, 68–70
advisory committee, for dissertations, 64–65, 69
aesthetic questions, 187
aesthetic theory
    in historical research, 74–75, 82
    in music education, 291–294, 332
    in philosophical method, 184
affective measures, as assessment dependent variable, 214, 232
African Americans. *See* ethnography
alpha error, in hypothesis testing, 106
alternatives, philosophical evaluation of, 181
ambiguity, in qualitative research, 177, 326
analysis
    in assessment, 234, 242
    conversational, 357
    in philosophical method, 191
analysis of covariance (ANCOVA), 114
    multivariate, 126–127
analysis of variance (ANOVA), 112–114
    cell size, 121
    comparisons in, 112–113
    error in, 115, 118
    example of, 113–114

factorial design concepts, 115–117
Kruskal-Wallis, 159
multivariate, 124–126
one-way, 115
other designs, 124
principles of, 112
randomized block designs, 121–122
repeated measures designs, 122–124
simple effects, 117–121
three-way, 115–116
two-way, 115–116
types of, 112
analytical complexity, 360–367
    analysis preceding theory for, 364–366
    concept mapping for, 363
    data mining and, 364–365
    dual scaling for, 364
    exploration-confirmation dynamic for, 366–367
    exploratory data analysis for, 365–366
    meta-analysis for, 361–363
    Rasch analysis for, 360–361
    as research trend, 344, 360
    single-case design and change measurement for, 361
    theory-confirming analysis for, 366
analytical thinking
    assessment of, 207–208
    in assumption evaluation, 180–181
antecedents, in qualitative research, 313
anthropology, qualitative research based on, 274, 280, 316–317
antinaturalist critique, of research, 21
appreciation, musical, 177–178
aptitude, musical, 206
    extant tests of, 218–219
    qualitative research on, 327–328